THE ASSOCIATION FOR SCOTTISH LITERARY STUDIES
NUMBER THIRTY-THREE

MODERNISM AND NATIONALISM: LITERATURE AND SOCIETY IN SCOTLAND 1918–1939

SOURCE DOCUMENTS FOR THE SCOTTISH RENAISSANCE

He canna Scotland see wha yet
Canna see the Infinite,
And Scotland in true scale to it.

Hugh MacDiarmid
A Drunk Man Looks at the Thistle

THE ASSOCIATION FOR SCOTTISH LITERARY STUDIES

The Association for Scottish Literary Studies aims to promote the study, teaching and writing of Scottish literature, and to further the study of the languages of Scotland.

To these ends, the ASLS publishes works of Scottish literature (of which this volume is an example); literary criticism and in-depth reviews of Scottish books in *Scottish Studies Review*; short articles, features and news in *ScotLit*; and scholarly studies of language in *Scottish Language*. It also publishes *New Writing Scotland*, an annual anthology of new poetry, drama and short fiction, in Scots, English and Gaelic. ASLS has also prepared a range of teaching materials covering Scottish language and literature for use in schools.

All the above publications are available as a single 'package', in return for an annual subscription. Enquiries should be sent to:

> ASLS, c/o Department of Scottish History, 9 University Gardens, University of Glasgow, Glasgow G12 8QH. Telephone/fax +44 (0)141 330 5309 or visit our website at **www.asls.org.uk**

A list of Annual Volumes published by ASLS can be found at the end of this book.

THE ASSOCIATION FOR SCOTTISH LITERARY STUDIES

MODERNISM AND NATIONALISM: LITERATURE AND SOCIETY IN SCOTLAND 1918–1939

SOURCE DOCUMENTS FOR THE SCOTTISH RENAISSANCE

Edited by

Margery Palmer McCulloch

GENERAL EDITOR—LIAM McILVANNEY

GLASGOW

2004

*

First published in Great Britain, 2004
by The Association for Scottish Literary Studies
Department of Scottish History
University of Glasgow
9 University Gardens
Glasgow G12 8QH

www.asls.org.uk

ISBN 0 948877 58 8 (Hardback), 0 948877 59 6 (Paperback)

A catalogue record for this book
is available from the British Library.

The Association for Scottish Literary Studies acknowledges
support from the Scottish Arts Council towards
the publication of this book.

Typeset by AFS Image Setters Ltd, Glasgow
Printed and bound by Bell & Bain Ltd, Glasgow

CONTENTS

CONTENTS

CONTENTS

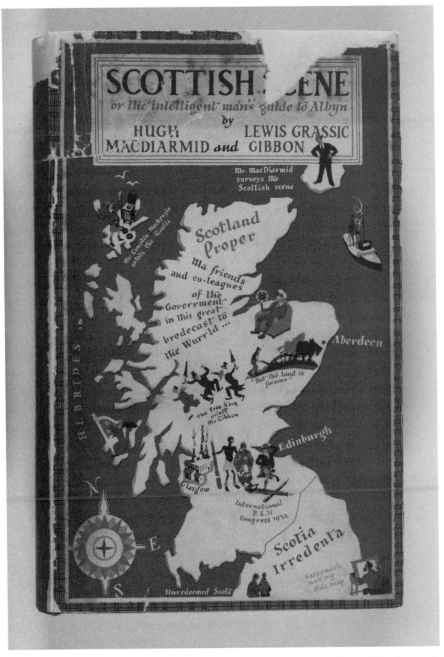

Original dust cover for *Scottish Scene or the Intelligent Man's Guide to Albyn* by Lewis Grassic Gibbon and Hugh MacDiarmid (1934)

THE CHAPBOOK PROGRAMME

*'Il far un libro meno e che niente
Se il libro fatto non rifa la gente. . . .'*

('To make a book is less than nothing unless the book , when made,
makes people anew.')

———————

The principal aims and objects of *The Scottish Chapbook* are:

To report, support, and stimulate, in particular, the activities of the Franco-Scottish, Scottish-Italian, and kindred Associations; the campaign of the Vernacular Circle of the London Burns Club for the revival of the Doric; the movement towards a Scots National Theatre; and the 'Northern Numbers' movement in contemporary Scottish poetry.

To encourage and publish the work of contemporary Scottish poets and dramatists, whether in English, Gaelic, or Braid Scots.

To insist upon truer evaluations of the work of Scottish writers than are usually given in the present over-Anglicised condition of British literary journalism, and, in criticism, elucidate, apply, and develop the distinctively Scottish range of values.

To bring Scottish Literature into closer touch with current European tendencies in technique and ideation.

To cultivate 'the lovely virtue'.

And, generally, to 'meddle wi' the thistle' and pick the figs.

The Chapbook Programme: 'Manifesto' for the flagship magazine of the new Scottish literary renaissance movement, printed in the inaugural issue of the *Scottish Chapbook* in August 1922, and in subsequent issues

INTRODUCTION

'The Scottish Renaissance' is the name by which the twentieth-century interwar revival movement in Scottish literature became known in its own period and has continued to be known into our time. First used by C.M. Grieve in the Book Reviews section of the *Scottish Chapbook* of August 1922, it was taken up by Professor Denis Saurat the following year in his essay 'Le Groupe de "la Renaissance Écossaise"' and thereafter quickly passed into common usage, even by those sceptical about the new movement's achievements.

What is significant about this literary revival, and what makes it so different from previous attempts at cultural renewal in Scotland, is that those involved believed that there could be no regeneration of the nation's artistic culture which did not also involve the regeneration of the social, economic and political life of the nation. Although there were different perceptions as to how such national renewal might be attained—from the belief in complete political and financial independence from England and the British State demanded by nationalists, to the socialist solution within (presumably) a socialist Britain advocated by those such as Edwin Muir—there was general agreement that the health of a nation's culture could not be separated from the health of the nation as a whole. This ideological position resulted in an unusually rich amount of critical, social, political and philosophical writing by the principal creative writers of the period, much of it unknown even to readers familiar with their poetry and fiction. It is also unusual in the context of the modernist period generally, in this respect having more in common with Shelley's belief in the poet or artist as 'unacknowledged legislator' than with modernist detachment.

Modernism and Nationalism: Literature and Society in Scotland 1918–1939 is therefore not a critical study of Scottish literary culture, but a collection of primary source documents which spans the period from the end of one war to the outbreak of another, and which brings us the debates and arguments not only about the future of Scotland's literature but about the wider cultural, social and political forces at work at home and abroad during this challenging transitional period. It may also be the case that a more acute understanding of the creative writing and writers of the period will be arrived at as a result of their work being seen in the context of such contemporaneous material.

An essential ingredient in any such exchange of ideas was the creation of a small magazine culture in Scotland, something noticeably absent in the period immediately after World War One. The great days of the *Edinburgh Review* and *Blackwood's* were over, and although these magazines were to continue for a few years longer, it was clear that they were in decline. In the first issue of his *Scottish Chapbook* in August 1922, C.M. Grieve— soon to become Hugh MacDiarmid—acknowledged the lack of 'the appearance in Scotland of phenomena recognisable as a propaganda of ideas', and he continued:

> None of these significant little periodicals—crude, absurd, enthusiastic, vital—have yet appeared in Auchtermuchty or Ardnamurchan. No new publishing houses have sprung up mushroom-like . . . It is discouraging to reflect that this is not the way the Dadaists go about the business!

This ironic comment points us towards the interest in cultural developments in Europe which was to become a hallmark of the Renaissance movement, and to Grieve's awareness of the avant-garde activities of the small magazines which had appeared in London in the pre-1914 period. He may have been over-optimistic in hoping to find such iconoclastic places of exchange in Auchtermuchty or Ardnamurchan, but they could reasonably have been expected to have made some kind of appearance in Edinburgh, a capital of cultural importance in eighteenth- and early nineteenth-century Scotland. The *Scottish Chapbook* became the first of a number of literary and cultural magazines instituted and edited by Grieve in the 1920s, shortlived, but with an influence far beyond their lifespan. In the early to mid-1930s the *Modern Scot*, edited by the American J.H. Whyte, took over Grieve's avant-garde role, while from the later 1920s onwards a number of social and political periodicals also came on the scene, such as the *Scots Observer*, supported by the Scottish Protestant Churches, the nationalist *Scots Independent*, the *Pictish Review* committed to Gaelic culture, and the *Free Man*, independent of specific affiliations but offering a platform to those who wished to explore new ways forward for Scotland. The *Scots Magazine* under J.B. Salmond published many energetic articles by the novelist Neil M. Gunn about the need for regeneration in the Highlands and about the complementary nature of nationalism and internationalism. All of these magazines, however, whether predominantly cultural or ideological, provided an interactive mixture of art, politics and social questions in their pages to which most of the principal creative writers at one time or another contributed, together with others in sympathy with the new movement. They thus became an important forum for the exchange of ideas about Scotland's future. Many of the excerpts in this collection of source documents are drawn from such magazines.

An important model for the periodicals edited by Grieve, and one which might be termed an honorary Scottish Renaissance periodical because of the influence it had on the self-education of at least two writers, Grieve himself and Edwin Muir, was the *New Age*, edited by A.R. Orage from 1907 until 1922: a 'Weekly Review of Politics, Literature and Art', as it styled itself. In the early years of Orage's editorship, the *New Age* was one of the liveliest weekly magazines in London, with its eclectic mix of arts, philosophy, politics and social concerns, and its bringing of European ideas and writers to an English-speaking audience. The young Grieve had been introduced to it when a pupil-teacher in Edinburgh and it was to be for him a principal source of education about avant-garde ideas and European artistic movements. He himself had a modest contribution published in it in 1911, but it was not until 1924 that he became a regular contributor. Edwin Muir also educated himself in philosophy and the arts through the *New Age* when he was a young man in Glasgow and he became a regular contributor during World War One under the pseudonym of Edward Moore. His first book, *We Moderns*, published in 1918, began life in the *New Age* as a series of aphorisms or short essays on modern life. It was followed by a regular series called 'New Values' in which Muir discussed, among other topics, the philosophy of Nietzsche (a strong influence on both Muir and MacDiarmid) and the 'modern science' of psychology; and between 1920 and 1922 he contributed the series 'Our Generation' which explored social and political concerns as well as the arts. The eclectic nature of the *New Age* was therefore a very relevant influence for a new intellectual and European-oriented movement in Scottish culture, which was also rooted in the social, economic and political soil of everyday contemporary Scottish life. It was especially influential on Grieve's second periodical, the *Scottish Nation*, to which Muir contributed the first English-language essay on the German poet Hölderlin in 1923. It was, however, its predecessor, the *Scottish Chapbook*—which shared its birth year with Joyce's *Ulysses*, Eliot's *The Waste Land* and the establishment of the *Criterion* under Eliot's editorship—which provided the platform for Grieve's development of his 'Theory of Scots Letters' with its advocacy of a revitalised Scots Vernacular as the principal poetic medium for a revival in literature.

This collection of source documents for the Scottish Renaissance has been divided into two general sections: *Towards a Scottish Literary Renaissance* and *Whither Scotland?*. It has then been subdivided thematically with the excerpts in each section presented chronologically in order to give a sense of the movement and changing nature of the debates as arguments interact with each other. The focus of the first overall section is, as its title suggests, predominantly literary, while the three subsections in the second part deal with social, economic, political and cultural questions in the Highlands, Lowlands and beyond Scotland. The structure of the collection has itself had to yield to the demands of the gathered material, with *Whither Scotland?*, for example, initially planned as a single

'Condition of Scotland' section. However, the extent and variety of material and viewpoints about politics and social and economic issues, and the amount of concern about the need to regenerate the Highlands and the Gaelic language, demanded a more expansive format. While 'contradiction' often seems the motto for these debates and arguments—especially when attempts to adopt a Celtic identity for the new Scotland come up against attacks on Irish immigration—shifting ideological positions also convey the fluidity of political nomenclature and understanding in a period when people were struggling to find alternative ways of organising society and of achieving power over social and economic problems. Terms such as 'fascism' and 'communism', for example, did not mean the same to those living in the 1920s and early 1930s as they do to us whose historical understanding includes awareness of the Hitler War and the Cold War. It is noticeable in these excerpts that while fascism in the 1920s seems to be entertained as a kind of super-successful nationalism, after the coming to power of Hitler in 1933 it is most often rejected as a dangerous political philosophy.

What may seem a surprising omission in the 'Competing Ideologies' section, given its influence on the English poets of the interwar period, is the Spanish Civil War. Grieve/MacDiarmid was one of several prominent UK writers who contributed a statement in support of the Republicans in Spain to a *Left Review* pamphlet in 1937 and in 1939 he wrote the long poem *The Battle Continues* attacking the poet Roy Campbell's support of Franco and the fascists (which unfortunately did not achieve publication until 1957). These have been noted in the commentary section of the collection. However, despite the wide coverage of the Spanish conflict in the newspapers of the time, specific items by Scottish writers have not readily come to attention. This may be in part because many of the small magazines associated with the revival movement had ceased publication by the later 1930s and partly, perhaps, because discussion among writers about political affairs beyond Scotland was increasingly taking place in personal correspondence, as is shown in later items in the final section of the collection. After a number of years when he had no magazine under his editorship, Grieve/MacDiarmid's last magazine of the interwar period, *The Voice of Scotland*, was edited by him from Whalsay in the Shetlands from the summer of 1938 until the outbreak of war in 1939.

Items by women writers have also been more difficult to find. In early studies of the period, the Scottish Renaissance movement was defined by its male contributors alone, and it is only in recent years that women poets and fiction writers have been given their place in assessments of the literary revival. An added complication is that, despite the fact that women were increasingly making their way into the workplace and had achieved entitlement to vote in 1918 and on equal terms in 1928, the continuing social perception of a woman's role in these years was a domestic one.

Women therefore did not on the whole take a public part in the literary and social/political debates of the time, and contributions by and about women were often confined to the 'Women's Interests' page of newspapers. Catherine Carswell, Willa Muir and Naomi Mitchison were unusual in their contribution to public debate, with Carswell in particular taking part in the revaluation of Scottish literary traditions after the publicity she achieved through her *Life of Robert Burns*. Some women were active principally as creative writers, some gave their time to nationalist organisations or to non-political cultural organisations such as Scottish P.E.N. and the Saltire Society. Helen Cruickshank, poet and Secretary of Scottish P.E.N., whose Corstorphine home, Dinnieduff, was a regular stopping-off place for visiting writers and cultural activists, was a civil servant and therefore most probably felt precluded from taking part in controversial public debate.

Where possible, contributions from women have been included throughout the various sections of the collection. However, section six, 'Women on Women: Gendering the Renaissance', has been completely devoted to excerpts which give perspectives on women, life and art from a female point of view, thus opening up uncharted areas of the Scottish Renaissance movement. It seems relevant to the *un*public role of women at the time that many of the most interesting insights come from correspondence between women friends or from personal journals.

My original intention was to end this collection of source documents with an 'Afterword' section, which would bring together comments from writers and scholars of later years as to what they considered the lasting significance of the interwar revival movement. However, as I put together the primary material, listening to the voices in the various sections interacting with each other, and often modifying my own procedures to meet their demands, it became clear to me that these writers and the events and perspectives of their period deserve to be evaluated on what they have to say to us in the excerpts given, not prejudged on the myths that have grown around them in intervening years. I have therefore left the excerpts to stand alone, apart from a short commentary section for explanatory purposes. We have most to learn if we listen to these voices in the context of their own time.

Margery Palmer McCulloch

A note on the text

Unless otherwise stated, all excerpts have been reprinted from the original sources and full source documentation has been given to enable readers to follow up a complete text if they wish to do so. The presentation of textual detail has not been standardised but given as in the original text, with the exception of small details such as the omission of the full stop in Mr, and, for clarity where necessary, the use of italics as opposed to inverted commas for the title of a published book. Thus, for example, M'Diarmid, McDiarmid, MacDiarmid appears in its various forms and s/z spellings are left as in the originals. Commentary notes are on the whole limited to giving explanatory information about writers and topics and, where possible, biographical information about less-familiar authors. Cross-referencing between topics has been indicated by giving the section and item numbers of related excerpts.

General Acknowledgements

I would like to express my thanks to all who have assisted with this project: to colleagues in Aberdeen, Glasgow and elsewhere who willingly answered queries; to Michel Byrne for help with Gaelic translations; and to Moira Burgess, Katherine Gordon and John Manson for their generosity in alerting me to material noticed during their own researches. I am grateful to Special Collections staff at the National Library of Scotland and Edinburgh University Library and to library staff generally at Glasgow University Library and the Mitchell Library, Glasgow. The Scottish Literature Department of Glasgow University has been supportive of the idea of this collection over several years and I am especially grateful to the Association for Scottish Literary Studies for adopting it as an Annual Volume. Duncan Jones of ASLS has given much assistance in translating it into print. Finally, but not least, I acknowledge a debt to Duncan Glen, whose ground-breaking *Hugh MacDiarmid and the Scottish Renaissance* (1964) laid down an information base which has been drawn on by all subsequent scholars of the interwar literary revival; and, on the home front, I thank Ian and Euan for their forbearance and for much practical help.

Copyright acknowledgements are given after the Commentary section.

MPM

TOWARDS A SCOTTISH LITERARY RENAISSANCE

Literary identity is the primary focus in the majority of the six sections presented under this collective heading. The first section, 'What *is* Scottish Literature?', sets the scene for the ensuing debates, since not only had the literary revolutionaries to fight against parochialism, but the very existence of a distinctive Scottish literary identity, as opposed to a provincial North British one, could no longer be taken for granted. Sections two to four, with their related and at times overlapping material, trace the discussions of language and identity and the emergence of a 'literary renaissance' from the attempt by the London Burns Club in the early 1920s to rescue the Scots Vernacular, through Grieve/MacDiarmid's hostility to and then advocacy of the use of Scots, to Edwin Muir's insistence in *Scott and Scotland* in 1936 that the only way forward for the ambitious Scottish writer was the English language and the English tradition. The third section, 'A Scottish Renaissance? Responses and Reviews', demonstrates how quickly the nomenclature and idea of a 'Scottish Renaissance' established itself, both on the part of enthusiasts and those more sceptical. This section also contains a number of important reviews of the new literature. 'Transforming Traditions' presents a selection of the attacks made on parochial Scotland and her past literary ikons, the 'sham bards of a sham nation', in the words of Muir's poem 'Scotland 1941'. This section also points to new ways forward and to the re-emergence of drama and the new art of film.

'Europe and the Impact of the Modern' and 'Women on Women: Gendering the Renaissance' are related to the previous sections, but have a slightly different emphasis. Re-engaging with Europe and engaging with the artistic and intellectual movements of the period were priorities for those attempting to regenerate Scottish culture. Section five therefore includes excerpts from the work of influential thinkers and from literary movements of what we now call the Modernist period, together with excerpts from Scottish writers of the time which show the impact on them of the modern movement in literature and ideas. Edwin Muir emerges from these excerpts as a key figure in the European dimension of the Renaissance as well as a powerful presenter and critic of 'the Modern'.

One shared element in Modernism and the Scottish Renaissance Movement is their predominantly male nature. Although the interwar period in general saw a significant increase in the number of women creative writers, especially fiction writers, women still did not find it easy to achieve public roles. While contributions by women have been included wherever possible throughout this collection of source documents, the final section of 'Towards a Scottish Literary Renaissance' is entirely devoted to perspectives by women writers: perspectives on their own female lives and on their responses to literature and society. These views, very often communicated in letters and private journals, add much that is important to our understanding of this transitional historical period, both in terms of gender and the wider social and political scene.

I

Preliminary: What *is* Scottish Literature?

1.1 Robert Louis Stevenson, from letter to S.R. Crockett (April 1888)

Don't put 'N.B.' on your paper: put *Scotland* and be done with it. Alas, that I should be stabbed in the house of my friends! The name of my native land is not *North Britain*, whatever may be the name of yours.

(Robert Louis Stevenson, letter to S.R. Crockett, Bradford A. Booth and Ernest Mehew eds, *The Letters of Robert Louis Stevenson* vol.6 New Haven and London: Yale University Press, 1995, p.156.)

1.2 W. MacNeile Dixon, from Introduction to *The Edinburgh Book of Scottish Verse* (1910)

'What is Scottish poetry?' one asks oneself; 'is it merely English poetry under another name, written by men of Scottish birth and descent, but otherwise in no way separable from the work of Dryden or of Keats? Or is it something very different, the poetry of an ancient kingdom north of Tweed, as distinct in theme and sentiment as in language, hardly, if at all, less separate and original than that of any other European people?' To confine it to the former class would be virtually to exclude the vernacular—an impossible proposition, since in the work of Burns, and often elsewhere, the vernacular is of classic excellence: to confine it to the latter would, on the other hand, impoverish the literary fame of Scotland by the omission of great names, names not readily to be yielded to the Saxon, names like those of Drummond of Hawthornden, of Campbell and of Scott. Though not indeed a problem of momentous consequence, the purposes of this book require an answer—how shall we here define Scottish poetry? And the matter seems to stand thus. An attempt to represent the mind and heart of a country, of a people as exhibited in its poetry, should be inclusive rather than exclusive, should avoid pedantry, should eschew cramping limitations and disputable principles. It should seek the plain and beaten path, the broad way of the daily traveller. We at least shall gain nothing by departure from it. Scottish verse, therefore, shall here mean verse which is the work of Scotsmen, whether in English or Scots. If the vernacular is more characteristic, more racy of the soil, the English poetry written by Scotsmen has something also to tell us of Scotland, of the literary or political influences to which she has most willingly and fully responded. If Fergusson and Burns are more truly Scottish, it is not uninteresting or uninstructive to recall the Italian grace of Drummond, or to remember that the most stirring of English martial lyrics were blown from a Scottish trumpet, the trumpet of Campbell. Nor is it the less desirable to claim for Scotland all that may justly be claimed, since, though as a nation she remained unconquered no doubt, she has never ceased to pay the tribute of a remote, if not subordinate, province of the Union. By a convention, carrying it here, as often, with a high hand, Scotland has given of her best in literature, and in some other things, without recompense of glory. The English editors of anthologies, for example, pleasantly and rightly enough assume that Scott or Stevenson are sufficiently English to enrich their collections, nor are they unwilling to accept Burns in certain of his moods; but unhappily reprisals are impossible,—this volume dare not draw from the works of Gray or of Wordsworth. Scottish may be English— when it is deemed of sufficient merit—but English can never be Scottish.

There is here, indeed, proposed no ground for quarrel, since the Scots language, though in its later history exposed to different influences, was Northern English, neither more nor less, an idiom perfectly dignified, perfectly fitted for the higher purposes of literature, unfortunate only in this, that it failed to establish itself as the language of the nation, as the speech of the majority. The speech of Chaucer, the East Midland variety of the language, grew to be English of the centre, and the other idioms, with them Scots, gradually passed into provincial obscurity. The poetry that claims to be indisputably Scottish must be content to pay the penalty, to be the more provincial the more it is characteristic, since it is poetry of a dialect, of Northern English, and not English of the centre. Let us not, however, exaggerate the seriousness of the penalty. The audience for poetry is never a mighty one, and the vernacular has still its audience. Let us be honest and outspoken, let us go further and say that if the vernacular contains a large body of poetry highly excellent, the difficulties of its dialect will assuredly be overcome by lovers of great art, as they are overcome by students of foreign literature. Great poetry, in whatever language it is written, will not suffer neglect; it is too precious, there is too little of it. Great poetry will continue to be studied, will continue to be current till the end of the world.

4

The critical question seems to be, 'What is the value of the Scottish vernacular poetry taken as a whole? Is it worthy the attention, not of those who understand it without effort, but of those who, knowing English, may easily, with the assistance of a glossary, come to understand it? Is it worthy the attention of the future which will find it more difficult to understand?' [. . .]

There is another literature in Scotland, neither English nor Scots, the literature of a wholly distinct language—the Gaelic. It might, indeed, be claimed as the only true national literature, uncontaminated by foreign influences for a thousand years. A representative book of Scottish verse could not overlook the Gaelic. Yet here translation is our only resource, and translations rarely, if ever, carry with them the spirit, and are powerless to reproduce the form or music of the original. And perhaps the problems of translation nowhere present themselves in more undisguised unfriendliness than to him who desires to give an English rendering of a characteristically Gaelic piece. How distinct is the Celtic from the Saxon genius!

(W. MacNeile Dixon, 'Introduction', *The Edinburgh Book of Scottish Verse* London: Meiklejohn and Holden, 1910, pp.vii–xv [vii–x, xiv–xv].)

1.3   G.R. Blake, from *Scotland of the Scots* (1919)

The living Scottish poets are few: Charles Murray, the poet of 'Hamewith', is one of the last representatives of a great strain. The literary product of Scotsmen is merged utterly into the mass of English literature, and the vernacular is practically moribund as a vehicle of thought: education and commerce have seen to that. There can only be one Burns, and the age of miracles of that description is past. The Scottish sentiment, *per se*, is in no imminent danger of expiring, but the means and modes of expression have changed utterly in the gradual transition of Scotland. The peasant is no longer illiterate; he can read and write in classical English; and the children of the folks in comfortable circumstances are now cosmopolitanised almost beyond recognition. This latter class possesses, of course, its singers, but they are vocal in the broad literary sense, not in the restricted national sense. And the younger lutes are still; for war is absorbing every activity and has choked the song in many throats with the clay of France and Flanders. [. . .] But the hope remains that out of the ashes of the conflagration will arise a spirit that will bring new life to the silent muse of Scotland.

(G.R. Blake, *Scotland of the Scots*, London: Pitman, 1919, p.99.)

1.4 G. Gregory Smith, from *Scottish Literature: Character and Influence* (1919)

Two considerations of contrary bearing present themselves at the outset. One is of encouragement; that the literature is the literature of a small country, that it runs a shorter course than others, and that there is no linguistic divorce between its earlier and later stages, as in southern English. In this shortness and cohesion the most favourable conditions seem to be offered for the making of a general estimate. But, on the other hand, we find at closer scanning that this cohesion, at least in formal expression and in choice of material, is only apparent, that the literature is remarkably varied, and that it becomes, under the stress of foreign influence and native division and reaction, almost a zigzag of contradictions. The antithesis need not, however, disconcert us. Perhaps in the very combination of opposites—what either of the two Sir Thomases, of Norwich and Cromarty, might have been willing to call 'the Caledonian antisyzygy'—we have a reflection of the contrasts which the Scot shows at every turn, in his political and ecclesiastical history, in his polemical restlessness, in his adaptability, which is another way of saying that he has made allowance for new conditions, in his practical judgement, which is the admission that two sides of the matter have been considered. If therefore Scottish history and life are, as an old northern writer said of something else, 'varied with a clean contrair spirit', we need not be surprised to find that in his literature the Scot presents two aspects which appear contradictory. [. . .]

One characteristic or mood stands out clearly, though it is not easily described in a word. We stumble over 'actuality', 'grip of fact', 'sense of detail', 'realism', yet with the conviction that we are proceeding in the right direction. We desire to express not merely the talent of close observation, but the power of producing, by a cumulation of touches, a quick and perfect image to the reader. What we are really thinking of is 'intimacy' of style. Scottish literature has no monopoly of this, which is to be found in the best work everywhere, and is indeed a first axiom of artistic method, no matter what processes of selection and recollection may follow; but in Scots the zest for handling a multitude of details rather than for seeking broad effects by suggestion is very persistent. [. . .]

The Scottish Muse has, however, another mood. Though she has loved reality, sometimes to maudlin affection for the commonplace, she has loved not less the airier pleasure to be found in the confusion of the senses, in the fun of things thrown topsyturvy, in the horns of elfland and the voices of the mountains. It is a strange union of opposites, alien as Hotspur and Glendower. [. . .] Does any other man combine so strangely the severe and tender in his character, or forgo the victory of the most relentless logic at the sudden bidding of sentiment or superstition? Does literature anywhere, of this small compass, show such a mixture of contraries as his in outlook, subject, and method; real life and romance, everyday fact and the supernatural, things holy and things profane, gentle and simple, convention and 'cantrip', thistles and thistledown? [. . .] There is more in the Scottish antithesis of the real and fantastic than is to be explained by the familiar rules of rhetoric. The sudden jostling of contraries seems to preclude any relationship by literary suggestion. The one invades the other without warning. They are the 'polar twins' of the Scottish Muse. [. . .] This mingling, even of the most eccentric kind, is an indication to us that the Scot, in that medieval fashion which takes all things as granted, is at his ease in both 'rooms of life', and turns to fun, and even profanity, with no misgivings. For Scottish literature is more medieval in habit than criticism has suspected, and owes some part of its picturesque strength to this freedom in passing from one mood to another. It takes some people more time than they can spare to see the absolute propriety of a gargoyle's grinning at the elbow of a kneeling saint.

(G. Gregory Smith, *Scottish Literature: Character and Influence* London: Macmillan & Co., 1919, pp.3–5, 19–20, 35.)

1.5   T.S. Eliot, 'Was There a Scottish Literature?' (*Athenaeum* August 1919)

We suppose that there is an English literature, and Professor Gregory Smith supposes that there is a Scotch literature. When we assume that a literature exists we assume a great deal: we suppose that there is one of the five or six (at most) great organic formations of history. We do not suppose merely 'a history', for there might be a history of Tamil literature; but a part of History, which for us is the history of Europe. We suppose not merely a corpus of writings in one language, but writings and writers between whom there is a tradition; and writers who are not merely connected by tradition in time, but who are related so as to be in the light of eternity contemporaneous, from a certain point of view cells in one body, Chaucer and Hardy. We suppose a mind which is not only the English mind of one period with its prejudices of politics and fashions of taste, but which is a greater, finer, more positive, more comprehensive mind than the mind of any period. And we suppose to each writer an importance which is not only individual, but due to his place as a constituent of this mind. When we suppose that there is a literature, therefore, we suppose a great deal.

Professor Gregory Smith assumes the existence of a Scottish literature more by the title of his book than by any assertion he makes. For in his treatment, which is fairminded, honest, intelligent and scholarly, he even supplies us with suggestions towards finding reasons to deny the existence of a Scottish literature. He has written a series of essays, dealing with what appears to be one subject, and the conclusion issues very honestly from his treatment that the unity of the subject is not literary but only geographical. What he has done is, because of the reflections it provokes, perhaps more interesting than either of two things he might have done. He might have written a handbook of writers who were born or flourished north of a frontier; such a book might have a practical utility, without giving occasion to any generalizations. Or he might have made a study of the Scotch mind. Such a study might have great interest on its own account, but at all events it is not part of Mr Gregory Smith's intentions. A book which contains no discussion of Scottish philosophy, which barely mentions the names of Hume and Reid, and only reports the personal dominance of Dugald Stewart in Edinburgh, does not pretend to be a study of the Scotch mind. It is only the Scotch mind in literature and belles-lettres that is charted. Because the book is neither a handbook nor a study of the Scotch mind, it is a study of Scotch literature in a sense which requires that there should be an organic formation.

What clearly comes out under Mr Gregory Smith's handling is the fact that Scottish literature falls into several periods, and that these periods are related not so much to each other as to corresponding periods in English literature. The way in which Scottish literature has been indebted to English literature is different from the way in which English literature has been indebted to other literatures. English literature has not only, at times, been much affected by the Continent, but has sometimes, for the moment, even appeared to be thrown off its balance by foreign influence. But in the long run we can see that the continuity of the language has been the strongest thing; so that however much we need French or Italian literature to explain English literature of any period, we need, to explain it, the English inheritance still more. Scottish literature lacks, in the first place, the continuity of the language. It is precisely in the years when English literature was acquiring the power of a world literature that the Scottish language was beginning to decay or to be abandoned. Gawain Douglas, in Tudor times, is perhaps the last great Scotch poet to write Scots with the same feeling toward the language, the same conviction, as an Englishman writing English. A hundred years later, a Scot unquestionably Scottish, one of the greatest prose writers of his time, Sir Thomas Urquhart, translated Rabelais into a language which is English.

Mr Gregory Smith makes it copiously clear that Scots literature was the literature of the Lowlands, and that the Scot of the Lowlands was at all times much more closely in touch with his Southron enemy than with the Gaelic occasional ally. Whatever aesthetic agitation may have taken place in the Highland brain, the disturbance was not communicated to the Lowlander. We are quite at liberty to treat the Scots language as a dialect, as one of the several English dialects which gradually and inevitably amalgamated into one language. Only Scotland, more isolated, and differing from the others more than they differed from each other, retained its local peculiarities much longer. The first part of the history of Scottish literature is a part of the history of English literature when English was several dialects; the second part is a part of the history of English literature when English was two dialects—English and Scots; the third part is something quite different—it is the history of a provincial literature. And finally, there is no longer any tenable important distinction to be drawn for the present day between the two literatures.

Even if we inspect the earlier Scottish literature alone—if we take it at the period following Chaucer when nearly all the poetry of any permanent value was being produced in Scotland and not in England—we can see that Scots literature was assimilating English influence with a very different tendency from that which is evident in the English (or English including Scottish) assimilation of foreign literature. English, the more it borrowed and imitated, the more significantly it became English; the inclination of Scots literature toward English is the curve of its development toward English. And as we examine the periods of Scottish (not Scots) literature we see that there is no common denominator between the periods when Scottish literature was most important. It was important as a dialect among the other English dialects; it was important in the fifteenth century when English poetry was not important; and it was important, or rather Edinburgh literature was important, as a *provincial* literature about 1800. The last is not the importance of a separate literature; it is the importance of a provincial capital which at a certain time happens to contain as many or more men of importance than the metropolis. Edinburgh in 1800, of which Mr Gregory Smith gives a pleasing glimpse, is analogous to Boston in America fifty years later. It was as interesting, perhaps for a moment more interesting, than London. But a provincial capital, even with the *Edinburgh* and *Blackwood's* of a hundred years ago, is the matter of a moment; it depends on the continuous supply of important men; the instant this supply falls off, the metropolis, even if suffering from a like poverty, gains the ascendant. And then the important men turn to the metropolis.

It is true that Mr Gregory Smith seeks for permanent characteristics of the Scottish mind which find expression in literature. But, with deference to his superior knowledge of the subject, the characteristics which he presents do not seem essential to literature, sufficient to mark any significant *literary* difference. Neither the love of precise detail nor the love of the fantastic, which he finds in Scottish literature, is a literary trait; on the contrary, they are both more likely to be hostile to artistic perfection. Nor has the passion for antiquities, nor the persistence of local metres in verse, any extensive significance. To the extent to which writing becomes literature, these peculiarities are likely to be submerged.

We may even conclude it to be an evidence of strength, rather than of weakness, that the Scots language and the Scottish literature did not maintain a separate existence. It is not always recognized how fierce and fatal is the struggle for existence between literatures. In this struggle there is great advantage to be won if forces not too disparate can be united. Scottish, throwing in its luck with English, has not only much greater chance of survival, but contributes important elements of strength to complete the English: as, for instance, its philosophical and historical prose. A literature does not maintain itself simply by a continual production of great writers. The historian of literature must count with as shifting and as massive forces as the historian of politics. In the modern world the struggle of capitals of civilization is apparent on a large scale. A powerful literature, with a powerful capital, tends to attract and absorb all the drifting shreds of force about it. Up to a certain limit of dissimilarity, this fusion is of very great value. English and Scottish, probably English and Irish (if not prevented by political friction), are cognate enough for the union to be of value. The basis for one literature is one language. The danger of disintegration of English literature and language would arise if the same language were employed by peoples too remote (for geographical or other reasons) to be able to pool their differences in a common metropolis. The chances of its survival, as a language and a literature in the tradition of European civilization, would be diminished against such a concentrated force as the French. For France, of course, a different danger, real or apparent, has been announced, we believe in an intemperate and fanatical spirit, by such apostles of French culture as M. Maurras: the danger of attracting foreign forces which might be received without being digested. That is at present, we trust, not an imminent peril for Britain.

(T.S. Eliot, 'Was There a Scottish Literature?', *Athenaeum* 1 August 1919, pp.680–81.)

2

Language, Identity and the Vernacular Debate

2.1 Extract from Minutes of the Annual Meeting of the London Robert Burns Club (June 1920)

Vernacular Circle: Mr Will proposed and Mr Anderson seconded that at this Annual Meeting of the London Robert Burns Club, held at Anderton's Hotel, on 7th June, 1920, there be formed, in connection with the Club, a Vernacular Circle, which will have for its principal object the consideration and adoption of methods for the preservation of the oral and literary language of Lowland Scotland. This was unanimously agreed to.

In moving the resolution, Mr Will said:

Ladies and Gentlemen—

I beg to move 'That this meeting confirm the decision of the Committee of March 1, 1920, that there be formed a Sub Committee or Vernacular Circle which will have for its object the preservation of the language of Lowland Scotland, in which the most important work of Robert Burns is enshrined.'

In moving this resolution, Mr Chairman, I should like to give in as few words as I possibly can, the reasons that actuated the Committee of the Club in coming to the decision it did, and the manner in which the Committee appointed to carry on the work of the Circle might act. I do not intend to advance any arguments in favour of the formation of such a Circle, for I believe there is complete unanimity on the matter of the advantages of such an organisation. If it were necessary to argue the point I think we should in one sentence justify the setting up of such a Circle. We should be able to say that if something be not done to arrest the decay of the language, Robert Burns's doric poems and songs will cease to be understood. That in itself should be sufficient to justify the London Robert Burns Club in setting the work afoot; indeed it would be a disgrace if the Club refused to undertake it.

Time and again it has been urged upon us at our Birthday Festivals—first by Mr John Buchan and last by Mr Charles Murray (Hamewith) that the Club might consider it to be its duty to seek every means in its power to foster the language of Lowland Scotland; and Miss Mary Symon of Dufftown, one of our foremost Scottish poetesses, has written repeatedly to me urging upon the London Robert Burns Club the desirability of taking action. It will thus be seen that this work has been thrust upon the London Robert Burns Club as being either the most likely organisation to carry it out, or as being the organisation whose duty it is to carry through such work. The Committee of the Club have shouldered the responsibility, and it is for you, ladies and gentlemen, if you think fit, to support their decision.

Members may ask what such a Circle as is suggested would do, and how they would do it. Well, my personal idea of this Circle is something like this:

It would be composed of members of the Club who would signify their wish to be enrolled.

Those members would meet, elect a chairman, secretary, and committee, and fix the annual subscription, something like half a crown per annum.

The Committee would be composed of enthusiasts representing different parts of Scotland, and would draw up finally the objects to be aimed at.

These objects might or might not embrace some of these suggestions:

To raise money for the purpose of founding at each of the Universities of Edinburgh, Glasgow, Aberdeen, St Andrews and Dundee an annual prize for a poem in the Scottish Vernacular, these prizes to be called the London Robert Burns Club Prizes.

To secure from individual ladies and gentlemen annual prizes to be given to schools in which they are interested locally for the best singers or reciters of pieces of prose or poetry in the Vernacular, the Committee of the Club suggesting the pieces.

To have every year certain essays or lectures as part of our winter programme, these lectures to be given by the greatest authorities on the subject in the country. [. . .]

Continuing the possible programme, I would suggest that we might extend our activities to the Colonies, where the Scottish element is so strong and where the heart beats true to the Homeland.

I need hardly continue, for there is no lack of ways in which we can move towards the continued use in speech at home and in literature at home and abroad of the auld Scots tongue.

As I have said, we shall have influential support. I believe a great acquisition to the membership of the Club the reflection that we are making a really good educational effort, and that we are assisting in perpetuating the message of Robert Burns.

Ladies and gentlemen, I beg to move the resolution.

Mr John Anderson, in seconding, said he most heartily approved all that Mr Will had proposed. He felt that the Club was undertaking a great educational and national work, and predicted great results from the scheme.

Other gentlemen supported the proposal, which was unanimously agreed to.

(Minutes of the London Robert Burns Club, 7 June 1920, Special Collections,
Mitchell Library, Glasgow.)

2.2 Representative Letters of Support for Vernacular Circle Proposal (1920)

a) Letter from John Buchan (March 1920)

35 & 36 PATERNOSTER ROW
LONDON. E.C.
31st March, 1920.

William Will, Esq.,
Tallis House,
Whitefriars, E.C.4.

My dear Mr Will,

I will be very willing indeed to be an honorary member of the Vernacular Circle of the Robert Burns Club. It is an excellent idea and I wish it every success.

Yours very sincerely,
John Buchan

b) Letter from Mrs Violet Jacob (April 1920)

Ladies Empire Club,
Grosvenor Street, W.
9.4.20

Dear Mr Will,

A hurried line to say that I shall have great pleasure in becoming an Hon. Member of the projected Vernacular Circle of the Burns Club. It seems to be an excellent idea.

Yours truly,
Violet Jacob

(London Robert Burns Club Papers, Special Collections, Mitchell Library, Glasgow.)

2.3 W.A. Craigie, from 'The Present State of the Scottish Tongue' (January 1921)

I have selected the subject of my discourse this evening—'The Present State of the Scottish Tongue'—in a spirit which I am afraid is not regarded as characteristically Scottish—in a spirit of some humility. This is one of the few things connected with the land beyond the Tweed of which the patriotic and reflective Scot has not full reason to be proud. If the Scottish tongue were in that flourishing state in which we would like to see it, would I be standing here—in the midst of a gathering of Scots, and in the very centre of that foreign capital which they have all but made their own—and yet be addressing you (as far as I can) in the language of the Southron? This is not as it ought to be; and yet if I had attempted to frame my address throughout in the 'haimert tongue', in the current speech of Forfarshire, it would not only have been a surprise, but perhaps something of a trial to you. It would certainly have demanded much more preparation on my part, and even more indulgence on yours than I trust I may rely upon while I unfold my views on this important subject.

The reason why I do not address you in our own tongue, even when speaking about it, can only be clearly understood by going back beyond our own time. It is no fault of ours, nor even of our fathers or grandfathers, but of still earlier generations, which allowed the germs of decay to creep into the fabric of the old Scottish tongue as it had grown up in the centuries when Scotland was a kingdom. In the sixteenth century, and especially in the first half of it, Scottish as a spoken and written language stood on a level with English, and in some respects even stood higher. The first real blow to it came through the Reformation. Whatever good that event may have done to Scotland in other respects, it not only failed to assist in the maintenance or development of the national tongue, but it materially helped to weaken its position by bringing with it the Bible and other religious works in English. The rapid rise of a new and interesting literature in England hastened the process still more, by placing new models before the Scottish authors, scribes, and printers of the day. It is surprising how quickly this influence made itself felt. An instance of it can be quite clearly seen in the two manuscripts containing the poems of Sir Richard Maitland (together with those of other Scottish poets). One of these, the folio, was finished in 1582; the other, the quarto, in 1586; and even in these four years the effect of southern models upon the language and spelling is very clearly marked.

With these preparations, the climax naturally came with the Union of the Crowns. After that date the former equality between the English and Scottish tongues was completely gone, and English was definitely recognised as the standard form for literary work, although the native tongue might persist in colouring it to a greater or less degree according to the taste or learning of the writer.

To a great extent, of course, Scots continued to speak after their own fashion, while trying to write as the English wrote. If this had not been so, the revival of dialect literature towards the end of the seventeenth century would not have been so natural or so easy. It is significant, too, that the precursors of this revival, the Semples of Beltrees, did not belong to the humbler part of the community—showing that the native tongue was still familiar in good society. It was, in fact, still only in a period of quiescence out of which it might have been fully aroused if circumstances had really been favourable, and out of which it did revive to a considerable extent.

In a gathering of Scots it is unnecessary to enter into details regarding the history of Scottish vernacular literature in the eighteenth century, marked as it is with the names of the great triad, Ramsay, Ferguson [sic], and Burns, and with those of many lesser lights. So far as it went, the revival of the native tongue for literary purposes was eminently successful, and the genius of Burns gave it a permanent place among the languages of the world. This was a great achievement, and compensates in no small degree for the loss of prestige which the language had previously sustained.

It is only when we critically examine the range of this Scottish literature of the eighteenth century that the weakness of the position becomes apparent. Of what does it really consist? Mainly of short poems and songs—narrative or lyric verse—of high quality at its best, but (much as we may enjoy it) outside the work of Burns seldom compelling the interest or admiration of those who are not born Scots. There are only a few attempts at longer poetic compositions, such as the 'Gentle Shepherd' of Allan Ramsay, or 'The Fortunate Shepherdess' of Alexander Ross. Of prose there is very little, and what there is, is of the trivial and humorous type that may serve to amuse, but certainly does nothing to impart dignity to the language in which it is written. It is here that the real nakedness of the situation is most clearly exposed. No Scottish writer of the eighteenth century who had anything important to say in prose attempted to say it in the language of his countrymen. He did it in his best English, and all the time he was haunted by an uneasy feeling that even his choicest English was not free from those dreadful solecisms known as Scotticisms, which would assuredly be pointed out and laughed at when his book had penetrated into the sister-kingdom.

In this respect, then, the eighteenth century did not mend the faults of the seventeenth; it made them worse. It helped to establish beyond remedy the feeling that for all serious and practical purposes—for all written and spoken discourses on formal occasions, even for familiar letter writing—the Scottish tongue was no longer admissible. Worse still, it established English as the only form of the language in which instruction was given, while the ability to read or write Scottish was left to be acquired by nature. If you remember what sort of education Burns had, the truth of this will be realised. Schoolmasters, it is true, sometimes continued to use the vernacular even in school, but merely as a matter of habit; what they were actually engaged in teaching was the reading and the writing of English. All things considered, I have little doubt that the ideas of culture which prevailed in the second half of the eighteenth century are largely responsible for finally reducing our old Lowland tongue to the position of a dialect, from which it has never since recovered. [. . .]

We have, therefore, a problem which occurs elsewhere in Europe at the present, as I hope to show later on. The language of the country—in this case the Scottish tongue—has steadily receded, and to all appearance is still receding, from actual use in everyday life, from all matters of business or administration, from school and church, and so on, but is still cultivated with success and even with enthusiasm for certain intellectual purposes and on sentimental grounds. How long can these tendencies co-exist without the second becoming purely artificial? That is the problem.

The question, of course, has two aspects. If Scots practically cease to use their tongue in their everyday talk, a knowledge of its form and vocabulary will soon only be acquired by reading—by a study of the existing literature. This affects both the writers and their readers. When the author has acquired facility in writing a language which he really does not himself employ, can he safely count upon an understanding public of readers whose knowledge of it is similarly artificial? No doubt this stage will only be arrived at by degrees, but in the end it is bound to come. I think it is not going too far to say that to some extent it has already arrived, and that it would not be difficult in recent Scottish literature to specify books which owe not a little to a close imitation of the older writers, and even a diligent use of the Scottish dictionary.

It is therefore a matter of some importance for those who believe that the Scottish tongue has a national value, to know exactly what the situation now is. It is nearly a quarter of a century since I ceased to live in Scotland, and I feel that I am not sufficiently acquainted with the circumstances of the present day to be perfectly definite on this point. Perhaps some of those present may be able to give useful information from a more recent acquaintance with the actual facts.

From all I can learn, however, the spoken tongue is not holding its own with that 'dourness' which we like to think of as particularly Scottish. The schoolmaster, the newspaper and magazine, and the novel, are proving too strong for it—to say nothing of ideas of culture which may be mistaken but are none the less powerful. There is, at least on the surface, sufficient justification for statements that the dialect is declining—even if 'dying out' may be too strong an expression. History has shown that it is never quite safe to say that any language or dialect is 'dying out'. In this respect languages are apt to prove like 'threatened men': they live long. A century after the Norman Conquest we find a historian stating (and probably with truth) that English barely survived as a language of the rustics in out-of-the-way districts. In the middle of the seventeenth century a Frisian scholar contemplated the speedy demise of the Frisian tongue; a Frisian schoolmaster constantly writes to assure me of the same thing at the present day, and this at a time when more Frisian is being written and printed than at any previous date. Even complaints as to the decline of the Scottish tongue are not new. Prefixed to the poems of Andrew Shirrefs, published in 1790, there is a piece written in 1788 entitled 'An Address in Scotch, on the Decay of that Language'.

This is a matter in which the schoolmaster is not entirely to be trusted, but it would be interesting and valuable to have a collection of reports from Scottish country schoolmasters as to the position which the dialect still holds as a living form of speech—and it would be equally valuable to have a statement of their own attitude towards it. In the past the schoolmaster has usually been indifferent or actually hostile; it would be interesting to know how far that attitude has been modified in Scotland, as it has been in some other countries where similar conditions have prevailed.

From the schoolmaster, too, we might learn how far a knowledge of the native tongue is being maintained among the younger generation by what they read. That this is not being done within the school is certain, so far as I am aware. I have not yet learned that the excellent *Readings in Modern Scots* by Alexander Mackie, published by Messrs Chambers in 1913, has become a favourite school book, as it richly deserves to be. I am also quite certain that the Scottish *Selections from the Waverley Novels* prepared expressly with a view to being used in schools, and published in 1916, has not yet penetrated within the walls of the school-room. One may, indeed, shrewdly suspect that the intrusion of such reading-books would rather embarrass than delight a considerable number of teachers, male and female, who have been accustomed to consider a careful avoidance, and even a complete ignorance, of their own native tongue as the prime essential towards a state of academic culture. [. . .]

Supposing, however, that those who assert the decline and ultimate disappearance of Scottish as a living form of speech are right in their view, what effect will this have upon the people of Scotland? [. . .] A nation which has no distinctive language lacks one of the most obvious features of nationality, and one which has lost its own language has to that extent allowed itself to become an appendage to another. This truth is very clearly expressed in a Frisian song, written some six years ago, when the Frisians began to take active steps to protect their language. 'We will not let our language go', it says, 'for without the Frisian tongue we are Frisians no more.'

If, however, the force of circumstances should justify the arguments of the practical unsentimental person, and a first-hand knowledge of Scottish should practically disappear in the course of the next generation or two, what effect will this have in relation to Scottish literature? Clearly it will create a new situation in this respect. Either the production of new literature in the dialect will cease altogether, or it will become a mere artificial form of composition, which will no longer have even the merit of local colouring, unless the scene is laid in the past. Even at the present day I could name an excellent scholar and critic born and bred in Scotland, who is inclined to believe that no man writes Scottish naturally, that its employment for poetry or prose is merely a conscious effort towards attaining a certain literary effect and not at all due to any natural impulse to use the tongue which lies nearest to him. I do not accept this view as absolutely correct even now, but we must certainly rapidly come to that stage if the written tongue has no longer the spoken one behind it.

We shall then have this anomalous situation: Scotland will continue to exist, and the glory of its past literature no man can take from it. But the Scottish people, having ceased to speak its own language, will be no more capable of understanding and enjoying that literature than any other portion of the English-speaking world. The Scot who wishes to read Burns will have to use the glossary as diligently as the Englishman of the present day: and I cannot readily imagine a more humiliating situation for a nation than to depend on a glossary for the understanding of its national poet. Worse still, the Scot will no longer, except by special training, be able to read aloud his national literature without mangling it in the most heart-rending (or ear-rending) manner. We have all, in our time, known what it is to hear Scottish poetry read, or a Scottish joke told, by one not born in Scotland, and we know how impossible it is for him to come anywhere near the real thing. But that is exactly what the Scot of the future will do if Scottish ceases to be a current form of speech—unless indeed the literature is buried along with the language. [. . .]

From these examples [Catalan, Provençal and Breton, Flemish, Frisian, Norwegian], which in several respects offer close parallels to the case of Scotland, we can learn several powerful factors in the revival of a language: first, school-teaching and school-books; second, cheap and popular books in the language of the people; third, scholarly work in the history of the language, and in the preparation of vocabularies and dictionaries; fourth, the cultivation of a new and national literature.

(W.A. Craigie, 'The Present State of the Scottish Tongue', a lecture given to the Vernacular Circle of the London Robert Burns Club, 10 January 1921; reprinted from *The Scottish Tongue: A Series of Lectures on the Vernacular Language of Lowland Scotland*, London: Cassell & Co., 1924, pp.3–46 [3–8, 10–14, 18–19, 20–22, 36–37].)

2.4 J.M. Bulloch, from 'The Delight of the Doric in the Diminutive' (December 1921)

When in a passing moment of easy-ozy disregard of my limited learning and leisure, I agreed to address the Vernacular Circle, it was much more than the temptation of alliteration that made me choose for my subject the delight of the Doric in the diminutive: for of all the visions entertained by the vernacularists, the one that has the most solid foundation in actual fact is the persistence in the use of the diminutive, more particularly in the north-east of Scotland, where by far the most vigorous and idiosyncratic form of the vernacular is retained.

Hundred of mothers throughout Aberdeenshire and Banffshire every night put their 'little wee bit loonikies' and 'little wee bit lassickies' to their 'bedies', while the infant of the household, described as the 'little wee eenickie', that is a 'teeny weeny eenie'—lies in its 'cradlie'. A thousand and one examples will leap to your minds:—'The boatie rows': 'sic mannie, sic horsie'; 'the ewie wi' the crookit horn'—as against Burns's 'Ca' the ewes tae the knowes'; a 'sheltie': a 'sheepie', a 'lammie', a 'burnie', a 'quinie' and so on through a whole catalogue of diminutives, sometimes five and six thick. Indeed, 'a little wee bit loonikie' represents five diminutives. These diminutives are, I say, just as frequently used as ever they have been. They are even employed by people who have sloughed nearly every other vestige of the vernacular, for the very simple reason that they cannot slough the mentality which the diminutive represents and which it can evaluate as nothing else can do. [. . .]

But in addition to the mere philological aspect of the problem, you will find, at any rate in the case of Scotland, many other applications which go deep down into national psychology. The diminutive, in short, is not an isolated phenomenon. It is simply one way, and merely the vocal way, of giving expression to a general method of minimising, which affects mind and matter alike. [. . .] It expresses itself very definitely in the Scot's religion, for Calvinism is based fundamentally on the conception of man as a puny creature struggling with a colossal predestined fate. [. . .] Curiously enough it is used to express two diametrically opposite emotions— Affection and Contempt—in which we as a people, who understand white and black—whereas the Englishman can see the whole spectrum at once—are particularly strong. [. . .]

Humour links up the third great use of the diminutive as an expression of contempt, and so far as I can gather our Doric is peculiar in using it for this purpose. It is, however, not difficult to understand how affection runs into humour, or rather wit, and then into contempt. We are constantly told that the Scot has no humour. What the Scot has got is wit, a very different quality. Humour is a quality of the heart: wit is the product of the head. It is not because the Scot has no heart. The trouble is he feels that he has too much of it. Thus he instinctively set his head to sentinel his heart, so that he may not go off at the deep end of rapturous enthusiasm or display too much affection. [. . .] Now there is nothing like the diminutive for expressing this mood, for, just as the diminutive is admirable for expressing the physical smallness of a child, and the child quality in the things we love, so it represents equally well all kinds of spiritual smallness and meanness. [. . .]

I have said that the use of the diminutive is most prevalent in the north-east of Scotland, particularly in Aberdeenshire and Banffshire, but it is also used in Kincardineshire, Forfarshire, and Fifeshire, and as far north as Ross-shire [. . .] This is so much the case that you will find the diminutive rarely printed. It is so natural, so much part of the common coinage that Scots 'makars', either of yesterday or of to-day, rarely employ it. They think it too common, too colloquial, not 'literary' enough. That is really one of our cruxes. The moment the Scot begins to write, he tends to become self-conscious, not least when he writes in English, because he does not write as he speaks, whereas the Englishman does. Even in Scots, a poetic convention tends to set itself up in print.

It is this more than anything that induces some critics of the Vernacular Circle, especially in Scotland, to regard us as so many Burkes and Hares, resurrecting the bones of a dead language. So vital a thing as our vernacular cannot die. Let it be freely admitted that it undergoes change precisely because it is alive; for, as Ibsen once said, the only thing that doesn't change is the law of change. True, the auld hoose of our Doric—which has extended beyond the old but and ben, tends to get out of the plumb, and the proud task of the Vernacular Circle is to do a bit of underpinning, mostly, however, by inducing our stay-at-home compatriots to write it as they speak it, for it shows far fewer cracks when it is spoken colloquially.

Certain it is, the diminutive changes least of all, because it expresses as nothing else can do the most marked characteristics of our mentality. Why, indeed, should the Scot abjure his thriftiness and cripple his vocabulary by casting aside an instrument of expression which saves the inspiration of his childhood from fading into the light of common day: an instrument so gracious, so expressive, so tender, so humorous; instinct with an element of that criticism of life which Matthew Arnold defined as the essence of poetry. The diminutive in our vivid vernacular makes all of us poets *in posse*, whether we know it or not, and the spirit of poetry, more than anything else, gives us greater power to face the prose of a work-a-day world and has made Scotsmen what they are.

(J.M. Bulloch, 'The Delight of the Doric in the Diminutive', a lecture given to the Vernacular Circle of the London Robert Burns Club, 12 December 1921; reprinted from *The Scottish Tongue*, pp.127–51 [127–28, 129–30, 139, 145–46, 148, 150–51].)

2.5   C.M. Grieve, from letters to *Aberdeen Free Press* (December 1921 and January 1922)

a) From letter of 15 December 1921

12 White's Place,
Montrose,
December 13, 1921

Sir,

The space you have given to Dr J.M. Bulloch's lecture on 'The Diminutive in Doric' encourages the hope that you will in fairness spare a corner for one who strongly differs from him.

Those who use what Dr Bulloch terms 'Albyn Place English' (whatever they may be) will probably—if they exist—have no difficulty in replying to the 'little Eccelfechanities of Peckham and Tooting' (whom we all know). But Dr Bulloch's plea for Doric infantilism is not worthy of the critical consideration of nursery-governesses. A critic capable of referring to 'Mr John Mitchell's delightful crack with his grandson' is capable of anything—and nothing. Most contemporary grandchildren would take steps to have us examined in lunacy if we afflicted them with such talks in Doric. [. . .]

The main objection to the Vernacular Circle's propaganda lies in the fact that it emphasises the part at the expense of the whole, and puts the cart before the horse. Had the aim been to encourage all that is finest and best in Scottish literature, whether written in Doric or English, the movement might have merited support—although, after all, prizes do not produce literature.

Is the expression of Scottish mentality in English—even Albyn Place English—essentially grotesque? Synge, Yeats, and other great Irish writers found no difficulty in expressing themselves in an English which they yet made distinctively Irish. Is the psychological difference between, say, Oscar Wilde and Joseph Conrad not as profound as the difference between an Englishman and a Scot?

Some of the 'perfervids' attached to the London Vernacular Circle (not themselves particularly distinguished as creative artists) are making claims for the Doric which even writers such as Mrs Violet Jacob, John Buchan, and Professor Alexander Gray—who have added to its glories—repudiate. The latter recognise its insuperable spiritual limitations, as Burns did, and as future writers must increasingly do.

b) From letter of 30 January 1922

12 White's Place,
Montrose,
January 27, 1922

Sir, [. . .]

I was brought up in a braid Scots atmosphere. No one relishes the

21

peculiar virtues of the Doric more heartily than I do. No one can be more anxious than I am that these should not be lost or Scottish vernacular literature cease to be read—dangers which I believe to be greatly exaggerated. But I am very much more anxious that the habit of reading should be controlled by literary factors alone. Mere patriotism is a Caliban's Guide to letters. What shall it profit a man if he remains a Scot but lose his own soul? The great need of every civilised country is for a thinking public. In Scotland there is ample reason to know that no intensive insistence on the Doric will conduce to that. The people do not think in the Doric or in any other language—and the problems that it is most urgently desirable that they should, if possible, be made to think about are those problems created by our industrial civilisation which there is no terminology in the Doric to deal with. For the most part the Doric tradition serves to condone mental inertia—cloaking mental paucity with a trivial and ridiculously over-valued pawkiness!—and bolsters up that instinctive suspicion of cleverness and culture—so strongly in all peasants—which keeps the majority of the Scottish public wallowing in obsolete and really anti-national tastes—anti-national, for the latent spirit of Scotland showed its potential stature when a determined effort was made (in the last half of the 18th century) to cast off the swaddling clothes of the Doric. Alas! reaction fastened them still more tightly about the unfortunate spirit (kept a Peter Pan of national consciousness against its will) and its struggles ceased—and are only now being resumed in a new and almost incredible access of hope! Compared with other countries comparable in size—Belgium, for instance—Scotland stagnates in an apparently permanent literary infancy owing to the operation of certain forces of which the Doric sentiment is the principal.

The Doric is as much mine as anybody's. I love it jealously. My accent could be cut with a knife. Not only so! I have had the temerity to address myself to the solution of the two great problems of the Doric—the facts that no serious Doric prose and no Doric drama ever evolved, in which respects Doric is singular amongst all European dialects and languages. I believe that both were capable of being evolved from the Doric. I believe I know exactly why neither ever did develop out of the Doric. And I believe that I can show that if certain factors had not operated, and if certain other factors had operated—and if history had followed a different course and Doric had today been exclusively used for all purposes in Scotland—how the difficulties which prevented the development of both would have been overcome. That thesis [. . .] I am now preparing for issue in book form—for private circulation only, for the simple reason that though (or perhaps because) I am interested very deeply in these matters myself, I consider that any attempt to create a Doric 'boom' just now—or even to maintain the existing vernacular cult in anything like its present tendencies—would be a gross disservice to Scottish life and letters.

(C.M. Grieve, Aberdeen Free Press 15 December 1921 and 30 January 1922;
reprinted from Alan Bold ed., The Letters of Hugh MacDiarmid, Athens:
Georgia University Press, 1984, pp.750–52 and pp.754–56.)

2.6 James Pittendrigh MacGillivray, from Preface to *Bog Myrtle and Peat Reek* (1921)

I have used the North and South dialects of our Scottish Vernacular in so far only as I have a living knowledge of their words, idiom, and accent; and I have done nothing in the way of making a curious mosaic of '*auld-farran*' and obsolete words, such as no Scot of any period or district ever spoke. There is, I believe, a modulation of tone and accent resulting from the habitual sequence of vowels used in the idiom of each district. These factors of tone and accent, shaped through generations by subtle feelings and sympathies, produce for the native the harmonious music of his Mother tongue. To assemble obsolete words from periods remote and from dialects of districts apart and strange to each other in idiom and in the pronunciation of the same words, may produce a kind of literary language of Scots for the scholarly appreciation of those who have no intimacy with the voice of any of our dialects; but the result, although often witty enough, and obviously truly sympathetic in intention, can never, I think, touch the heart like a true native diction from any one of the quarters.

(James Pittendrigh MacGillivray, Bog Myrtle and Peat Reek, published privately by the
author, 1922, pp.v–ix [vi–vii].)

2.7 C.M. Grieve, from *Dunfermline Press* (August and September 1922)

a) From 5 August 1922

If there is to be a Scottish literary revival the first essential is to get rid of our provinciality of outlook and to avail ourselves of Continental experience. [. . .] Most of it [Scottish literature] is, of course, and must continue to be, written in English. But it is not English on that account, although it is denounced on that score by the ardent minority bent upon the revival of the Doric [. . .] It is no more English in spirit than the literature of the Irish Literary Revival, most of which was written in the English language, was English in spirit.

b) From 30 September 1922

[Sir James Wilson's *Lowland Scotch*] was still uncut when my friend [Hugh MacDiarmid] discovered it in the corner of a book-shelf. I had forgotten all about it. I admit that it deserved a better fate, although I am little interested in phonetics [. . .] I have strong views in regard to the literary uses of the Vernacular which I have on more than one occasion expressed at length in this column and elsewhere in the Scottish Press. At the same time, I possess a great delight in words; and the obsolete, the distinctively local, the idiomatic, the unusual attract me strongly. [. . .] My friend, as I have said, busied himself with the book, and a jotter and pencil; and later on passed over to me the two sets of verses which I have pleasure in re-producing here ['The Watergaw' and 'The Blaward and the Skelly']. They serve a useful purpose, I think, in rescuing from oblivion and restoring to literary use forgotten words that have a descriptive potency otherwise unobtainable. Not only so, but apart from that philological interest they have, in my opinion, some genuine poetical merit too.

(C.M. Grieve, 'Scottish Books and Bookmen', *Dunfermline Press*, 5 August 1922, p.6, and 30 September 1922, p.7.)

2.8   C.M. Grieve, from *Scottish Chapbook* (October 1922)

One of the objects of *The Scottish Chapbook* is to supplement the campaign of the Vernacular Circle of the London Burns Club for the revival of the Doric. This issue will, I hope, prove unusually interesting to every student of the Vernacular. [. . .] I do not support the campaign for the revival of the Doric where the essential Scottish diversity-in-unity is forgotten, nor where the tendencies involved are anti-cultural.

The work of Mr Hugh M'Diarmid, who contributes a poem and a semi-dramatic study to this issue, is peculiarly interesting because he is, I think, the first Scottish writer who has addressed himself to the question of the extendability (without psychological violence) of the Vernacular to embrace the whole range of modern culture—or, in other words, tried to make up the leeway of the language. It is an excessively difficult task, and I envy him his enthusiasm. What he has to do is to adapt an essentially rustic tongue to the very much more complex requirements of our urban civilisation—to give it all the almost illimitable suggestionability it lacks (compared, say, with contemporary English or French), but *would have had if it had continued in general use in highly-cultured circles to the present day*. A modern consciousness cannot fully express itself in the Doric as it exists. Take a simple case. What is the Doric for motor-car? It is futile to say 'mottor caur'. The problem that faces a conscientious literary artist determined to express himself through the medium of the Doric is to determine what 'motor-car' would have been in the Doric had the Doric continued, or, rather, become an all-sufficient independent language. He must think himself back into the spirit of the Doric (that is to say, recover it in its entirety, with all the potentialities it once had, ridding it, for his purpose, of those innate disabilities and limitations which have brought it to its present pass)—and then, appropriately to the genius of the language, carry it forward with him, accumulating all the wealth of association and idiom which progressive desuetude has withheld from it until it is adequate to his present needs—the needs not of a ploughman but of a twentieth-century artist who is at once a Scotsman (as distinct from an Englishman or a negro) and a 'good European' or 'Western World-Man'. . . . From this point of view the value of the Doric lies in the extent to which it contains lapsed or unrealised qualities which correspond to 'unconscious' elements of distinctively Scottish psychology. The recovery and application of these may make effectively communicable those unexpressed aspects of Scottish character the absence of which makes, say, 'Kailyaird' characters shallow, sentimental, humiliating travesties.

   Doric economy of expressiveness is impressively illustrated in the first four lines of Mr M'Diarmid's poem ['The Watergaw']. Translate them into English. That is the test. [. . .] Not only so; but the temper of the poem is modern and the Doric is adequate to it. It is disfigured by none of the usual sentimentality. It has a distinctively Scottish *sinisterness* for which expression is too seldom found nowadays. [. . .] The whole trouble with the Doric as a literary language to-day is that the vast majority of its exponents are hopelessly limited culturally—and that the others (such as Mrs Violet Jacob, Mr Charles Murray, and Miss Mary Symon) only use it for limited purposes.

(C.M. Grieve, editor's 'Causerie', *The Scottish Chapbook* 1:3 October 1922, pp.62–63.)

2.9   Edwin Muir, from 'A Note on the Scottish Ballads' (*Freeman* January 1923)

No writer can write great English who is not born an English writer and in England; and born moreover in some class in which the tradition of English is pure, and it seems to me, therefore, in some other age than this. [. . .] And because the current of English is even at this day so much younger, poorer and more artificial in Scotland than it is in England, it is improbable that Scotland will produce any writer of English of the first rank, or at least that she will do so until her tradition of English is as common, as unforced and unschooled as if it were her native tongue. [. . .]

Whether the Scottish genius will ever return to some modified form of the ballad as its preordained medium it is useless to consider to-day. Probably Scottish writers are fated hereafter to use English, and to use it, taking all things into account, not with supreme excellence. But it is difficult to avoid two conclusions: that the ballads enshrine the very essence of the Scottish spirit, and that they could have been written only in the Scottish tongue.

(Edwin Muir, 'A Note on the Scottish Ballads', *Freeman* [USA] 6, 17 January 1923; reprinted from Edwin Muir, *Latitudes* London: Andrew Melrose, 1924, pp.12–30 [15, 30].)

2.10   C.M. Grieve, from 'Causerie: A Theory of Scots Letters', *Scottish Chapbook* (February and March 1923)

a) From February 1923

We base our belief in the possibility of a great Scottish Literary Renaissance, deriving its strength from the resources that lie latent and almost unsuspected in the Vernacular, upon the fact that the genius of our Vernacular enables us to secure with comparative ease the very effects and swift transitions which other literatures are for the most part unsuccessfully endeavouring to cultivate in languages that have a very different and inferior bias. Whatever the potentialities of the Doric may be, however, there cannot be a revival in the real sense of the word—a revival of the spirit as distinct from a mere renewed vogue of the letter—unless these potentialities are in accord with the newest and truest tendencies of human thought. We confess to having been discouraged when thinking of the Vernacular Movement by the fact that the seal of its approval is so largely set upon the traditional and the conventional. The real enemy is he who cries: 'Hands off our fine old Scottish tongue'. If all that the Movement is to achieve is to preserve specimens of Braid Scots, archaic, imitative, belonging to a type of life that has passed and cannot return, in a sort of museum department of our consciousness—set apart from our vital preoccupations—it is a movement which not only cannot claim our support but compels our opposition. The rooms of thought are choc-a-bloc with far too much dingy old rubbish as it is. There are too many vital problems clamouring for attention. . . . It is a different matter, however, if an effort is to be made to really revive the Vernacular—to encourage the experimental exploitation of the unexplored possibilities of Vernacular expression. 'The letter killeth but the spirit giveth life.' Only in so far as the Vernacular has unused resources corresponding better than English does to the progressive expression of the distinctive characteristics of Scottish life—however much these may have been submerged, subverted, or

26

camouflaged, by present conditions (we shall deal later with the question of the relationship between literature and politics)—has it possibilities of literary value. If the cultural level of work in the Doric is not capable of being raised to equal that in any other living language—if the Doric has not certain qualities which no other language possesses and qualities as that of consequence to modern consciousness as a whole—then all that can be hoped for is a multiplication of equivalents in the Vernacular to work that has already been better achieved in other languages without any special contribution at all from Scotland to the expressive resource of modern life. The Doric unquestionably has a past and, to a very much more limited extent, a present. The question is whether it has a future which will enable it successfully to compete, at any rate along specialised lines, with other languages. Our interest, therefore, should centre not so much in what has been done in the Doric as in what has not but may be done in it. No literature can rest on its laurels. [. . .] For our part we frankly confess that a living dog is worth any number of dead lions, and we unreservedly accept Thomas Hardy's definition that 'literature is the written expression of revolt against accepted things'.

We have been enormously struck by the resemblance—the moral resemblance—between Jamieson's Etymological Dictionary of the Scottish language and James Joyce's *Ulysses*. A *vis comica* that has not yet been liberated lies bound by desuetude and misappreciation in the recesses of the Doric: and its potential uprising would be no less prodigious, uncontrollable, and utterly at variance with conventional morality than was Joyce's tremendous outpouring. [. . .] And one of the most distinctive characteristics of the Vernacular, part of its very essence, is its insistent recognition of the body, the senses. [. . .] This explains the unique blend of the lyrical and the ludicrous in primitive Scots sentiment [. . .] and the essence of the genius of our race, is, in our opinion, the reconciliation it effects between the base and the beautiful, recognising that they are complementary and indispensable to each other.

b) From March 1923

The Scottish Vernacular is the only language in Western Europe instinct with those uncanny spiritual and pathological perceptions alike which constitute the uniqueness of Dostoevski's work, and word after word of Doric establishes a blood-bond in a fashion at once infinitely more thrilling and vital and less explicable than those deliberately sought after by writers such as D.H. Lawrence in the medium of English which is inferior for such purposes because it has entirely different natural bias which has been so confirmed down the centuries as to be insusceptible of correction. The Scots Vernacular is a vast storehouse of just the very peculiar and subtle effects which modern European literature in general is assiduously seeking and, if the next century is to see an advance in mental science equal to that which last century has marked in material science, then the resumption of the Scots Vernacular into the mainstream of European letters in a fashion which the most enthusiastic Vernacularist may well hesitate to hope for, is inevitable. The Vernacular is a vast unutilised mass of lapsed observation made by minds whose attitudes to experience and whose speculative and imaginative tendencies were quite different from any possible to Englishmen and Anglicised Scots to-day. It is an inchoate Marcel Proust—a Dostoevskian debris of ideas—a inexhaustible quarry of subtle and significant sound. [. . .] The revival of Scots Vernacular is being retarded simply because of the fact that the majority of writers in the Vernacular have only a patois knowledge of it—not an educated knowledge—and are not to any useful extent in possession of its literary traditions apart from Burns: while they confine their efforts to a little range of conventional forms. [. . .] we have lost (but may perhaps reacquire) word-forming faculties peculiar to the Doric for the purposes of both psychological and nature description. There are words and phrases in the Vernacular which thrill me with a sense of having been produced as a result of mental processes entirely different from my own and much more powerful. They embody observations of a kind which the modern mind makes with increasing difficulty and weakened effect. Take the word 'birth', for instance, meaning a current in the sea caused by a furious tide but taking a different course from it—a contrary motion. It exemplifies a fascinating, exceedingly adroit and purely Scottish application of metaphor. Then there are natural occurrences and phenomena of all kinds which have apparently never been noted by the English mind. No words exist for them in English. For instance—watergaw—for an indistinct rainbow; yow-trummle—meaning the cold weather in July after the sheepshearing; cavaburd—meaning a thick fall of snow; and blue bore—meaning a patch of blue in a cloudy sky. Another feature of the Doric which I will not illustrate here is the fashion in which diverse attitudes of mind or shades of temper are telescoped into single words or phrases, investing the whole speech with subtle flavours of irony, commiseration, realism and humour which cannot be reproduced in English. In onomatopoetic effect, too, the Doric has a wider range and infinitely richer resources than English while the diversity of inherent bias is revealed in unmistakeable fashion.

Whatever the potentialities of the Doric may be, however, there cannot be a revival in the real sense of the word—a revival of the spirit as distinct from a mere renewed vogue of the letter—unless these potentialities are in accord with the newest tendencies of human thought.

(C.M. Grieve, 'A Theory of Scots Letters', *Scottish Chapbook* 1:7, February 1923, pp.182–84; 1:8, March 1923, pp.210–12.)

2.11 'The Scottish Vernacular in Music' (*Glasgow Herald* October 1923)

Mr Percy Gordon, B.Mus., Glasgow, who lectured to-night to the members of the Vernacular Circle of the Burns Club of London, has a very poor opinion of the broad Scots spoken by people in Glasgow. Having lived nearly all his life there, he apologised to his audience for being deficient in the pure Doric. In Glasgow, he said, the vernacular is horribly corrupted by Irish and by a refusal to pronounce any consonants unless it cannot be avoided. Turning to his subject, he contended that music is a form of language, and accordingly must have a vernacular aspect. For that we have to go to folk music, involving to some extent the pentatonic scale and the 'Scotch snap'. Neither of these, however, he showed, are peculiarly Scottish, and the vernacular in Scottish music is very much a matter of mood. That consists of feeling and the poetry and association connected with certain tunes. Mr Gordon, with the aid of the piano, illustrated how certain feelings are expressed in Scottish music.

(Unsigned report of lecture to the Vernacular Circle of the London Burns Club, *Glasgow Herald* 18 October 1923, p.9.)

2.12 John Buchan, from Introduction to *The Northern Muse* (1925)

A century and a half have passed since Burns wrote, and the vernacular, confined to an ever-narrowing province, has suffered a further detrition. Old words and constructions have lapsed from use; modes of speech which were current so late as thirty years ago among the shepherds of Ettrick and Galloway are scarcely intelligible to their successors; in the towns the patois bids fair to become merely a broadened and dilapidated English; and though the dwellers north of Tweed will be eternally distinguishable from their neighbours by certain idiosyncrasies of speech, these idiosyncrasies will be of voice and accent, and not of language. The Scots vernacular ceased in the sixteenth century to be a language in the full sense, capable of being used on all varieties of theme, and was confined to the rustic and the parochial; capable, indeed, in the hands of a master of sounding the depths of the human heart, but ill suited to the infinite variety of human life. Even from this narrowed orbit it has fallen, and is now little more than a robust rendering of colloquial English. The literary Scots which Burns wrote is more than ever a literary tongue, far removed from any speech in common use. It is understood by many, not because it is in their ears from hearing, but because it is in their memories from reading. To restore the Scots vernacular is beyond the power of any Act of Parliament, because the life on which it depended has gone. Thirty years ago I learned in the Tweedside glens to talk a Scots, which was then the speech of a people secluded from the modern world; to-day if I spoke it at a Tweeddale clipping I should find only a few old men to understand me. Scots can survive only as a book-tongue, and it is to that purpose that I would bespeak the efforts of my countrymen. The knowledge of the book-tongue is still fairly common, and if, in the mill of a standardized education, it should ever be crushed out, we shall lose the power of appreciating not only the 'makars', but the best of the Ballads, Burns, and Sir Walter Scott—that part of our literary heritage which is most intimately and triumphantly our own.

(John Buchan, *The Northern Muse: An Anthology of Scots Vernacular Poetry* London: Thomas Nelson and Sons, 1925, pp.xix–xxxi [xxiv–xxvi].)

2.13 Lorna Moon, from letters to David Laurance Chambers, Bobbs-Merrill Publishers (August 1928)

a) From letter of 20 August 1928

Dear Mr Chambers [. . .]

Do you think it would be advisable for me to write a preface about the complete omission of dialect? You see I have come to the conclusion that it is never justified. Indeed if it *is* correct to write in dialect then *all* conversation should be in dialect, since there is nobody, not even the Oxford Don who pronounces English according to the dictionary. I use the idiom common to Scottish people but I see no reason to stress their mispronunciation which is all dialect is. Ne'est ce pas?

It is possible though that the reviewers may want to show how clever they are by pointing out that Divot Meg would say 'dinna' for 'don't', and 'ken' for 'know' etc. A preface would jump them on this. Or do you think that it is not necessary? [. . .]

LORNA

b) From letter of 30 August 1928

Dear Mr Chambers [. . .]

I whooped with delight over your remark that I 'handled the dialect' well. Because this shows me that I did what I tried to do: that is: create the impression that the characters spoke in dialect while keeping strictly to English. Do you know that in the whole book there are only six Scotch expressions and only two of those are used in conversation? The six are:

'bairn': 'kirk' 'brae': 'mycerties': 'kist': 'havers': and one other which I forget at the moment.

But it is no wonder that I tricked you, because, I also put it over on a Scotch professor, just over! When he had read the thing he said: 'Yon's a grand book. Yon's a Scotch book.' (which you know is simply wild praise from a Scot). I said: 'You didn't miss the dialect?' He misunderstood me, thinking I meant, 'you could not understand the dialect', and answered: '*miss* it, would I be forgetting my mother tongue in a twae month think ye?'

'But you know', I said, 'there are only six Scotch expressions in the book. The whole thing is written in English.'

'Niver! Niver!' he cried 'I woulda seen it at a glance!'

'But I'm telling you' I urged.

'Oh maybe the lassie, she was educated, but Divot Meg was Scotch as peat—'

When he re-read Divot Meg, he was fairly winded:

'I couldna hae believed it!' he cried.

And that is the answer! I use the idiom and *they* supply the pronunciation. If the reader knows the Scotch pronunciation he will supply it himself without realizing it. If he doesn't he will think he is reading English as spoken by the Scot and never be a bit the wiser. So I think there is no need for a preface. Do you? [. . .]

Yours,
LORNA

(Lorna Moon, *The Collected Works of Lorna Moon*, ed. Glenda Norquay, Edinburgh: Black & White Publishing, pp.260, 262.)

2.14 Gordon Leslie Rayne, from 'This Scottish Tongue: The Renascence and the Vernacular' (*Scots Magazine* May 1933)

[Our younger people] have, like most Scottish children of the last few decades, become rather less noticeably and pointedly Scottish; they are smoother, more polished, more dexterous with the English tongue, which to them is less alien than to their sires; alien it is hardly at all, save for a few, born in geographical remoteness, or in social circumstances that encourage the survival of the dialect, for with no possibility of denial the normal speech of the modern Scot, even of the poorly educated, is English, and English alone.

This is a matter of incalculable moment for the future of Scottish letters. Among school children I have been struck with the increasing decay of dialect forms and phrases. The natural medium of the lower strata of society is still, it must be admitted, a corrupt and clippit speech, but it is English for the most part, not Scots. The use of the vernacular has for long been condemned by genteel standards; it implies a kind of social stigma still to employ the braid tongue of the farm or the close. Ever since the Union the heavy weight of social recognition has been thrown upon the side of English, and even Dr Johnson remarked that 'the conversation of the Scots grows every day less unpleasing to the English; their peculiarities wear away; their dialect is likely to become in half a century provincial and rustic even to themselves'. Johnson's time limit was wrong, but his prophecy is none the less near fulfilment. Even in the 'sixties of last century many Scottish ministers were still in the habit of preaching in the broadest Scots, but that habit has long ago died out. It is a significant fact, which I commend especially to the exponents of the Renascence among us, that the vernacular is still at its best in facetiousness and humour. In the comedian and in the pantomime it survives, broader and coarser than anywhere else, and I must confess that when I hear it so employed, I feel dismayed and discouraged, to think that the last home of pithy and pungent dialect is to be the boards of the third or fourth class theatre. Years ago, I used to notice that a lad o' parts, when he stood up to translate a bit of Virgil or Horace, had sometimes difficulty in finding the right word in English for what he knew the Latin to be, but he could always give you the dialect form. I can remember boys who, with a little hesitation, would confess that a certain word meant 'breenge', but could not say just what was the accurate English equivalent. That state of things is changing now; the radio and the cinema, from both of which they hear English as she is talked, have done much to raise the level of speech and to sound the knell of the vernacular.

My point in all this is simply the absurdity of harking back to the pedantic tongue of Dunbar, whom I hear now mentioned as the great well of Scottish undefiled. This is sheer sentimentality. It brings ridicule upon a national aspiration which, however ludicrously misguided, has still some justification for its life and works. All I would here humbly do is to suggest the pertinent reflection that the development of the Scottish nationality has nothing whatever to do with the continuance of the Scottish vernacular. I leave outside for the moment the further query whether that development be at all related to the recovery of political autonomy. As I see it, the Scottish character presents as one of its most consistent and most striking virtues that of being by far the least insular in these islands, if not on this continent. Scotsmen have everywhere and at all times shown an easy adaptability to the habits, the thoughts and the speech of other nations. They have shown within my own lifetime an increasingly rapid adaptation to the standard of English speech and English culture, and within that period the discarding of vernacular and dialect, just like the discarding of the continental pronunciation of Latin that used to be normal in Scottish schools and universities, has proceeded apace. Whatever this nationality of ours consists in, it is not irrevocably bound up with the preservation of what is uniformly looked upon as a provincial and rustic mode of utterance, but it is irrevocably bound up with the preservation of other qualities and gifts, of which the glorious company of the self-styled revivalists have yet to think and learn.

(Gordon Leslie Rayne, 'This Scottish Tongue: The Renascence and the Vernacular', *Scots Magazine* 19:2, May 1933, pp.107–110 [109–110].)

2.15   Dane M'Neil [Neil M. Gunn], from 'The Scottish Renascence' (*Scots Magazine* June 1933)

[Mr Rayne] should know that the harking back to Dunbar is professedly not a harking back for language so much as a harking back for greatness. Dunbar is great in breadth, in variety and ingenuity, in largeness of conception and utterance, after the fashion that Chaucer before and Shakespeare after him were great. It is this lost greatness that the renascent Scot would strive to see restored, recognising that its manifestation in a nation at any time is due not so much to the odd appearance of an individual genius (generally forced to dissipate his best energies in rebellion), as to the existence within the nation itself of that aptitude for greatness out of which genius naturally flowers.

Finally, that the development of the Scottish nationality 'has nothing whatever to do with the continuance of the Scottish vernacular', may be correct. Scottish nationality may have nothing to do with the Gaelic tongue and literature. Having at last acquired English, it may be able to dispense with all history and tradition; it may indeed develop all the better for the lack of roots of any sort. Something of this parasitic conception of Scotland is common enough. All that can definitely be said is that the greatest poetry produced in Scotland since Dunbar has been in the Scottish tongue, that our only poetry to-day of European importance is being written in that tongue, and that, with all due deference to Mr Rayne, great poetry in whatever tongue makes a nation neither ridiculous nor ludicrous. For the rest, it would appear that Scotsmen have the chameleon-like quality of 'adaptability to the habits, the thoughts, and the speech of other nations'. Yet, adds Mr Rayne, our nationality is irrevocably bound up 'with the preservation of qualities and gifts of which the glorious company of the self-styled revivalists have yet to learn and think'.

If only Mr Rayne had helped us by explaining when his chameleon is not a chameleon, and how! Unless, of course, all the 'qualities and gifts' had already been summed up by him in our genius for music-hall comedy, complete with deep chuckle and grin of merriment (continuing).

(Dane M'Neil [Neil M. Gunn], 'The Scottish Renascence', *Scots Magazine* 19:3, June 1933, pp.201–204 [204].)

2.16 Lewis Grassic Gibbon, from 'Literary Lights' (1934)

For, however the average Scots writer believes himself Anglicized [. . .] it is not English. The English reader is haunted by a sense of something foreign stumbling and hesitating behind this smooth façade of adequate technique: it is as though the writer did not *write* himself, but *translated* himself.

Often the Scots writer is quite unaware of this essential foreignness in his work; more often, seeking an adequate word or phrase he hears an echo in an alien tongue that would adorn his meaning with a richness, a clarity and a conciseness impossible in orthodox English. That echo is from Braid Scots, from that variation of the Anglo-Saxon speech which was the tongue of the great Scots civilization, the tongue adopted by the basic Pictish strain in Scotland as its chief literary tool.

Further, it is still in most Scots communities, (in one or other Anglicized modification,) the speech of bed and board and street and plough, the speech of emotional ecstasy and emotional stress. But it is not genteel. It is to the bourgeois of Scotland coarse and low and common and loutish, a matter for laughter, well enough for hinds and the like, but for the genteel to be quoted in vocal inverted commas. It is a thing rigorously elided from their serious intercourse—not only with the English, but among themselves. It is seriously believed by such stratum of the Scots populace to be an inadequate and pitiful and blunted implement, so that Mr Eric Linklater delivers *ex cathedra* judgment upon it as 'inadequate to deal with the finer shades of emotion'.

But for the truly Scots writer it remains a real and a haunting thing, even while he tries his best to forget its existence and to write as a good Englishman. In this lies his tragedy. He has to *learn* to write in English: he is like a Chinese scholar spending the best years of his life in the mystic mazes of the pictographs, and emerging so exhausted from the travail that originality of research or experiment with his new tool is denied him. Consequently, the free and anarchistic experimentations of the progressive members of a free and homogeneous literary cultus are denied him. Nearly every Scots writer of the past writing in orthodox English has been not only incurably second-rate, but incurably behind the times. [. . .]

With a few exceptions presently to be noted, there is not the remotest reason why the majority of modern Scots writers should be considered

Scots at all. The protagonists of the Scots Literary Renaissance deny this. They hold, for example, that Norman Douglas or Compton Mackenzie, though they write in English and deal with un-Scottish themes, have nevertheless an essential Scottishness which differentiates them from the native English writer. In exactly the same manner, so had Joseph Conrad an essential Polishness. But few (except for the purpose of exchanging diplomatic courtesies) pretend that Conrad was a Polish writer, to be judged as a Pole. [. . .] Modern Scotland, the Gaels included, is a nation almost entirely lacking a Scottish literary output. There are innumerable versifiers, ranging from Dr Charles Murray downwards to Mr W.H. Hamilton (he of the eldritch glamour); there are hardly more than two poets; and there is no novelist at all. [. . .] The chief Literary Lights which modern Scotland claims to light up the scene of her night are in reality no more than the commendable writers of the interesting English county of Scotshire.

Let us consider Mrs Naomi Mitchison. She is the one writer of the 'historical' novel in modern English who commands respect and enthusiasm. Her pages are aglow with a fine essence of apprehended light. *The Conquered* and *Black Sparta* light up the human spirit very vividly and truly. And they are in no sense Scots books though written by a Scotswoman. Their author once wrote that had she had the command of Scots speech possessed by Lewis Grassic Gibbon she would have written her Spartan books (at least) in Scots. Had she done so they would undoubtedly have been worse novels—but they *would* have been Scots books by a Scots writer. [. . .]

Another writer hailed as a great Scots novelist is Mr Neil Gunn. The acclamation is mistaken. Mr Gunn is a brilliant novelist from Scotshire who chooses his home county as the scene of his tales. His technique is almost unique among the writers of Scotshire in its effortless efficiency: he moulds beauty in unforgettable phrases—there are things in *The Lost Glen* and *Sun Circle* comparable to the best in the imaginative literature of any school or country. He has probably scarcely yet set out on his scaling of the heights. . . . But they are not the heights of Scots literature; they are not even the pedestrian levels. More in Gunn than in any other contemporary Anglo-Scot [. . .] the reader seems to sense the haunting foreignness in an orthodox English; he is the greatest loss to itself Scottish literature has suffered in this century. Had his language been Gaelic or Scots there is no doubt of the space or place he would have occupied in even such short study as this. Writing in orthodox English, he is merely a brilliantly unorthodox Englishman.

Once again, a writer who has been hailed as distinctively Scots, Mrs Willa Muir. So far she has written only two novels—*Imagined Corners* and *Mrs Ritchie*—and both show a depth and distinction, a sheer and splendidly un-womanly power which stir even the most jaded of enthusiasms.

[. . .] She has promise of becoming a great artist. But a great English artist. The fact that she is Scots herself and deals with Scots scenes and Scots characters is (to drive home the point ad nauseam) entirely irrelevant from the point of view of Scots literature. [. . .]

Mr John Buchan has been called the Dean of Scots letters. Mr Buchan writes mildly exhilarating romances in the vein of the late Rider Haggard (though without either Haggard's magnificent poetic flair or his imaginative grasp), commendable essays on a variety of topics, uninspired if competent biographies of Sir Walter Scott, the Marquis of Montrose, and the like distinguished cadaver-litter on the ancient Scottish scene. He writes it all in a competent, skilful and depressing English: when his characters talk Scots they do it in suitable inverted commas: and such characters as do talk Scots are always the simple, the proletarian, the slightly ludicrous characters.

Mr Buchan represents no more than the great, sound, bourgeois heart of Scotshire. He has written nothing which has the least connection with Scots literature except a few pieces of verse—if verse *has* any connection with literature. In compiling *The Northern Muse*, however, a representative anthology of Scots 'Vernacular' poetry, he turned aside from other pursuits to render a real service to what might have been his native literary language. Yet even in that service he could envisage Braid Scots as being only a 'vernacular', the tongue of *a home-reared slave*. [. . .]

[This] brings us at last to consideration of the two solitary lights in modern Scots Literature. They rise from men who are writers in both Scots and in English—very prolific and controversial writers, men occupied with politics and economic questions, poets in the sense that life, not editors or anthologists, demand of them their poetry. [. . .] One of these two is Hugh MacDiarmid and the other Lewis Spence.

MacDiarmid's poetry in Braid Scots came upon a world which had grown accustomed to the belief that written Scots was a vehicle for the more flat-footed sentiments of the bothy only; it came upon a world pale and jaded with the breathing and rebreathing in the same room of the same stagnant air of orthodox English. He demonstrated, richly and completely, and continues to demonstrate, the flexibility and the loveliness of that alien variation of the Anglo-Saxon speech which is Braid Scots. [. . .] Mr MacDiarmid, like all great poets, has his in and out moments—some of them disastrous moments; his care to set this planet aright has laid waste some of his finest poems—but, working in that medium of Braid Scots which he calls synthetic Scots, he has brought Scots language into print again as a herald in tabard, not the cap-and-bells clown of romantic versification.

Of an entirely different order, but a genius no less genuine, is Mr Spence in his Scots poetry. [. . .]

How far these two are isolated phenomena, how far the precursors of a definite school of Scots literature is still uncertain: they have their imitators in full measure: in William Soutar the Elijah of MacDiarmid may yet have an Elisha. When, if ever, the majority of Scots poets—not versifiers—begin to use Braid Scots as a medium that dream of a Scots literary renaissance may tread the *via terrena* of fulfilment, enriching (in company with orthodox English) the literary heritage of that language of Cosmopolis towards which the whole creation moves.

An experiment of quite a different order from MacDiarmid's writing in synthetic Scots, or Spence's in deliberate excavation in the richness of the antique Scots vocabularies, may be noted here. As already stated, there is no novelist, (or, indeed prose writer,) worthy of the name who is writing in Braid Scots. The technique of Lewis Grassic Gibbon in his trilogy *A Scots Quair*—of which only Parts I and II, *Sunset Song* and *Cloud Howe*, have yet been published—is to mould the English language into the rhythms and cadences of Scots spoken speech, and to inject into the English vocabulary such minimum number of words from Braid Scots as that remodelling requires. His scene so far has been a comparatively uncrowded and simple one—the countryside and village of modern Scotland. Whether his technique is adequate to compass and express the life of an industrialized Scots town in all its complexity is yet to be demonstrated; whether his peculiar style may not become either intolerably mannered or degenerate, in the fashion of Joyce, into the unfortunate unintelligibilities of a literary second childhood, is also in question.

> (Lewis Grassic Gibbon, 'Literary Lights' in Lewis Grassic Gibbon and Hugh MacDiarmid, *Scottish Scene or The Intelligent Man's Guide to Albyn* London: Jarrolds, 1934, pp.194–207 [196–97, 198, 199–201, 203–205].)

2.17   Edwin Muir, from 'Literature in Scotland' (*Spectator* May 1934)

In Scottish poetry there has been a change of a different kind. The most gifted poet writing in Scots at the beginning of the century was Charles Murray. He was a poet in the peasant tradition; he played skilful variations on immemorial simple folk themes which had been used hundreds of times by Burns and his many predecessors and successors. The real originality of 'Hugh McDiarmid' is that he employs Scots as any other poet might employ English or French: that is, to express anything which a modern writer may have to say. This has not been done in Scotland since she ceased to be a nation, since about two centuries, that is to say, before Burns. 'Hugh McDiarmid' is an extremely erratic and uneven writer; but he is probably the most gifted poet who has written in Scots since Burns, and the innovation he has made (if it should turn out to be a true innovation, that is, if it is carried on and consolidated after him by other writers) is clearly of major importance. But here again Scottish criticism has failed. 'Hugh McDiarmid's' use of Scots has been much praised and much blamed; but

37

the question whether he has succeeded in reinstating Scots as a language capable of expressing the whole world of contemporary experience and thought just as satisfactorily as English or French has never been seriously considered. He has very successfully expressed his own individual talent, with all its excellences and defects; and as the result is original, that is sufficient to justify his means. But that Scots will ever be used again as an independent language capable of fulfilling all the purposes of poetry and prose is, I should think, very doubtful. It is not impossible, for Scots was once an autonomous language, and inherently there is no reason why it could not be an autonomous language again. But there is against that an overwhelming balance of probability. And if a language cannot be used for all the normal literary purposes of a language, no serious argument can be advanced for using it for poetry. 'Hugh McDiarmid' is a poet of great originality, but if Scots does not become an independent language he will probably be known as a writer who fashioned a speech of his own, which has to be specially learned before he can be appreciated.

The question of language in contemporary Scottish literature is a very difficult one. Apart from 'Hugh McDiarmid', the names most commonly connected with the Scottish Renaissance are those of Neil M. Gunn, Eric Linklater and Lewis Grassic Gibbon. Mr Gunn's sensitive style is more obviously influenced by D.H. Lawrence than by Neil Munro; Mr Linklater writes vigorous Elizabethan prose; Mr Gibbon has struck out a style which does succeed in giving the rhythm of the Scottish vernacular. But all use English as their natural utterance; their literary inspiration is the great English writers, not Dunbar or Burns. On the other hand, they write about Scottish life for a Scottish audience, and not for an English one, like Stevenson. They write for this audience in English, it is true, but there they have little choice; for the Scottish people are a people who talk in Scots but think in English. These writers are, in any case, more intimately Scottish than Stevenson was, and that justifies one in calling the literary revival to which they belong a Scottish one. It is obviously only at its beginning yet; the promise for its future lies in the fact that for some time Scotland has been becoming more and more conscious of itself as a separate unity, and that this tendency seems bound to continue.

(Edwin Muir, 'Literature in Scotland', *Spectator* 25 May 1934, p.823.)

2.18   Neil M. Gunn, 'Preserving the Scottish Tongue: A Legacy and How to Use It' (*Scots Magazine* November 1935)

'If I desired to make a testamentary bequest of the income of a sum of £2,000, to be applied to keep up an interest in the knowledge of the

Scots Vernacular, what would be the most satisfactory form of application?'

Neil M. Gunn's response

Unlike Communism or other social creed or manifestation, the Scots Vernacular is an affair exclusively Scottish, and to keep it alive, Scotland must be kept alive. For if Scotland dies, then not only the Vernacular but everything that gives her separate meaning and identity dies with her. In looking therefore for something to keep the Vernacular alive, I should look for whatever body existed with the object of keeping Scotland the nation alive. If no such body existed, then I should know that any concern of mine to finance the Vernacular would be purely antiquarian and of no living value whatsoever.

The logic of this is to me unavoidable. Whenever the conception of the nation is reborn, immediately everything that distinguishes that nation is reborn, including in particular its forms of expression. Take such diverse countries as Norway, Czechoslovakia, and the Irish Free State. In each case when nationhood was resumed, the native language or languages, long fallen into desuetude, became the active concern of the whole people. That is the fact, whether we like to honour it or not.

I know that all this points to the Scottish National Party as the home for the bequest, and to the dread word politics! I cannot help that. I am concerned here only with the honest logic of the business, and logic says it is futile to attempt to stimulate any part of the body when the whole is giving up the ghost.

Let it be admitted, even for the fun of it, that with the Scottish National Party it would be a gamble, but at least it would be a real gamble; and it is just conceivable that a man might feel, here or hereafter, that once in his life he had made a gesture, none the less glorious because it had been both adventurous and hardheaded! But as with the Vernacular, so with the adventurous spirit: it is dying. We want to play safe in a little way. Instead of the living word on our lips, we want the dead word in a dictionary.

(Neil M. Gunn, 'Preserving the Scottish Tongue: A Legacy and How to Use It', *Scots Magazine* 24:2 November 1935, pp.105–14 [110–11].)

2.19 Edwin Muir, from *Scott and Scotland* (1936)

a) From 'Introductory'

But behind this problem of the Scottish writer there is another which, if not for the individual author, for Scotland itself is of crucial importance.

This is the problem of Scottish literature, and it is clearly a question for the Scottish people as a whole, not for the individual Scottish writer; for only a people can create a literature. The practical present-day problem may be put somewhat as follows: that a Scottish writer who wishes to achieve some approximation to completeness has no choice except to absorb the English tradition, and that if he thoroughly does so his work belongs not merely to Scottish literature but to English literature as well. On the other hand, if he wishes to add to an indigenous Scottish literature, and roots himself deliberately in Scotland, he will find there, no matter how long he may search, neither an organic community to round off his conceptions, nor a major literary tradition to support him, nor even a faith among the people themselves that a Scottish literature is possible or desirable, nor any opportunity, finally, of making a livelihood by his work.

b) From 'Language'

Scottish literature, considered linguistically, may be divided into Early Scots, Middle Scots, and Anything At All. The first two periods exhibit a certain homogeneity of language and as a result of that a definite style; the third, which began tentatively with Knox (the first Scotsman to write good English prose), and definitely with the acceptance of the English translation of the Bible, signalizes a disintegration of the language of Scottish literature and the disappearance of a distinctive Scottish style. Scotland continued to produce writers, but they wrote in a confusion of tongues ranging from orthodox English to the dialects of the various Scottish districts. The only speech which they did not continue to use was Scots, for that had disappeared. Consequently, since some time in the sixteenth century Scottish literature has been a literature without a language. Middle Scots survived Sir David Lyndsay for a while in the lyrics of Alexander Scott and Montgomery. But a little later Drummond of Hawthornden was already writing in pure English, and since then Scottish poetry has been written either in English, or in some local dialect, or in some form of synthetic Scots, such as Burns's, or Scott's, or Hugh M'Diarmid's. Scottish prose disappeared altogether, swept away by Knox's brilliant *History of the Reformation* and the Authorized Version of the Bible.

The reasons for this disintegration of the language of Scottish literature are controversial, and I have no space to enter into them here. But it is clear that the Reformation, the Union of the Crowns, and the Union of the Kingdoms had all a great deal to do with it. I must confine myself, however, to certain of its consequences. The pre-requisite of an autonomous literature is a homogeneous language. If Shakespeare had written in the dialect of Warwickshire, Spenser in Cockney, Ralegh in the broad Western English speech which he used, the future of English literature must have been very different, for it would have lacked a common language where all the thoughts and feelings of the English people could come together, add lustre to one another, and serve as a standard for one another. A common language of this kind can only be conceived, it seems to me, as an achievement continuously created and preserved by the highest spiritual energy of a people: the nursing ground and guarantee of all that is best in its thought and imagination: and without it no people can have any standard of literature. For this homogeneous language is the only means yet discovered for expressing the response of a whole people, emotional and intellectual, to a specific body of experience peculiar to it alone, on all levels of thought from discursive reason to poetry. And since some time in the sixteenth century Scotland has lacked such a language.

Every genuine literature, in other words, requires as its condition a means of expression capable of dealing with everything the mind can think or the imagination conceive. It must be a language for criticism as well as poetry, for abstract speculation as well as fact, and since we live in a scientific age, it must be a language for science as well. A language which can serve for one or two of those purposes but not for the others is, considered as a vehicle for literature, merely an anachronism. Scots has survived to our time as a language for simple poetry and the simpler kind of short story, such as 'Thrawn Janet'; all its other uses have lapsed, and it expresses therefore only a fragment of the Scottish mind. One can go further than this, however, and assert that its very use is a proof that the Scottish consciousness is divided. For, reduced to its simplest terms, this linguistic division means that Scotsmen feel in one language and think in another; that their emotions turn to the Scottish tongue, with all its associations of local sentiment, and their minds to a standard English which for them is almost bare of associations other than those of the classroom. If Henryson and Dunbar had written prose they would have written in the same language as they used for poetry, for their minds were still whole; but Burns never thought of doing so, nor did Scott, nor did Stevenson, nor has any Scottish writer since. In an organic literature poetry is always influencing prose, and prose poetry; and their interaction energizes them both. Scottish poetry exists in a vacuum; it neither acts on the rest of literature nor reacts to it; and consequently it has shrunk to the level of anonymous folk-song. Hugh M'Diarmid has recently tried to revive it by impregnating it with all the contemporary influences of Europe one after the other, and thus galvanize it into life by a series of violent shocks. In carrying out this experiment he has written some remarkable poetry; but he has left Scottish verse very much where it was before. For the major forms of poetry rise from a collision between emotion and intellect on a plane where both meet on equal terms; and it can never come into existence where the poet feels in one language and thinks in another, even though he should subsequently translate his thoughts into the language of his feelings.

Scots poetry can only be revived, that is to say, when Scotsmen begin to think *naturally* in Scots. The curse of Scottish literature is the lack of a whole language, which finally means the lack of a whole mind.

c) From 'Criticism'

The usual defence of Scots poetry is that it is lyrical, and that all poetry should be lyrical, should be as spontaneous as a song. That is in the last resort the critical standard on which all Scots poetry is judged. [. . .] Even admirers of Hugh M'Diarmid praise him chiefly for his first two books of lyrics, whereas easily his most original poetry is to be found in the long semi-philosophical poem, 'A Drunk Man Looks at the Thistle'. They praise his lyrics at the expense of his poetry because they think that poetry should be simple and spontaneous, because there is an admirable canon of Scottish song in the simpler mode, by keeping to which one cannot go far wrong, or indeed far in any direction, and finally because their emotions speak one language and their minds another. If the English were to judge all their poetry by that, say, of Campion, they would be using a standard roughly resembling that which is used for Scots poetry indiscriminately. The result is that a really original Scots poet like Hugh M'Diarmid has never received in Scotland any criticism of his more ambitious poems which can be of the slightest use to him.

d) From 'Conclusions'

Yet no Scottish writer can regard the present state of Scottish literature without sorrow or exasperation, and a wish to do something about it. I shall therefore describe the direction in which I think it should develop; but I cannot expect general agreement with my suggestions, and I claim no particular consideration for them.

First, as to the language of Scottish literature. I have tried to show that the chief requisite of a literature is a homogeneous language in which everything can be expressed that a people wishes to express. Scotland once had such a language, but we cannot return to it: to think so is to misunderstand history. That language still exists, in forms of varying debasement, in our numerous Scottish dialects; but these cannot utter the full mind of a people on all the levels of discourse. Consequently when we insist on using dialect for restricted literary purposes we are being true not to the idea of Scotland but to provincialism, which is one of the things that have helped to destroy Scotland. If we are to have a complete and homogeneous Scottish literature it is necessary that we should have a complete and homogeneous language. Two such languages exist in Scotland,

and two only. The one is Gaelic and the other is English. There seems to me to be no choice except for these: no half-way house if Scotland is ever to reach its complete expression in literature. And of these two alternatives English is the only practicable one at present, whatever Gaelic may become in the future.

To say this is to say that Scotland can only create a national literature by writing in English. This may sound paradoxical: in support of it I can only advance my whole case in regard to the Scots language, as outlined in the first part of this book, and the contemporary case of Ireland. Irish nationality cannot be said to be any less intense than ours; but Ireland produced a national literature not by clinging to Irish dialect, but by adopting English and making it into a language fit for all its purposes. The poetry of Mr Yeats belongs to English literature, but no one would deny that it belongs to Irish literature, pre-eminently and essentially. The difference between contemporary Irish and contemporary Scottish literature is that the first is central and homogeneous, and that the second is parochial and conglomerate; and this is because it does not possess an organ for the expression of a whole and unambiguous nationality. Scots dialect poetry represents Scotland in bits and patches, and in doing that it is no doubt a faithful enough image of the present divided state of Scotland. But while we cling to it we shall never be able to express the central reality of Scotland, as Mr Yeats has expressed the central reality of Ireland; though for such an end the sacrifice of dialect poetry would be cheap. The real issue in contemporary Scottish literature is between centrality and provincialism; dialect poetry is one of the chief supports of the second of these two forces; the first can hardly be said to exist at all. And until Scottish literature has an adequate language, it cannot exist. Scotland will remain a mere collection of districts. [. . .] But meanwhile it is of living importance to Scotland that it should maintain and be able to assert its identity; it cannot do so unless it feels itself a unity; and it cannot feel itself a unity on a plane which has a right to human respect unless it can create an autonomous literature. Otherwise it must remain in essence a barbarous country. That sense of unity can be preserved by an act of faith, as it was preserved in Ireland. Our task is to discover how this can be done; and I have tried to show how important the possession of a homogeneous language is for that end.

(Edwin Muir, *Scott and Scotland: The Predicament of the Scottish Writer*
London: Routledge, 1936, pp.14–15; 17–22; 38–39; 41–42; 177–80; 182.)

2.20 William Soutar, from 'Debatable Land' (*Outlook* October 1936)

Keats in one of his letters rightly asserts that a proverb is not a proverb to us until it has been 'proved upon our pulses', and this book is a similar assertion by which Mr Muir would initiate us into the truism that only a nation can have a national utterance. [. . .]

In the concluding section of his book Mr Muir, by the accumulated findings of his analysis, is able to offer a solution to the riddle with which he was confronted when considering Walter Scott, and asserts that 'the curious emptiness beyond the wealth of his imagination' was a necessary concomitant to the fact that Scott 'lived in a community which was not a community, and set himself to carry on a tradition which was not a tradition; and the result was that his work was an exact reflection of his predicament. His picture of life had no centre, because the environment in which he lived had no centre'.

But, having thus intercorroborated from the life of a most gifted individual what he had already exemplified from language and the various departments of literature, Mr Muir is unwilling to leave his readers merely with the negative, if profoundly disturbing, conclusion that Scotland is a country within which, for something like four centuries, there has been no organic reciprocity between the people and their representative men. Therefore he outlines in conclusion the directions of development, social and linguistic, which in his estimation must be followed if Scotland is to regain her national status. These are political autonomy, classlessness, and the acceptance of English as the only practical medium of expression at present. He is well aware of the controversial nature of the last of these contentions, and not without ample justification: and it may not be unprofitable to limit the remainder of this notice to a brief consideration of what Mr Muir's suggestion implies, namely, 'that Scotland can only create a national literature by writing in English'. Were this quotation but an isolated phrase one might have overlooked the confusion of national values evident within it, but it is echoed a few pages later in the words, 'Meanwhile . . . it [Scotland] cannot feel itself a unity on a plane which has a right to human respect unless it can create an autonomous literature. . . . that sense of unity can be preserved by an act of faith. . . .' To underline the lack of emphasis upon the necessary priority of nationhood to national utterance evinced in these sentences might appear to be quibbling were it not possible for the reader to correlate them with two significant omissions from Mr Muir's book. Flodden is never named, and there is no consideration of the work of MacDiarmid. Yet it is from the former that we must trace the beginning of the process of disintegration under discussion; and it is in the poetry of the latter that we recognize the contemporary act of faith which Mr Muir demands. His own alternative seems perilously near a ready-made solution, and consanguineous to the credulity of certain Douglasites who would heal the social cancer by the application of an economic poultice. But a repudiation of Mr Muir's prognosis in no way invalidates the excellence of his dissection upon the broken corpus of the Scottish language; an investigation which makes his book not only one of the most valuable contributions to contemporary Scottish studies, but also a challenge to every Scottish writer.

(William Soutar, 'Debatable Land', *Outlook* 1:7 October 1936, pp.87–90 [87, 89–90].)

2.21 Neil M. Gunn, from review of *Scott and Scotland* (*Scots Magazine* October 1936)

Mr Muir's attempt, in this book and elsewhere, to find in the Reformation the major destructive force of the old native concord, is finally as unsatisfying as any of his other individual factors. For what Mr Muir does not seem to see is that the 'rigours of Calvinism' were a symptom equally with other national phenomena like, for example, the rigours of the industrial revolution. England and Germany were reformed countries, yet their literary tradition continued and deepened. Ireland was never a reformed country, yet its ancient literary tradition disappeared with the loss of its nationhood. When Ireland once more fought for her nationhood and regained it, her literature reappeared (and in English, if with a difference) and Mr Muir uses names like Yeats and Joyce for critical conjuring on the highest plane. I am not concerned here with any argument for Scottish Nationalism. I am merely striving to find the principle which includes the facts and reconciles all opposites. The loss of nationhood does this. No other single factor or cause mentioned by Mr Muir does it.

If Mr Muir had faced up to this (as he does every now and then, and particularly in the case of Scott) and accepted all its implications, he would have saved us the last page of this book—surely one of the most signal instances of the Caledonian Antisyzygy run amok. 'I do not believe', he writes, 'in the programme of the Scottish Nationalists, for it goes against my reading of history, and seems to me a trivial response to a serious problem.' That can only mean that any deliberate action for the regaining of nationhood is trivial, for he immediately goes on: 'I can only conceive a free and independent Scotland coming to birth as the result of a general economic change in society, after which there would be no reason for England to exert compulsion on Scotland, and both nations could live in peace side by side.' In other words, we are to lie down under compulsion until other peoples bring about an economic change (whatever that may mean) which may permit a free and independent Scotland to be born. Is the idea, then, of a free and independent Scotland not 'trivial' after all? Apparently not, for Mr Muir at once proceeds: 'But meantime it is of living importance to Scotland that it should maintain and be able to assert its identity; it cannot do so unless it feels itself an entity; and it cannot feel itself an entity on a plane which has a right to human respect unless it can create an autonomous literature.' What do the words 'identity' and 'entity' mean here? Do they mean the nationhood of a free and independent Scotland, or do they mean some vague literary ideal to be perpetuated in a vacuum? How does a country *assert* its identity? And how, in particular, can the broken image of a lost kingdom 'create an autonomous literature' now, if it failed, as Mr Muir has so brilliantly shown, in the case of Scott, our greatest genius? But Mr Muir goes on: 'That sense of unity can be preserved by an act of faith, as it was preserved in Ireland.' Not economics now, but an act of faith! In Ireland, of course, they never troubled their heads about an economic change. They did not even bother about an act of faith; they simply acted with faith. But they *acted*. And their action was concerned solely with the restoration of nationhood. And Mr Muir holds them up as our example! Was ever unreason so varied within such short compass by so eminent a writer? [. . .]

It gives no pleasure to indulge in this sort of controversy. But it is important, I feel, that a writer who faces up to the absolutes in literary criticism should not hesitate over their implications when they are brought into the light of our common day. What was true in the case of Scott must apply surely with infinitely greater force to Mr Muir himself and to the Scottish writers of his time. If Mr Muir is certain in his mind that the dialectic of history has made consideration of Scottish nationhood 'trivial', then he would have been justified in asserting that as his expression of faith, and should have stopped there. But to have done that would have made of his book an antiquarian effort, a species of indulgence in 'nonsensical trash'. And Mr Muir—like the rest of us—knows it is too vital for that.

(Neil M. Gunn, review of *Scott and Scotland*, *Scots Magazine* 26:1, 26 October 1936, pp.72–78 [76–78].)

2.22 Catherine Carswell, 'The Scottish Writer' (*Spectator* December 1936)

How account, without too deeply wounding Scottish self-esteem, for the unsatisfactoriness of Scottish literature as a whole, and for the predicament in which the particular Scottish writer finds himself?

This is the problem Mr Muir has set himself in his contribution to the survey of Scottish problems embodied in the *Voice of Scotland* series. Justifiably he uses Sir Walter Scott merely as an example in the theory he evolves. Not what Scott did for Scotland, but what Scotland did not do for Scott is his theme. Why, he asks, is so great a literary artist also so disappointing a writer in certain respects? Briefly the answer is that Scott is not to blame, because he was obliged to think in one language and to feel in another.

A divorce between intellect and emotion is, as I think most thoughtful people will agree, an underlying cause of our literary shortcomings. But whether it can be attributed to circumstances of language in that degree which Mr Muir would have us believe, is another question. Mr Muir argues well and has picked his examples with care. Yet here and there we feel a sense of strain, as though there were doubts in his own secret mind, and as though he were aware of inconvenient truths which, if allowed full play, might interfere with the nice woof and warp of his fabric. And we ask ourselves whether that fabric is not devised less to demonstrate one defect in the Scottish body than to hide another. Language is a kittle subject, and lends itself to both sides of many an argument.

For example, Mr Muir points to Dunbar and Henryson as examples of Scottish poets who, had they been followed up, would have founded a Scottish literary line instead of ending in the air. But to make his point here he is compelled to exaggerate the difference in language between these poets and their English contemporaries. Yet was this more than a question of spelling, and of some turns of thought and phrase? Was it more, for instance, than the difference between the mother tongue of a Dorset or a Northumbrian man and literary English? It is certainly not so wide a gap as that which was successfully negotiated by Provençal men who have written in Parisian French and in the dialects of Sicily or of Tuscany. With Gaelic it is, of course, another story. But were not Dunbar and Henryson, for all their Scottish birth and sentiment, in the true body of English literature, and hence English writers with Scottish souls? Is not the same true of Sir Thomas Urquhart? Have not Scottish ministers been able to preach in the mother tongue with all the force of their emotion and intellect combined? Yet there is scarcely a Scottish sermon worth reading today, which sad circumstance, to my mind, points to one thing only, namely that Scotsmen lack a religious genius, for all their concern with theology.

The very fact, however, that one feels inclined to argue with Mr Muir, is the proof of how provocative and stimulating he has been in this book.

(Catherine Carswell, 'The Scottish Writer', *Spectator* 11 December 1936, pp.1054, 1056.)

2.23   David Daiches, from 'Dialect and the Lyric Poet' (*Outlook* May 1936)

The difference between the Scots and the English poems of a modern Scots writer is not quite that between the Scots and English poems of Ramsay, Fergusson, or Burns. With the earlier poets it was largely a case of knowing the dialect from childhood and acquiring the polite tongue by reading and even by study: further, the medium of poetry in the eighteenth century was adequate and comfortable—a situation quite the opposite to what we have today. Eighteenth-century English poetry, before the beginnings of the 'Romantic' movement made themselves obvious, was in a very balanced and self-satisfied state. But Burns approached it from the outside and never wrote it with ease. His English poems were written in what to him was a quite artificial mode. That mode was artificial in a sense even to Pope but not in the sense that it was to Burns. To the English it was the natural and legitimate *poetic* way of writing; far more natural, and certainly far easier, to Burns was a composite Scottish dialect poetry, though this, too, was to some extent artificial to him in the sense that English poetic diction of the time was to Pope.

To Burns, then, dialect poetry gave an opportunity to be natural (as far as a conscious poetic artist can be natural). To modern Scottish poets it gives an opportunity to be unnatural—often they search Dunbar and Henryson and the dictionaries to get the right word. Unnatural in this way the contemporary writers are, but that matters little if the language is used properly. Today dialect gives a poet a chance to be lyrical without losing dignity; in Burns's day it gave him a chance to be poetic without being artificial. That is the important difference.

What are poets who have a dialect at their command making of this opportunity? More perhaps than the critics are inclined to admit. There have been some admirable things in a small way produced these last few years by talented writers whose judicious use of Scots raises them to a level they could not attain to in English in the present state of English poetry. It is easy to sneer and say that these are remnants of the 'Whistlebinkie' school, persistent kailyarders who are carrying on with the old sentimental stuff. The best of them are not. William Soutar's most recent volume is as fine a justification as we need—there is a poetic ease and vigour here together with a genuine lyrical quality which we just do not find in more distinguished English poets who, able handlers of language though some of them are, are far too troubled about the very fundamentals of their art (as well as about everything else) to abandon themselves to simple poetic passion. Who among our English poets can today write a poem which is at the same time a *song*? Our Scots poets can do this perhaps better than anything. Four moving lines of Doric with little fuss and concealed art may have a more cogent appeal than 'The Orators'. The latter is highly important transition stuff, while the former has 'got there' right away. What English poet would today even attempt renderings of Heine as Alexander Gray has done and, in parts, done so effectively? It is what Pound might have done at the time when he was translating such a lot, but it is not very probable that the right touch would have been found even there.

So long as the dialect poet keeps his eye on the object, knows clearly and feels keenly what he has to say, he will be able to avoid the obvious defects of the sentimental kailyard tradition. Let him be classical in restraint while genuine in emotion, not too ambitious in theme, and cogent yet simple in expression, and he will be able to exploit admirably a field left perforce untilled by his English contemporaries. And not only is this age of transition an opportunity for the Scottish dialect poet; a similar field lies open to his southron neighbour, though, largely because of lack of example and a tradition, there is very little activity shown here. It would be interesting to see English dialect poets stealing behind the backs of their preoccupied brethren. Not that they could produce anything shattering or immensely valuable, but they could perhaps do something in this field of song and lyric. Perhaps again even this—and a great deal it is, too—would be a difficult achievement in an English dialect, because there is in England no such tradition of song-writing in the vernacular as there is in Scotland, and dialect itself has not the precedent for use in *educated* speech that the Scots possess. [. . .] And then there is Hugh M'Diarmid with his Jamieson [. . .] What seems to matter most is not where or how the materials are gathered but in what mood and with what degree of felicity the poet uses the materials. Certainly one of the essentials of good dialect poetry is a *classical* handling of the theme: there must be no nonsense about it, nothing tawdry or slobbery or shown. The emotion may be as deep as you like, but well under control—a touch of excess in a Scots dialect poem and back we go with a rush to 'Whistlebinkie'. True, the dialect poet can be simple without being trite, forthright without being silly—but he must mind his step. These virtues are his at a price, and the price is excessive caution, a finely-adjusted balance between self-surrender and self-control, between spontaneous lyrical emotion and constant regard for 'proportion'. For sentimentality in dialect becomes over-sentimentality (let the psychologist say why) and exuberance tends to become hysteria. It may be because the emotional values of dialect words are so strong and obvious compared with those of standard English, and their associations are frequently so much more vivid. In fact, dialect has the defects of its qualities, and the freshness and vigour which make it potentially lyrical also make it potentially flamboyant. And it is to be noted with pleasure that the best of contemporary Scots dialect poetry is not flamboyant or facile; the poets do not ring the obvious emotional changes on an expressive word but use it with delicacy and restraint. Not always so—in some of the women poets especially there is a tendency to emotional overstress which is so dangerous in this type of writing—but the best of Charles Murray, Marion Angus, William Soutar, and Professor Gray do show admirably restrained handling of emotional dialect. There is a lot of inferior stuff, of course, in the work of contemporary dialect poets and few besides Hugh M'Diarmid are accepted as more than 'highly talented' (though M'Diarmid himself nods often enough, especially when writing in English), but time will tell and perhaps more than we think is going to survive as worthy

49

products of the Scottish genius. [. . .] It would be a mistake to lose a sense of proportion in discussing these poets, but an even greater mistake to ignore them and the *potentialities* of their work as so many critics are doing.

(David Daiches, 'Dialect and the Lyric Poet', *Outlook* 1:2 May 1936, pp.76–83 [79–82].)

2.24 William Soutar, 'Faith in the Vernacular' (*Voice of Scotland* June–August 1938)

The incongruities associated with the Scottish vernacular renaissance are byproducts of discussion rather than inherencies, and manifest the futility of seeking to evaluate the movement merely from the linguistic viewpoint. The revival of Scots as a literary potential is a very debatable affair; but its significance as an act of faith is beyond equivocation: it is our temporary necessity. Unless we recognise the relativeness of this faith we are forced to misinterpret our present need by anticipating experience; in other words we rationalise the process; assuming therefrom, and reason can hardly do otherwise, that Scots cannot be an adequate medium for contemporary thought; and that consequently it is a misguided enthusiasm which prompts us to preserve it. If, however, we are conscious of the relative nature of this effort towards vernacular rehabilitation we are also made aware of its paradoxy: namely to be the symbol of a process which, in fulfilment, offers no promise of its own: but to appreciate this we must look beyond Scotland.

We live in a period of transition and disintegration and are given the choice of two pathways towards stability—Fascism and Socialism; nationalism is integral to both but in the former it is an end in itself; in the latter a means or subsumption. This world-wide struggle is peculiarly complicated in Scotland which is but a pseudo-entity and therefore confronted by a choice which demands an epicyclic response. Symptomatic of this dilemma is the movement to rehabilitate the vernacular which not only testifies to the need for the rediscovery of our national roots but also for an alignment with the worker: nor is it over-fanciful to see the dilemma embodied in synthetic Scots itself; which by its virtue, namely the increasing comprehensiveness of its vocabulary, tends to alienate the ordinary reader. One can sympathise with critics who maintain that the Scottish poet must accept the ready-made vehicle of English as his only solution to a linguistic impasse; but these have failed to recognise the symptomatic nature of the renaissance of Scots which has been indicated above. In a transitional period there are temporary loyalties which are necessities for faith; such a loyalty at this moment in Scotland is the effort to re-establish the vernacular, and ought to be accepted even with the self-consciousness that it is but temporary. In England the embarrassment which confronts the New Signature poets is the compulsion to speak for a class to which they do not belong; and it was inevitable that they should recognise in Hopkins a conditional affinity. For Hopkins also was a man halted between two worlds albeit these were metaphysical; and the integrity of his utterance created a technique which, even in imitation, retains something of the spiritual tension which informed it.

Poetry in English, by contemporary Scots, exhibits little or nothing of Hopkins' influence; and it may be fairly assumed that this is so not only because the poetry is written by individuals reared in working-class homes but also by reason of the linguistic complexity which is their peculiar problem. This comparison is worth emphasising since it illustrates the synchrony of frustration and ready-made solutions; and bears this social implication that only an autonomous Scotland can co-operate unequivocally in the establishment of a classless world.

The paradox of faith in a transitional period, such as our own, is that it becomes self-conscious; this is concomitant upon its temporaneousness. It follows, therefore, that although the preoccupation with Scots is recognised to be a necessary declaration of faith, now, it is not pursued in the assumption that Scots must become established in a corporate Scotland. Let us be fulfilled as an integrated people and we shall find our true speech whatever it may be. At the moment the revival of Scots is indicative of the desire for nationhood and, by reciprocality, would increase that desire. It is therefore imperative that faith in the vernacular be maintained at present and that it be orientated beyond nationality; since the parable of the man who swept his house is also applicable to a people.

(William Soutar, 'Faith in the Vernacular', *Voice of Scotland* 1:1 June–August 1938, pp.22–23.)

3

A Scottish Renaissance?
Responses and Reviews

3.1 From *Scottish Chapbook* (August 1922)

a) C.M. Grieve, from Editor's 'Causerie'

In my opinion, then, for several generations Scottish literature has neither seen nor heard nor understood what was taking place around it. For that reason it remains a dwarf among giants. Scottish writers have been terrified even to appear inconstant to established conventions. (Good wine would have needed no 'Bonnie Brier Bush'.) They have stood still and consequently been left behind in technique and ideation. Meanwhile the Scottish nation has been radically transformed in temperament and tendency; Scottish life has been given a drastic reorientation, with the result that Scottish literature today is in no sense representative or adequate. [. . .] Sadly the preface to *Lyra Celtica* was recalled. Therein William Sharp declared, 'All Ireland is aflame with Song. . . . Scotland is again becoming the land of Old Romance.' He wrote with a passionate prematurity. Only those who kept their eyes on Paisley were rewarded—although, as one critic remarked, 'no attempt at renascence has ever been better equipped than that undertaken in the Lawnmarket of Edinburgh by Patrick Geddes and Colleagues', and another said of the forgotten *Evergreen*, that, while the organ of a band of social reformers in one of the poorest quarters of Edinburgh, it also touched an international note, and kept up the spirit of the best ideals in literature and art. Naturally, this being so, it speedily became defunct, and the movement of which it was the organ scarcely outlasted it. 'It is no exaggeration to say,' Sharp also wrote no longer ago than 1896, 'that at this moment there are more than a hundred Gaelic singers in Western Scotland whose poetry is as fresh and winsome, and, in point of form as well as substance, as beautiful as any that is being produced throughout the rest of the realm.' He must have imagined that miraculous band in some inconceivable moment of transition between himself and 'Fiona Macleod'. They were never heard of before, nor afterwards. No examples of their work were included even in *Lyra Celtica* itself. The Scottish literary revival proved to be a promise that could not be kept.

To-day there is a distinct change in the air, however. An access of curiosity and imprudence may work wonders.

b) From 'Book Reviews'

What Belgium did, Scotland can do. Literary Scotland, like Belgium, is a country of mixed nationalities. Instead of two languages, Flemish and French, we have Braid Scots, Gaelic and English. Let the exponents of these three sections in Scottish Literature to-day make common cause, as the young Belgian writers, despite their acute nationalistic and technical differences, did in 'La Jeune Belgique' and elsewhere; and the next decade or two will see a Scottish Renascence as swift and irresistible as was the Belgian Revival between 1880 and 1910.

(C.M. Grieve, editor's 'Causerie', *Scottish Chapbook* 1:1 August 1922, pp.3–4;
'Book Reviews', p.28.)

3.2 Denis Saurat, from 'Le Groupe de "la Renaissance Écossaise"' (*Revue Anglo-Americaine* April 1924)

Un nouveau mouvement littéraire se prononce en Écosse, qui est une des choses les plus intéressantes et les plus riches en promesses dans le groupe des littératures anglo-saxonnes à l'heure présente. Tout récent, ce mouvement a déja produit une quantité d'oeuvres assez considérable, particulièrement dans la poésie lyrique. Il prétend d'ailleurs se rattacher à un renouveau du sentiment national écossais.

Le mouvement a trois organes: Une revue hebdomadaire de combat et de propagande, *The Scottish Nation*, à ses débuts surtout politique, mais où la littérature a fini par prendre une place prépondérante; une revue mensuelle exclusivement littéraire: *The Scottish Chapbook*; et une anthologie annuelle de poésie écossaise: *Northern Numbers* qui paraît depuis 1920. C'est le même écrivain, C.M. Grieve, qui dirige les trois organes, et ce jeune et fougueux tempérament de révolutionnaire intellectuel et de poète mystique mériterait à lui seul toute une étude.

L'idée centrale qui a groupé plus de cinquante écrivains—dont quelques-uns déjà célèbres—est l'idée de l'autonomie écossaise. Nous laisserons ici de côté l'autonomie politique pour nous occuper exclusivement de la littérature. L'Écosse—nous disent les théoriciens du groupe—a quelque chose d'original à apporter à la littérature européenne; quelque chose d'aussi distinct de la littérature anglaise, en une autre direction, que les oeuvres de l'école irlandaise dans les quarante dernières années. L'Écosse doit se libérer intellectuellement de l'influence anglaise et jouer son rôle indépendant dans la culture mondiale. On voit immédiatement la noble ambition du nouveau groupe: il ne s'agit pas de se renfermer en Ecosse, de limiter l'horizon intellectuel à une résurrection des coutumes, des croyances, des traditions locales: cette résurrection est certes au centre du mouvement; mais on veut donner aux esprits écossais, outre la conscience de leur race, une culture universelle. Tout ce que fera le monde entier, en fait de culture, devra être jugé d'un point de vue écossais; et, inversement, il faudra faire prendre au monde l'habitude de se demander, lorsque quelque chose d'important se préparera en littérature ou en art, non plus seulement: 'Qu'en penseront les Anglais?' mais aussi: 'Qu'en penseront les Écossais?'

(Denis Saurat, 'Le groupe de "la Renaissance Écossaise" ', *Revue Anglo-Americaine*
April 1924, pp.1–13 [1–2].)

3.3 George Kitchin, M.A., D.Litt., from 'The "Scottish Renaissance" Group: What It Represents' (*Scotsman* November 1924)

Complaint was made recently that, while any amount of care and money is lavished on keeping green the memories of our older writers, none of this gracious stream is directed to the task of encouraging our new school of Scottish writers. It is really an old protest this—the cry of the present-day artist who appears a pigmy against the clutching *mortmain* of the giants of the past. As a rule, it is met by scant sympathy. Partly the public apathy, partly the manners of the newcomers, succeed in beating down their cry, and as often as not, unless the true matter is in them, they retire disgruntled from the stage, and rail with the melancholy Jacques against an unfeeling world. For all that, it behoves us to look carefully at the work of any group that challenges a place in the sun lest, by hardening our hearts, we miss something that is destined to endure. There are as many instances of a dull age rejecting good work, as of literary impertiments wearying the public into a sort of sullen recognition.

It cannot be said that this present group of Scottish writers lack confidence. The august title they have assumed—*The Scottish Renaissance Group*—alone might terrify some people; more serious, the character of intellectual revolutionaries which some of them adopt is not calculated to conciliate opinion at the present moment. The remembrance of what has happened in Ireland largely as the result of an aggressive, self-sufficing, race-culture, is not likely to make things easy for them. But, on the other hand, they have this to exploit, the feeling that we have subsisted too long on worship of the great writers of the 19th century, the feeling that this ancestor-worship has gone far enough, and that it is time we were looking round for new ideas and a new manner, if Scotland is to contribute anything to European thought and art. That is the very valuable asset of the new school.

A Parallel with Spenser

One remembers how Spenser was acclaimed by an enthusiastic group of friends as the New Poet, and how eager the Elizabethan public was to greet him after the long period of Chaucer worship. One remembers how Ronsard and his friends prepared themselves for the French laurel, and how they dethroned the preceding age of poets. The parallel with Spenser—in other respects an absurd one—is close enough when we consider that the work with which the new poet determined to storm his public—*The Shepherd's Calendar*—was a *dialect* poem, making its appeal to what was perdurable and native in the English life and habit. For this matter of dialect lies at the root of the modern movement. One of the chief voices in the *Northern Numbers* group says:—'The trouble to-day when one tries to remake from dialect a literary language is the desperate lack of culture of the vast majority of those who use it. . . . It is necessary to make it express the needs, not of a workman, but of an artist of the 20th century, who is at the same time a Scotsman (and not an Englishman or a negro), and a good European or Occidental.'

It is a little boastful this manifesto, and will naturally alienate those who do not realise either the sunken riches of dialect or the fact that there is a special Scottish psychology which can be expressed only through dialect, and which is Scotland's contribution to European culture. But, after all, the Elizabethan group which supported young Spenser had a supreme poet to present to the public of that day. Have our young Parnassians any such golden-mouthed poet? We are told that they have. They have Mr Hugh M'Diarmid. He is the new poet. His followers will have it that he is the new Burns, and this time a Burns who is in the European movement, not as our Burns was, at least as Matthew Arnold painted him, a mere local deity.

A French Critic's Admiration

Now comes the one piece of genuine encouragement our new group has received. They have compelled for Mr M'Diarmid—and the group in general—the extreme admiration of a very cultivated group in France, of which M. Denis Saurat is chief. Edinburgh is not likely to underrate the industry and penetration of this distinguished stranger, who has been within our gates this very week. His work on Blake and on Milton—the subject of his lecture at the University—is of a high class. One would say he is not likely to go off on forlorn crusades and get stupidly this strange admiration for our group of unthought-of writers! It is true, as his work on Milton shows, that M. Saurat is of the adventurous type of scholar and critic. Standing on Masson's lecture platform, he dared to impugn that great man's view of John Milton. But we were all prepared for that. 'Another light gone out', is all we murmur. We don't mind M. Saurat putting out Masson's light, but we are amazed at him assisting at putting Mr M'Diarmid's light in and actually going the length of translating him into classical French! But, then, has he not told us that before we can hope for a genuine Scottish renaissance we must burn our Scotts, Carlyles, Stevensons? And we are afraid he is right! [. . .]

Not a Literary Movement Only

It is impossible to judge here of the claims made for Mr M'Diarmid. No doubt some of them are extravagant, but there are certain pieces of his which raise him above the common level of writers in dialect—above (in the writer's opinion) Mr Charles Murray. He has—it is strange to say it of a dialect poet—a certain high seriousness which Mr Murray never attempts. For Mr Murray's craft, delightful as it can be, definitely accepts the local limitation, whereas it is the ardent aim of the new group to be something more. And the spirit they represent is not confined to verse. Painters, sculptors, and musicians are enlisted in this movement, which is at once intensely local and European at the same time. It is the age of folklore, of the hearth as opposed to the salon. But it is no longer the simple singing of the loom and the hearth. The most subtle technique is applied to folk themes and folk dialect. The movement has appeared in every country in Europe. It was bound to come to us, who have one of the richest dialects. To liberate Scottish art from being the lackey of English art, so that Scotland can play her separate part in European culture, is the ambitious idea—in other words, to reverse the process of the 18th century, when men of letters sought to be English and to speak like Englishmen. It remains to be seen whether those who have applied themselves to this task have the necessary pertinacity and vision.

(George Kitchin, M.A., D.Litt., 'The "Scottish Renaissance" Group: What It Represents', *Scotsman* 8 November 1924, p.8.)

3.4 W.P. [William Power], from 'Follow the Gleam' (*Glasgow Herald* November 1924)

Genius and talent do not thrive in a vacuum, nor can they distribute themselves indiscriminately over the wide world. They find their necessary complement, their condition and indeed their reason of being, in a national spirit and a definite national environment. In these we realise ourselves. Without Scotland, the brightest Scot amongst us were only a stray x, an unknown and unknowable quantity. It is the existence of Scotland that gives meaning to his personal symbol and raises it to the hundredth, thousandth, or ten millionth power. The study of general literature is necessary to the enrichment of our being, but without a national centre of our own we are like bees without a hive, sipping honey that we cannot store. The study of the history and literature of our own country gives a central meaning and a definite direction to general culture. It justifies our being and gives it character. The dormant fibres of our nature reawaken one by one as we realise our spiritual affinity with Barbour, Blind Harry, Dunbar, Gavin Douglas, Henryson, Buchanan, the Melvilles, Ramsay, Fergusson, Burns, and Hogg. We feel the very roots of our being in the wistful pathos and elemental tragedy of the old Ballads, and in the homely and intimate touches of rustic life in the old songs. Scotland itself becomes something more than a mere geological feature, more even than an extension of our own being; it becomes an integral part of the national life in which our own life has lost itself in order to find itself more completely. From a valiant past which is not dead, since it lives in us, we gather courage for the present and hope for the future. How can anything daunt us if we have made our lives continuous with those of Scottish men and women who faced existence with so frank and brave an appreciation of its grimness, its tragedy, its pathos, but also of its undying soul of beauty and of humour?

But the past has no meaning unless in relation to the present and the future. For over a century Scotland has attempted to put her past definitely behind her, except for tourist purposes, and to devote herself exclusively to large-scale industry, the letting of shootings, the breeding of prize-stock and the export of whisky. Empire-builders, and heids o' depairtments. There is something not unalluring about this decline into complacent provincialism. Gear-gathering and purely individual aims make smaller demands upon the average mind than a full national life. Literary renaissances are bothersome things. Best to assume that Scottish history ended with the Union and Scottish literature with Scott. Put your feet on the fender, 'ferlie at the folk in Lunnon', and turn with a tranquil mind to the chartularies of Pluscarden, the fluctuations of the price of fish at Leith in the sixteenth century, the witch-burnings of James VI, Lockhart's *Scott*, and the History of the U.P. Church.

Nations, however, do not retire from business quite so easily. The past has a propellent power undreamt of by antiquarians. Ghosts from our emptied countrysides flit through the industrial areas, where two-thirds of our population are bunched. They squeak and gibber quaint Babylonish nonsense about land values, municipal this and that, and the exploitation of the proletariat. What they really want to say, but they have the lost the language for it, is that a nation in which three-fourths of the population are completely divorced from the land and from the sanative variety of rural life is not in a healthy state. The same idea haunts the mind of the middle-class Scot who has not been drugged by an English public school education. Also, he begins to feel the personal need for a spiritual centre of national life. He wants to give a present and a future tense to the things that constitute the real soul of the Scottish nation. Our young men have visions, and our old men dream dreams. The flower of Scottish song blooms upon the slag-heaps of Lanarkshire. The rustic Muse reawakens in Buchan and on Donside. A Scottish Chap-book emanates from Montrose. The *Northern Review* has bravely lived and bravely died. The *Scots Magazine* continues its more sober career. In Glasgow a gallant effort is being made to establish a Scottish Stage. The signs of a national literary renaissance are plainly evident in the literary columns of our daily papers. Our poets and essayists have definitely moved away from the flat-footed moralising, maudlin sentiment, chortling 'wut' and cosy prejudice that degraded so-called Scottish literature in the period between Scott and Douglas Brown. They have realised that art is not an evasion of life but a brave and closely studied attempt to get at its essentials. It is *la vraie verité*. Even Edinburgh, that beautiful cenotaph of metropolitanism, is beginning to be invaded by faint stirrings of national life. The Porpoise Press has established itself in the very shadow of the Scott Monument.

The champions of provincial slumber and facile imitativeness, who put up their umbrellas in Edinburgh when it is raining in London, find it easy to pour cold water on the idea of a Scottish literary renaissance. Art, they say, should be spontaneous. A literary renaissance that tries to root itself in a national impulse is like a tree standing on its head. But the Scottish literary renaissance has already begun to root itself in Scottish life, which includes the whole history of Scottish literature. All it demands that it cannot itself supply are critical sympathy and the primary requisites of material encouragement. Authors cannot write, even for nothing, without publishers and a public. The existence of a stage is the chief inspiration of a dramatist. If the Elizabethan stage had not been built up by cultured English noblemen long before Shakespeare left Stratford-on-Avon, *Hamlet* and *Macbeth* and *King Lear* would never have been written. An endowed Scottish stage with enlightened directors would not produce a Scottish Shakespeare. But it would give Scottish writers the opportunity, the training, and the motive for lack of which Scottish drama has failed to develop.

The misunderstanding that has arisen between literary scholars and creative writers is artificial and futile. It is like a rivalry between historians and statesmen. It is as if the administrative departments of an army were to withhold supplies from the fighting forces, and the combatants were to reply: 'Keep your old guns and your mouldy stores; we'll fight with our fists and live on the country.' The Scottish Text Society and the *Scottish Chapbook*, the *Scottish Historical Review* and the *Northern Review,* are integral and complemental parts of the same movement; each is meaningless without the others. We cannot have too much sound Scottish history. We have far too little of good Scottish literary criticism. We are doing well in Scottish anthologies: Mr Buchan's is a model of its kind. But there is urgent need for good cheap editions, not only of Henryson, but of Dunbar (the late Professor W.P. Ker's favourite poet), James I, Gavin Douglas, and Sir David Lyndsay, and of Scottish prose-writers like Pitscottie, Buchanan, Knox, the diarist Melville, and Patrick Walker. The way for these has been prepared by Mr Robb's excellent *Book of Scots* for school use.

And what of Gaelic and the Scottish vernacular? Gaelic is dying as a spoken tongue [. . .] But as a subject of literary study, along with Irish Gaelic, it is of priceless value. Really good translations of Gaelic poetry, by a Scottish Douglas Hyde, would send a rich tributary stream of inspiration into Scottish literature. Glasgow ought to be the world-centre of Celtic scholarship.

The Scottish vernacular is also dying from popular speech. For that reason it can have no future in prose literature. 'Johnnie Gibb' is a unique tour de force. It lacks transparency and melodic flow; it is a conglomerate of quaint opacities that cloud the sense and hold up the narrative; it is everything that good prose is not. Like German, only more so, Scots is chaotic in prose and spontaneously formful in verse. It is loaded to the muzzle with gnomic, homely, comic, tragic, and romantic suggestion. It is an arsenal of spells and evocations. Its inspiration power was manifested two centuries ago, when a small group of vernacular poets in Scotland brought about the Romantic Revival and the Return to Nature in Europe.

The power of Scots is still undiminished. In the hands of Stevenson and other writers it has become that unique phenomenon, a language unspoken but sung and felt, and alive with all the elemental forces that lie behind the huge mechanism of intellect and civilisation. Reproaches about resort to Jamieson need not trouble our Scottish poets: accuracy and an approach to standard Scots are the first essentials; localisms should be banned: if a word is 'felt', and the feeling of it is conveyed to the reader, then its use was justified. With Dr Craigie to keep them right in verbal detail, the poets will go ahead in Scots, never fear. They are handling something bigger and more vital than Provençal, Catalan, or even, in some respects, than modern English. And the English prose of Scottish authors will derive strength from the stream of vernacular poetry that flows beside it: not so much by the taking over of savoury words and expressive phrases, as by the inspiration of perpetual contact with the elemental soul of a nation.

Europe, wounded and weakened and disillusioned by the war, is a prey to parasitical influences of morbidity, spiritualism, freakishness, pseudo-psychology, and deadly materialism. Her aeroplanes cleave the clouds, but her soul remains below. Once again, as two centuries ago, after the dreadful wars of Louis XIV, she looks around for springs of healing. May she not find them once again in the waters called forth by Scottish poets from the rocks of their native land?

(W.P. [William Power], 'Follow the Gleam', *Glasgow Herald* 15 November 1924, p.4.)

3.5 Unsigned review of *The Northern Muse: An Anthology of Scots Vernacular Poetry*, arranged by John Buchan (*Burns Chronicle* 1925)

This book comes opportunely on the eve of the promised Scottish Renaissance, for the proper understanding of which it will be a great help to the general reader who has not made a special study of Scottish literature, and whose library of Scottish vernacular poetry is consequently limited. In presenting his carefully chosen examples of the Scottish Muse from the earliest times down to the present day Mr Buchan has arranged them, not in chronological order, but according to their subject-matter, in eighteen divisions or 'Books', as he calls them, each division dealing with the same subject, as, for instance, 'Youth and Spring', 'Love', 'The Hearth', 'Human Comedy', 'Bacchanals', &c., &c. Under each heading examples are given characteristic of its treatment by authors as far apart in time as Dunbar and Henryson from Burns, Sir Walter Scott, and Charles Murray. Hence, in the 533 pages of the book more than a superficial acquaintance is made with the works of Dunbar, Montgomerie, James I, Henryson, Sir David Lyndsay, Barbour, Blind Harry, Sempill of Beltrees, Gavin Douglas, and some of the anonymous Makars who have done so much for the Scottish lyric. Nor are recent, and poets still with us, left out. Ramsay, Tannahill, Fergusson, Outram, James Hogg, Logie Robertson, R.L. Stevenson, Neil Munro, Violet Jacob, Charles Murray, George Macdonald, Wingate, Thomas Smibert, &c., are all represented by choice examples chosen with the best of taste. The 'Introduction', and the 'Commentary', at the end of the book—scholarly productions in Mr Buchan's best style—are worth, in our opinion, the price of the whole book.

No better, handier, cheaper, and more tasteful compendium of the Scottish poetic vernacular has ever been compiled, and we would strongly advise every lover of our national literature to add the volume to his library.

(Unsigned review of *The Northern Muse*, *Burns Chronicle* 1925, p.6.)

3.6   C.M. Grieve, from *Scottish Educational Journal* (September 1925 and April 1926)

a) From 'Edwin Muir' (September 1925)

Comparing Sir George Douglas and George Brandes I questioned whether Sir George might not have achieved more, if he had had a different conception of the critic's function—'a conception', I said, 'that it is to be hoped some Scottish critic in however small a measure will soon begin to show'. But as a matter of fact we have that already in Edwin Muir—a critic incontestably in the first flight of contemporary critics of *welt-literatur*. He differs from Brandes and from the Brandes-like critic I desiderated for Scotland, however, in that he has not yet become effective in his own country. That will come. Muir is still a young man: and the problems that have to be solved before a Scottish Renaissance can be got thoroughly under-weigh have already been engaging his attention. His interest lies there: but the movement has not yet reached the point at which it can give him a sufficient—and sufficiently suitable—audience to make it worth his while (I do not mean merely financially—though the matter of *modus vivendi* is involved) to devote himself either wholly or in large measure to it. Muir's critical apparatus is not designed for the spade-work that has yet to be done. Infants cannot profitably be sent direct to the Universities: and, relatively speaking, interest in literature in Scotland is infantile, while Muir is a Pan-European intervening in the world-debate on its highest plane. The number of readers in Scotland capable of following his arguments is extremely limited—proportionately to population much smaller than in any other country in Europe or in the United States: as is indicated by the fact that it is only within the last two or three years that his name has become known to any extent at all in what may be called our uppermost class of readers, whereas his outstanding ability has long been recognised in London, he is known in Germany as the translator of Gerhardt Hauptmann and as a thoroughly qualified international interpreter of German literature, he has a big following in America, where he has contributed a great deal to most of the leading literary periodicals. A prominent French critic writing on the Scottish Renaissance and remarking on Muir's connection with the movement, is careful to add *nota bene* after his name, as if that in itself were a sufficient guarantee—as it is—that, however unknown the names of the other prime movers in this 'News from the North' may be, 'there is something in it'. And so forth. In short, he has already the makings of a world-reputation, which he is rapidly consolidating. His name is to be encountered everywhere—in the *Nation and Athenaeum* almost every week, in *The Calendar of Modern Letters*, in the *Adelphi*, in the *Saturday Westminster Gazette,* in the *North American Review*, in *The Dial*, in the *New York Nation*. And always over distinctive work—work that, however diverse in its point of departure, is obviously making irresistibly for that common rendezvous where ultimately it will be found to be assembled as a four-square body of criticism challenging comparison with the best of its kind produced by any contemporary—and by all but two or three forerunners—in the English language. Since the collapse of the *Scottish Nation* and the *Northern Review*—to both of which he contributed—Scotland has ceased to offer any suitable medium for his work. There is nothing for him in Scotland.

b) From 'Neil M. Gunn' (April 1926)

Practically the only young Scottish prose-writer of promise manifesting himself to-day is Mr Neil M. Gunn, whose first novel, *The Grey Coast*, is published by Messrs Jonathan Cape, Ltd—the only Scottish prose-writer of promise, that is to say, in relation to that which is distinctively Scottish rather than tributary to the 'vast engulfing sea' of English literature. As a writer of short sketches and short stories, he has contributed largely to the *Glasgow Herald*, to the *Scottish Nation* and *Northern Review*, to *Chambers' Journal*, to the *Dublin Magazine*, to, above all, the *Cornhill*, and many other periodicals: and is our nearest equivalent to the Irish Liam O'Flaherty. [. . .] There is an allied reason for his special significance from a purely Scottish point of view—a double-barrelled reason. His un-Scottish preoccupation with pure technique; and his constant endeavour to apply it to the purely Scottish scene. In other words, he is showing an ever-lessening tendency to subscribe either in style or in subject-matter to the un-Scottish conventions of all British editors and almost all British publishers. He is, in fact, tending in the opposite direction: and having got rid of the attitude at once to life and to letters which has characterised the period of Scotland's nationalistic and literary nadir, his artistic integrity is bringing him into unmediated relations with Scottish nature, human and otherwise. The process is not yet complete. He has not wholly found himself nor has Scotland reacquired entire autonomy in his consciousness. His work remains unequal—now almost anonymous in its resemblance to 'current fiction' in the mass, now falling into a Kailyard rut, now tinged with the Celtic twilight. Above these levels, at its second-best, it manifests a point of view not dissimilar to George Douglas Brown's, but more humane, more *divers et ondoyant* than his, but, at the same time, less organic. It is this style—of attitude to life, not of writing—which comprises most of *The Grey Coast*. But the best things in the book are pure Gunn—something new, and big, in Scottish literature.

('Edwin Muir', *Scottish Educational Journal* 4 September 1925; 'Neil M. Gunn',
2 April 1926; reprinted from *Contemporary Scottish Studies*, a centenary reprinting by
the *Scottish Educational Journal* (1976), pp.29; 97.)

3.7 Theta [Thomas Henderson], from 'The Scots Renaissance and Mr C.M. Grieve' (*Scottish Educational Journal* October 1925)

Probably few readers of the Journal see eye to eye with Mr C.M. Grieve in the judgments he has expressed in his series of articles, yet it is to be hoped that the majority of those who disagree more or less violently with him do so for better reasons than those offered by some of his critics [. . .] It is true that Mr Grieve lays himself wide open to misunderstanding. He is continually obscuring the light of his critical principles, derived for the most part from Saintsbury, by irrelevancies. Far too frequently he blurs his effort by uncouth contortions of phrase and clause that remind us, in their writing awkwardnesses of the less admirable writers of Elizabethan prose. He has not the serenity of spirit that is the best quality of the best critics. He is too fond of killing squirrels with a howitzer. He has a more than Hibernian fondness for trailing his coat before his chosen enemies. His curious pedantry leads him to buttress his opinions by pointless and platitudinous quotations from insignificant foreigners. Worst of all, his style of prose-writing is one of the worst ever devised by a critic. It seems to be borrowed, in part at least, from Saintsbury, but it has added to his ungainliness a more than Boeotian heavyfootedness.

On the other hand, it is fair to Mr Grieve to point out that it is far from being an easy task to blaze a new trail. He has, with good reason, set himself to bring about a revaluation of our literature. He has not set his hand to that very necessary piece of work from purely critical motives. He avows his intention of initiating a Scottish Renaissance. Our land is to blossom in more than its former glory. Our tongue is to become the medium of a genuine literature, fit to rank with the greatest in Europe. We are to be set free from the bondage of Anglicisation. The spirit is to work mightily in us—and the sacred fire is to purge the dross of materialism from our hearts. Surely a not ignoble dream—or ambition and one that might well excuse even more bad temper and lack of grace than Mr Grieve reveals. It is, we believe, the bare truth that our chief national weakness is what might be our chief national strength. Our guid conceit of ourselves once spurred us on to fight our way to primacy in many fields. To-day, save for rare, individual exceptions our conceit takes the decidedly humiliating form of Burns Suppers, imitations of imitations of Burns, a wearisome exposition of themes long since exhausted and a definite abandonment of the very qualities—fierce independence, resolute individuality alike in man and in nation, fiery, but whimsical, pride, a humour that was of earth and a poetry that was of the sky—that once made Scotland great. The difference is that of Hyperion and a Satyr.

Mr Grieve is like many of us profoundly discontented and disgusted with most of what has for many years passed as Scots literature. It is, of course, easier to express discontent and disgust in ephemeral articles than in the best way—by creative work, inspired by higher ideals than those of the market-place. Yet we are not without the hope inspired by the existence of genuine literature. Mr Grieve is severe on Neil Munro—much too severe in our opinion, though like Mr Grieve we believe that Munro has not given his native land more than a tithe of what he could. Still, in all his books, the vision beautiful lifts up our hearts, if but for a fleeting moment, and in his *Gillian the Dreamer* it is with us all the way. No doubt that early book was his worst seller, and equally without doubt, he has never again attempted to write a book of the kind, but it is true that he never has quite lost the poignant sense of beauty and the secret of *lacrimae meae* he revealed in that almost-masterpiece. [. . .] Mr Grieve, it is now well known, is the Hugh M'Diarmid whose *Sangschaw* has been recently published. The secret was always an open one. It may now be considered no longer a secret in any sense since John Buchan printed the first poem in *Sangschaw* in his fine anthology *The Northern Muse*. Mr Grieve is to be congratulated in the first place on having the courage to face his numerous critics with a book of poems for them to assail. No doubt they will avail themselves greatly of the privilege.

What of the poems? Personally, I rank them high—much higher than the average of most of the Scots verse of recent years. Their diction is, save for one feature to be considered anon, extremely simple, clear, attractive. As a poet he is ever so much happier than a prose-writer. This is not unusual. Wings are not handy when one is walking. Take, for example, the poem already referred to:—THE BONNIE BROUKIT BAIRN [. . .] Can anyone deny that the central thought is poetic, and that the treatment is successful in making the reader realise that it is poetical, that it lifts the whole subject beyond the realm of the trivial into the sphere of the universal, that, in other words, it gives to the mood of a moment something of the quality of the eternal?

Most of the poems in the book reveal the same capacity to fix in permanent form the thought that would otherwise pass. For the most part Mr Grieve keeps to the lyric which is, of course, the simplest and, in most respects, the easiest of poetic forms. The only exceptions—'I Heard Christ Sing' and 'Au Clair de la Lune'—are more apparent than real, for they can fairly be regarded as lyric sequences, which probably owe something of their form to Heine. It remains for Mr Grieve to prove that his lyrical gift and his remarkable endowment of terse pointed phrase can be applied on a more heroic scale. [. . .]

One thing remains to be said. Mr Grieve has with malice aforethought (or with far sighted wisdom, according to the point of view) chosen to eke out the resources of the vernacular by using obsolete words and what look uncommonly like fabrications of his own. He is perfectly entitled to do so. He has no precedents to appeal to. The beautiful work of Gerard

Hopkins owes much to the poet's choice of strange words and combinations of words. Still, this freedom has its danger, and I am not convinced that Mr Grieve gains much from his 'eemis stane' 'yow-trummle' 'amplefeyst', and the rest of them.

(Theta [Thomas Henderson], 'The Scots Renaissance and Mr C.M. Grieve', *Scottish Educational Journal* 30 October 1925, pp.1170–71.)

3.8   Edwin Muir, from 'The Scottish Renaissance' (*Saturday Review of Literature* October 1925)

It is known only to a few people in England, it is probably not suspected in America at all, that for about three years there has existed what has been termed a Scottish Renaissance. The beginnings of all movements are obscure; they only attain that burst of splendor which convinces the cultivated public after they have struggled on against opinion, against all reason, through a long and painful apprenticeship. [. . .]

Recently a volume of poetry which claims to be the fruit of the Scottish Renaissance has been published. It is *Sangschaw*, by Mr Hugh M'Diarmid. It is written in Scots, and it has the best of justifications; it is perfectly original. That is to say, it could have been written by no one but Mr M'Diarmid, by no poet of any nationality other than the Scottish, and in no language save that language. It is even more unlike contemporary English poetry than that of Mr Yeats and Mr Russell, and it is as little as theirs parochial. Mr M'Diarmid's intellectual competence cannot be gainsaid, nor his modernity, to use an awkward but necessary word. He is by no means a mere dialect poet, a successor of the host of sentimental rhymers who have written in all the dialects of Scots because they have not known any other language. He has chosen Scots, rather, as a serious vehicle for all that a writer may desire to express. He has partly chosen it, partly created it; for the language he uses is one derived from all the Scots dialects, a composite language. To experiment with speech in this wholesale way was hazardous; yet in the present state of Scottish letters it was necessary. There is an essential difference between literary language and spoken language; we can use naturally in poetry, for instance, words which in everyday speech would sound artificial. But in Scottish poetry since the time of Burns (whose Scots was really artificial, a composite language, like Mr M'Diarmid's) there has been no literary language, the speech which the dialect poet, the village bard, has used for poetry has been the same which his neighbors used every day; and it is this primal limitation which has made his utterance invariably provincial: he has had no language for the order of experience with which poetry is chiefly concerned. There has been no Scottish literary instrument for over a century, no larger speech transcending the bounds of everyday speech, and capable of dealing with every variety of experience. In combining the riches of all the dialects and in using them purely with an eye for their literary values Mr M'Diarmid has created for himself such a language. This language has not yet been tested on a grand scale, but to the extent to which it is used in this volume it is an adequate, natural, and original vehicle for what Mr M'Diarmid has to say. This may turn out to be a fact of great importance for Scottish letters, if one may talk of an entity which at the moment scarcely exists. For if a Scottish literary language is possible then a Scottish literature is possible too.

The idea of a Scottish literary revival was first publicly advanced by Mr M'Diarmid's friend and colleague, Mr C.M. Grieve, about three years ago. It was associated at first in the *Scottish Nation*, a weekly journal, with a political policy of Home Rule for Scotland. The *Scottish Nation* was short-lived; the writers whom Mr Grieve expected to arrive did not appear, and the public was cold. The *Scottish Chapbook*, a monthly miscellany of Scottish poetry, ran the same course and had to be discontinued at the same time. It was in the main very poor, and decisively below the level of even the worst English reviews; but it was redeemed by the occasional appearance of Mr Grieve's prose, of poems by Mr M'Diarmid, and of various contributions by Mr G.R. Malloch. These represent thus far the net literary achievement of the Renaissance; other writers have appeared, but their performance has been no more than respectable, and often scarcely that. Of these three writers Mr M'Diarmid is, I think, easily the most important, as he has been the last to emerge. The only other figure of equal importance in the movement is the composer, Mr F.G. Scott, who is attempting to do for his branch of art what Mr M'Diarmid is trying to do for poetry. Mr Scott's music has force, originality, wit, form; it is modern in technique, and Scottish in idiom; and it has an emphatic charm which is to be found in no other music written in the British Isles. It is as unlike contemporary English music, in other words, as Mr M'Diarmid's poetry is unlike contemporary English poetry.

The renaissance has crystallized thus far, then, in Mr Scott and Mr M'Diarmid. Here I am concerned only with the latter. If Mr M'Diarmid is the representative contemporary Scottish poet, how does his poetry compare with the English poetry of our time?

For purely descriptive purposes Mr M'Diarmid's poems may be divided under four headings: the decorative, the mystical, the descriptive (*genre* pieces), and, most characteristic, perhaps, the curiously reflective. These divisions are not, of course, definite; the decorative poems are sometimes touched with mysticism, the decorative and descriptive alike are seldom entirely without a flash of the author's almost eccentric thought. One of the best of the decorative poems is this:

> *Mars is braw in crammasy,*
> *Venus in a green silk gown* [. . .]

This poem is strangely felicitous; the mood, a fleeting one, is perfectly rendered; but Mr M'Diarmid is more characteristic and I think more incontestably a poet in poems such as 'Country Life':

> *Ootside! . . . Ootside!*
> *There's dooks that try tae fly*
> *An' bum-clocks bizzin' by* [. . .]

Here it is an almost fantastic economy, a crazy economy which has the effect of humor, and yet conveys a kind of horror, which makes this poem so original and so truly Scottish. It is a pure inspiration; nothing could be better of its kind, and the kind is rare. This vision is profoundly alien to the spirit of English poetry; the thing which resembles it most, outside other Scottish poetry is perhaps the poetry of Villon. It is the product of a realistic, or more exactly a materialistic, imagination, which seizing upon everyday reality shows not the strange beauty which that sometimes takes on, but rather the beauty which it possesses normally and in use. There is in this perception of beauty less magic and less exaltation than in that of romantic poetry; but on the other hand it has more toughness, vigor, and fulness. The romantic note is of course often heard in Scottish poetry, and with supreme force in the Ballads, but it is this other note that is most essentially Scottish; it is this that sets aside the Ballads, the poetry of the Makars and of Burns, the prose of Carlyle and George Douglas, from the literatures of all other peoples, and gives these nationality and character. It is this note, too, that peculiarly characterizes Mr M'Diarmid's poems.

How, then, does Mr M'Diarmid compare with his English contemporaries? In curious speculation and half-fantastic thought he is certainly as original as Mr Graves; his descriptions are more economical and, I think, more vivid, that Mr Blunden's, and his mysticism more organic with his general mood than Mr de la Mare's. In the *quality* of his work he is not unworthy to be compared with these poets; but the question is whether he has a power, like theirs, of sustained imagination. This has still to be seen. Each of these poems is a single flash, vivid but brief. We wait for the further volume which will establish Mr M'Diarmid's title to our most serious attention.

(Edwin Muir, 'The Scottish Renaissance', *Saturday Review of Literature* [USA], 31 October 1925, p.259.)

3.9 From unsigned review article 'A Scottish Renaissance' (*Times Literary Supplement* January 1926)

The present century has witnessed a remarkable revival of interest in the

Scots vernacular. It has taken several forms, lexical, dramatic, and poetic. The ambition to compile a scientific Scots dictionary owes its inspiration to Professor Craigie, who has himself undertaken the earlier period, leaving the later to the Scottish Dialects Committee. The dramatic movement belongs partly to Glasgow, partly to the North-East, where the influence of the late Gavin Greig still survives. But there has also been a remarkable efflorescence of pure poetry. To most English, and to many Scottish, readers Mr Robb's anthology will come as a revelation. A hundred and thirty-eight poems by fifty-three different authors—surely a rich posy to be culled in so narrow a field! [. . .]

Most of these new poets have kept to that lowly path which Scots poetry has followed ever since the eighteenth-century revival, confining themselves to such homely themes, sentiments, and verse-forms as are supposed to appeal to the common folk who alone retain Scots as their mother tongue. But there is a left wing to the movement which cherishes a loftier design; no less, indeed, than the revival of Scots as a general literary instrument, for poetry at least, if not for prose. To this wing Mr Hugh M'Diarmid evidently belongs. His little volume sounds a challenge: he will show the world what Scots can do to treat high themes in a serious spirit. There is nothing intrinsically absurd even in the larger aspiration. In our own time Norse, Frisian, Afrikaans, not to speak of Welsh and Erse, have shown what a few resolutes can accomplish when carried forward on a strong wave of national or local sentiment. But such a wave there must be. The literary severance of Norway from Denmark was due to the same forces that presently brought about its political separation from Sweden. Without such forces—and there is little sign of them in Scotland—the aspiration after a *general* revival of literary Scots will remain a dream. The decay of Scots prose set in at the Reformation; it became irremediable when the adoption of the Authorized Version and the Shorter Catechism established English firmly in the pulpit and the schoolroom. Thereafter serious Scottish speech—the 'stately speech' that Wordsworth admired—owed its elevation mainly to the English Bible. [. . .]

But in verse, on the whole, the prospects are less depressing. The language of verse is not abstract and technical, but concrete and passionate; and these qualities Scots does possess. The difficulties here belong to a different order. To the poet words are not bare significants; they carry also an emotive charge; their logical meaning is not more important than their associations. Unhappily, Scots has kept humble company so long that it has not only suffered impoverishment in its vocabulary but contracted associations too homely, too trivial, sometimes too vulgar for high poetry. If it is to be used again for that purpose, at least on a grand scale, it must break these low associations and form new. In other words he who aspires to reform Scots poetry must first do what Spenser did for English: he must create a new poetic diction. And this in fact is the task to which Mr

M'Diarmid has addressed himself. He has had to find his own method. The example of Burns does not greatly help. It is true that Burns, by reinforcing traditional Scots from his own 'hamely Westlan' dialect, did in a sense create a new diction; but he did not apply it to new purposes; he only showed that Scots could do superbly what it had always done pretty well. Since Burns, Scottish poets have generally founded on their own local dialects, eked out from a traditional stock that wore thinner year by year. Mr M'Diarmid casts his net wider. He founds, apparently, on the traditional Lothian Scots; but he admits good dialect words from any quarter, and he has searched the dictionaries for what Rossetti used to call 'stunning words for poetry'. This was how Åsen went about it with Norse; and the principle is probably sound, though Mr M'Diarmid's choice of vocables is not always happy. Independent dialect words are administered for his purpose; but not mere dialectal forms like 'loonikie', still less sheer vulgarisms like 'wi'in', 'wi'oot'. [. . .] Obsolete words revived have at first neither meaning nor associations except for the scholar; yet if they are good words they may take root and blossom afresh: there is nothing for it but time and use. [. . .]

It is hard to form a purely aesthetic judgment on these poems, so often do literary and linguistic considerations cross one another in the reader's mind. And not in the reader's mind only: the writer himself, it is plain, has frequently been distracted by his twofold purpose of writing high poetry in Scots and of making Scots to write it in. Slender as it is, the volume displays considerable variety of mood and manner. There are realistic vignettes like 'Country Life', and macabre sketches like 'Crowdieknowe', vividly touched but not new in kind. At the other extreme are two mystical poems. 'I heard Christ sing' reveals the propensity already noted to turn to English for the expression of exalted moods. 'The Ballad of the Five Senses' is the most ambitious poem in the book, but not the most convincing: the uninitiate will be left suspecting that towards the end mysticism passes into mystification. Between these extremes lies a group of poems—'The Watergaw', 'In the Hedge-back', 'Reid-e'en', 'Wheelrig', 'Farmer's Death'—in which some natural scene, intensely observed, becomes the setting or the symbol of a poignant spiritual experience. These are the poems which establish Mr M'Diarmid's claim to be regarded as an original poet. Within this circle he can conjure; outside it he is more derivative than his new diction lets appear, and he tends to force the note, as if he thought to take the kingdom of poetry by violence.

Still, there is a true vein of poetry in Mr M'Diarmid—how rich, or how thin, his future work will show. And he has entered upon a fascinating if doubtful enterprise. Its success will depend above all on the early emergence of a poet of commanding genius; for the way to show that high poetry can be written in Scots is to write it. Mr M'Diarmid may not be the destined conqueror; neither his substance nor his form gives much

69

promise of that; but he merits the praise of the pioneer. He writes in the faith without which there can be no conquest; the belief that Scotland still has something to say to the imagination of mankind, something that she alone among the nations can say. And can say only in her native tongue.

(Unsigned review including *A Book of Twentieth Century Scots Verse*, selected by William Robb and *Sangschaw* by Hugh M'Diarmid, *Times Literary Supplement* 7 January 1926, p.8.)

3.10 Lewis Spence, from 'The Scottish Literary Renaissance' (*Nineteenth Century* July 1926)

Scottish literature, through native impulse no less than artificially applied endeavour, is presently experiencing a phase of revival which in some respects has almost the character of renaissance. A well-directed and ingenious effort is seeking to raise it from the slough of the commonplace in which it has lain for nearly a century, and the distinguishing features of this movement have already been widely criticised and debated in the Scottish Press, sometimes with but little sympathy and insight, at others with all that philosophical desire to arrive at a fundamental comprehension which is typical of the Caledonian intellect.

But, had analytical examination as well as creative capacity not been applied to it by a certain group, Scottish literary endeavour to-day might not have been recognisable as a stream of considerable force which is gradually excavating a new channel for itself. It would, of course, have been evident that its volume was presently much greater than at any time during the past three centuries, and that, as in the case of English letters, a much higher degree of technical achievement was being manifested. It would also have been abundantly clear that composition in the Scots vernacular was once more coming greatly into favour after a period of neglect and vitiation. But, lacking the searching scrutiny to which the 'Scottish Literary Renaissance', as it has been termed, has been subjected, it would scarcely have been apparent to English or European men of letters that the new tendency in Scottish literature was actually of the nature of a rebirth, that it was, in fact, a manifestation of the reawakening of Scottish sentiment and national spirit.

During the last quarter of a century Scottish literature failed to attract the attention of the world of culture. It certainly did not appeal to European imagination as did the Irish or Norwegian literatures. The crass sentimentalism and undistinguished banalities of the Kailyard school alienated from the first the sympathies of critics of taste and insight. Scotsmen of perspicacity and experience could not but feel depressed at the popular vogue of a cult which, they were aware, frequently afforded only a base caricature of their countrymen, paving the way for the even grosser tradition of Lauderism. Nor to Scotsmen of liberal view did the somewhat artless impulse to concentrate the entire literary thought and homage of the nation upon the achievement of Robert Burns, however admittedly great, appear as likely to be conducive to the healthy or catholic expansion of Scottish literary life and activity. Those of them more familiar with the genius and tradition of the older and more courtly Scottish poets—Douglas, Henryson, Dunbar, and Lyndesay [sic]—and with the tradition, magical and intense, of the northern balladeers, recognised in these a spirit as genuinely native and technically more worthy of affection and close study than that of their successors. While worshipping Burns 'this side idolatry', they wholeheartedly detested the host of uninspired plagiarists who succeeded him, and deplored the descent of Scots poetry into an abyss of infamous *cliché* and mechanical reiteration.

The initial effort to define a theory of modern Scottish letters, and to ring its recent manifestations into one corpus, is due to Mr C.M. Grieve of Montrose, author of *Annals of the Five Senses*, a young writer of great resource and tireless energy, and a poet whose work reveals better than that of most of his contemporaries the opportunities which the Scots vernacular affords to skilful appreciation of its possibilities. Both under his own and under his pen-name of 'Hugh M'Diarmid', Mr Grieve has recently created a veritable *kulturkampf* in Scottish literary circles, a tumult in which his ideas have been greeted with the most savage condemnation mingled with praise almost extravagant. Impatient of Kailyairdism and the cult of Burns, Mr Grieve was among the first to recognise that post-war Scotland was ripe for a new literary dispensation. Although then almost unknown, he seized upon the situation with coolness and address and soon dominated it. Briefly, he has accomplished three things. He has shepherded together such Scottish versifiers of ability as exist into a single flock—in other words, he has 'clubbified' Scots poetry, drawing it willy-nilly into some such semblance of a 'school' as Mistral did with the literature of his Langue d'Oc. Secondly, he has advanced an enthusiastic claim for the status of the Scots vernacular as a language, advocating its enlargement from the condition of *patois*, in which it presently languishes, by the revival of older forms, the creation of new ones, and the amalgamation of its several dialects into a species of 'generalised' or 'synthetic' tongue. Lastly, he has with marked critical ability, if in rather too diffuse a manner, formulated an admirable working philosophy or 'theory' of Scottish letters, chiefly with reference to the psychological differences which distinguish the Scottish mentality from those of neighbouring peoples.

This David with the sharp-shooting sling has naturally aroused the whole camp of Philistines into furious war. Not that Scotland is without its wise Sophetim who recognise the justice of much of this young champion's argument. But the Goliaths of the Kailyard, the 'Greybeards' of the Poets' Corner, those who affect 'wut' of the maundering order as found in

Johnnie Gibb o' Gushetneuk, and the whole tribe of Perfect Burnsians, smarting beneath the bruises dealt by his missiles, have inveighed in chorus against the innovator and blasphemer. Generally speaking, criticism seems to have been confined to contemptuous phrases, ability to compose a reasoned counterblast being scarcely conspicuous in Mr Grieve's opponents. Better equipped critics might have indicated that Mr Grieve in his enthusiasm has pressed some rather raw recruits into his phalanx, excellent as its general standard is; that his efforts to enrich Scots and raise it from its present grovelling dialectal levels to the status of a language have been somewhat haphazard and required a greater philological and selective skill than he is perhaps capable of bringing to the task; and that his theory of Scots letters is too greatly burdened with philosophical and psychological argument, and facile erudition, to commend itself as sufficiently practical. It might also have been said that the style in which his essays are couched is a little vague, and prone to the manufacture of reiterate and somewhat far-fetched phrases.

But if it is not always a good medium for literary polemic, it is, indeed, one of rare richness and eloquent of real penetration. Mr Grieve resembles Mr Gordon Craig's actor—'he gasps, he pants, he raves'. But, unlike that Thespian, he 'gets there'. He carries you with him by sheer force of brain-power, added to a species of Demosthenean eloquence, in which the pebble in the mouth is somewhat distressingly apparent. With every page you either gain increased confidence in him or execrate him the more. He is a kind of literary Winston Churchill whom one must either love or detest, and as I happen to be of his way of thinking it is quite easy for me to do the former, though I can comprehend something of the frenzy he has stirred up in the narrow and outmoded generation of senile rhymesters, and in the breasts of those purists who, affecting a close acquaintance with Scots, are almost totally ignorant of it. [. . .] The central fact regarding the Scottish Renaissance is that the rising generation of Scottish poets are beginning to recognise that they must be bilingual—and although English is in many cases a suitable medium for their work, it must be reinforced by Scots as an adjunct for use in those circumstances where they find English fail them. They have, indeed, rediscovered in Scots a natural and psychological speech capable of expressing a more intimate point of view, and holding for them many shades of feeling which English does not hold. It was, indeed, inevitable that they should arrive at such a conclusion. It may be objected that Scots poets have been bilingual for more than two centuries. But at no time within that period has Scottish opinion, both educated and popular, evinced such marked interest in the vernacular, and it can scarcely be doubted that the endeavour to enlarge and enrich Lowland Scots and to employ it more frequently as a medium of cultured verse is, after all, one of those developments which men of letters plume themselves on creating, but which, when all is said and done, are merely the reaction of popular tendencies upon the sensitive mind of the artist.

(Lewis Spence, 'The Scottish Literary Renaissance', *The Nineteenth Century*, July 1926, pp.123–33 [123–26, 133].)

3.11 Edwin Muir, from 'Verse' (*Nation and Athenaeum* January 1927)

The year 1926 has produced an unusual number of long poems. [. . .] The reaction against short forms seems to be spontaneous, and though except in one or two cases its success has not been striking, its mere existence gives one a sense of greater potentiality.

Mr M'Diarmid's poem in Scots is by far the most remarkable in the present list. For one thing, it never gives one the impression [. . .] of being too long for the imaginative energy which seeks expression through it. For another, its form is characteristic and original; it is not a given mould into which a personal content has been poured, but a construction put together—sometimes indeed, with some sign of improvisation—revealing the contours of the chief character's mind. We do not feel in it the resisting weight of a scheme which the poet must follow whether he is in the mood or not; the scheme and the expression seem to arise out of each other; the form is at once fluid and logical. Consequently the author is never monotonous [. . .]

'A Drunk Man Looks at the Thistle' is a long monologue, varying from realistic narrative through satire, invective, humour, nonsense, philosophical speculation and mystical apprehension of the thistle's significance. In the earlier poems Mr M'Diarmid showed that he was as much interested in the possible as the actual. The form of the present poem, fixed by the psychological state of the principal character, permits him to express with their appropriate degree of conviction his various intuitions of the world, some of them realistic, some of them fantastic or grotesque. The scheme of the poem might be called indifferently psychological or philosophical; it is the picture of a mind; it is an image of the world as symbolized in the thistle. The world changes its shape, is lost, appears again as Mr M'Diarmid follows the transitions, daring and yet natural, in the mind of the monologist. Some idea of the variety of the poem may be given by saying that it contains translations from Russian, German, and French, parodies of contemporary poetry, love songs, sacred and profane, pictures of Scottish life, satire on the Kailyard School, and a long address to Dostoyevsky. Such a mixture of elements might easily appear impossible; but Mr M'Diarmid manages his characters' psychology so admirably that his effects of surprise and contrast are almost always convincing. To achieve this must have been difficult enough; but the whole is written in a synthetic Scots which the author has created himself, and which he uses now with ease and force. The flow, vigour, variety, wit, and originality of the poem are its greatest virtues; it is never dull, and there are very few poems of over four thousand lines which are never dull. Its main fault, making every allowance for several beautiful passages, and for an instinctive rightness of form throughout, is a frequent carelessness of style; the rhymes are sometimes scrambled into their places in a hasty, slipshod manner. In spite of that, however, this is probably the only poem of importance which has appeared in Scots since the death of Burns. There is a glossary at the end which unfortunately is not complete; but as it stands it should make the poem easily readable even by those who are not accustomed to Braid Scots.

(Edwin Muir, 'Verse', *Nation and Athenaeum* 22 January 1927, p.568.)

3.12 Unsigned review, *'Penny Wheep'* (*Times Literary Supplement* March 1927)

In *Penny Wheep* Mr McDiarmid prosecutes the double enterprise begun in *Sangschaw* of writing serious poetry in Scots and of creating a new poetic diction in which to write it. While the new volume contains nothing quite so good as the best things in *Sangschaw*, it has, on the whole, the same merits—an unusual sense of the movement and changing aspects of the earth in its diurnal round, a gift for seeing familiar things from new angles and illuminating poignant situations by flashes of imaginative insight. Two short poems addressed to children strike a new and pleasing note. But there are the old faults too—pretentiousness, bravado, an affected robustness, not to say coarseness, of taste, a penchant for ugly words and subjects, and that over-emphasis which has been the bane of Scottish literature from the first.

Linguistically the book marks an advance on *Sangschaw*. True, at his second dip Mr McDiarmid has dredged up no pearls to match 'hazelraw' and 'yowdendrift'; but he has recovered some racy serviceable words that had passed, or were passing, out of literary use: some others also that might well have been left in oblivion. Not all old words are good words for poetry; but Spenser himself did not create his new poetic diction at a stroke. The Glossary, though fairly complete, is not always reliable. In standard Scots 'beek' is 'bask', not 'expose one's self'; 'boot' is 'had to' not 'should'; 'cude' is 'tub' not 'barrel'; 'downa' is a verb, not an adjective (it is correctly used in the text); 'nesh' is 'sickly', 'delicate', 'fastidious', not 'full of awareness', 'spald' is 'shoulder', 'limb', 'joint', not 'backbone'; 'thringin' is 'squeezing', not 'hoisting'. The renderings of 'gallus' by 'callous' and of 'santit' by 'swallowed up in sand' suggest derivations which are quite unsupported. 'Raun for the yirdin' is defined by Mr McDiarmid as 'frightened to death', as if 'yirdin' = 'earthing', *i.e.* burial; but Jamieson, our sole authority for the phrase, which was unknown to Wright's correspondents, spells it with no apostrophe, and explains it as 'afraid of the thunder'. ('Yirdin' means also earthquake, and in fact may possibly be two words—(1) = air-din, (2) = earth-din.) Oddest of all is Mr McDiarmid's idea that 'loans soup' means 'charity soup'; according to the lexicographers the phrase has nothing to do either with 'lend' or with 'soup' but means 'a sup (of milk) given in the milking-loan', and therefore fresh from the cow.

(Unsigned review, *'Penny Wheep'*, *Times Literary Supplement* 24 March 1927, p.214.)

3.13 Catherine Carswell, *'Morning Tide*, Mr Neil Gunn's Novel' (*Scottish Country Life* February 1931)

It is good that this novel, Neil Gunn's third and best, issued in a very pleasing small green shape by the Porpoise Press (7s.6d.) should have been chosen by the Book Society as the Book of the Month. I mean it is good, not merely for Mr Gunn and for the Porpoise Press, but for the Book Society, which does not always make, or even perhaps have the chance of making, so happy a choice. Between the variable quality of the 'possibles' on one hand, and on the other the limitations imposed by considerations of family reading, popular appeal and an appearance sufficiently modern, the monthly pronouncement must be a ticklish job. In this case the Society has all it can want, with some stimulating, yet not alarming, extras thrown in. Let us examine both aspects of the book.

To begin with, it truly fulfils its title. It has a morning fragrance. With its opening we seem to sniff the air over wet seaweed newly left bare by the tide. And it recaptures and renders youth—the youth of a normal but sensitive country boy of twelve. We get to know him inside and out—his moods, terrors, dreams, absurdities, the expressions of his face, the texture of his torn, blood-stained jersey: we share the feel of his frozen fingers, his smarting eyelids, swollen nose and hungry stomach. The story gives us only three days—not consecutive—from his life, but each separate stretch of narrative is built round a central incident that is crucial in his development, and these incidents are set amid so much of talk, event, emotion and description that they form together a rich picture.

Part One shows the child alone on the shore in the early morning gathering bait for his father, carries him through a fight with a school-mate to the genial atmosphere of his home, and culminates in a great storm. This is one of the most impressive storms I remember in fiction—a storm seen from the shore by watchers who are devoured by a double fear. The smacks containing their men may not come back at all, or, coming back they may be smashed in full view within a yard or two of safety. As each heaves into sight before the gale the man at the helm has to decide whether he will save the human lives within at the sacrifice of his boat by running it on the shingle, or choose the risky feat of seamanship involved by trying for the harbour. The thrill when a boat wins clear through the too narrow entrance on the crest of a wave alternates with the more shattering thrill when another boat crashes on the bared masonry. It is finely done and very exciting.

Part Two is overshadowed by the coming departure of Alan to Australia. To celebrate his last night at home the young man goes salmon-poaching, and he does his young brother the honour to include him in the moonlight raid. This too is good, and the departure itself one of the best passages in the book.

Part Three contains another schoolboy fight, and a lover's meeting between Kirsty the dairymaid sister and a young Don Juan of the parish, which meeting is half-willingly witnessed by Hugh from an ambush. But its main theme is the serious illness of the mother who is troubled with her heart. Her illness, and indeed her whole character, are extremely moving so long as we regard them through Hugh's eyes. When he has to run for the doctor and fails to get him, we endure the nightmare ordeal of a child's helplessness. We are as sure as he is that his mother will die and that it will be his fault. But she does not die. And that she does not die is again right, just as it is right that not one of the storm-swept fishermen should be drowned. For it is not, I take it, the sense of all-powerful fate that the author wishes us to feel, but the unprotected, exaggerated reactions of a half-grown being as he finds himself faced one by one and for the first time with such things as real danger, love and illness, each one of these being at one remove from himself but near enough to affect him powerfully. If even one of the fishermen had been drowned (instead of drenched and injured); if Charlie Chisholm, as well as being a village Don Juan had been a calculating seducer; if Hugh's mother had not taken a turn for the better and demanded a cup of tea; Hugh's ecstasy of boyish experience would be at once less true and less typical.

And yet! With all this rightness and charm there is something that is wrong, something that is more typical than true, something even that is cinema where cinema should not be. Clearly the author is acutely sensitive to sights, sounds, smells and sensations, and he remembers exquisitely how these affect the growing boy. . . . But it seems as if he doubted his power of conveying his reminiscence to the reader. He often overloads and sometimes over-states. He is both too anxious and too little exact. We get a hint of this in the opening sentence—'The boy's eyes opened in wonder at the quantity of sea-tangle, at the breadth of the swath which curved with the curving beach on either hand.' Now this boy is a fisherman's son; he is not awakening from sleep; he is alone and on business. Would not the less conscious—'The boy's eyes wondered', or even 'the boy wondered' or possibly 'the boy's eyes were opened to wonder for the first time' have an honester ring? Again, describing a dish of steak—'the ardent smell of it stung his eyes. His stomach flattened in a lean hunger.'—Mr Gunn writes neither prose, poetry nor sense. I am sorry to read that Hugh 'laughs huskily', and of Kirsty that 'courage always thrilled her'. As a close to the magnificent storm-scene we could well do without the caption, 'O red ecstasy of the dawn', and we feel all the discomfort of a sentimental recitation when Kirsty tells her little brother of their mother's recovery—'I heard a voice saying, "Kirsty", I looked up. It was our mother! And her pale worn face was smiling. . . . Oh, Hugh, my heart leapt!'

Here is too much of the fade-out. And though I intend it as no dispraise when I say that this novel is well suited for adaptation to the needs of the screen, I do suggest as a criticism that screen procedure is too prevalent in the novel. Her low voice sings: the home atmosphere often goes sugary like the dear little old home out yonder: it can too often by said by the reader what is once said by the writer, that 'everything was slightly exaggerated, with a curious air of unreal tension'. The sisters in particular—dark, violet-scented Grace, and red-haired, too-eloquent Kirsty, have only a flickering, film-studio life. They are not like any Scotch girls.

Which brings me to my last word of criticism. Mr Gunn has been so careful to generalize his scenery, his language and his characters, that it would be easy for the casual reader to miss the fact that this is a Scottish novel. And even the careful reader will be hard put to it to guess what part of Scotland it refers to. I believe this to be intentional on Mr Gunn's part. He wishes to pass beyond Scotland and to become universal. But here his effort defeats itself, and the absence of local colour brings about not universality but a certain emasculation. It is all a little too beautiful, a little too noble and sweet, a little too generalized to be as true as the emotion from which it has evidently sprung. Something has got lost in the process. The fact that this absent element will enormously add to the popularity of the novel permits the critic to insist upon it without offence, especially when the critic is a friendly Scot. Mr Gunn is a novelist whom Scotland will find no difficulty in cherishing. His book has loveliness and the power to move. But some of us are asking something more from him. I, for one, believe he can give it if he will.

(Catherine Carswell, 'Morning Tide, Mr Neil Gunn's Novel', Scottish Country Life February 1931, p.50.)

3.14 Neil M. Gunn, from letter to Catherine Carswell (February 1931)

Larachan,
Dochfour Drive,
Inverness.
6/2/31

Dear Mrs Carswell,

The publishers of *Scottish Country Life* have sent me the copy with your review of my novel *Morning Tide*, and I am moved at once to thank you for the pleasure I've got from your penetrating criticism. You see so far and so clearly that I am positively prompted to talk. Not a frequent experience, as you can imagine, for reviews mostly are depressing, good, bad or indifferent. But yours raises a sparkle. And your preliminary praise I accept naturally, of course, were it only to get at your 'and yet!' How Marian McNeill will chuckle at your display of my verbal inexactitudes, for she suffered rather at my hands on the subject of the cliché.

And yet (if you will allow me) I wonder just how far you have worked out some of the issues you raise in this art of the novel? It's not that I would defend what I was at (for to do so would be to proclaim artistic failure!) so much as to find out your fixed canon of condemnation. For I am not quite satisfied with your analysis; I am not in any final sense convinced; as though there were something really 'fixed' in your attitude and the least trifle facile in declaring itself. And yet I am so very nearly convinced.

Possibly I am entirely to blame for having written in certain places so badly that you failed to see what I was at. Take, for example, that 'O ecstasy of the dawn!' You are kind to call it a 'caption'. Compton Mackenzie calls it 'literary bathos'. Splendid! The idea that the writer stood aside & wrote it deliberately as a fitting climax makes even my laughter hot! My intention, which was rather different, is so obviously hopelessly obscure. Or again, and in the same sentence, you say that you 'feel all the discomfort of a sentimental recitation' . . . but then so did Hugh, the boy, who even silently cried out against 'this assault'. Now what's to be done there? Should I also have added that extra touch of ironic detachment in order to protect the onlooker? Or would that be to play safe, to be superior with that elusive air of a commiserating omniscience? [. . .]

All of which is the merest quibbling. But there is a really profound criticism (cheers!) in your cinema conception. You cannot mean, of course, that there was any intention here to write for the screen, for the book has no story and represents the very antithesis of the commercial scenario. You bring this flickering, fascinating conception, however, to a *fixed* point when you say that the two girls 'are not like any Scotch girls'. Not verbally inexact or dishonest quite, but you are to me meaningless—in the sense that you have switched from what looked like a flash of spiritual illumination to the wart on the nose. As though Scotch girls could be known only by their exteriors & accents. Certainly they would be 'known' on the street by these. But even the most brilliant author of exterior accent and 'local colour' (merci!) would be beat hollow by a second-rate talkie machine, particularly when it came to honesty! If your 'Scotch girl' isn't some sort of spiritual something she's nothing. I am not here implying that I have got through any spiritual quality at all; but it would look as if I were trying to imply that you forgot to expect it! And here I have reached the really fascinating point as to what Scots character or spirit is going to mean, or how it's to be done afresh, in our imaginative writing. But I've taken so long to reach it that I'm shamed to a finish. I accordingly forgive you the dreadful imputation that I was trying to pass beyond Scotland & become universal. I am even dreading being attacked for writing about our particular little place! But for your pretending to perceive a mythical universality, I thank you!

And for bearing with me while amusing myself like this I would also thank you, were it not that I have heard so much about you from Flos Marian McNeill that it all sounds like a continued argument. Perhaps I am merely protecting myself from being overwhelmed by the brilliance and understanding you have wasted on so slim and unobtrusive an effort as *Morning Tide!*

Your *Burns* is a great bit of work. I talked about it with O.H. Mavor in Glasgow the other day & he agreed with me. And he's a wit.

Yours very sincerely,
Neil M. Gunn

By the way, J.C. Squire was more patronising to Burns than he was to you, so your ironic detachment must have been pretty good!

(Neil M. Gunn, letter to Catherine Carswell 6 February 1931, Catherine Carswell Archive, Special Collections, Mitchell Library, Glasgow.)

3.15   Neil M. Gunn, from letter to F. Marian McNeill (March 1931)

Larachan,
Dochfour Drive.
30/3/31

My dear Marian, [. . .]

I read Catherine Carswell's *Open the Door*. It's a splendid piece of work in every way. First class stuff in it. Why that woman did not go on writing novels, seeing she has taken writing as her job, heaven alone knows. One is almost tempted to wonder as to failure of inspiration or imagination or whatever it's called. Otherwise she was an ass. For it obviously is not laziness. Her energy, in detail, is remarkable. She has, however, two besetting sins: honesty and sincerity. That is a more damning charge than may appear. 'Honesty is the best policy as the following story will tell.' Ah these Scots Puritans—no wonder she loves Grieve! And no wonder the Highlander laughs within himself—and turns tender! But they mistrust tenderness these terrible people who love the truth and are honest! Yet they talk of being 'continental' and gay and ever 'free'—anything indeed but honest-sincere-Calvinist! So we can forgive them a lot! [. . .]

Yours,
Neil M. Gunn

(Neil M. Gunn, letter to F. Marian McNeill 30 March 1931, reprinted from J.B. Pick ed., *Neil M. Gunn: Selected Letters* Edinburgh: Polygon, 1987, p.12.)

3.16   Edwin Muir, from review of *To Circumjack Cencrastus* (*Criterion* April 1931)

The author of this poem is, I think, the most considerable Scottish poet since Burns; but for two reasons he has not so far won the recognition in England, nor the popular name in Scotland, which Burns secured very soon after the publication of the Kilmarnock edition. The first is that he writes in a Scots which, while like Burns' an artificial literary language, is far less watered down with English; and the second is that in his later poetry he deals with somewhat abstruse themes. His first two volumes, *Sangschaw* and *Pennywheep*, were collections of lyrics in which he used a synthetic Scots formed out of words and idioms taken from the Makars and such modern Scots dialects as suited his purpose. In his next volume, *A Drunk Man Looks at the Thistle*, a long poem of some 3,000 lines, this language had become a natural medium with little or no trace of its artificial origin, a language capable of great poetic as well as broad humorous effects. 'Hugh M'Diarmid' writes it now with the ease of one brought up in it, and the freedom of one continually forming and modifying his vehicle. The result is a poetic speech which in freshness and daring is, I think, quite unique to-day.

A new or a renewed language brings with it a new world of feeling and thought; and the intellectual fancies in *To Circumjack Cencrastus* could never have been put into contemporary English, for the shades of meaning in its speech come from different psychological roots. But neither could they have been put into Scots as it was written before 'Hugh M'Diarmid' fashioned his new speech, for ever since Burns Scottish vernacular poetry has been local, treating only a few humble and conventional themes; the poverty of its vocabulary, indeed, making it incapable of anything more. Consequently, in the present poem we see a modern poet undertaking the task of treating for the first time in his own language the world of modern life and thought; of rendering that world with all the peculiar shades of emphasis which the spirit of his nation and his language imposed upon him.

The world of modern knowledge is too provisional and too vast, as I think was demonstrated in Robert Bridges' *Testament*, to be treated in the old systematic way; and in both his long poems 'Hugh M'Diarmid' employs a more indirect method. He takes a symbol and pours his mind into it. In the present poem his symbol is the great curly serpent Cencrastus, the symbol of the thing which the mind always pursues and always falls short of; and his attack is a sort of catch-as-catch-can, resulting in a series of abortive attempts, reverses, modified successes, arguments with himself and his antagonist; in short, a confrontation of himself and his enemy, sometimes wildly humorous, sometimes serious; the whole making by oblique routes to a clearer apprehension of the ways of Cencrastus and a recognition of the primacy of the reason which is employed in discovering them. The poem begins with a long invocation whose refrain is

There is nae movement in the warld like yours.

Then it sweeps in everything, great or small, which might throw light on that movement: Scotland and Gaelic poetry (these being the author's most immediate pre-occupations), Professor Einstein and relativity, Rainer Maria Rilke and Sir Harry Lauder, the author's private affairs, politics and religion, scenes from low life, and speculations on the nature of reality. The scope of the poem is encyclopaedic, but its arrangement is deliberately grotesque [. . .] An encyclopaedia sometimes rejoicing, sometimes in labour, sometimes topsy-turvy: this is the object of the author's attack, and he deals with this heterogeneous mass of material in a variety of ways: by speculation, satire, parody, soliloquy, rhapsody. Yet the poem remains completely in character throughout, and is obviously the full expression of an individual mind.

Scottish poetry at its best has never run to sweetness or magnificence like English, but to a sort of wild play with imagination and technique, coming from an excess of energy which expends itself both recklessly and surely. It is seen at its most characteristic in Dunbar, the greatest craftsman in Scottish poetry; but it is seen in Burns too, though he was only an apprentice in his art compared with the older poet. It is displayed in Dunbar's almost endless and yet effortless surplus of internal rhymes, his 'showing-off', and in such grotesque fantasies as 'The Seven Deidly Sins' with their wild but extremely skilful mixture of the coarse and the terrible. This kind of poetry by a natural twist, a 'thrawnness', combines the most violently opposed elements out of an intellectual relish in the contrast. 'Hugh M'Diarmid's' poetry is of this kind; for though there are passages in the present volume where he rises to magnificence, they are always broken into by some deliberate incongruity reminding us that he is simultaneously dealing with the greatest and the meanest things. To show this, however, I should need to quote at greater length than is possible here; yet this quality is the mainspring of all the transitions and contrasts which make the poem so various and so continuously interesting. His wit is more quotable, as when he finds the brief title of 'the apprentice deid' for the living [. . .]

'Hugh M'Diarmid's' more serious passages are too long for quotation; unfortunately, for it is in them that the extent of his powers is displayed. He has, I think, in greater measure than any other poet to-day, the impetuous force which sweeps the reader away on long and rapid flights. But he has also a great skill in descending, and in keeping our minds occupied until he is ready for another ascent; for his invention never seems in danger of flagging, nor the great variety of measures he uses look like coming to an end. There are careless lines in this long poem, but there is scarcely one which does not give the delightful shock of originality. A poem so long, so various, and so sustained as this, written on such a theme, could only have been written by a man of poetic genius.

To Circumjack Cencrastus is in Scots, but I imagine it should give no very great difficulty to an English reader. It is a pity that the author has not provided a small glossary, for then there need not have been any difficulty at all.

(Edwin Muir, review of *To Circumjack Cencrastus*, *Criterion* 10:40, April 1931, pp.516–20.)

3.17 Rebecca West, review of *The Three Brothers* by Edwin Muir (*Modern Scot* Spring 1931)

This book has not only qualities which would claim their own high measure of esteem at any time; it has a peculiar value for this moment. I picked it up when I had just laid down a book in which a gentleman took seventy thousand words to assert, in a style that was the horrid literary equivalent of what is known as a 'rueful smile', that nothing ever happens to a Civil Servant; and I had before that been bathing in the tepid flood of a review conducted under the influence of Mr T.S. Eliot, which reduced man's religious and philosophical thinking to the dimensions of a sick headache. Turning to *The Three Brothers* was to advance into an age when literature had regained its normal state of healthy virility, when it could hope to achieve comedy and tragedy once more, instead of eternally dwelling in a twilight state where the mind is just sufficiently awake to push away the dreams that are messages from its deeper self, but still too sleepy to engage in any intellectual process.

It has the initial advantage of being a well-built novel. I do not mean by this that it is 'well constructed' in the ordinary sense, because that it hardly is. The second part of the story, which deals with the entrance into adult life of the three brothers is disproportionately short compared to the first part, which deals with their childhood. It runs to nearly the same length in pages, but there is much more material to be included, and therefore some of the most important phases of the story—such as David's love-making—are hurried along in too perfunctory a manner. But the story is well built by reason of its sound style, admirably appropriate to a novel that is narrative but not superficial, which beautifully balances the subjective and the objective. Henry James did a great deal of harm through his assertion (developed at length in his prefaces to the 'New York' edition of his collected works and repeated in *The Craft of Fiction*, by his disciple, Mr Percy Lubbock) that the way to write a novel is to use the consciousness of one of the characters as a lens through which the action is observed. This has caused a whole-hearted abandonment on 'the stream of consciousness' method which is not altogether desirable. If the author desires to show his subject as a part of a group too much 'stream of consciousness' leaves the group hazy and unestablished in the reader's mind; and in any case it may lead, if considered as an absolute good, to a crazy solipsism. But here is an admirable compromise. A vigorous style, which has its roots surely in *Weir of Hermiston*, looks inside David's mind, but also keeps an eye on the world outside, which is the world of Fife and Edinburgh in the time of Queen Mary; and fuses the two into a very solid universe.

The Three Brothers is primarily a book about religion. This lies to some extent on the surface in the discussions in which Sandy and Archie and David canvass the merits of Calvinism and Anabaptism, and the implicit strife between Blackadder, their Free-thinking father, and their Romanist mother. It lies to a greater degree, however, in the symbolic significance of the characters. Sandy represents man overwhelmed by his primitive phantasies and fears, a neurotic unable to live graciously because of his suicidal desire to hand himself over to suffering and hate. Archie represents man who has not even risen to the level of being a neurotic, whose primitive phantasies and fears vex and pass like a dog's dream. David represents man who wants to rise above his neuroses, who wants life to lead to joy and love instead of suffering and hate. In the mother, feeble-forcible, greeting and girning, we see an embodiment of fecund humanity, always complaining of the miseries of life, never ceasing to increase and multiply. In the father, loving and stern, we see an embodiment of the Creator as man has always imagined him, as distinct from the servant who sits in his kitchen, begetter of bairns all over the parish, a drunkard without dignity, embodiment of mere nature, whom man cannot allow to be all that is behind the universe. This father dominates his children. Sandy would like to love him, David loves him. There is a shadow of guilt in his relationship with them. Was there not sin in the conceiving of Sandy, which caused the dark spot in him? Was he not cruel in engendering the sensitiveness of David unless he could protect him from pain? The situation is largely and gravely stated. It reminds one of Kafka's *The Castle*, that unfinished masterpiece which Mr Muir recently translated, which also aims at a statement of man's relationship with God; but it is in no sense an imitation. Peculiar to Mr Muir are the poetic and pictorial power which makes him able to evoke the beauty and violence of old Edinburgh; and the strokes of characterisation which make some of Archie's speeches such masterly revelations of egotism. One must register a complaint that Mr Muir's people know too well what is the matter with them. At any moment they can analyse their psychological conditions with perfect detachment and practised eloquence. In life few can diagnose their disease so cleverly without being well on a way to recovery. But that flaw is a trifling matter compared with the splendid seriousness and ambition of this novel.

(Rebecca West, '*The Three Brothers* by Edwin Muir', *Modern Scot*
2:1 spring 1931, pp.85–87.)

3.18 'Mrs Muir's First Novel', unsigned review of *Imagined Corners* (*Modern Scot* Summer 1931)

Presumably Mrs Muir's book derives its title from Donne's

> At the round earth's imagin'd corners, blow
> Your trumpets, Angells, and arise, arise
> From death, you numberless infinities
> Of soules. . . .

but the precise significance of her use of the words 'imagin'd corners' eludes us. It is an appropriate title, however, inasmuch as, like Donne, she writes about transublunary things, and though the setting of her story is the mean Angus seaside town of 'Calderwick', where minds are for the greater part as narrow as the streets, she is concerned with psychological and philosophical problems of moment, and shows her characters in relation not only to the petty standards of the township but to the complex modern consciousness.

Mrs Muir's characters are indubitably Scottish, in fact indubitably Angus. Where she scores over so many Scottish writers is that she uses such characters for the major tasks of literature. The much disputed question of what characters and topics are worth writing about is seldom fairly put:

it does not resolve itself into the question of whether one should write about the unintelligent or clever, or the subtle or simple, or the high or the lowly. The important thing is that the ever so lowly and simple and stupid characters can be used for major fiction if they are given a certain cosmic significance. Emma Bovary was a vulgar, illiterate, unimaginative, morbid, worthless little besom—and who has read Flaubert and not wept for her? Flaubert makes Emma the vehicle of a great 'force', and Mrs Muir has the gift of similarly writing about her 'Calderwickians'. That is not to say that Mrs Muir is a writer on a par with Flaubert, but she is definitely the same kind of self-conscious artist, an aristocrat of letters, compared to the democrats who never lift their eyes from the kailyard to contemplate in imagination the 'round earth's imagin'd corners'.

The chief of her characters, Elizabeth Shand, is intelligent, well-educated in bookish matters although naïve in other more important respects, and sensuous. Were the period of the story not pre-war she would be shocking the local librarian by revelling in the novels of D.H. Lawrence. In her ignorant Scottish way she has fallen in love with and married the good-for-nothing Hector Shand, because of the physical satisfaction he gives her. Hector is also a type common in puritanical Scotland—a man who fornicates promiscuously as circumstances allow, whose sexual activities run to waste and who marries someone who is not so much a wife as a mother to him, someone to tether him to respectability. Mrs Muir, who describes him as always engaged in either lifting a woman's skirts or sheltering behind them, depicts him to perfection. The other chief characters are Hector's sister Elise, John Shand and his empty-headed wife Mabel, with whom Hector would like to commit adultery, and the Reverend William Murray and his sister and demented brother. The minor characters include two prim spinsters, excellently drawn, a village atheist, and several others all more than competently handled. The story at first embraces the township as represented by a dozen or more characters, and finally centres round Elise and Elizabeth—the former a sophisticated, disillusioned widow, who makes a splendid foil for the other. In concentrating the interest on these two characters in the concluding chapters, something is lost and the balance of the novel is to some extent upset, since some of the preceding events described at length scarcely impinge on these two women's lives; but the psychology of the two women is so convincingly described that what is lost on the swings, so to speak, is made up on the roundabouts.

Some of the best passages in Mrs Muir's tragedy are humorous passages. When it comes to dealing with the parochial and trivial—the U.F. Church sale of work, the local doctor's dinner-party, back-door gossip in the High Street; beyond which point the average Scottish novel seldom ventures—Mrs Muir beats the kailyard writers at their own game. Moreover, she goes on to deal with the big problems beyond such *trivia* in a way that reveals the writer's rare intellectual and philosophical calibre. *Imagined Corners* is a 'novel of ideas', and is really to some extent a sort of Scottish *Point Counter Point*, in which provincial Scottish types corresponding to the Bloomsbury and Chelsea types Mr Huxley assembled for his purpose work out their destiny according to a similar formula. Having mentioned *Point Counter Point* one should perhaps add how very different *Imagined Corners* is in other respects. Mrs Muir's characters in 'real life' are much less explicit, making her task more difficult, and they are, perhaps as a consequence, less of intellectual abstractions than Mr Huxley's creations. They are creatures of flesh and blood, even when thwarted and inhibited; Mrs Muir writes about them with warm understanding, scolding at them sometimes, but never turning up a disdainful nose. We shall look forward to her second novel.

(Unsigned review of *Imagined Corners* by Willa Muir, *Modern Scot* 2:2 summer 1931, pp.171–73.)

3.19 Edwin Muir, 'A New Scottish Novelist', review of Fionn MacColla's *The Albannach* (*Modern Scot* Summer 1932)

The author of this book has very remarkable gifts. He is, first of all, a born writer; he uses words sensitively, forcibly and exactly, and at times with great poetic power. His observation of character and physiognomy is extraordinarily subtle, his rendering of half-conscious feelings and sensations full of definition. He has the very rare ability to create characters completely, from the crown of their heads to the soles of their feet, so that they give an illusion of almost physical reality; and he can evoke a scene just as solidly. He has humour, passion, sincerity, and an extremely effective turn for satire. Yet although *The Albannach* is a brilliant performance, and should receive an unequivocal welcome from a country not remarkable for brilliant performances in literature, it has too many faults to be satisfying, the worst of these being that it has really no effective construction.

This may be partly due to the fact that it is an autobiographical novel. For one of the faults of the autobiographical novel is that it is apt to end inconclusively, like Lawrence's *Sons and Lovers*, for example and Joyce's *Portrait of the Artist as a Young Man*. The author is presented with the problem of breaking off his story of one human life at some point, and there is no point conceivable by him (except death, which would involve a sort of vicarious suicide) that is decisive enough to serve as the final conclusion of a work of art. Lawrence ends *Sons and Lovers* with his hero's resolve to lead a different life; Joyce ends the *Portrait* with Stephen's dedication to literature. But the end is not really an end, but a beginning,

86

the beginning of a dispensation which we are asked to assume will be better than the former one; and that assumption is never capable of convincing us, for no matter how sincere aspiration and resolution may be, we know that life goes on. 'Fionn MacColla' has also rounded off his story by a device of this kind; the hero, having sunk into drunken apathy, is rescued by an idea which he sees springing up round him, the idea of nationalism. But to end on that note is to plunge us into the midst of the ordinary illusions of life, to deliver us up to their undifferentiated blind force after we have been living in a world in which they were merely objects of contemplation.

The construction of the book is unconvincing, then, and the conclusion false. There is also an occasional weakness in characterization; the figure of the kindly Glasgow priest is the worst example. But having said this one must return again to the virtues of a very remarkable book. It contains a whole gallery of portraits of an almost startling life-likeness. The father and mother of Murdo, the hero, are the best in that gallery; but the Highland minister with his unction, his gluttony and his lecherous little eyes is almost as good, and the various deracinated Highlanders whom Murdo encounters in Glasgow are completely convincing though outlined with a few strokes. To come to the various scenes, the funeral of John the elder is the best I have read in a literature well packed with funerals. The description of the row in the Glasgow café is also extremely vivid. But the passage that shows best the author's extraordinary power and sincerity of imagination is the one describing his half-mad terror in Glasgow after discovering that he was physically tainted. One may legitimately complain that here the author does not explain adequately the nature of the pollution (he is frank enough elsewhere, as is right); but the description of Murdo's state of mind is nevertheless the work of a writer of first-rate powers. These powers are undisciplined as yet, which is natural enough, seeing that this is a first novel; but they are unquestionably there, they make the reading of this book an exciting experience, and they are sufficiently extraordinary to make one wonder whether in 'Fionn MacColla' there may not be the making of a writer of first class.

(Edwin Muir, 'A New Scottish Novelist', review of *The Albannach* by Fionn MacColla, *Modern Scot* 3:2 summer 1932, pp.166–67.)

3.20 From 'Two Scottish Novels', unsigned review of *Poor Tom* and *Sunset Song* (*Modern Scot* Autumn 1932)

Mr Muir's new novel is the most interesting work in prose written by a Scotsman since—the war, if you like—or even the year in which *The House with the Green Shutters* was published.

The reader who knows his *Marionette* and *The Three Brothers* will recognize in *Poor Tom* the same qualities that made the earlier books notable—extreme economy of statement, a painstaking attention to the purely formal demands of the novel, exquisitely subtle analyses of character, and the mood of quiet contemplation that pervades all the author's chapters and gives his stories almost a dream-like quality. This last quality is of enormous value. Mr Muir has the faculty of so transfixing an attitude, in a moment of aesthetic vision, that it is seen as if in a dream, bereft of its purely temporal qualities, of all the crowded naturalistic details that clutter up the scene when seen in the flux of waking hours. He imposes an artist's order on his material, recalling Percy Lubbock's words in *The Craft of Fiction*: 'Instead of a continuous, endless scene, in which the eye is caught in a thousand directions at once, with nothing to hold it to a fixed centre, the landscape that opens before us is whole and single; it has passed through an imagination, it has shed its irrelevancy, and is compact with its own meaning'. Such a scene is, for instance, the Socialist procession or any other of a score of episodes in *Poor Tom*.

Reading *Poor Tom* one is reminded of Mr Muir's poetry: it is not that Mr Muir writes 'poetic prose', but that his prose, in addition to bearing the stamp of the same personality, as is inevitable, is as carefully designed and executed as his verse. The perfection of his form tempts one, so few are the novels of formal excellence, to judge of *Poor Tom* along with poetry and drama, just as the strain of mysticism in all his work—more genuine than in any other modern writer known to us—prompts one to compare it with the work of seventeenth-century mystical poets. [. . .]

Poor Tom is Mr Muir's finest achievement as yet. The course of Tom's thwarted passion, his accident, his disease and death; his brother's anguish, his socialism; the girl who is false to both of them; the Calvinist background—all are described with profound feeling and a nice precision. The frequent philosophical interludes fit into place in the novel like the choruses in a Greek tragedy, and the sole flaw in the work is the occasional disparity between the characters shown in action in one chapter—for the most part, not very clever and ill-educated—and the fascinating thoughts that in the next chapter are described as passing through their heads. The meditations on Socialism, Puritanism and so on, challenge comparison with any contemporary English prose.

There are several novelists who are more richly endowed than Mr Muir with the gifts of eye and ear that enable the novelist to gather his material, but who fail to make such good use of it. Such is Lewis Grassic Gibbon, who attempts—like the majority of novelists—to handle a mass of material which would require tremendous gifts to organize into a fully satisfying art-form. The dialogue of *Sunset Song* recaptures admirably the clipped, racy speech of the Mearns; the anecdotes of bed and bothy have the stamp of truth; the characters are lifelike. But the tragedy moves jerkily to its close, with a very big jerk before the magnificent epilogue, and the style is, in the words of one reviewer, 'a little . . . hot in the collar'. [. . .] For all its entertainment value, and its moving account of life on a croft, the reader feels that Mr Gibbon is making his novel, especially the first part, as Mr Shaw says Sir James Barrie makes his plays—as a milliner makes a bonnet, by matching and sewing together the materials—not by transmuting his impressions into an art-form. Mr Gibbon's story of Kinraddie is like the map drawn on the boards of the novel: it has not, in Mr Lubbock's words, 'shed its irrelevancy', has not 'passed through an imagination'. It is readable, and probably the best recent Scottish story of its kind, but it leaves the novel where it was thirty years ago.

(Unsigned review of *Poor Tom* by Edwin Muir and *Sunset Song* by Lewis Grassic Gibbon, *Modern Scot* 3:3 autumn 1932, pp.250–52.)

3.21   Some further responses to *Sunset Song* (1932)

a) From George Malcolm Thomson to Helen Cruickshank (August 1932)

If you have not already done so, get hold of a novel *Sunset Song* by L.G. Gibbon, whoever he or she may be. It seems to me the pioneer of something new and very interesting in Scottish letters. Perhaps the first really Scottish novel.

(Helen Cruickshank, quoting from letter from George Malcolm Thomson, Helen B. Cruickshank Papers, MS2 folder 7, University of Stirling Library.)

b) From Donald Carswell to Lewis Grassic Gibbon (August 1932)

I don't know who you are, though I have several suspicions, all involving your sex. But that's nothing. The only thing that matters is that you have written a damn good book—the best Scotch book since Galt. I started on *Sunset Song* with a violent prejudice. 'Oh, another of the bloody awful Scottish renascence abortions—frightfully stylised'. But I soon changed my tune. There's no doubt you have got the essential Scotland. [. . .] I suddenly realised that the book must be read aloud with something like a Mearns accent. I did my best in a Scotch girl who is living in our house just now— the incident of the Reverend Gibbon and the chamber-pot. The effect was amazing!

(Donald Carswell, letter to author of *Sunset Song*, 17 August 1932, quoted by Ian Munro in *Leslie Mitchell: Lewis Grassic Gibbon* Edinburgh: Oliver and Boyd, 1966, p.74.)

c) Compton Mackenzie, from review in *Daily Mail* (September 1932)

I have no hesitation in saying that *Sunset Song*, by Lewis Grassic Gibbon, is the richest novel about Scottish life written for many years. Mr Gibbon is the first of our contemporary Scottish writers to use the dialect with such effect. [. . .] There is internal evidence that he had already struggled hard to acquire a mastery of English prose before he ventured to approach his present task. It is experience which has given him the right to experiment.

The language is often coarse and sometimes brutal, and the statement of facts is always unequivocal. Mr Gibbon can summon Robert Burns as witness for the defence. Indeed the comparison with Burns is constant in the reader's mind, for Tam o' Shanter runs through Mr Gibbon's prose all the time.

The theme is the extinction of the crofters by the conditions of the modern world. I am myself optimistic enough to believe that Mr Gibbon's epic elegy is premature, but such optimism only makes me more grateful for this superb lament which shows what is in danger of being for ever lost.

(Compton Mackenzie, *Daily Mail* 13 September 1932, quoted in Munro, p.75.)

d) Letter from James Barke to Lewis Grassic Gibbon (December 1932)

43, Glanderston Drive,
Glasgow, W.3.
12th December, 1932

Man Gibbon,

Yon was a great masterpiece: *the* greatest Scottish book in the English language. How can I, a poor bit scribbler indicate to you how much he appreciated *Sunset Song*?

Perhaps you have interjected: why the hell should I be interested in what *you* appreciate? Who the hell are you anyway? And instantly I retort (the poor bit scribbler pose falling away instantly): I am a Scotsman reared among coo-sharn and horses and ploughed fields and the scent of wet larches and the dawn on the hills at morning, with as keen an appreciation of the fine things of this earth as anybody—bar none. Of course that's no excuse for writing you. And I paid three sweet half-crowns for your book—and that's no excuse either. So there seems to be nothing for it but to write without any excuse at all—which may be better.

Well, Gibbon man, I read *Sunset Song* with greater and richer and fuller and deeper enjoyment than anything I can ever remember reading. With the possible exception of the *Communist Manifesto*—on a different plane. And I'd be a mean scrunt if I didn't tell you so.

And Chae Strachan and Long Rob of the Mill and Chris, poor quean, will be in my consciousness for ever. Rich—but not strange. Warm and intimate as the rich red blood of life itself.

And Blawearie and Peesie's Knapp and Alex Mutch's big ears.

A friend of mine in a big literary way of his own said (after I'd deaved him to read the book) I got an alternative title to *Sunset Song*. And I said: Aye. And he said Kinraddie's Hurdies! And instead of a map of the district it should have been a map of all their hurdies. I should have mentioned that my friend is a kind of sexual introvert or I would have hung up the receiver (which, after all, is like hitting a man in the privates). And it was a good joke too in its way, though I mention it only as in illustration of the prejudices that still survive in places one would least expect it.

I'll leave it at that. You know how fine *Sunset Song* is without me telling you. I sincerely hope you will give us many more like it.

Yours sincerely,
[signed James Barke]

P.S.   You'll have seen, of course, where the printers made a mess of 'The Flowers of the Forest': but where in God's name did you get such a poor, dribbling version of it for the pipes? For a tune like that you want something with good heavy fundamental ballast in it.

(James Barke, typed copy of his letter to Lewis Grassic Gibbon 12 December 1932, James Barke Archive, Mitchell Library, Glasgow.)

3.22   Lewis Grassic Gibbon, letters to James Barke (January and July 1933)

a) Letter of 21 January 1933

28, Edgar's Court,
Welwyn Garden City.
21.1.33.

My dear J.W.B.,
I've a letter of yours dated the 12th of December, and I'm ashamed to find it unanswered. Don't blame me too much, but a variety of wanderings

about from my home, plus a doze of 'flu on my return. Now that I'm more or less recovered I'm attempting to catch up with correspondence.

Glad you liked *Sunset Song* and I hope you'll like its successor, *Cloud by Day*. Three half crowns is indeed a damnable price to pay for a novel (I never do). And one can get the *Communist Manifesto* in a sixpenny pamphlet!

Anyhow, I'd prefer a comparison with the C.M. to almost anything else. Glad there is at least one soul in Scotland unspotted by this dreary rash of nationalism.

Your friend (was it Edwin Muir?) who found S.S. a bit too-too, must have the usual constipation complex. Don't know if Vienna has discovered that one yet, but it's rampant.

I see you were hied away to hospital as you finished the letter. Do hope you're better and that you'll write me again.

Good wishes,
Sincerely,
Jas. Leslie Mitchell
(L. Grassic Gibbon)

(Letter of 21 January 1933 on notepaper headed 'From: J. Leslie Mitchell'; James Barke Archive, Mitchell Library, Glasgow.)

b) From letter of 26 July 1933

107, Handside Lane,
Welwyn Garden City
26.vii.33

My dear Barke,

Many thanks for your amusing letter. [. . .]

Don't agree about *Image and Superstition* (as the genteelly pawky *Times Lit Supp* called it.) Conception was OK (wasn't I present at the birth?) but it's badly slung together. I'm sorry for that, because it didn't pitch over the Diffusionist propaganda properly. I think I've managed better in a historical novel of this autumn (a Mitchell book, not a Gibbon) on the rebellion of the Roman slaves under Spartacus. . . . though I'm vaguely ashamed of it also.

Cloud by Day had been used by another of my publisher's authors— damned impudence, wasn't it? So I clouded the Howe instead. Don't think the English should have much difficulty in pronouncing it. It's a much better book than *Sunstroke Song*—a fact confirmed by the preliminary rumbles of disapprobation I hear all around me from Burnsians and Scots ministers who lapped up Vol.1. . . . Seriously, I think it suffers a bit from the necessity to demolish so many superstitions in order to clear the way for the blatant communism of *Grey Granite*.

Best wishes,
Yrs,
[signed with initials]

My wife says you 'sound thrilling'. So if you're down London way this year you're invited for a week-end.

> (Letter of 26 July 1933 on notepaper headed 'From J. Leslie Mitchell' and signed with
> initials in what appears to be an iconic amalgamation of Gibbon and Mitchell;
> James Barke Archive, Mitchell Library, Glasgow.)

3.23   Edwin Muir, from 'New Novels' (*Listener* August 1933)

In coming to *Cloud Howe* [after *Ordinary Families* by E. Arnot Robertson] one feels at once that the level of intelligence required from the reader has sunk. Miss Robertson would be incapable of writing such lyrical generalities as these:

> So she'd heard it all as she sat knee-clasped there, in the play of the wind and the sun, a tale so old—oh, old as the Howe, everlasting near as the granite hills, this thing that brought men and women together, to bring new life, to seek new birth, on and on since the world had begun. And it seemed to Chris it was not Cis alone, her tale—but all tales she harkened to then, kisses and kindness and the pain of love, sharp and sweet, terrible, dark and wild, queer beauty of the hands of men, and their lips, and the sleeps of desire fulfilled, and the dark, strange movements of awareness alone, when it came on women what thing they carried, darkling, coming to life within them, new life to replenish the earth again, to come to being in the windy Howe where the cloud-ships sailed to the unseen south.

Mr Gibbon can go on like that for a long time in a hypnotic anapoeotic chant, signifying nothing or something which would sound outrageously sentimental or obvious in ordinary language. It is not that he is without intelligence; he simply shuts his eyes with determination every now and then and relapses into a trance into which he tries to lure his readers with him. The beginnings of this habit could be seen in *Sunset Song*; in the present volume, which is a sequel of that story, it has disastrously grown and elbowed out a great deal of the author's delightful Rabelaisian humour. Whether there is any connection between the two facts it is hard to say; but in *Cloud Howe* the lyricism has grown sweeter and the humour bitterer. The book continues the story of Chris Guthrie, now the wife of the Reverend Robert Colquhoun in the little spinning town of Segget. The picture that Mr Gibbon draws of the inhabitants of that little place is consistently sordid and mean and should logically lead to complete disillusionment with human nature. [. . .] Nevertheless, the part of the book dealing with the ignominious humours of the Segget people is admirable, except for an occasional over-eagerness to prove that they are worse than they could well have been. The part dealing with Chris Colquhoun and her husband, on the other hand, is quite unconvincing, and consists mainly of an infuriating and persistent lilt. Robert tries to 'save' Segget; then he throws in his lot with the Socialists, then he withdraws from his wife and the world, begins to see visions, and finally collapses one Sunday in the pulpit and dies as he has lived, melodramatically. How a man of Mr Gibbon's gifts can write such things is a mystery. [. . .] Fundamentally—if one is to take the author seriously—*Cloud Howe* is an unusually bad novel; but it is worth reading for its realistic and humorous passages.

(Edwin Muir, review of *Cloud Howe* included in 'New Novels', *The Listener* 9 August 1933, p.222.)

3.24 From 'Four Story-Tellers', unsigned book review (*Modern Scot* Summer 1933)

Judged from the point of view of the connoisseurs of character who form the majority of the reviewers of fiction in these islands, *Mrs Ritchie* is a masterpiece. The puritanical Mrs Ritchie, of Calderwick, is 'as large as life'. Everyone in Protestant Scotland must have known her type—the embodiment of the puritanical, conserving, order-loving strain in mankind, as Emma Bovary was the embodiment of the romantic, dissipatory strain. Born with an inferiority complex, the God-fearing daughter of a washer-woman and a drunkard father, she escapes into an atmosphere of Bible-class rectitude, and nags her husband into the grave, her shell-shocked son to suicide and her daughter out of the town. Here, in *Mrs Ritchie*, is one of the grimmest challenges offered to puritanical Scotland since *The House with the Green Shutters*. But more important, if your concern is literature, is the fact that here is a beautifully wrought piece of imaginative prose. The book has a unity that *Imagined Corners* lacked. Mrs Muir takes every technical difficulty in her stride; she has solved for her present purposes the problem of naturalism in which so many writers stand bogged; and her occasional transition into symbolism is excellently achieved. In every way, it is a memorable Scottish novel.

Sun Circle makes difficult reading by comparison, not (as somebody has said) because it is too introspective, but because Mr Gunn's use of words is frequently vague. There is too much in his story, besides much that is vigorous and powerful, that is 'artistic' and pretentious in the manner of the interlude preceding the fire that descends on his village (to take one piece of 'fine writing' at random). [. . .] Words there are used in the romantic, associative manner we think of in connection with the 'nineties'. Writing of the kind has not been absent from some of Mr Gunn's previous books, but its presence in what is perhaps his most ambitious work, depicting the clash between Druidism and Christianity in north-east Scotland in the time of the Vikings, is doubly regrettable.

Those persons who reckon *Sunset Song* a masterpiece—the publishers put on record some of their names—will also like *Cloud Howe*, for it is written in the same galumphing style as the earlier story, and with most of the same irritating mannerisms. With the praiseworthy aim of giving his narrative coherence, Mr Gibbon writes in a colloquial fashion based on the rhythms and vocabulary of the everyday speech of the Mearns, indicating the dialogue by italics: the experiment is tiresome, in spite of all the author's vivacity: the medium does not afford the novelist the range he ought to require. It so happened that the present reviewer picked up *Cloud Howe* after dipping afresh into Joyce's *Ulysses*, which brings to the depicting of Dublin life practically every refinement of the novelist's technique—the contrast (if one may use a steam-hammer to crack a walnut) was instructive. Joyce does not merely titivate the low life of Dublin: the life he depicts may be for the most part simple and rude, but the texture of his prose is that of a highly intellectual literary technician. There is not the crude identification of subject-matter and method that there is in *Cloud Howe*, which recalls the programme-music that is content to imitate the sounds of nature instead of transmuting them into a Pastoral Symphony. The two volumes of *A Scots Quair* so far published, in spite of all the eulogiums on the wrapper, have more to offer to the student of the country-life between Stonehaven and the Grampians than to the reader who at this time of day expects from a novel some considerable degree of literary sophistication.

Mr Linklater's *The Crusader's Key* is an ingeniously indecent little tale, unpretentious, concise and highly amusing.

('Four Story-Tellers', unsigned reviews of *Mrs Ritchie* by Willa Muir; *Sun Circle* by Neil M. Gunn; *Cloud Howe* by Lewis Grassic Gibbon and *The Crusader's Key* by Eric Linklater, *Modern Scot* 4:2 summer 1933, pp.157–59.)

3.25 Lewis Grassic Gibbon, from 'Scots Novels of the Half-Year' (*Free Man* June 1933)

I suppose other Scots novels have been issued since January, but I haven't read them, and the plan of this book-page is to devote it to books the reviewer has actually read. This, I am aware, is by far the most revolution-ary intention ever expressed by a protagonist of the Scots Renaissance.

Of the four novels listed above, one *might* have been very good, one *is* good, and two are the dreich yammer of a culture's second childhood.

Mr James Barke is my man. He has all the Scots virtues and most of the faults; he is apt and acute and passionate, and an excellent hand with a claymore. And he preaches and proses and halts through long stretches to tell the bored reader, over and over again, just how his hero felt and considered and was spiritually uplifted and spiritually tormented (generally tormented) by Life and Fate and Fortune and the vagaries of Mr Bernard Shaw. Had Mr Barke pushed Bernard into the dust-bin, shorn his hero of much fluffy verbiage, through which he peers like a calf through a whin bush, and faced him up to facts at the end—then, what a novel this might have been!

As it is, it surely gives promise of good things to come, unless Mr Barke, like his hero, has fled to a Balcreggan from the terrors of Glasgow. In dealing with life in that deplorable city, the vomit of a cataleptic commercialism, Mr Barke is at his best, however he may long to describe the banks and braes and couthy knowes, and kye in sunset clover and the beauty of a pibroch. Duncan, the hero is brought up in a gamekeeper's cottage, schools, dreams, fights, reads. Then his father dies, and Duncan goes to Glasgow, and encounters socialism and capitalism and Bernard Shaw as the Intelligent Guide. He sinks far down in the grimy no-life of the Gorbals, and scrambles unconvincingly from the pit, and escapes to a Highland cottage again, complete with heather in the foreground, pibrochs in the distance, and a girl undressing indoors for his delight.

And great fun, too. But more of the Gorbals next time [. . .]

Miss Orr deals with Edinburgh, Edinburgh of the Literary Revival, its poseurs and poetasters and Community Drama players. And she is oh-so-nice and gently-satirical, and generally quite damnably dead about it. [. . .] How it failed to be a selection of the English Book Society is the strangest of puzzles. [. . .]

Mr Neil Gunn, like Mr James Barke, has also the real thing. He can write a lovely prose. In an arrangement of a half-dozen words, he can give you a moment of the purest aesthetic joy. His hills and his islands shine with the light that never was on land or sea, but eternally and very beautifully in the vision of the poet.

But I cannot find belief in this antique Scotland of his; this time of brooding heat and tenebrous terror and bright, sharp cruelty—cruelty fashioned into shining codes and philosophies, Norse and native. Raiding Norsemen butchered wounded men, sacrificed them, even, but not even the aberrant Nahua were cool and philosophic in their butcheries; they were mixed and muzzy and muddy-souled, that was all. Mr Gunn's Norse and natives both suffer from the author's learnings in an antique and out-dated anthropology. If I had the power I would banish Mr Gunn, Mrs Mitchison, and Mr Eric Linklater to St Kilda for a year to read the works of Elliot Smith, Perry, and H.J. Massingham. Antique man was a beast enslaved by cult and creed—but originally a kindly beast.

Miss Nan Shepherd writes about farm life in Kincardineshire, a farmer's pretty granddaughter, a prima donna who disturbs the peace, and God alone knows who. I extend my sympathy to the Almighty. This is a Scots religion and Scots people at three removes—gutted, castrated, and genteelly vulgarised.

Read Mr Gunn and Mr Barke. They are neither of them, *Sun Circle* and *The World His Pillow*, books to stir you as with a trumpet-cry. But they *are* Scots and they *are* real. Mr Barke I see assailed by some of the funny little quarterlies which keep up an illiterate ape-chatter at the heels of the Scots Renaissance. Nuts to them, Mr Barke!

(Lewis Grassic Gibbon, 'Scots Novels of the Half-Year', reviews of *The World His Pillow* by James Barke; *Immortal Memory* by Christine Orr; *Sun Circle* by Neil M. Gunn and *A Pass in the Grampians* by Nan Shepherd, *Free Man* 2:21, 24 June 1933, p.7.)

3.26   C.M. Grieve, from 'Seeds in the Wind' (Free Man July 1933)

Under this happy title has been published the third volume of poems by William Soutar, the previous two being *Gleanings from an Undergraduate*, and *Conflict*. The latter contained some notable poems in English—poems of a high philosophical order. The new volume is in Scots, and, as the sub-title implies (Poems in Scots for Children), most of the poems are no more than they purport to be—bairn rhymes, pretty jingles, almost meaningless trifles. They spring from certain superficial predilections rather than from deep conviction, and Soutar's work as a whole has not that consistency, that drive, that 'roust', of which I have spoken elsewhere. Yet how definitely related he is to the real aim and object of the Scottish renaissance movement is well enough known to readers of *The Free Man* where many of his brilliant satirical and political poems and biting epigrams have appeared. In his use of Scots he illustrates what many of us do—Gibbon, A.D. Mackay, Adam Kennedy, and others—the return to, and new use, of Scots or the Gaelic or of Scots and Gaelic idiom in order to break away from inherited and Anglified habits of thought, achieve a closer contact with the objects actually around us, in Scotland here, and in relation to conscious Scottishness furth of Scotland itself, and to define the reactions of our sensibilities to our unexplored environment as Scots. And in this connection Soutar's contribution as manifested in this book and elsewhere is a very valuable one. He has a masterly grip of many phases of Scots; and the glossary to even this slim—and excellently produced—

volume runs to some hundreds of words. Frequently the content and the verbal dress of his verses are in splendid keeping; the spirit of the poem is as purely Scottish as the words. [. . .]

But *Seeds in the Wind* contains at least half-a-dozen short poems which ought to be included in any new edition of Mr John Buchan's *Northern Muse*, and once we are in a position to survey as a whole Mr Soutar's considerable output of poems of many kinds in English and Scots, critical and philosophical articles, epigrams and pasquils, there will be a good deal left in each of these categories of permanent value—a very definite and valuable contribution to the new Scottish Movement, and shrewdly, if not in many cases very obviously, related to the purposes which I have declared all we younger Scottish writers worth a rap have—and necessarily so—in common.

(C.M. Grieve, review of *Seeds in the Wind* by William Soutar, *Free Man* 2:26, 29 July 1933, p.8.)

3.27 Lewis Grassic Gibbon, from 'New Novels: Mr Barker [sic] and Others' (*Free Man* February 1934)

[Mr Barke's] story is a story of the modern Highlands—the strangest of Highlands, so that even the accustomed novel-reader, entering its pages, gasps at the unaccustomed tang of the air. For something, undoubtedly, has gone wrong. Where are the claymores of the '45? Or the wealthy returned emigrant? Or the sweet-voiced, gentle priest? And where—oh, where?—is Nurse Elspeth, the faithful, fatuous, flat-footed Elspeth who throughout the last three hundred Highland novels has reared the young laird in godly ways until he attains to manhood, and thereafter acts as his devoted housekeeper (inevitably he weeps in her lap in the penultimate chapter)? . . . . Here, instead, are the Highlands of apprehended reality, viewed through the eyes of a realist so sure in his task that ever and again his technique employs the tool of symbolism. In another age Mr Barke might have been a great epic poet; in this one, with poetry the most minor and affected of the arts, he employs the major art of the novel with a fine skill and freedom.

His crofters and fishers and village folk are faithfully living and life-size; the Wild MacRaes themselves—four sons of a gamekeeper—are heroic figures of myth, and not the less real for that. They centre and epitomise the struggle of the classes that is waged just as bitterly in the remote glen as in the nearby factory; for a time, sheep-stealing, land-raiding, they almost dominate their landscape. Their countryside, oppressed under the demands and restrictions of clownish lairds, alien and Scots, seems on the verge of rising to their leadership in a miniature peasant rebellion. . . . There is this glimpse of a possibility, then it fades, as in real life it would fade. The weakness of even heroic peasants without a definite creed or code of revolt destroys them; one by one they are lopped down, farcical or tragic in their fall.

The whole story is told—or I should say tells itself—with a bleak precision that is fascinating, style and stuff in perfect equipoise. Because first readings are sometimes unfortunate, I try—inadequately—to restrain my enthusiasm. Certainly from that first reading it seems to me that *The Wild MacRaes* is the best Highland novel I have ever encountered.

(Lewis Grassic Gibbon, review of *The Wild Macraes* by James Barke, *Free Man* 3:4, 24 February 1934, p.6.)

3.28 Edwin Muir, from 'Literature in Scotland' (*Spectator* May 1934)

It is now about ten years since the Scottish Renaissance began to be talked about. There was no sign of a renaissance at the time except in the work of 'Hugh McDiarmid', the writer who talked and wrote most indefatigably about it. He started several reviews, some weekly and some monthly, which never lasted for very long but produced work by young writers which otherwise might never have been produced. Most of that work was bad, but some of it was good: for instance, Mr Neil M. Gunn's first stories, so far as I can remember, appeared in one of those short-lived magazines. After the last of them had stopped came *The Modern Scot*, a quarterly edited by Mr James H. Whyte, which is the best literary review that has appeared in Scotland for many decades, and has now maintained for several years a critical level which is unique there. At the same time there has been a far more intensive literary production than the first twenty years of the century could show, as well as a considerable public interest in it. No doubt the growth of nationalist feeling in Scotland has helped greatly to canalize that interest. There is now, at any rate, an increasing public prepared to give a special welcome to Scottish work, and that is quite a new state of things, and provides for the first time for a century the possible conditions of a literary revival. But this is probably the most that can be said: there is a great deal of literary activity in Scotland; there is no Scottish literary movement to compare with the Irish movement whose chief figure was Mr W.B. Yeats.

The main reason for this, I think, apart from the absence of genius in any great abundance, is that the Scottish Renaissance is a renaissance without a centre, either social or intellectual. It has no convenient meeting point like Dublin where writers can discuss their aims, and no common literary purpose which would give directions to their production. The result is that Scottish writers receive no effectual criticism, and consequently no real help in their work. It is well known that the general level of book-reviewing in the English Press is very low; but in Scotland it is considerably lower. Again, there are in England several reviews in which intelligent criticism can be had if one wants it; while in Scotland there is only one, and it a quarterly. In a country where criticism is indiscriminating or almost absent the work of its creative writers may be remarkable, but it is likely to be uneven. Scotland has three or four writers of original talent, but their work is far more uneven than it has any right to be, or than it would have been had they written for a country which possessed an acknowledged standard of serious criticism as well as the popular one represented by the Press. This lack of criticism is probably the chief danger to the present revival of literature in Scotland. With a little more enthusiastic complaisance it may end in a complete uncritical morass.

But though the present literary production in Scotland has no definite direction, there is one thing which clearly distinguishes it from that of Stevenson, Barrie, Crockett and Ian Maclaren at the end of last century. The Scottish characters in which these writers dealt were intended primarily, like Sir Harry Lauder's humour, for foreign consumption. They were designed for the popular English taste; they were exports. This was not true to the same degree of Neil Munro's Highlanders, who came later, and it cannot be said at all, I think, of Mr Neil M. Gunn's or Mr Lewis Grassic Gibbon's or 'Fionn MacColla's' Scottish characters. These writers address themselves first of all to a Scottish audience, and not incidentally, as their predecessors did. Certainly Stevenson should not be blamed too much for his literary strategy, for such an audience did not exist in his time. And the fact that it does exist now is a clear proof of an immense increase in national self-consciousness.

(Edwin Muir, 'Literature in Scotland', Spectator 25 May 1934, p.823.)

3.29 Eric Linklater, 'The Novel in Scotland' (*Fortnightly*, November 1935)

Mr Edwin Muir recently suggested that 'the most vital work in prose fiction for some time now has been done on the periphery of the novel. . . . When people no longer believe very strongly in a society they cannot believe very strongly in representations of it either. They do not want a skilful picture of a scene that has ceased to convince them'.

That there is more vitality—and by inference more scope for vitality—on the periphery of the novel than in its traditional circumscription is, I think, a matter for argument. The activities of extra-galactic space, because of their unexpectedness, have a liveliness that may seem to outshine the more familiar luminaries; but the Galaxy does not necessarily grow dimmer. This, however, is an extraneous debate. When Mr Muir says we cannot very strongly believe in literary representations of a society we have ceased to believe in, he is on firmer ground; and this firm ground may be a useful vantage point from which to consider the Scottish novel of to-day.

Social life in Scotland has at present no peculiar and individual significance. It has no essentially native culture to inspire it, no sense of independent nationality to integrate it. It is derivative and provincial. To pretend that everyone in Scotland is conscious of this provincialism and, in a special sense, of insignificance, would of course be an overstatement; but Scottish writers, almost without exception, are painfully aware of it. Their reaction to the Scottish scene is therefore likely to be evasive, or lacking in conviction, or minutely selective. They may avoid Scottish themes; or deal with them in a parochial spirit that belittles what is already small enough; or confine themselves to some remote parcel of geography, to some distant fragment of life, and find in that solitary corner a significance that is clearly lacking in the whole. Naomi Mitchison, for example, has done her best work in Sparta, and on the antique shores of the Black Sea. The parochialists are too many to count. And among the selectivists Neil Gunn is easily the first with his *Grey Coast* and *Morning Tide*: in these books he has done work that is artistically satisfying, but which has little relation to the main stream—such as it is—of Scottish life; they are not Scottish novels in the sense in which Sinclair Lewis's novels are American.

An interesting attempt to meet the need for a large-canvas novel was recently made by George Blake in *The Shipbuilders*. He chose for his background the declining riches and importance of the Clyde. The theme is large enough, and his stage is properly set with the scenery of tragedy. But his principal characters are insufficient either for scenery or argument. They are three in number: a shipbuilder faced with the regrettable fact that, for him, shipbuilding is no longer profitable; his wife, surrounded by the boredom of Scottish society; and a riveter, sometime the shipbuilder's batman, confronted with unemployment. The shipbuilder, despite care in his creation, obstinately resembles someone seen in a passing first-class carriage. His wife is a mere pencil sketch, a conventional outline of something in which Mr Blake is clearly not very interested. The riveter, however, has been created with much more vigour. He is a living and likeable person, and in his amusement and among his friends a dependable guide to the manners of Scotland's industrial majority. But as if unsure even of his importance, Mr Blake undermines his character with sentimentality. He makes him a little bit too good to be true, and a little bit too true to certain fictional standards to be good for art.

Now there must be some reason for this failure to create characters congruent with the strength of the story, for Mr Blake can write, think, see, and feel with all the necessary skill, clarity, percipience, and emotion. When he writes of the Clyde itself, with its empty yards and its world-pacing history he is magnificent; he can make a list of dead shipbuilders' names sound like a Homeric catalogue of heroes; he can find abundant riches in crowded places or in a small domestic atmosphere; and he can create minor figures with certainty and economy. Why, then, does he fail with his principals?

Surely the reason is to be found in Mr Muir's diagnosis: he is not able to believe very strongly in the specific importance of Clyde shipbuilders, their wives, and their conservative employees, and therefore he has not given his representations of them sufficient force. They are decaying orders that Mr Blake has written of, and he had not the excitement of publishing a new thing when he described their decay; for that was already too well known.

A dozen rural counterparts to this picture of industrial decline could be found in any Scottish bookshop, and most of them would at least mention, if they did not depend on, the depopulation of the Highlands, the Circean men-into-sheep translation of the nineteenth century, and the ingenious discovery of deer-forest and grouse-moor when the sheep-runs had become too sour for mutton. The confectioners of these country matters are mostly young, and a laudable indignation often breathes life into characters that are otherwise of no great interest. But their range of characters is necessarily small—shepherds and crofters, a dissatisfied young man, a girl or two for seduction, some English visitors seen and heard from a distance—and genius itself cannot make bricks without straw. Here we come to more sterile ground than Mr Muir was speaking of. Here is not society no longer able to convince, but society scarcely able to exist. Had Balzac been born in the Scottish Highlands he might have become a northern Gilbert White, but he could never have been the author of a Human Comedy, for the sufficient reason that there is not enough humanity to make such comedy.

It is true that in Ireland, where certain districts may superficially resemble the Highlands, there are writers of abundant vigour, talent, and significance. But Irish writers have two advantages; they had, not long ago, a capital in which a group of people were definitely and perhaps defiantly intellectual in their interests; and they have now a sense of national achievement, of national importance and individuality, of being alive in the midst of significant and largely successful effort. You cannot easily find in Scottish letters of today anything that equals the literary vitality of Seán O'Faoláin and Francis Stuart, for example. There is passage after passage in their work that reads as though the rising sun were behind it; they are excited by loveliness as one can only be at the renewal of the year. But it is more than a century since Edinburgh was a home for intellectual interests or for speculation—save on the Stock Exchange—while athletic exploits at

Murrayfield and on the golf-links are all that can give us a feeling of national achievement.

There was, till a few months ago, when he most untimely died, a Scottish novelist who had made, out of his own intensity of feeling and the seemingly unpromising material of the eastern lowlands of Scotland, something that came as near as makes no difference to being a really great novel. I mean Lewis Grassic Gibbon, whose Scots quhair [sic]—the three novels *Sunset Song, Cloud Howe*, and *Grey Granite*—is *sui generis*. In the first place Gibbon invented a prose rhythm that successfully evoked the sound and temper and physiology of country speech; and in the second place he had a definite historical conception of society and a definite philosophy. He believed in the primitive beatitude of mankind, and he believed in the possibility of a return to happiness through Communism. He did not believe in Communism as a social terminus. He once wrote to me: 'I loathe organization, control, the state, and the voice of the serjeant-major. As the sole surviving specimen of Natural Man to be found in these islands, I'm naturally an anarchist. But how you or I, or—more to the point—our unfortunate progeny, can attain real freedom and fun without the preliminary conditioning of Communism is beyond me. Communism's merely a means to an end—a nannie enforcing on the dirty little boy who calls himself Man the necessity for scrubbing the back of his neck and keeping his regrettable bowels in order. When he grows adolescent and can do these things automatically, and has ceased to smell quite so badly, he'll be a much better equipped specimen for his chosen mission of playing football with the cosmos.'

Whatever one may think of his politics, it may safely be said that Gibbon was the only Scots writer of his generation to dare suppose that playing football with the cosmos was his chosen mission. But he was an audacious person. To invent a new prose rhythm and write three full-length novels in it was plumed and high-horsed audacity; and to come so near success as he did was to demonstrate the genius that justified it. The best of his writing, that in the words of one man may evoke the speech of a whole countryside, has a spell-like quality. It marvellously presents the flavour of speech, and suggests a life in which speech, not writing, is still the proper means of communication. But when, in the third volume, the story comes to town, the ingenious rhythm has to some extent to be abandoned; while Communism, as a literary inspiration, seems hardly so useful as the life of the soil that innervates the earlier volumes.

Gibbon's death was a grievous loss to Scotland, and I can see no signs even of a cosmic skittle-player among those who survive him, unless perhaps in John Allan, whose *Farmer's Boy* has a quality of delight that is rare in Scottish writing. A rich, native, rather lazy, but whole-hearted delight in men and women, food and drink and the Scottish countryside, is indeed the salient characteristic of his book. It begins, 'I was born on the afternoon of the day on which my grandfather signed his third Trust Deed on behoof of his creditors . . . the only form of literature in which our family have ever achieved distinction'. Such contempt for polite conventions—the book is a kind of autobiography—has not for a long time been the mark of Scottish authors; and Mr Allan has set a noble example in jilting respectability.

(Eric Linklater, 'The Novel in Scotland', *Fortnightly*, November 1935, pp.621–24.)

3.30 Robert Bain, from 'Scottish Poetry of To-day' (*Burns Chronicle* 1939)

Poetry is the most powerful of all forces in keeping alive the spiritual faith of a nation in the hour of defeat or triumph. It is the only treasury of her best thought. When good, it—and it alone—reveals all the nation's greatness. But no poet can deliberately set out to add to this. He cannot say 'I will reform this or that', as a politician might, for he cannot tell what slightest thing may move his spirit to action. He cannot bind himself to any particular scheme which professes to set right the world. The best of good intentions will not make a poem. A poem ends all argument, for it never argues. It is an instantaneous revelation of the poet, his country, and of the heart of man—that heart in which all 'isms' are one. It is the failure to accept this truth that has been the weakness of Hugh MacDiarmid. And he knows it. He is beyond question our foremost poet, but half the time he is cursing his own people for being sunk in the slough of ineffective sentimentalism and for regarding poetry as a substitute for toddy. But he made poetry a matter of fierce discussion, and that was a blessed revolution, for he rushed to conflict with a clatter of lost Scots words which roused antagonism by their foreignness. Now our poetry had really become thowless, and had Mr MacDiarmid let all his hates, his gospels and foreign enthusiasms go hang, and kept to his poetry, there is no saying what might have happened. But he had too many gods to serve. And he still has. His latest book, *Stony Limits*, shows him at his best and worst. It has enough science to gravel all but a specialist. The beginning of 'On a raised beach' is meaningless except to a geologist. The same applies to his poem on Cancer. Neither is in any form of current speech. His longer poems are thickets of scientific terms. Yet every now and then we break through the entanglement of these and come on astonishing glades of the purest and loveliest poetry. [. . .] Mr MacDiarmid's devotion to Scotland is a magnificent thing, and from this book alone I could make a little anthology of passages packed with revelation, of lines full of critical discernment, and of small lyrics, emotionally deep, yet clear as deep waters are. No man knows better than he what poetry is, but he is so intolerant of mediocrity and man's indifference that poetry is lost in bitterness and satire. He makes me blazing wild one moment and exultant the next when, forgetting self, he becomes poet and poet only. And then I forgive him all his faults, for poetry is the great reconciler.

The contrast presented by Edwin Muir's poetry is startling. In his two most recent books *Variations on a Time Theme* and *Journeys and Places* we feel as if we were looking at a horse and rider on a theatre stage or in a heraldic picture. The pace of the horse is steady but as the stage is going backward the horse does not change its position. So, if one could stand still in time and watch the years go backward or forward at will, or sit on a hill and see in fancy its past or conceive its future, we should be in the right mood to open Mr Muir's books and win his vision of the unchangeableness of human story—man ever riding into the unknown on a dimly-guessed-at-quest. Life is seen as a continuous journey, with men the ever-changing travellers, each generation beholding a new horizon which will presently vanish behind it. And while there is here no trumpet-call to some sudden great achievement, there is a sense of human triumph in the sheer persistence of man the traveller. *Journeys and Places* might be regarded as notes on stages of that time-long wandering, and each, however distant from us, is clear as if it were to-day. We see Troy falling, and the chief mourners are they who were never trusted to fight for it—its slaves. They were the real folk of the city and not its legendary great ones—Helen or Paris or Hector or Priam [. . .] But even the slaves did not know their oneness with Troy till they had lost it, for only rarely—and this is another of Mr Muir's revelations—does a man recognise that he has come to what the poet calls 'The Sufficient Place', a central peace outside of which lies the tumult of the world.

Poetry of this quality is not easy to absorb. But it is poetry, singularly pure, as a living statue might be, in its repose, yet definite and vivid to eye and thought. [. . .]

In William Soutar's poetry we come into a world that is wholly Scottish, and even with the opening lines of his *Poems in Scots* he dismisses a great deal of the past:–

> 'Orion and Aldebaran,
> And a' the sterns that gang their gate,
> What ken they o' the thochts of man.
> Or fash about his fate.'

Yet in his very next poem he brings in symbolism—but with a difference—and writes a ballad that is of the same blood and being as those old Scots ballads which are our country's most outstanding gift to poetry. [. . .]

Equally fine as poetry, and as richly symbolic, is 'The auld tree', dedicated to Hugh MacDiarmid, and so acknowledging what we owe to him, for his Thistle comes into the poem, and has now become, miraculously,

> a tree,
> Younglin' and braw wi' fullyery. [. . .]

I am not going to dwell further on Mr Soutar. The rest of his work has the same clear vision of actuality, and he keeps true to that singing word which on the right lips is the real flaming sword of the spirit. He uses symbols, but they are those which are the breath of our own national being, and in his poetry they become living. [. . .]

It was my intention to deal with three other poets, Nan Shepherd, Helen Cruikshank [sic] and W.D. Cocker, but these must be left for another occasion. But I may remark that our women poets are much more direct than the men. They get off their mark more quickly, and go straight as an arrow, with sight unimpaired by the conflicting theories of the world. They come nearest to the methods of the Balladists in vision and sincerity.

(Robert Bain, 'Scottish Poetry of To-Day', *Burns Chronicle* 14, 1939, pp.86–94.)

4

Transforming Traditions

Bards of a Sham Nation?

4.1 Edwin Muir, from 'Robert Burns' (*Freeman* May 1923)

'Few men had so much of the poet about them', said the father of Alan Cunningham, 'and few poets so much of the man: the man was probably less pure than he ought to have been, but the poet was pure and bright to the end.' It is the only humane judgment passed on Burns by a contemporary: all the others have a touch of cant in them, something morally or socially superior. The most dully respectable circle in literary history sat and watched Burns in his sober hours, driving him regularly to the extreme where goodfellowship was not very strongly flavored with decency. The goodness of his father early drew to the house people with an affectation of deliberate virtue. It attracted the pious Murdoch, the model dominie, who loved to recollect in after years the admonitions he had given to genius. Later Burns, now a young man, was permitted for a time to breathe the musty controversial air of liberal theology as it was propounded in his county, and he found it so good that he was moved to poetry. This was, however, his only experience of emancipated society. His fame and his journey to Edinburgh again enveloped him in the stupendous Scots respectability of that time; the elegant and priggish minister Blair, the virtuous and respectable Dugald Stewart, 'the historian Robertson', sat beside him wondering visibly whether their young genius would become a really respected poet and a prosperous and godly farmer. Their society must occasionally have appeared to him like the reading of an interminable, dull tract. But indeed his educated friends, except for one or two women, had only virtue to recommend them, while his boon companions were equally without sense and sensibility. In spite of a lifelong desire for friends, he found only moralists and tipplers; and although he could move these by the astonishing spectacle of his thoughts and passions, so that when he spoke from his heart they wept, he received nothing back from them to give him happiness, nor, except in states of drunken effusion, any direct human comprehension. As his life grew poorer he turned to these states more and more rather than to the intelligent men of virtue who had less than nothing to give him, and who gave grudgingly.

It was after his visit to Edinburgh that his nature, strongly built and normal, disintegrated. He had hoped, in meeting the first shock of his astonishing triumph in the capital, that escape was at last possible from the life of hardly maintained poverty which as a boy he had foreseen and feared. He left Edinburgh recognizing that there was no reprieve, that hardship must sit at his elbow to the end of his days. Fame had lifted him up on the point of an immense pinnacle; now the structure had melted away and, astonished, he found himself once more in his native country, an Ayrshire peasant. Some fairy had set him for a little in the centre of a rich and foreign society; then, calmly and finally, she had taken it from under his feet. There is hardly another incident in literary history to parallel this brief rise and setting of social favor, and hardly one showing more the remorselessness of fortune in the world. The shock told deeply on Burns, working more for evil than the taste for dissipation which he was said to have acquired from the Edinburgh aristocracy. His character gradually fell to pieces. The more narrowly decent want constrained him, the more he took to the drink; yet to the last a little good fortune was sufficient to set him back for a time in a self-respecting life. [. . .]

He desired above all things to love and to be loved, yet it is doubtful whether once in his life he had a deep and sincere passion. His imagination demanded something more than the dairy-maids and mason's daughters of his parish could give him; but when he dreamed of the Edinburgh women whom he was later to know, his realistic mind quickly cut the reverie short. But it was not only the imperfections of mason's daughters that kept him from loving; there was an obstacle also within himself, a thirst for love which probably no single love affair could have quenched, a too great desire to love which by its vehemence defeated itself. [. . .]

His vision of the world was unusually complete. Generally praised as a lyric poet, he was more truly a kind of dramatist. He expressed very seldom in his songs the emotions of Robert Burns, and when he expressed them, he often did it badly. 'To Mary in Heaven' and 'Man was made to Mourn', poems obviously composed under the stress of deep personal emotion, were among the worst he wrote, and had none of the absolute sureness of dramatic lyrics like 'Tam Glen' or 'Whistle and I'll come tae ye, my lad'. In his songs he put himself in a certain attitude, or rather, a certain number of attitudes, and the voices which spoke through them were those of the entire Scots peasantry of his time. All his songs written for women were especially exquisite; in throwing the emotion of a woman into a song he did not once fail. But even in his songs for men the voice was not often Burns'; it was generally that of the ideal young Scots peasant who is one of his chief creations. He himself became this Scots peasant, generalizing himself in his race and in his class [. . .] So complete, so universal was he here that it may be said of him that he created the modern Scots peasant. He did not make the Scots peasantry any better morally, perhaps, but he gave them something which is more valuable than morality, an aesthetic consciousness of their joys and griefs, their nature and destiny, and left them with some added touch of humanity and of poise.

His songs showed this strong and true dramatic power; but its main achievement was 'The Jolly Beggars'. In spite of its bestiality (a word, as good as any other, which Arnold was to find for it a hundred years later) that poem was of all his works the most full of 'the glory and the joy' which he found as he walked

> Behind his plough upon the mountain side.

He filled it with a sense of Bacchanalian ecstasy in which lust became a form of rapture, and every kind of freedom was possible; but all was seen with a sort of divine carelessness, with a charity which had become impartial. [. . .]

In sense of life, in humour, in dramatic force and truth, in organic vigour of style, he was great; but his most divine power was probably that of putting into words more simple and unalterable than any others in Scots or English literature, emotions and thoughts felt by every one. [. . .] More than any other poet of the last two centuries he has helped to humanize his own countrymen and the English-speaking peoples generally, and to instill into them not only a more sensitive manner of feeling, but also a more philosophic habit of thought. No one was better fitted than he for the task; no one was farther removed from all perversity of feeling, all singularity of thought. He was a norm of humanity, a model, in everything but his life, for all men. As a consequence there is no writer on whom the blame of succeeding generations lies more lightly; Burns will always be loved, except by a few timid Presbyterians like Stevenson, with a special, warm indulgence. This attitude is one of the lessons which his poems have taught mankind.

(Edwin Muir, 'Robert Burns', *Freeman* [USA] 7, 9 May 1923; reprinted from *Latitudes* London: Melrose, 1924, pp.1–11[1–4, 7–9, 11].)

4.2 C.M. Grieve, from *Contemporary Scottish Studies* (1926)

a) From 'Conclusion: I'

The Burns Movement—The Next Step? Within the past year or so the Burns Cult, with its world-wide clubs, has been rapidly reorienting itself, and has put the revival of the Vernacular in the forefront of its programme.

It is becoming to an increasing extent a Scottish literary and national movement and not just an organisation for maintaining an Annual Dinner and orgy of indiscriminate eulogy, and for the bibliographical and antiquarian study and preservation of Burnsiana. It may be that through a new address to Burns' great ideal of Universal Brotherhood the Scottish psychology will yet realise in a higher fashion than is connoted in mere ubiquity or even in success in commerce and engineering its world-function, and become, not merely cosmopolitan, but—they are part and parcel of each other, and opposed to cosmopolitanism or imperialism—national and international. Alongside this reorientation has come a new attitude to Burns himself—not the old stupid provincial idolatry, but a reconsideration of his place and power on purely literary grounds. The new disposition of the activities of the Cult is attracting a new type of speaker and writer of a higher cultural calibre. It is becoming widely recognised that the day is past for rehashing the personalia—rewhitewashing or redenigrating the Bard— and that the time has come to consider his quality and methods as a poet, his comparative international status, the influence he has had on Scottish life and letters, the way in which he handled the Vernacular, to appreciate his limitations as well as his powers, and to resume him into his proper historical setting and see him in that. The application of modern critical methods to Burns and his work cannot be long delayed.

b) From 'Conclusion: II'

Is it desirable that there should be a return, especially on the part of the Scottish people, to Scott? Efforts are being made in certain quarters to revive interest in his work, and, in particular, the Waverley Novels. Very diverse writers have recently been claiming that he is greater than Burns, with the implication that Scott and Burns ought to be drastically regraded in popular esteem. It is noteworthy, however, that the writers in question (scarcely one of whom, incidentally, is even a second-ranker either as critic or creator) are all either English or Anglo-Scottish litterateurs (meaning by Anglo-Scottish litterateurs writers whose reputations, such as they are, are bound up with the English literary tradition rather than with the quite distinct, if admittedly infinitely inferior, Scots literary tradition). The movement to reinstate Scott in critical esteem and popular regard must therefore be regarded as one designed to conserve and reinforce certain elements in English culture, while taking it for granted that Scotland and England have identical cultural interests. But should this be taken for granted?

English literature to-day may be tending in directions that are undesirable in themselves or, at all events, at variance with its great central traditions; and some such corrective as that which has spontaneously generated this re-appreciation of Scott (or some qualities in Scott) in certain quarters, may be required. To these central traditions of English literature as distinct from Scottish, the bulk of Scott—all but an almost infinitesimal residuum—may, or rather must, be conceded; Burns, on the other hand, belongs mainly to Scots literature. At the moment when, belatedly, tendencies, however tentative to a Scottish Literary Revival, are manifesting themselves, it is peculiarly necessary to ensure that English literary traditions are not recouping themselves by means which are likely to prevent the emergence of the diametrically opposed tendencies upon which the development of distinctively Scottish literature depends. In Scotland itself, at any rate, there should be jealousy to see, since distinctively English forces have so long and so tremendously dominated British literature, that the continued paramountcy of the Southern partner in our most unequal alliance is not any longer ensured by any failure to detect and urge the specific, if contrary, interests of those purely Scottish elements which may have the potentiality of liberating forces capable in the long run of redressing the cultural balance between the two nations.

(C.M. Grieve, Contemporary Scottish Studies London: Leonard Parsons, 1926,
'Conclusion: I', pp.314–15; 'II', pp.316–17.)

4.3   C.M. Grieve, 'Hiatus' (*G.O.C. Magazine* January 1929)

'The Scott Country', 'the Burns Country', 'the Barrie Country'. How I hate these fixations of parts of Scotland so that one cannot go into them without being compelled to entertain a certain set of associations. One can scarcely see the landscapes in question without having one's impressions largely pre-determined by these authors; their spirits interpose between us and the objects of vision. It is intolerable—if one wants to see the Borders or Ayrshire or Kirriemuir as they actually are (to us—for everybody sees them differently in proportion to his or her individuality), and not an open-air cinematograph performance of certain novels or poems. But it is subtler than that; one does not really see Barrie's characters in the streets of Kirriemuir; one is only conscious of a certain atmosphere drawn from his writings.

On respire un goût mental

How is one to escape from this? Unless we are titanic geniuses we cannot escape out of the past thought of a few individuals by whom our mentality, such as it is, has been almost wholly pre-determined, and all that we can see anywhere selected in advance out of the inexhaustible materials actually in existence. We do not see any part of Scotland; we only see what our optical limitations and the quality of our sensibility permits us to see. But all that is a very large question; what I am principally concerned with here is how a visitor can go to the Burns country, the Scott country, or the Barrie country (taking it for granted, of course, that they have heard these terms and read these authors) and yet evade these powerful influences at will and see the scenes made famous by certain literary associations with 'their own eyes' or under aspects opposed to the traditional ones.

It is obvious that this must continually be done or certain districts would get completely used up. Nobody else could deal with them in future without being hopelessly imitative. Fortunately it is only a very little that a Scott or a Burns can write even about a chosen locality; genius itself cannot circumscribe reality and put its impress upon it. It is only an aspect here, an element there, that is affected—but our minds lag so far behind our lives that whole generations can have their attitude to Nature and to other people and to themselves dictated to them by a single writer or group of writers. Scottish life has changed completely since Burns's day and Scott's; yet most Scots even yet cannot escape from the literary conventions these writers established, and the greater part of contemporary Scottish fiction and verse deals with a type of life few, if any, of the writers have actually lived, and which, so far as the great majority of our countrymen are concerned, is gone for good and need not be regretted. The problem of Scottish arts and letters to-day is to bring the Scottish scene into accord with modern mentality—to bridge the gulf between the lives we actually lead and the superannuated conceptions which still so largely dominate our consciousness. [. . .]

Burns and Scott belong to the bad old days before the development of modern labour-saving devices. The Scottish Renaissance Movement is the literary equivalent of S.M.T.—or is trying to be. It is not easy. We feel that to read Crockett or 'Ian Maclaren' nowadays is like being thrown suddenly out of fourth into reverse. But it is not easy to 'move with the times' intellectually. Pointing out how slowly and with what difficulty the railway train has made its way into literature—Wordsworth called it 'Motions and Means', 'Nature's lawful offspring'; Tennyson was forced to accept it, but handled it very gingerly; Browning was a little bit more courageous, but even he introduced it through the back door of serio-comic verse— Robert Graves shows how a Scottish poet, John Davidson, ultimately accepted it more 'naturally'—but even then there was a very long way to go before it could be treated with perfectly modern nonchalance and written about quite casually and without self-consciousness in serious poetry.

Scottish poetry, and literature generally, has still a long way to go. It appertains to conditions of life long since—happily—revolutionised. Our poets are still scraping the ground with a wooden stake instead of using a motor-plough. The best way to keep the influences of the Past in their proper place is to imagine oneself whirring round a corner at 40 m.p.h. and sending headlong into the ditch for safety the astounded figures of Scott and Burns. But, as it is, most of us, even in our high-powered cars, only take

> *winding*
> *Roads whose dust seems gilded binding*
> *Made for . . .*

the 'Bonnie Brier Bush' or 'langsyne in Braefoot'.

(C.M. Grieve, 'Hiatus', *G.O.C. Magazine*, January 1929, pp.58–9.)

4.4 John Buchan, from letter to Donald Carswell (July 1929)

Elsfield Manor,
Oxford,
12th July, 1929

My dear Carswell,

I need not tell you—for you know very well already—how good this thing of yours is. I have read it with the greatest admiration and delight. It is one of the freshest and most searching things ever written on the subject. [. . .] Of the speculative and introspective intellect he had, of course, nothing; but he had very large solid reasoning powers, to which I should be sorry to deny the name of intellect. [. . .] I am constantly struck with the really massive rationality of the man. So if you deny him intellect, you must define the word specially. [. . .] Also, when you give Lockhart the lie, as unfortunately is sometimes necessary, I think you ought to give your authority.

(John Buchan, letter to Donald Carswell of 12 July 1929 apparently responding to pre-publication draft of Carswell's *Sir Walter* (1930), NLS Acc. 6571.)

4.5 Donald Carswell, from *Sir Walter: A Four-Part Study in Biography* (1930)

If Mr Scott as a man of sixty could have been induced to give a candid opinion on the business of bringing up a family, he would probably have replied that, like most things, it partook largely of vanity and vexation of spirit. Anne Rutherford had, more or less cheerfully, borne him twelve children, of whom the first six died in infancy. The second six—five boys and a girl—were hardy enough to grow up, but they did not inspire their father with enthusiasm. They were certainly a plain-looking lot, though he could not complain of that: after all, he had not chosen Anne Rutherford for her looks, and the Scotts had never been beauties. [. . .] On the whole Mr Scott got most comfort from the contemplation of his third son and namesake, Walter, who was at the Bar, wherein was great cause for satisfaction and gratitude to the Power which directs even our afflictions to our good, for Wattie was of so venturesome and restless disposition that he would assuredly have gone for a soldier had not Providence ordained him to hobble about on a stick all the days of his life. As it was, the lad had consented readily enough to be bound to the law, and, when his time was up, had pleased his father still more by electing to proceed to the Bar instead of sticking to a desk in George's Square. [. . .]

Those were great days for the high-flying romantics. Goethe and Schiller had at last joined forces. Bürger had died at the height of his reputation in 1794, and in the same year Mrs Radcliffe had curdled the blood of young ladies to an ecstasy, exquisite but strictly chaste, with the *Mysteries of Udolpho*. Less exquisite and not at all chaste was a romance called *Ambrosio* or *The Monk*, which a very young, very undersized and very odd-looking gentleman in the Diplomatic service, Lewis by name, had seen fit to throw upon the world in 1795. He got great fame by it. Robert Burns was dying at Dumfries, working even on his deathbed at his beloved task of preserving and restoring his country's folk-songs, and steadfastly refusing payment, though pinched for money. But Scott, absorbed in contemplation of his skull and crossbones, had lost interest in the national poet. As a lad he had been bitterly disappointed at the miscarriage of Tom Grierson's plan for a real meeting with Burns. As a young man, brimming over with literary enthusiasms and eager to make literary acquaintances, he could easily have repaired the omission. He knew Burns's friends the Riddels. Year after year, for months at a time, he was within an easy day's ride of Dumfries. Once, if not twice, in 1795 he was actually in the town. But he never sought out the poet, who would cheerfully have drunk with him till dawn. When Burns was dead, none was more earnest than Walter Scott in the empty business of his apotheosis. But Burns alive in Dumfries, broken in health and reputation, was a different proposition. Naturally, a socially ambitious young advocate would not seek the company of a crapulous Exciseman, with his shabby-genteel household, his peasant wife, his many bairns (not counting his bastards), who had disgraced himself among the local gentlefolk and was capable of advertising in shameless verse his amour with a blowsy barmaid at the Globe tavern. Scott's instinct was sound. A dubious contact was avoided. It is unlikely that he would have been happy with Burns. It is certain that Burns would have detested him. [. . .]

So died, in his sixty-second year, Walter Scott, the simplest, sincerest and greatest of all romantics. To others romanticism might afford a metaphysic or an artistic theory or a gesture; to him it was a religion, a creed to be accepted and a life to be lived. But the romantic life is not a practical proposition: indeed, like raising oneself by the hair of the head, it is a contradiction in terms, for the essence of romance is that the life it reveals was never lived on sea or land. Scott never understood that. He never really understood anything, for though he had solid reasoning powers, he had little insight. He lived in terms of feeling and believing and willing, and spent his days pursuing incompatibles with unremitting diligence and spectacular, if sometimes sad, results. He was a professional man who aspired to be a feudal lord and could not keep his fingers out of trade; a Jacobite whose devotion to the House of Hanover became a byword; an enthusiastic admirer of the material progress of his age who would not accept its social and political consequences; an Anglophobe in principle who in practice found England altogether admirable; an historian who knew everything about history except its meaning. To a moderately clever man these absurdities would have been obvious, but Scott was not even moderately clever. Of the metaphysical diathesis that is said to distinguish his countrymen he had not a trace. He loved to talk, but was never at ease in a discussion and never said anything worth remembering. His writings are as bare of ideas as his conversation was.

But if he conspicuously lacked the higher intellectual qualities, he had the endowment most suited to express his genius—an inexhaustible invention, a formidable memory, a sharp, though superficial eye for character, a gusto for the human pageant and a power of application that enabled him in ten years to produce more than Dickens produced in twenty. To discuss the quality of his genius is no part of the present study, and merely to extol its magnificence would be an idle and impertinent display of brave words. It is enough to say that in the history of prose fiction there are but two epoch-makers—Cervantes, who did the ancient and beloved art of pure story-telling to a cruel death, and Walter Scott, who brought it to a glorious resurrection.

(Donald Carswell, *Sir Walter: A Four-Part Study in Biography* London: John Murray, 1930, pp.8–9, 18–20, 160–62.)

4.6 C.M. Grieve, from 'Scotsmen Make a God of Robert Burns' (*Radio Times* January 1930)

C.M. Grieve, in an unusual article, asks, 'Is that god clayfooted?'

A couple of years ago the present writer made an attack on the Burns cult, on the ground that Burns was by no means so great a poet as his idolaters claimed, and that his influence on Scottish life and letters had been thoroughly bad and largely responsible for the obstinate provincialism of both. A furious controversy ensued, but there have been many signs since that the attack was timely and effective. On three points there could be no rebuttal. Burnsians may make the most exaggerated claims for their hero but the percentage of poetry-lovers in the English-speaking world who know anything of his work is unquestionably tiny, and they appreciate it inverse ratio to their interest in, and knowledge of, poetry in general. Even in Scottish schools little Burns is taught, and a great deal more Wordsworth, Shelley, Keats, Coleridge, and Tennyson. Is Burns taught in English schools? How many non-English-reading poetry-lovers have ever heard of Burns—and has this materially affected their knowledge of poetry? Of course not. Burnsians need only consult a representative collection of important modern studies of poets and poetry to see that Burns is seldom mentioned, and practically destitute of influence or interest. Poets such as Blake in England, or Baudelaire, or Rimbaud in France are the subjects of an endless flow of critical studies. Burns occasions no such technical research, or aesthetic or philosophical speculation, while, as Mr Augustine Birrell pointed out some time ago, the spate of Burns orations every January seldom yields a paragraph that is not hopelessly beneath the standards of literary criticism, even in the *Nation and Athenaeum*, or *New Statesman*. Few of the 'orators' have any ability or standing, or would ever be invited to expatiate on any other literary subject. Critics of repute have always held aloof. Scottish writers of more than parochial merit—such as John Davidson, R.B. Cunninghame Graham, Norman Douglas and F.W. Bain—have evaded the cult; and not one of the younger Scots writers of promise today will have anything to do with it. It is significant, too, that almost all the Burns Clubs have ceased to feature 'Scots literature', or 'Other Scottish Poets' on their toast lists.

The Burns sentiment is one of the principal opponents of the new movement in Scottish arts and affairs. It is not good for any country to be so long and completely dominated by a single writer as Scotland has been dominated by Burns; but the concern of the Burns Movement is to keep Scotland 'thirled' to certain values, entirely unrelated to its greatest or most distinctive periods, or those of any other culture. These values are bound up with obsolete conditions of rural life, 'romantic love', and the emergence of that spirit of democracy which is today being so comprehensively challenged and overthrown. The implications of this have recently been stressed by another bearer of the Bard's own name—Dr C. Deslisle Burns, who, lecturing in Glasgow and elsewhere, has contended that 'a simple poetry might supply the needs of simple minds if men still believed that the Universe had its centre in their village, or even on our very significant earth, but the larger view opened up by modern knowledge made a grander poetry possible which could not be expressed in the traditional terms'.

It is along these lines that the new movement is at last joining issue with the Hildebrandism which has been Scotland's curse for centuries, and bringing to bear on 'The Immortal Memory' the force of that destructive work of the free intelligence of the last half-century, manifested in such writers as Ibsen, Nietzsche, Shaw, James Joyce, Aldous Huxley, and scores of others, and in the developments of contemporary psycho-analysis and science in general, which, in the words of one of the ablest of living Scottish writers, Mr Edwin Muir, has brought about 'a sense of the questionableness of the most simple emotions, the most sanctioned relations, the most stereotyped experience', which the poetry of Burns is peculiarly unfitted to withstand. The spirit of the age is increasingly repudiating the social, moral, and political bases of Burns's work, a process which is quickly undermining the so-called 'Immortal Memory!' Burns has nothing to contribute to the crucial problems of today and tomorrow. His work is part of a stream of tendency which has practically exhausted itself and is now the subject of a widespread reaction.

The Burns cult in literature is like Bill Boanerges in Shaw's *Applecart*, but listeners are increasingly aware of two radically opposed elements in Scottish programmes. The B.B.C. has done a great deal for recent developments of Scottish life and literature, by broadcasting the poems, short stories, and dramas of the younger writers and such addresses as those in the *What's Wrong with Scotland* series. It is still inevitable that there should be such things as the St Andrew's Night broadcast and the annual Burns celebration. But the tension between the two is increasing, and the new tendencies are more and more at variance with the old-fashioned 'coamic' and 'kailyaird' tradition, and apt, when confronted with the Burns cult, to cry, 'Not Burns—Dunbar!' or, still more disconcertingly for those to whom Gaelic literature is unknown, to claim that Alasdair MacMhaighistir Alasdair stands in the same relation to Burns as Paul Valéry to Beranger, or Alexander Blok to Apollon Maykov (who, as Prince Mirsky says, 'satisfied the taste of the average Russian poetry-reader of his day for tame ideas, tame picturesqueness, and mild realism'—just as Burns has done in Scotland). [. . .]

Burns himself was no Burnsian and clearly foresaw what has continued ever since when he wrote: 'My success has encouraged such a shoal of ill-spawned monsters to crawl into public notice, under the title of Scottish poets, that the very term Scottish poetry borders on the burlesque.' The general influence of his work on Scottish character and culture has been equally unwholesome.

(C.M. Grieve, 'Scotsmen Make a God of Robert Burns', *Radio Times* 17 January 1930, p.137.)

4.7 Catherine Carswell, 'The "Giant Ploughman" Can Withstand His Critics' (*Radio Times* February 1930)

I do not propose to score off Mr Grieve on debating points. It would be so easy that it would be a shame to take the money. All I need point out is that he begs the only question that really matters about Burns, which is: Even supposing (what isn't true) that contemporary literary criticism does not regard him as a great poet, why does he continue to occupy that enviable position in the estimation of innumerable unliterary persons all over the world? There is no poet that has not his periods of neglect by the *fashionable* critics. Equally, no poet who maintains his place in the affection of the unliterary can at any period *fail* to inspire the interest and respect of the few critics who count in any generation. Burns, who in the past has earned the passionate homage of Jeffrey, Byron, Keats, Carlyle, Taine, Henley, Arnold—to mention a very few names—is not going to be sneered out of the company of the great simply because he does not strike the book-makers of one or any generation as good for a monograph.

It will be useful to see what is at the root of the grudge which confuses Mr Grieve's mind. Mr Grieve is sad, as any good Scot well may be, about the condition of his country. He sees the failure of Scotland—among other failures—to recognize her contemporary poets (of which he himself is one under the name of McDiarmid). He feels the need and believes in the imminence of a Scottish Renaissance. But somehow it is uphill work. He will not blame Scotland or himself for this, but he must blame somebody and something. His eye is caught by the Burns cult, with its absurdities, vulgarities, sentimentalities and unrealities. From that his eye travels to the figure of the ploughman with its dwarfing effect upon other Scottish figures. It drives him mad. But he has found something to blame. He shouts 'Down with Burns!'.

If by shouting he and I could knock down the false image and overwhelm the smug folly at its foot, I would shout louder than Mr Grieve—in the sure knowledge that Burns would soon climb to a greater as well as a more desirable eminence. But I have more regard for my larynx. It cannot be done—that way.

Scottish writers, Mr Grieve says, will have nothing to do with the cult. Why should they? But, confusing the cult with the poet, he goes on to infer that therefore Scottish writers despise Burns. On the contrary, the fact is that they take his greatness a little too much for granted (I refer Mr Grieve to Edwin Muir's admiring essay on Burns). In what other country would serious writers have been deterred by the existence of a cult from constant discussion and re-examination of so remarkable a phenomenon.

The failure of Scotland in this respect shocks such 'foreign' writers as D.H. Lawrence. For some time Lawrence, in his veneration of Burns as man and poet, had the intention of repairing it himself. He gave it up, though with reluctance, only because he felt that the task demanded a knowledge of Scotland that no 'foreigner' could possess.

Yet he might have written his book if the critical and biographical ground had been in any degree prepared by Scotsmen. To take only one instance, where can one find a complete, accurate, critical text of Burns's extant letters? How can we look for a Scottish Renaissance, when a man like Mr Grieve, who should be a leader in it, is blind to facts that are obvious to the rest of the world?

As to what the rest of the world feels about Burns, an infallible test is provided by the world prices of Burnsiana in the saleroom.

If Mr Grieve thinks that Scotland's recent comparative poverty in drama, fiction, poetry and criticism is not Scotland's own fault (or misfortune) but Burns's, he is unable to think straight. Literary creativeness is not so easily checked as all that.

(Catherine Carswell, 'The "Giant Ploughman" Can Withstand His Critics', *Radio Times* 14 February 1930, p.376.)

4.8 Catherine Carswell, from *The Life of Robert Burns* (1930)

Among the Tarbolton girls it became understood that when Rab from Lochlie started to talk they should gather round to listen and laugh and watch his face. Often unpromising and heavy, it could, as they had learned, transform itself upon occasion, and their presence was usually occasion enough. Emboldened by his Irvine experiences he made love with great success at home and abroad. He knew—as the girls knew, but as Sillar with all his amorousness would never know—that love was the single flower of life for poor country people. It began to be whispered that an hour with him in the dark was worth a lifetime of daylight with any other lad. [. . .]

But Lizzie Paton he could not see as his wife. Neither could Gilbert nor his sisters. If they had been of their mother's opinion the united family might have been too much for Robert. But Gilbert was emphatic. The like of Lizzie Paton was no match for a Burnes. As for the sisters, one at least was to be of the Mossgiel household, and she wanted a particular girl friend of her own to live with them and help. There would be more than enough young women on the farm; besides a bachelor brother makes an easier master than one with a wife. Agnes Burns having been reduced to a disapproving silence, Lizzie was packed off to her widowed mother.

She made no complaint. She had, it appeared, a clear—some called it a masculine—outlook on life. She admitted that she had not been taken advantage of or misled by promises. She had merely been heartily, perhaps hopefully in love. [. . .]

True to his promise he saw Jean. He even went to the Cowgate to see her under the eyes of her parents. The interview was not a success. Jean did not seem to comprehend how basely she had acted. All she could see was that it was not yet too late for a securer marriage ceremony. Robert's inability to see this baffled her and put more power into her parents' hands.

Little did she or they guess that through their action he had now given himself irrevocably elsewhere. Had they so guessed, his leave-taking might have been unpleasanter than it was. As it was, Mr and Mrs Armour told him they never wished to see him again.

Yet he returned across the kirkyard with feelings for the faithless one that surprised him by their tenderness and passion. He had seen easily enough (Jean was not one to hide such things) that she still loved and quite simply wanted him. She wanted him even more than she wanted marriage, which was very loveable of her. Besides she was imbued with most endearing common-sense. As she must pay, why should she not have her fill of love? Somehow she had managed at parting to convey this view to him, and it was a view in which it was impossible for him not to rejoice. Mary had been gone a month, and a month is in certain respects a long time. He was certainly going to marry Mary. But there was still the attic window of Johny Dove's. He loved, he revered, he worshipped Mary. But an honest loving lass is an honest loving lass, for a' that and a' that.

(Catherine Carswell, *The Life of Robert Burns* (1930); reprinted from Edinburgh: Canongate Classics, 1990, pp.103, 119, 163.)

4.9 'Burns *Life* Furore' (*Daily Record* September 1930)

a) 'BAD SORT BUT—LOVABLE'

HIGHLAND LADY DEFENDS MRS CARSWELL'S BURNS

'A HIGHLAND WOMAN' writes:

I am astonished that so many of your readers express themselves as profoundly shocked or disillusioned by the extracts you have published from Mrs Carswell's *Life of Burns*.

My own reactions were entirely different and I cannot believe I am alone in this respect.

So far from being an 'attack' or a 'catalogue of peccadillos', her study struck me as unusually sympathetic and understanding. It is so splendidly free from moralising—the vice of nineteenth century biographers.

Of course, by Y.M.C.A. standards, Burns was a bad, sad young fellow—but *how* lovable!

Abnormal psychology? Is the capacity to love more than one woman a sign of abnormality? Shade of Holy Willie! The only sign of abnormal psychology I can detect in Burns was his ability to make immortal songs. [. . .] As for Highland Mary, I thought Mrs Carswell's picture very lovely and tender. Whether or not she gave herself to Burns in the fullest sense of the phrase, it is obvious that Mary was a chaste woman.

Chastity and virginity are not synonymous terms as the wrath of some of your correspondents would seem to imply.

To one of your readers at least Burns has emerged from your pages as one of the most lovable and tragic figures in the history of letters.

A HIGHLAND WOMAN

b) 'MODERN WOMAN AND BURNS'

'SUCH TRASH'

Sir,—Mrs Carswell may be a brilliant writer, but of what use is her brilliance when she tackles a subject that is obviously beyond her? [. . .] We are perfectly aware of all the facts she uses, but no discriminating critic would study Burns from the worst side of his nature, and it is regrettable that she has aimed for sensationalism rather than for truth. It is perhaps more regrettable that there is a public ready to read such trash.

Does Mrs Carswell represent the modern woman, or does she dare to think that her view of Burns is shared by the majority of her sex?

I have met few women who gloried in hearing of the seamy side of Burns, and if any exist they are, I am sure, few and far between.

Is purity of thought not of some biographical value? Where can one find purer songs than those of Burns? Has his great work in this field ever been truly estimated?

ALEX. MUTCH, PRESIDENT, SCOTTISH LITERATURE AND SONG ASSOCIATION, ABERDEEN.

c) 'ANT AND VESUVIUS'

Metaphorically, I would compare Mrs Carswell to an ant endeavouring to consume Vesuvius by nibbling at its base.

No, Mrs Carswell, Burns is too big for you. Try something or somebody else.

S.R. MILLAR

d) 'BOYCOTT NEW BURNS "LIFE"'

'PIECE OF FICTION'
'WOMANHOOD DEGRADED'

Sir,—It seems to me Burns lovers and admirers have the most effective answer in their own hands—*refrain from buying this book*. That, I venture to say, would affect Mrs Carswell more than all the adverse criticism being hurled at her.

Naturally, she wanted to produce a 'best seller', and being keenly alive to the drawing power of the magical name of Robert Burns, did not hesitate to attach it to what is largely a piece of fiction.

If the extracts already published are a sample of the terminological inexactitudes within its covers, then no bookshelf will be any the poorer for want of it.

Among the few who delight to wallow in the mud, Mrs Carswell's scurrilous book may find support.

JEAN ARMOUR, AYR

> (Responses to Catherine Carswell's *Life of Robert Burns*, correspondence pages
> *Daily Record*, 26, 27, 29 September 1930.)

4.10 Catherine Carswell, from letter to S.S. Koteliansky (September 1930)

> 3 Parkhill Studios,
> Parkhill Road, NW3
> 23 September

My dear Kot, [. . .]

I'm so glad you think well of the Burns so far as you have gone—it is to be taken primarily as a *book*, though of course it sets out to be a biography as well.

This morning (through the newspaper where it was serialised) I had an anonymous letter containing a *bullet*, which I was requested to use upon myself that the world might be left 'a brighter cleaner and better place'. So evidently the fun has started. Oh Scotland, oh my country!

> (Catherine Carswell, letter to S.S. Koteliansky 23 September [1930], British Library,
> Add.MS 48975, no.174.)

4.11 F. Marian McNeill, from 'The New Burns' (*Scots Independent* December 1930)

If any additional argument were needed for the re-establishment of a cultural centre in Scotland, it is provided by the spate of letters that followed the publication in the *Daily Record* of parts of Mrs Carswell's *Life of Robert Burns*. Here we have the inevitable chorus of the 'bodies', who provide a running commentary on Scottish life and letters, in the manner of a Greek chorus—but with what a difference! For whereas one speaks in the accent of ancient Athens, the other speaks in the accent of Drumtochty and Thrums.

Well, so long as we continue to export our aristocracy and intelligentsia en bloc, and to drive from the land, slumwards, shipwards, that sturdy population whose very proximity to the soil keeps their judgment in essential matters sound, so long must we thole the ascendancy of the 'petit bourgeois' or parish-pump mentality.

'What Scotland needs is brutal young men', the reviewer recently heard an Anglo-Scot remark—a man whose devotion to his 'pays d'origine' is tempered with something approaching despair at her complacent provincialism. Happily the 'brutal young men' are emerging—C.M. Grieve and his 'alter ego', Hugh McDiarmid, George Malcolm Thomson and Donald Carswell, to mention the most prominent—and at every brickbat they throw there is a burst of righteous indignation from the 'bodies'. And who can blame them? It isn't very pleasant to have one's cherished headgear knocked off and displayed to the world as a 'lum hat wantin a croon'. Later, perhaps, they may discover that some of the missiles that so sadly disturbed their complacency are of considerable intrinsic worth.

And now comes Mrs Carswell. It is not, of course, her first appearance. Her prize novel, *Open The Door!*, caused something of a sensation in those Glasgow circles whose gentility and humbug she satirises; in her second novel, *Camomile*, she seems almost deliberately to 'pull a long nose' at those same circles, like a high-spirited girl who has escaped from a tiresome governess; her *Burns*, however, is the work of a woman to whom freedom has become the air she breathes. She has not aimed at the 'bodies'; she had, in fact, forgotten their existence until 'as bees bizz out wi' angry fyke' they sallied forth in print.

Since bees sting, there must be balm in the thought that Burns himself would have loved this book, with its fearless sincerity and understanding. One can detect a strong bond of sympathy, almost an affinity, between the biographer and her subject—a common antipathy to shams and humbug, to the 'contumelious sneer' of gentility, and to cramping, ready-made codes; a common conviction that a man *is* a man 'for a' that'; a common charitableness to the sins of the flesh and abhorrence of the sins of the spirit; and, above all, a common love of 'fulness of life'. [. . .]

Mrs Carswell's writing is a sheer delight—cool, crisp, and invigorating as a fine harvest day—and her pages have a vividness reminiscent of *The House with the Green Shutters*. But surely her sketch of eighteenth-century Scotland in the Prelude is unjustifiably gloomy. She speaks of the 'dismal poverty of Scotland's inhabitants'. Poverty, yes. But dismal? 'I pitied their poverty', writes an English visitor in 1704, 'but observed the people were fresh and lusty, and did not seem to be under any uneasiness with their way of living'. We are told that 'the English traveller was shocked by their rags, their filth, their damp and smoky hovels.' No doubt, just as the English, or for that matter the Scottish visitor to-day, is shocked by the rags and filth, the damp and smoky tenements of Glasgow. But there is more to Glasgow than slums, and there was more to eighteenth-century Scotland than hovels. [. . .] And as for the lairds' houses 'with nothing of grace and little of comfort', in practically every county in Scotland to-day there stand delightful eighteenth-century houses with evidence of having possessed all the comfort of their period. The Adam brothers were not an isolated phenomenon. [. . .]

Apart from its unduly sombre tones, the Prelude is an admirable vignette and provides a fitting background for the warm and glowing life depicted in the book itself. [. . .]

Mrs Carswell has scandalised the 'bodies'; but in time—who knows— she may be regarded as a Joan of Arc who came to deliver Scotland from the deadly 'respectability' that is stifling not only the art of the nation, but also its morality which should be positive, not negative; dynamic, not static; and its religion, which should provide not a barred window, but a magic casement. Nothing would have pleased Burns more. When half-gods go, the gods arrive.

(F. Marian McNeill, 'The New Burns', *Scots Independent* December 1930, p.29.)

4.12 Edwin Muir, from 'Robert Louis Stevenson' (*Modern Scot* Autumn 1931)

In the general eclipse of Victorian reputations no one possibly has suffered more than Stevenson. For while the fillip of ironical or hostile criticism has galvanized his colleagues into a new life—a life which is probably unwelcome to them—Stevenson has simply fallen out of the procession. He is still read by the vulgar, but he has joined that band of writers on whom, by tacit consent, the serious critics have nothing to say. So extraordinary, indeed, is the neglect into which he has fallen that when one surveys his literary period, the period of Meredith, Hardy, Swinburne, Bridges, Pater, Henry James, Mr George Moore, Mr Kipling and Mr Shaw, it is only by an effort of memory that one contrives to include him. [. . .]

Stevenson died in 1894 in his forty-fourth year. That is to say, he was still, for a novelist, a young man. Moreover he was younger than his years, for he had spent his childhood and youth in a country where everything combined to prevent an imaginative writer from coming to maturity. After three centuries of a culture almost exclusively theological, imaginative literature in Scotland in Stevenson's time was tolerated, where it was tolerated at all, only as an idle toy. That a novel should influence the character or humanize the emotions was an un-Scottish idea; and if Stevenson's relatives and advisers had contemplated such a secular operation it would have seemed to them illegitimate and insidious; for by its working, morality, which should come uncontaminated from its pure source in religion or philosophy, entered the character by clandestine ways, indeed stole past conscience by lulling it to sleep, and took the soul by carnal wiles.

So one of the earliest ideas which must have been implanted in Stevenson's mind by universal suggestion was that storytelling was an idle occupation, and could be tolerated only as long as it remained so. He had before him, moreover, the example of his great countryman Scott, and he was probably too young, and too securely enclosed in national literary prejudice, to see that Scott's immense powers too were made idle by the general expectation of his countrymen that they should be idle. [. . .]

He shared another fault with Scott, and he has been nauseously praised for his boyish irresponsibility. This too may largely be put down to his early environment. A society which makes a writer a mere entertainer tacitly deprives him of any civic status, puts him among the superior mountebanks, and, if he is a man of independence, drives him into a showy Bohemianism. The defiantly picturesque pose which Stevenson assumed was in part at least the cloak under which he hoped to conceal his humiliating function, that of having to please everybody.

(Edwin Muir, 'Robert Louis Stevenson', *Modern Scot* 2:3 Autumn 1931, pp.196–204 [196–99].)

4.13 C.M. Grieve, 'The Scott Centenary' (*Free Man* October 1932)

No intelligent person can have witnessed the Edinburgh procession in connection with Scott's centenary without a sense of shame. It was a deplorable sight. There is nothing more intolerable than to see a file of nonentities dressed in pretentious robes. They were for the most part physically decrepit and mentally null—utterly unrepresentative of the realities of Scotland to-day, but, for that reason perhaps, in keeping with the occasion. Such an antiquarian cortege was appropriate to Scott's fame and an adequate commentary on its true character. The defensive note in most of the Centenary speeches was significant. Even if, we were told, Scott is little read and found intolerably prolix, dull, and full of false romanticism, he was a great man even more than a great writer and, while his financial dealings are ingeniously excused in one way or another, we are asked to admire his debt-paying feat. But being thus conventionally honest entailed a dishonesty to something infinitely greater, and no writer of world-wide fame had less artistic integrity or more snobbish contempt for his craft than Scott. His best work is in Braid Scots; would he had given us more of it. [. . .] Scottish realities are at last breaking through the haze of the false romanticism in which Scott wrapped them up. Scott, as Professor Gordon said, 'died in the gravest fear that the Scotland he had known and loved was launched on a course which would lead to ruin'. Precisely; he persisted in thinking of it in terms of the past—but it is just for that reason that there has been such a gulf between the generally accepted myth of Scotland to which he gave currency and the actual Scotland. He had no profound and progressive sense of his country yet here and there gave a glint of genuine mettle just as, in the enormous mass of his writing, he soared at times incalculably above his general level. It is all the more [note]worthy therefore that while speakers like Professors Paterson and Gordon could not keep some of the momentous developments impending in Scotland now out of their speeches, none of them referred to Malachi Malagrowther and Scott's unmistakeable stand in regard to the Scottish pound note. Surely Scott's attitude to what is now the crucial issue—the financial system—might have been stressed so that Scott would have been more effectively related to the current situation. And it would have been well to remember too that he was the last Scottish direct actionist prior to the development of the present Movement. Those of us who are all for militant tactics can claim that he once had sufficient intelligence to be of our company, and when fools deride us for our seditious talk remember that he erred like us and was determined to resort to arms. His intuitions were right but he did not ensue them. Would that he had! Facts like these are conveniently forgotten by the nit-wits who run such Centenary palavers.

(C.M. Grieve, 'At the Sign of the Thistle: The Scott Centenary', *Free Man* 1: 35, 1 October 1932, p.5.)

4.14   Edwin Muir, from *Scottish Journey* (1935)

a) On the Burns Cult

The whole problem of the Burns cult in Scotland is a peculiar one, and I may as well animadvert upon it here, since no book about Scotland can avoid it. Burns was a great poet, and a character of great likeableness and charm. He was also a man whose life and poetry are very difficult to separate; for the best of his poetry sprang directly out of his life. He expressed more perhaps than any other poet his workaday character in his poetry, throwing into it his daily hopes, fears, humours, affections, lusts, repentances, despairs, sentimentalities. With such a figure to work on, it was easy for the popular imagination to substitute the man, or an idealised effigy of him, for the whole Burns, forgetting that the poet was an essential part of him and that his actual life could not have been what it was if he had not possessed genius. This is roughly what has happened. To every Scotsman Burns is a familiar figure, a sort of household god, and most Scotsmen, I suppose, could reel off a few proverbial tags of his poetry, and one or two of his songs set to music. But that is all. This public effigy, in which the lover, the boon-companion and the democrat are the main ingredients, with a hard-working farmer in the background, but all subdued to respectability by time, is the real object of worship of the Burns cult. It is not a literary cult, but a social one. It has very little to do with Burns, and is concerned chiefly with the perpetuation of a myth. In that myth Burns becomes an ordinary man like his devotees, which he was not. He also becomes a successful lover and a free and glorious companion, which everybody would like to be. His myth is thus based on a firm foundation of sanctified illusion and romantic wish fulfilment. This legendary figure is a Scotsman who took upon him all the sins of the people, not to redeem them, but to commit them as ideally as they should be committed, that is, freely and guiltlessly, in an imaginary world beyond good and evil, a Paradisal Kailyard with a harmless domesticated serpent; for even to the most respectable of Burns's worshippers, to elders and ministers of the Kirk, Burns's sins are in a special category, and his fornications have the prescriptive right of King David's. He was a scapegoat driven out to sweet pastures, while the people elected to remain in the wilderness; a god who sanctified the meagre indulgences of the many by unlimited loving and drinking.

This is not an unfair description of what Burns means to Scotland as a racial myth. The Burns of popular legend is an imaginative incarnation of a people's desires, unfulfilled in life. It has no fundamental resemblance to Burns himself.

b) On Scott's Abbotsford

Abbotsford is a very strange house. It is a place certainly well-suited to be displayed, to astonish, to stagger, and to sadden; but that it should ever have been lived in is the most astonishing, staggering, saddening thing of all. One feels, while wandering through it, that one is on the track of a secret more intimate than either Scott's biography or his written works can tell; and that if one stayed here long enough one would at last understand the mania which drove him to create this pompous, crude, fantastic, unmanageable, heartless, insatiable, comfortless brute of a house, and sacrifice to it in turn his genius, his peace of mind, his health and his life. Everything in it, except the study with its secret stair, where Scott slipped down in the early morning to write his romances unknown to his guests, is designed for ostentation; it is a huge showroom of vulgar romantic properties. The library, a long wide hall with high windows looking down on the Tweed, is like a public library. The house itself, with its persistently repeated turrets, might be a railway hotel designed in the baronial style. In this barracks antique swords, armorial bearings, ancient suits of mail, dungeon keys, and all kinds of rusty lumber meet one at every turn. Archbishop Sharp's fire-grate and Balfour of Burley's snuff-box; the pulpit of the old kirk of Dunfermline and the door of the old Tolbooth Prison; Burns's toddy tumbler and Napoleon's pen and writing-case; a German heading-sword and the crucifix which Mary Stuart bore on her way to execution; Rob Roy's purse, sporran, claymore and dirk; Prince Charlie's quaich; the keys of Selkirk jail and Lochleven Castle; sabres, cutlasses, daggers, pistols, blunderbusses: Scott, it seems, could not have enough of such things, and could swallow the most crude and worthless lumber if it was only sanctified by history. The ceiling of the library is a bad copy of the carvings in Roslin Chapel. The walls of the drawing-room are covered with emerald-green Chinese wall-paper. It shows scenes of Chinese life interwoven with floral scrolls, and near the door Mr George Bernard Shaw, in a Chinese robe, can be seen talking a century before his time. It is an astonishingly faithful likeness; easily, indeed, the best I have ever come across.

The study, a smaller, square, high room, is the place in the house which one can most nearly believe in. The desk is enormous, being both high and massive, and makes one realise that Scott was almost a giant. Here, to use his own phrase about Byron, he 'wielded his pen with the negligent ease of a man of quality'. One imagines him stealing down in the morning before his guests were awake, finishing off a paper duel, changing, and appearing in the dining-room surrounded by his dogs, a Border laird more convincing than nature. A fantastic life in a fantastic house.

To realise how fantastic that life was one has only to look at Raeburn's magnificent portrait which hangs in the Chinese drawing-room. Chantrey's bust in the library, said to be the best likeness of Scott, shows us merely the laird. But Raeburn's portrait is that of a very remarkable man. The fine eyes have a gipsy fire beneath the overhanging brows, but the whole expression is one of passion so firmly suppressed that it seems to darken every feature, giving out smoke instead of flame except through the eyes. The body, leaning forward as if preparing to spring, looks twisted and dwarf-like in spite of its bulk, and the arms have a contorted look, as if they were straining against invisible fetters. This broad and twisted body surmounted by the powerful head with its flashing eyes is both menacing and pathetic; expressing simultaneously consciousness of power and of defeat. The face might be that of a lifelong outcast or a lifelong prisoner who has never resigned himself to his lot.

As impressive in another way is the death mask that lies in the turret-room. It shows the face of a man who, after struggling on courageously and drawing on his powers to the end, has found that that is not enough; so that all the features are fixed in painful surprise. The mouth is pulled down like that of a hurt child; but the rest of the face expresses steady offence.

This mask, like Raeburn's portrait, shows passion in every line: offended pride, hurt vanity, defeated ambition, frustrated hope. Abbotsford impresses one as the concrete expression of this passion; for only that can make it comprehensible, and Scott's strong and deadly attachment to it; explaining its fantastic tastelessness and ostentation, even its comfortlessness. [. . .] It must have been the *Ivanhoe* side of Scott that built and furnished Abbotsford. Consequently it is both real and unreal, like *Ivanhoe*, and has the inspired tastelessness of a substitute which is indispensable. It is surely the saddest and strangest monument that Scott's genius created.

(Edwin Muir, *Scottish Journey* London: Heinemann, 1935, pp.89–91; 57–60, 61.)

4.15 Edwin Muir, from *Scott and Scotland* (1936)

a) From 'Introductory'

The riddle which confronted me in approaching Scott himself, by far the greatest creative force in Scottish literature as well as one of the greatest in English, was to account for a very curious emptiness which I felt behind the wealth of his imagination. Many critics have acknowledged this blemish in Scott's work, but have either made no attempt to account for it, or else have put it down to a defect in Scott's mind and character. Yet men of Scott's enormous genius have rarely Scott's faults; they may have others but not these particular ones; and so I was forced to account for the hiatus in Scott's endowment by considering the environment in which he lived, by invoking the fact—if the reader will agree it is one—that he spent most of his days in a hiatus, in a country, that is to say, which was neither a nation nor a province, and had, instead of a centre, a blank, an Edinburgh, in the middle of it. But this Nothing in which Scott wrote was not merely a spatial one; it was a temporal Nothing as well, dotted with a few disconnected figures arranged at abrupt intervals: Henryson, Dunbar, Allan Ramsay, Burns, with a rude buttress of ballads and folk songs to shore them up and keep them from falling. Scott, in other words, lived in a community which was not a community, and set himself to carry on a tradition which was not a tradition; and the result was that his work was an exact reflection of his predicament. His picture of life had no centre, because the environment in which he lived had no centre. What traditional virtue his work possessed was at second hand, and derived mainly from English literature, which he knew intimately but which was a semi-foreign literature to him. Scotland did not have enough life of its own to nourish a writer of his scope; it had neither a real community to foster him nor a tradition to direct him; for the anonymous ballad tradition was not sufficient for his genius. So that my inquiry into what Scotland did for Scott came down finally to what it did not do for Scott. What it did not do, or what it could not do. Considered historically these alternatives are difficult to separate.

Having traced Scott's greatest fault to his geographical and historical position as a writer, I began to wonder what he might have been, given his genius, if he had been born into a genuine organic society such as England, or even into a small self-subsistent state like Weimar. Could he possibly have left his picture of life in such a tentative state, half flesh and blood and half pasteboard, unreal where he dealt with highly civilized people, and real where he dealt with peasants, adventurers and beggars? Would he not have been forced to give it a unity? or rather, would not a sociological unity at least have been there without his having to make a specific effort to achieve it? To ask such questions is not criticism; but the object of this book is not criticism. I wish merely to define the position of the Scottish writer, and then to inquire by what means he can come to completeness, what help Scotland can give him in doing so, and what obstacles she puts in his way. There is at present a general disposition in Scotland to blame Scottish writers who turn to the English tradition when they are faced with this problem. I shall have to consider whether they should do so, or rather whether they have any choice but to do so.

b) From 'Scott and Scotland'

Scott's first important work was the *Minstrelsy of the Scottish Border*. This book was essentially an attempt to save something of a Scotland that was disappearing. 'By such efforts,' Scott said, 'feeble as they are, I may contribute something to the history of my native country; the peculiar features of whose manners and character are daily melting and dissolving into those of her sister and ally. And, trivial as may appear such an offering to the Manes of a kingdom, once proud and independent, I hang it upon her altar with a mixture of feelings which I shall not attempt to describe.'

There is no mistaking the emotion in these words, and I think it is not hard to guess at the mixture of feelings which Scott shrank from describing. He was a man to whom the established order was sacred. The Union between Scotland and England was an accomplished fact, a solid part of the established order. He accepted it as such, and although Jacobite sentiment still excited his imagination, it had no effect on his practical judgment. [. . .]

At the same time he saw 'the peculiar features of [Scotland's] manners and character . . . daily melting and dissolving into those of her sister and ally'. His strong instinct for continuity showed him Scotland as 'a kingdom, once proud and independent'. It is clear from this passage that Scott regarded with acute concern the inevitable melting and dissolving of Scotland's manners and character into those of England [. . .] One has the impression already that Scott can find a real image of Scotland only in the past, and knows that the nation which should have formed both his theme and his living environment as a writer is irremediably melting away around him. He was nearer the beginning of that process than we are, he saw its end more clearly, and had a more complete image of what was involved. [. . .]

I began this inquiry by asking what Scotland did for Scott, and I have tried briefly to show what it was able to give him and what it could not give him. Nature endowed him with a genius universal in its scope. Scotland provided a body of heroic legend for that genius to work upon. But it could not give him a complete framework of living experience on which to nourish his powers and exercise them; in other words, it could not give him a basis for the profound criticism of life of which there is no doubt that he was capable, as can be seen from a few of his lyrics, drawn from his secret world, and such scenes as the climax of *Redgauntlet*. It could not give him a tradition, for its tradition was melting and dissolving away; so it offered him a legend instead. Yet his essential gift was for the delineation of contemporary life, and his work is greatest where we feel in it the shock of immediate experience. [. . .]

I have said nothing about Scott's relation to the Scottish vernacular, since his relation to the society or no-society in which he lived seemed to me of far more importance. But his attitude to Scots was pretty much the same as I have outlined already in the first part of this essay. Where he wished to express feelings of more than ordinary seriousness and range, or feelings modified by thought, he employed English, using Scots for the simplest purposes of humour and pathos. His Scots, it is true, was far better than his English, and he produced in his dialogue the best Scots prose that has ever been written. But as the Scots vernacular did not come out of a unity, he felt that it could not express a unity; so for the structural, the unifying, part of his work he relied upon English. This again is bound up with his divided allegiance and his final acceptance of the established order. But the determining fact was a social and political one: that he lived in a country which could not give an organic form to his genius.

(Edwin Muir, *Scott and Scotland: the Predicament of the Scottish Writer*,
pp.11–14; 136–37, 138–40, 172–75.)

4.16   Neil M. Gunn, from review of *Scott and Scotland* (*Scots Magazine* October 1936)

Scott was so great a genius that what he dealt in must have some reality to the mind of living men. It is not that the history was untrue or was inadequate subject matter for his genius; it was that it no longer enriched or influenced a living national tradition; it had not even the potency of pure legend; it was story-telling or romance set in a void; it was seen backwards as in the round of some time spyglass and had interpretive bearing neither upon a present nor a future.

(Neil M. Gunn, review of *Scott and Scotland*, *Scots Magazine* 26 October 1936, pp.72–78 [73].)

New Directions

4.17   Reah Denholm, from 'The National Theatre Movement' (*Scots Magazine* July 1924)

To-day a new movement is afoot. Three years ago, with very little money and that little raised by means of a guarantee loan, and with practically no beating of drums, a small band of people, calling themselves The Scottish National Players, made their first bow to the public in a hall in Glasgow, and intimated with a modest gesture that their object was nothing less than to found a National Theatre and aid in the creating of a national drama.

The actual inception of the movement dates back to 1913. At that time the Repertory Theatre in Glasgow was still in active existence, but a feeling was abroad that something might be done to establish a company which would deal more directly with Scottish themes, for, although the Repertory people, a brilliant and able band, were registered as The Scottish Playgoers Company, they seldom produced Scottish plays or work by Scottish authors. The first impulse to provide Scotland with a drama emanated from a few active spirits in the Saint Andrew Society (Glasgow)—among them the movement's present chairman and one of its vice-chairmen, Mr D. Glen MacKemmie and Mr W. Ralph Purnell—and crystallised in discussion; a sub-committee of the parent body was appointed, a company was formed, and plays were advertised for. Everything was in readiness for a beginning in 1914, when the war cloud broke over Europe, and for the time being blotted out all such activities. When peace came at last and the personnel of the movement drifted back from war service, that first simple venture I have spoken of was made in January, 1921, in the Royal Institute Hall, with three little plays—*Châtelard*, by C. Stewart Black; *Cute M'Cheyne*, by Joseph Laing Waugh; and *Glenforsa*, by John Brandane and A.W. Yuill. That first attempt was successful; but a second, equally modest, experiment, still under the wing of the Saint Andrew Society, was tried three months later, which again resulted in enthusiastic houses as a sign from the public, and praise and encouragement on the part of the press. A move was then made to the Athenaeum theatre, where five new plays were staged, and then, and not till then, The Scottish National Players ceased to be a sub-committee of the Saint Andrew Society, and, taking their courage in both hands, faced the future and its responsibilities alone and unaided.

In January of the following year a public meeting was held, and the Scottish National Theatre Society formed. To-day that Society numbers nearly eight hundred members on its roll. The birth of the new organisation took place, luckily, at the passing away of the Glasgow Repertory Company, and most of the shareholders in the older movement handed over the dividends on their holdings to the new Society. Among these supporters were Lord Howard de Walden, Sir J.M. Barrie, Mr John Galsworthy, and Dr Neil Munro. Thus the Scottish National Theatre Society, its players, its members, and its supporters, are in one sense the legitimate descendants of the Glasgow Repertory Theatre.

The aims of the Society are, briefly, threefold: (1) to develop Scottish National Drama, (2) to encourage in Scotland a public taste for good drama of any type, (3) to found a Scottish National Theatre.

The new movement, it will be seen, is anxious to reverse the policy of its predecessor, the Glasgow Repertory Theatre. That Company's way of doing was to produce one Scottish play to twenty or thirty alien pieces. That is a rough guess. What I want to convey is that productions of 'native' drama by that company were very rare. The Scottish National Theatre Society, on the other hand, make this their primary object. As every reader of this article, however, is a potential playwright, it may be as well to state two facts at this point. This first. The Reading Committee of the Society is not seeking for plays of the kailyard school, nor for pieces modelled on 'Rob Roy' or 'Cramond Brig', nor for conventional caricatures of the 'pawky' Scot such as we have all grown accustomed to see portrayed on the English stage; it does not hunger after dialect nor thirst particularly for 'but-and-ben' atmosphere or room-and-kitchen squalor. Its aim is to present in dramatic form the real life of Scotland, past and present, of every grade and shade, from every angle. It is looking for plays national in essence and outlook and atmosphere, but free from exaggeration of any kind. Secondly, this. The Society is non-political. In its ranks the Conservative 'lamb' lies down with the Socialist 'lion', all shades of party feelings are merged in a nationalism and a patriotism that are entirely free from political or international arrogance. It seeks to create rather than to destroy. It is anxious to call forth a national spirit that, while keeping green the memory of its own greatness, will add its quota to the accumulative wealth of all the nations. At the same time the Society is quite willing to produce plays dealing with political life or any phase of it in Scotland, because political life is part of Scotland; but these plays must have the red blood of drama in their veins, they must have stage value, historical accuracy, and literary merit. [. . .]

When the Scottish National Players set their movement afoot three years ago, they had to look across the sea to Ireland to find a tradition, an inspiration, a model, call it what you will. They found it ready to their hand in the works of J.M. Synge, W.B. Yeats, Lady Gregory, and the others who gave the Irish Players the stuff of which their drama is made. The Irish movement made the mistake of wandering for three years in the wilderness with English professional players, after which it came to itself and organised a trained company of native Irish actors, amateur in the sense that they were not paid. Then, and only then, did it make its histrionic mark. The Scottish movement wisely made use of this valuable piece of experience. It formed a native company at the beginning, and can now claim that it has travelled a little way along the road which leads to its heart's desire. [. . .]

I see there is a call from one quarter for the Scottish National Theatre Society to seek a new and distinctive form for the Scots drama, 'to approach problems of releasing Scots psychology into dramatic forms . . . unfettered by the stale commercialised conceptions of alien theatredoms'. Perhaps there is something in the idea, but it is not, of course, new. All down the history of the world's stage, someone somewhere has been calling for a new form, and sometimes, as Ibsen is claimed to have done, finding it. But these so-called new forms, once they have had their little day, are either dropped or assimilated into the older methods. Form is important, but the play as a whole is still the thing; and after all, the oldest methods of all have produced dramas unsurpassable. The *Medea* and *King Lear* are finer and more terrible plays than *Brand*. What the newer methods that are being tried here and there to-day can do remains to be seen, but this can be said on behalf of the Scottish National Theatre Society: if a dramatist of vision and imagination and passion, who can scale all the heights and plumb all the depth of Scots psychology, cares to break out into a new form, that will not prejudice his work in the eyes of the Society. Genius can make its own form in any art. But to pour scorn on accepted forms is of little use until you have something better to put in their place.

(Reah Denholm, 'The National Theatre Movement', *Scots Magazine* July 1924; reprinted from subsequent publication as pamphlet, Glasgow University Theatre Archive, Special Collections, Glasgow University Library.)

4.18   From inaugural editorial (*Modern Scot* Spring 1930)

If the pronouncements of such 'good Europeans' as Gide and Keyserling, and the alterations made in the map of Europe by the treaty of Versailles can be taken as truly representative of the spirit of the age, autonomy of race and not a United States of the World is the ideal of both the philosophers and the politicians of to-day. The progress made by the new European states both in economic and intellectual spheres is sufficient indication as to the successful results of racial self-government.

It is our own firm conviction that whatever lasting benefits Scotland may receive will come through the re-establishment of an independent government and of an individual Scottish culture. Nothing will be gained from the imitation of such cultural institutions as the English provinces now enjoy: little theatres, repertory cinemas, Sunday concerts, and the like, unless these are actively used as a means of exploiting Scottish talent and of raising the present standards in Scottish music and drama. We believe that in spite of the gradual centralisation in London of both Scotland's government and intellect, the fundamental differences between Scottish and English character have remained unchanged, and that both the vernacular and the Gaelic can still effectively be used as national media of expression.

In spite of the immense amount of spade work for the movement which has already been done by such pioneers as the Hon. Ruaraidh Erskine of Marr, C.M. Grieve, and others, the Scottish Renaissance is still in its infancy. Although the new Vernacular movement in poetry is now firmly on its feet, although there are now Scottish artists and critics who have acquired a European reputation without having to sacrifice their nationality, there are still vast fields in the arts and in literature which have yet to be explored and developed. It will be the purpose of the *Modern Scot* to provide an organ for those artists and writers whose experiments are most valuable to Scotland to-day and through whom our new culture may come into being.

(Inaugural editorial [J.H. Whyte], *Modern Scot* 1:1 spring 1930, p.5.)

4.19 'The Porpoise Press' (*Modern Scot* Spring 1930)

One of the chief causes of Scotland's present intellectual dependence upon England and the reason why so little original Scottish thought and literature appears is that, apart from the small but excellent presses of Aeneas Mackay at Stirling and Alexander Gardner, of Paisley, there is not one publishing firm in the country exclusively devoted to books on Scotland or by Scots authors. And this is in spite of the fact that Scottish printing is well known to be of extremely high standard and that a large proportion of English publishers have their books printed in Edinburgh.

The re-establishment, therefore, of the Porpoise Press in Edinburgh under the management of George Blake and George Malcolm Thomson is an important event in the course of Scottish Letters. Until recently in the hands of Mr Charles Graves, the Porpoise Press has hitherto confined its activities to the artistic production of poems by prominent Scottish poets, but under

135

the new management its scope is to be considerably enlarged. The Press will shortly issue a series of pamphlets dealing with Scottish topics, and it is hoped that in the autumn it may publish a new novel by a well-known Scottish writer.

('The Porpoise Press', *Modern Scot* 1:1 spring 1930, p.55.)

4.20 'Scotland and the Cinema' (*Modern Scot* Spring 1930)

This last winter has definitely proved that the cinema has at last been recognized in Scotland as an art form. Two film societies have been started in Glasgow and Dundee on similar lines to those in England, and have shown many Russian and German films of great artistic value which under ordinary circumstances would never be seen. The workers' Film Society recently founded in Edinburgh has already shown *Mother*, *Turksib*, and *The End of St Petersburg* to large and appreciative audiences.

Owing to the uncertainties of transport and the scarcity of first-class silent films available in this country—not to mention the spasmodic activities of the ever-watchful civic authorities—it is extremely difficult for Scottish Film Societies to be certain of securing the films they really want and of receiving them in time. It is, however, to be hoped that the Atlas Company, who have recently been formed in order to import German and Russian films of outstanding merit, will help to increase the number of good films and also that the parliamentary commission which is at present sitting to discuss the troubled question of film censorship will soon remove the official ban from Soviet films.

Two films on Scottish subjects have been shown publicly within the last year, *The Loves of Robert Burns*, a talkie, produced in Elstree by Alfred Hitchcock, with Joseph Hyslop in the title role, and *Drifters*, a silent picture produced by John Grierson for New Era. The first film, in spite of excellent singing by Mr Hyslop, did not run for long in London; even the English critics found the story unconvincing. *Drifters*, on the other hand, has received praise from all parties and was shown to the Film Society in London on November 10th. In Mr Grierson's own words, 'it is about the sea and about fishermen, and there is not a Piccadilly actor in the piece. The men do their own acting and the sea does its—and if the result does not bear out the 107th Psalm it is my fault.' Mr Grierson, who comes from Glasgow, has studied American and Continental film technique, and is better acquainted than any other director in this country with the problems of photography and montage. His next film, on which he is at present engaged, is to be a multi-lingual record of British industry entitled *Smoke and Steel*.

(Unsigned article, 'Scotland and the Cinema', *Modern Scot* 1:1 spring 1930, p.53.)

4.21 Murray McClymont, 'A Scottish Theatre: The Need for a New Form' (*Modern Scot* Winter 1930)

When I speak of a Scottish theatre I do not mean a playhouse. I mean a distinctive manifestation of the national consciousness in terms of theatrical art.

The more one thinks about a Scottish theatre, however, the more one realises the futility of discussing it at all while yet the view prevails in Scotland that the drama must precede the theatre, the cart the horse. For, so long as this sequence obtains, so long will our theatre societies, drama groups, producers and players continue to labour under the stagnating delusion that our dramatists have 'let them down'. Such is their constant cry. Actually, of course, it is they who are letting not only dramatists but Scotland down, for the theatre must come before the drama, the theatrical medium before the dramatic expression. Dramatic literature is not written literature but oral literature, and authors who are dramatists have no option but to write their plays, as Mr St John Ervine has phrased it, for available 'machines'.

Here in Scotland the national consciousness manifests itself in our religion, in our laws, even on our 'rugger' and 'soccer' fields. But does it do so theatrically? Do we act, produce, and interpret plays in a manner peculiar to ourselves? Are there discoverable in all our present-day activities—from the polished productions of the S.N.T.S. down to the crudest efforts of our village groups—any distinctive habits which might conceivably be called Scottish? I know of none. I know of only one theatre in Scotland, the English theatre, which has been established here for over two hundred years and is the true explanation of our dramatic poverty. Scotland has no national drama because she has failed to provide her writers with a national medium for the release of Scottish genius in terms of drama. There is no Scottish theatre: there are merely obstructionists who delay its coming by asserting its existence without proof.

National drama is universal drama. Drama whose appeal is national is parochial drama. I commend the distinction to the notice of the S.N.T.S. Universality in drama is, however, a matter of emotional and intellectual content, not of form. Form is national. It is national because tastes differ, no two races think alike, each must approach the universal in a manner consistent with itself. Form is therefore an expression of the national consciousness, a manifestation of the racial need. All forms may lead to the universal and one be as good as another, but each nation (if it be a nation and not a tribe of denationalized humbugs) must approach the universal in its own peculiar way. That way attainment lies. The alternative, as our drama proves, is imitation and defeat. [. . .]

Scattered creative endeavours will not, of course, constitute of themselves a Scottish theatre. They will, however, call for uniformity. Thus we arrive at the point to which in the end all discussion of our dramatic poverty returns—a Scottish playhouse. There can be no Scottish theatre without it. For it has been found elsewhere that in order to raise the level of art in a country and give meaning and direction to group enthusiasm it is necessary that there be one consummate scene of action for the purposes of development and example. But just as the theatre must come before the drama, so must the creative efforts precede the unifying authority. When our theatre societies, drama groups, producers and players have apprehended, as sooner or later they must, why no Maecenas like Morozov in Russia and Miss Horniman in Ireland has appeared on the Scottish horizon since wee Allan Ramsay made his costly gesture in Carrubber's Close, the day of Scotland's dramatic renaissance will have dawned.

(Murray McClymont, 'A Scottish Theatre: The Need for a New Form', *Modern Scot* 1:4 winter 1930, pp.5–9 [5–6, 9].)

4.22 William Power, 'Community Drama and the Renaissance: A New Theatre Public' (*Scottish Stage* March 1932)

James Bridie, not long ago, wrote an icily scathing letter to a London paper about the ape-like behaviour of a Glasgow audience which, through some collective misapprehension, found itself at a really good play.

Once at least I have witnessed that kind of thing. It is an appalling experience—from the humiliating horror of which one seeks evade by trying to figure out how all those well-fed and well-dressed people had contrived to escape any tincture of education, imagination, or manners; and how, in a city with over 100,000 unemployed, they managed to justify their economic existence.

'There', one can imagine a Russian Communist exclaiming, 'are your precious bourgeois! Do you wonder we despise them?'

Frankly, I don't, if the Russian Communist believes that the bourgeois are typified by our chocolate audience.

On its favourite sweetmeat alone, with which it stays itself during a performance, our chocolate audience spends more money each year, I should think, than would be required to keep going a first-rate repertory theatre. That is the kind of reflection that has been gall to idealists in all ages. [. . .]

When one considers, also, the notorious decline in the financial support for orchestral concerts and good opera, one is compelled to face a big social fact. The 'moneyed' audience, on which good drama and music have hitherto tried to depend—the audience that can afford big prices for seats, not to speak of chocolates and ice-cream—is hopeless. Money and taste have definitely parted company. We have to set ourselves, in Scotland at least, to the creation of a new audience—fit and not few.

May we not take it that the Scottish National Theatre Society represents largely a gallant but vain attempt to win over a section of the 'moneyed' audience to the cause of good native drama, and that the Community Drama movement represents a going down to the root of the matter?

From the point of view of the highbrow purist, the Community Drama Festival may be only a kind of 'parlour game'. But it is also a kitchen game, a factory game, a mine game, a byre game. Not slowly, and surely, it has diffused awareness of truths the moneyed audience never knew—that all the world's a stage, and all the men and women merely players; and that the essence of drama is inner fidelity to actual life.

Hundreds of companies, with an equal number of intimately interested audiences, and thousands of actors and actor-aspirants, have been called into being, mostly in regions that had known nothing better than the poorest American films. The poorest of the plays being performed are intrinsically better than the plays that draw the chocolate audience.

It was in much the same fashion, from village orchestras and choirs, and private quartets and quintets, that German music was built up. The Elizabethan theatre arose out of the amateur performances of the old guilds.

The people that sat in darkness have seen a great light. Permanently valuable in itself, Community Drama is also creating for the 'professional' theatre a huge new public which financially will balance or outweigh the chocolate audience.

For this new public, I hope, new theatres will be built, all pit and gallery, in the cities and big towns; and from the Community companies there will be a large accession to the numbers of professional actors with whom the artistic quality of plays is a consideration as well as the amount of salaries.

That aspect of the Scottish Renaissance was undreamt of by the founders of the Scottish National Theatre Society. They went out after asses and were the means of finding a kingdom. Yet the process was unconsciously anticipated in the nature of some of the Scots plays for which a 'moneyed' audience was vainly sought and which, or plays like them, are being acted by Community players.

The time is about ripe for entering on the 'European' phase of the Renaissance in the field of drama by garnering for a professional and established Scots Theatre some of the fruits of Community Drama.

(William Power, 'Community Drama and the Renaissance: A New Theatre Public', *Scottish Stage* March 1932, p.7.)

4.23 'James Bridie on the Theatre: Address to Glasgow Students' (*Glasgow Herald* November 1933)

Rhetoric in the theatre was the subject of the presidential address which was delivered last night to the Glasgow University Dialectic Society by Dr O.H. Mavor, known to the theatre-going public as James Bridie. Dr Mavor defined rhetoric as declamatory speech, which, he said, consisted of formally built sentences containing one or more conventionalised climaxes, and intended to be declaimed or even shouted in a highly emotional manner. Having quoted passages from various dramatists in order to illustrate his meaning, Dr Mavor proceeded to discuss the question—What do you want from the theatre? It was obvious, he remarked, that some people were interested in surface anatomy, others in dirty jokes. To some the theatre was a place in which one could digest a heavy meal. To some it was a cross between a laboratory and a church. To many it was a gilded frame for the beloved form of well-graced actor or notorious actress.

But these wants were superficial, limited, and easily satisfied. There must be something more fundamental about an art that had lain closer to the hearts of the people than any of its more reputable sisters—that had attracted to its service some of the most magnificent minds capriciously put by Providence into human skulls. The novel made a poor show against the drama. In the theatre most of us seemed to want one of two things—a vision of life or an escape from life. And the preference to which we leaned was a fair index of what sort of people we were.

SIR JAMES BARRIE'S APPEAL

Only people who were unfit for life wanted to escape from it. Healthy people wanted to control it or to use it and feel it more intensely. Sir James Barrie, whose great contribution to the theatre and literature was his revival of the witchcraft of the old ballad, could produce an unexpected effect upon us by a turn of phrase or twist of an idea that was almost stunning in its impact. But we must be moralists first and aesthetes afterwards, and Barrie was a thoroughly immoral and decadent writer. He was the dramatist of Escape. He appealed to the child in all of us—that was to say, to the fantastic, amoral, lying, cruel, treacherous, wicked little shirker and coward who was the living justification of the doctrine of original sin. The boy who would not grow up was a familiar figure in psychiatry, and he had none of the charm of Peter Pan. He had introduced Barrie because Sir James really could write the Drama of Escape, and that was not so easy as some people supposed. To produce illusion it was necessary to have a fairly steady stance on the good hard ground.

140

ESSENTIALS OF A PLAY

Strong, self-satisfied, hard-headed people knew the Drama of Escape for what it was and they had no use for it. They wanted interpretation, or, at least, translation, and not dope. It could be as graceful as they liked, as oblique and subtle as they liked, but it must translate real life. It must propose them problems. It need not, as some buffle-headed idiots of dramatic critics thought, solve them. A play was only a story, and they could not solve a problem in a story. If everything was not done to hold our interest, to utilise to the full the pleasure of the eye, the ear, and the mind a play was not a play at all. A play should be entertaining, always remembering that, to grown-up people, the raising of a salacious giggle was not the only available form of entertainment.

(Unsigned report, 'James Bridie on the Theatre: Address to Students', *Glasgow Herald* 16 November 1933, p.2.)

4.24 Lewis Grassic Gibbon, 'A Novelist Looks at the Cinema' (*Cinema Quarterly* Winter 1934/35)

Perhaps, in the interests of truth and alliteration, this should read A Philistine looks at the Films.

As becomes a good Scots novelist, I live in a pleasant village near London; and, in the intervals of writing novels for a livelihood and writing history for pleasure, I attend of an evening the local cinema. It is popularly known as the bug house; the jest having long staled, there is no longer even a suggestion of vocal quotes around this insulting misnomer. For it is certainly a misnomer. The seats are comfortably padded, even for ninepence; a girl with trim ankles and intriguing curls comes round at intervals with a gleaming apparatus and sprays the air with sweet-smelling savours; the ashtrays are large and capacious; and it is amusing, in the intervals, to brood upon one's neighbours and consider the wild growth of hair which furs the necks of women who neglect the barber.

But at this point the Big Picture comes on. In the first hour we have witnessed two news reels; a speech by Signor Mussolini, simian and swarthy (why has Hollywood never offered him adequate inducements to understudy King Kong?); shots of a fire in a London factory, taken from the roof of a nearby building which was surely a public-house owned by a pressing philanthropist, so desperately poor is the photography and so completely moronic the camera-man in missing every good angle of vision; and No.CVII of Unusual Jobs, showing the day-to-day life of an Arizonan miner who has turned an empty gallery into a home for sick and ailing bats. Then has followed the Travelogue.

Travelogues in English bug houses (for I'll keep the homely misnomer) deal with only two portions of this wide and terrible planet of ours. We are never shown the Iguazu Falls or the heights of the Andes or the snows on Popocatepetl; or North Africa and the white blaze of sunlight across Ghizeh; or S. Sophia brooding over Constantinople; or Edinburgh clustered reeking about its hill; or London in summer; or the whores' quarters in Bombay; or the bleak and terrible tracks that were followed by the Alaskan treks of '98' or Mophenjo-Daro, the cradle of Indian civilization; or the manger in Bethlehem at Christmas time, with the pilgrims swopping diseases on the holy stones; or the pygmies of the Wambutti; or the Punak of Borneo, a quarter of a million of them, naked, cultureless, happy, the last folk of the Golden Age; or the dead cities of Northern England, cities of more dreadful night than that dreamt by Thomson; or. . . .

We are shown instead, wearyingly, unendingly, *ad infinitum* and *ad nauseam*, the fishers of Iceland and the dancing-girls of Bali. A strange, unrecorded tabu has smitten the travelogue-makers; the rest of the earth, those two islands apart, is forbidden their observation. So, with faith and fortitude, twice a week, we sit in the bug house and watch Iceland—mostly female Iceland—grin upon us over the salted cadaver of the unlucky cod; we gaze upon unending close-ups of gigantic buttocks bent in arduous toil; we blink upon geysers and giggling Scandinavian virgins. . . . Or, in Bali, we watch the Devil Dance. The girls appear in masks; the novice film-fan deplores these masks till later he sees a group of the girls without them. Then he understands that even the devil has an aesthetic eye. . . .

Next, Mr Laurel and Mr Hardy have entertained us with a desperate vigour. They have sawn themselves in halves, fallen down chimneys, eaten gold-fish, married their sisters, committed arson, or slept in insect-infested beds. And gradually, whatever the pursuit, the grin has faded from our faces. We are filled with awareness of a terrible secret unknown to the lords of the films: that the dictum on art being long and life short was never intended for injudicious application to a single-reel comedy. . . . Mr Hardy has discovered fleas in his bed. Excellent! We laugh. The flea has infested the skirts of the Comic Muse since the days of Akhnaton. But Mr Hardy is still horrified or astounded. Yard upon yard of celluloid flicks past, and we await fresh developments. There are no fresh developments. The film, we realize, was made for the benefit of a weak-eyed cretin in whose skull a jest takes at least ten minutes to mature.

Then we have had Mickey Mouse . . . and remember Felix the Cat. Rose-flushed and warm from heaven's own heart he came, and might not bear the cloud that covers earth's wan face with shame, as Mr Swinburne wrote. But some day, surely, he will return and slay for us this tyrant. How long, O Lord, how long?

But now the Big Picture is coming. First, a lion has growled convincingly or a radio tower has emitted sparks or a cockerel has crowed in a brazen

I-will-deny-thee-thrice manner. The heraldic beasts disposed of, we come to the names of the producer, the scenario-writer, the costumier, the sound-effects man; we learn that Silas K. Guggenheimer made the beds, Mrs Hunt O'Mara loaned the baby, and Henryk Sienkiewicz carried round drinks. The fact that we here in the bug house care not a twopenny damn for any of these facts, that we never remember the names except as outrageous improbabilities in nomenclature, is unknown to Hollywood or Elstree. . . . It is bad enough to have the printer's name upon one's novels. But what if he printed page after page in front of the title, telling how Jim Smith set the type and Rassendyll Snooks read the proofs and Isobel Jeeves typed the correspondence, and the printer's boy who had belly-ache was treated with a stomach-pump in St Thomas's?

Lists of actors and characters, confusing, and (a noted name or so apart) quite meaningless. Then, with tremolos, a distant view of New York— always the same view, film directors gallop madly round to each other's studios to borrow this shot . . . or a distant view of London; also, always the same view. Then—the picture. . . .

Like most intelligent people I prefer the cinema to the theatre. Stage drama has always been a bastard art, calling for acute faith from the audience to supplement its good works. The film suffers from no such limitations; it presents (as is the function of art) the free and undefiled illusion. A minor journalist and playwright of our time, St John Ervine, denies this with some passion. His flatfooted prose style (relieved by a coruscation of angry corns) is employed week by week in a Sunday sheet to carry bulls of denunciation against the Whore of Hollywood. (Can it be that Hollywood has refused to film Mr Ervine's works as—with a far greater ineptness—it has refused to film mine?) But Mr Ervine's poor tired feet are needlessly outraged. The Whore has righteously our hearts—if only she would practise the courtezan to the full, not drape her lovely figure in the drab domestic reach-me-downs of stage drama.

Too often—in fifteen out of twenty of the Big Pictures that reach our bug house—she is clad not even in reach-me-downs. Instead, she is tarred and feathered or sprayed with saccharine in the likeness of a Christmas cake; and unendingly, instead of walking fearless and free, she sidles along with her hands disposed in a disgustingly Rubens-like gesture.

But—we had *Le Million*, and enjoyed its cackle; we had *Gabriel Over the White House*, the courtezan in dust-cap and mop, spring-cleaning her back-garden as even a Muse must do. We had *Man of Aran* which—apart from the fact that the characters never had any sleep and the sea suffered from elephantiasis, and every gesture and every action was repeated over and over again till one longed to go for the projector with a battle-axe— was a righteous film. And a month ago we had *As the Earth Turns*, which ought to be crowned in bay, in spite of some deplorable photography and an occasional sickly whiff of sugar-icing.

Between whiles our Big Picture is the Muse in tar and feathers.

(Lewis Grassic Gibbon, 'A Novelist Looks at the Cinema', *Cinema Quarterly* Winter [1934/]1935, pp.81–85.)

4.25   Neil M. Gunn, from 'The Theatre Society of Scotland' (*Scots Magazine* December 1938)

I have just received a circular letter from the secretary of a new association which is in process of being formed with a view to establishing 'an endowed professional theatre in Scotland'. I have been interested from time to time in so many new 'movements' within our country, and have got so used to seeing them run their short race and fade out, that my first approach to still another effort is inclined to be tinged with scepticism. [. . .] And the latest is this effort to form a 'Theatre Society of Scotland'. Those who first conceived the project obviously made up their minds that it was to be no hole-and-corner affair of parochial enthusiasm. Apparently the conception of Scotland is widening. Even in 'movements', there is no avoiding the general law of learning from our mistakes and defeats. After all, presumably it is a big affair or nothing; it is of national size, with international implications, or it isn't worth bothering about. So amongst patron advisers, we find names like Ashley Dukes of London, Hilton Edwards of the Gate Theatre, Dublin, Tyron Guthrie now of the Old Vic; in organisation, names of University principals, and of city fathers like Will Y. Darling and P.J. Dolan: in playwriting, Bridie and Robins Millar; in literature, Eric Linklater, Hugh MacDiarmid, Edwin Muir, to select a contrasted trio; and so on for painting, sculpture, and the learned professions. Of the long list of printed names, only a small minority is Scottish Nationalist in politics. It is as if it had been decided to approach the national problem from the international point of view.

Now, let me make it quite clear that the promoters do not explicitly recognise a 'national problem' at all. In their prospectus there is no suggestion that Scotland needs a theatre through which she may express her essential self. They merely want to 'bring together all who believe in the social and artistic value of the theatre, in order that a united effort may be made to establish an endowed professional theatre in Scotland'. This theatre 'would form a permanent centre for the pleasure of audiences and the advancement of the art of the theatre'. Amongst its services to the community, it would 'explore the theatrical possibilities of Scottish intonation and movement, as shown in national speech and dance' and 'interest Scottish artists and art students in the work of scene and costume design'. 'Plays of all nations, types and tendencies' would be performed, as well as ballet, opera, and even the right sort of revue.

In short, what is envisaged here is a professional theatre for Scotland, through which the whole art of the stage would be made manifest; a national theatre such as countries of less population than Scotland, and with very much less material resources and educational endowment, possess normally in Europe. Even down in the Balkans, where a city may not have half the population of Edinburgh and a tiny fraction of its wealth, one naturally looks for its Opera House or its National Theatre. From the Balkans to Norway, where every budding dramatist thinks in terms of Ibsen. And from Norway to Dublin, where the endowed Abbey Theatre has produced drama that has had no small effect in recent years in revivifying the English stage and in setting a certain fashion to Europe.

Surely it should be possible to endow one such theatre in Scotland. Think of Glasgow with its enormous population and industrial wealth—the boasted second city of the earth's greatest empire—and then think of it or its citizens unwilling to endow one small theatre. For the moment, do not let us quarrel over the reason for this. Let us simply realise the fact, and see in this Theatre Society a body of Scottish men and women, representative of all the arts and of learning, endeavouring to bring an endowed Scottish theatre into being. Anyone can join this Society by paying half a crown and so help to realise the great aim. Are we capable of doing it?

As I began by saying, my first reaction was one of scepticism. But there are factors undoubtedly favourable to the scheme. The idea of Scotland as a unit for such an experiment is emerging. The swift and vast spread of the Community Drama Festival Movement implies that we have been starved of true dramatic nourishment. And there is, in satisfaction of what I have called the general Scottish attitude, the negative factor that the scheme is not 'nationalist'. For all those who assert that political nationalism is nonsense, and that what we want is a purely cultural revival, then here surely is their perfect opportunity to prove their case in at least one direction, that of the drama. Will they do it? Those of us who incline to scepticism, because of an analysis of the Scottish situation such as I have earlier indicated, shall await the results with interest: and meantime, let it be said, shall assist in every way possible.

For we in Scotland are labouring under difficulties. In Dublin, Irish national life was so strong that it created a drama out of itself. It had not to appeal to patrons by promising foreign plays and ballet and opera. It did not say: Endow us so that we may give you artistic satisfactions. It said: We will show you your own life translated into drama, and make you sit up, and look at it, and realise it as you have never done before. Here is Ireland, here is Cathleen ni Hoolihan, here are your conflicts and your slums, the plough and the stars, and there goes the all-wide Juno, and there her drunken Paycock asking: 'What is the moon; what is the stars?' I have seen most of the great Abbey plays in the Abbey, and remember vividly still the shock I got when, at my first visit many years ago, I heard the Irish voices in the *Shadow of a Gunman* coming over the footlights into the darkened auditorium. I had forgotten, if I had ever known, that contemporary drama could act on one like this.

But we cannot expect anything like that in Scotland, because there has been neither a sense of national conflict nor of national travail; there has not been that high movement of the country's spirit out of which great drama is made. That is not a vague emotional statement; it is simple fact, and can be checked, as I say, by reference to the experience of Ireland and, even still more recently, by the experience of Russia and the remarkable drama that is appearing in that country, a drama that makes most of our British pieces look like sophisticated trifling about sweet or nasty nothings.

How, then, can an endowed theatre in Scotland be of any real use to us, apart of course from providing those so-called artistic satisfactions? What do we want a national theatre for if we have nothing in ourselves, nothing national, to express there?

In a sentence, is this to be another petit-bourgeois effort at keeping abreast of other peoples' conceptions of the drama of life? Looking ahead, I think not. Because of our position, as I have attempted to hint at it, we need a theatre first, to which Scottish writers may bring their conceptions of life, born out of a heredity and environment peculiarly their own. These conceptions may be defeatist, disruptive, rebellious, constructive, but at least they would refer to elements of conflict in our country that are profoundly real, from the tragic and heroic sea-fisheries of the north to the desperate industrialism of the south, from the Highland glen to the Lowland farm, with all the vital inter-play of character and thought and aspiration such scenes inevitably imply, for portrayal through the essential Scottish conception of fantasy, comedy, and tragedy. At present a Scottish writer has no theatre to which he can take any such drama. Just as his country suffers from having no focal point, no vitalising heart, so the native playwright suffers, in this single element of the drama, from having no central stage, no national theatre, to which he may bring the fruits of his talent and have them read and judged as drama, not as hopeful commercial efforts at understudying the London stage. Even in the immense growth of the Community Drama Festival Movement, he has proved to himself already that only a certain type of play is preferred for competitive purposes. To a large degree it has become a game of acquiring marks, and the more cunning amateurs have become expert at the game.

What the Scottish playwright, who feels he may have something to say or to evoke, needs is a theatre, run by professional players, to whom he can entrust the expression of adult thought and irony and imagination. Without such a theatre he is crippled in expression or simply does not write plays at all and turns to some other medium, like the novel. Such a theatre needs to be endowed, if we are going to get the best.

Again let it be said that this Theatre is not being founded with a view to encouraging the Scottish playwright. It will encourage him for all that, and the seeing of first-class work will be no disadvantage to a developing technique. If he comes away with plays, as the Irish and the Russians have done, there will be much more fun going around than is usually found in a milieu for providing social and artistic values. But that smile must remain directed towards the lap of the gods.

Meanwhile there are doubting but still hopeful Scots who will watch with considerable interest what is going to happen to the Theatre Society of Scotland.

(Neil M. Gunn, 'Nationalism in Writing: II—The Theatre Society of Scotland', *Scots Magazine* 30:3 December 1938, pp.194–98.)

5

Europe and the Impact of the Modern

5.1   Sigmund Freud, from *The Interpretation of Dreams* (1900)

Every attempt that has hitherto been made to solve the problem of dreams has dealt directly with their *manifest* content as it is presented in our memory. All such attempts have endeavoured to arrive at an interpretation of dreams from the manifest content or (if no interpretation was attempted) to form a judgement as to their nature on the basis of that same manifest content. We are alone in taking something else into account. We have introduced a new class of psychical material between the manifest content of dreams and the conclusions of our enquiry: namely, their *latent* content, or (as we say) the 'dream-thoughts', arrived at by means of our procedure. It is from these dream-thoughts and not from a dream's manifest content that we disentangle its meaning. We are thus presented with a new task which had no previous existence: the task, that is, of investigating the relations between the manifest content of dreams and the latent dream-thoughts, and of tracing out the processes by which the latter have been changed into the former.

The dream-thoughts and the dream-content are presented to us like two versions of the same subject-matter in two different languages. Or, more properly, the dream-content seems like a transcript of the dream-thoughts into another mode of expression, whose characters and syntactic laws it is our business to discover by comparing the original and the translation. The dream-thoughts are immediately comprehensible, as soon as we have learnt them. The dream-content, on the other hand, is expressed as it were in a pictographic script, the characters of which have to be transposed individually into the language of the dream-thoughts. If we attempted to read these characters according to their pictorial value instead of according to their symbolic relation, we should clearly be led into error. Suppose I have a picture-puzzle, a rebus, in front of me. It depicts a house with a boat on its roof, a single letter of the alphabet, the figure of a running man whose head has been conjured away, and so on. Now I might be misled into raising objections and declaring that the picture as a whole and its component parts are nonsensical. A boat has no business to be on the roof of a house, and a headless man cannot run. Moreover, the man is bigger than the house; and if the whole picture is intended to represent a landscape, letters of the alphabet are out of place in it since such objects do not occur in nature. But obviously we can only form a proper judgement of the rebus if we put aside criticisms such as these of the whole composition and its parts and if, instead, we try to replace each separate element by a syllable or word that can be presented by that element in some way or other. The words which are put together in this way are no longer nonsensical but may form a poetical phrase of the greatest beauty and significance. A dream is a picture-puzzle of this sort and our predecessors in the field of dream-interpretation have made the mistake of treating the rebus as a pictorial composition: and as such it has seemed to them nonsensical and worthless. [. . .]

The first thing that becomes clear to anyone who compares the dream-content with the dream-thoughts is that a work of *condensation* on a large scale has been carried out. Dreams are brief, meagre and laconic in comparison with the range and wealth of the dream-thoughts. If a dream is written out it may perhaps fill half a page. The analysis setting out the dream-thoughts underlying it may occupy six, eight or a dozen times as much space. This relation varies with different dreams; but so far as my experience goes its direction never varies. As a rule one underestimates the amount of compression that has taken place, since one is inclined to regard the dream-thoughts that have been brought to light as the complete material, whereas if the work of interpretation is carried further it may reveal still more thoughts concealed behind the dream. [. . .] Even if the solution seems satisfactory and without gaps, the possibility always remains that the dream may have yet another meaning. Strictly speaking, then, it is impossible to determine the amount of condensation. [. . .]

How, then, are we to picture psychical conditions during the period of sleep which precedes dreams? Are all the dream-thoughts present alongside one another? or do they occur in sequence? or do a number of trains of thought start out simultaneously from different centres and afterwards unite? There is no need for the present, in my opinion, to form any plastic idea of psychical conditions during the formation of dreams. It must not be forgotten, however, that we are dealing with an *unconscious* process of thought, which may easily be different from what we perceive during purposive reflection accompanied by consciousness.

(Sigmund Freud, 'The Dream-Work', *The Interpretation of Dreams* (1900); reprinted from the Penguin Freud Library Volume 4 *The Interpretation of Dreams*, translated by James Strachey and edited by Angela Richards Harmondsworth: Penguin Books, 1991, pp.381–83, 385.)

149

5.2   W.B. Yeats, from 'The Symbolism of Poetry' (1900)

Symbolism, as seen in the writers of our day, would have no value if it were not seen also, under one 'disguise or another, in every great imaginative writer', writes Mr Arthur Symons in *The Symbolist Movement in Literature* [. . .] and he goes on to show how many profound writers have in the last few years sought for a philosophy of poetry in the doctrine of symbolism, and how even in countries where it is almost scandalous to seek for any philosophy of poetry, new writers are following them in their search. [. . .]

All writers, all artists of any kind, in so far as they have had any philosophical or critical power, perhaps just in so far as they have been delicate artists at all, have had some philosophy, some criticism of their art; and it has often been this philosophy, or this criticism, that has evoked their most startling inspiration, calling into outer life some portion of the divine life, or of the buried reality, which could alone extinguish in the emotions what their philosophy or their criticism would extinguish in the intellect. They had sought for no new thing it may be, but only to understand and to copy the pure inspiration of early times, but because the divine life wars upon our outer life, and must needs change its weapons and its movements as we change ours, inspiration has come to them in beautiful startling shapes. The scientific movement brought with it a literature which was always tending to lose itself in externalities of all kinds, in opinion, in declamation, in picturesque writing, in word-painting, or in what Mr Symons has called an attempt 'to build in brick and mortar inside the covers of a book'; and now writers have begun to dwell upon the element of evocation, of suggestion, upon what we call the symbolism in great writers. [. . .]

Besides emotional symbols, symbols that evoke emotions alone—and in this sense all alluring or hateful things are symbols, although their relations with one another are too subtle to delight us fully, away from rhythm and pattern—there are intellectual symbols, symbols that evoke ideas alone, or ideas mingled with emotions; and outside the very definite traditions of mysticism and the less definite criticism of certain modern poets, these alone are called symbols. Most things belong to one or another kind, according to the way we speak of them and the companions we give them, for symbols, associated with ideas that are more than fragments of the shadows thrown upon the intellect by the emotions they evoke, are the playthings of the allegorist or the pedant, and soon pass away. If I say 'white' or 'purple' in an ordinary line of poetry, they evoke emotions so exclusively that I cannot say why they move me; but if I bring them into the same sentence with such obvious intellectual symbols as a cross or a crown of thorns, I think of purity and sovereignty. Furthermore, innumerable meanings, which are held to 'white' or 'purple' by bonds of subtle suggestion, and alike in the emotions and in the intellect, move visibly through my mind, and move invisibly beyond the threshold of sleep, casting lights and shadows of an indefinable wisdom on what had seemed before, it may be, but sterility and noisy violence. It is the intellect that decides where the reader shall ponder over the procession of the symbols, and if the symbols are merely emotional, he gazes from amid the accidents and destinies of the world; but if the symbols are intellectual too, he becomes himself a part of pure intellect, and he is himself mingled with the procession. [. . .]

If people were to accept the theory that poetry moves us because of its symbolism, what change should one look for in the manner of our poetry? A return to the way of our fathers, a casting out of descriptions of nature for the sake of nature, of the moral law for the sake of the moral law, a casting out of all anecdotes and of that brooding over scientific opinion that so often extinguished the central flame in Tennyson, and of that vehemence that would make us do or not do certain things; or, in other words, we should come to understand that the beryl stone was enchanted by our fathers that it might unfold the pictures in its heart, and not to mirror our own excited faces, or the boughs waving outside the window. With this change of substance, this return to imagination, this understanding that the laws of art, which are the hidden laws of the world, can alone bind the imagination, would come a change of style, and we would cast out of serious poetry those energetic rhythms, as of a man running, which are the invention of the will with its eyes always on something to be done or undone; and we would seek out those wavering, meditative, organic rhythms, which are the embodiment of the imagination, that neither desires not hates, because it has done with time, and only wishes to gaze upon some reality, some beauty; nor would it be any longer possible for anybody to deny the importance of form, in all its kinds, for although you can expound an opinion, or describe a thing, when your words are not quite well chosen, you cannot give a body to something that moves beyond the senses, unless your words are as subtle, as complex, as full of mysterious life, as the body of a flower or of a woman. The form of sincere poetry, unlike the form of the 'popular poetry', may indeed be sometimes obscure, or ungrammatical as in some of the best of the *Songs of Innocence and Experience*, but it must have the perfections that escape analysis, the subtleties that have a new meaning every day, and it must have all this whether it be but a little song made out of a moment of dreamy indolence, or some great epic made out of the dreams of one poet and of a hundred generations whose hands were never weary of the sword.

(W.B. Yeats, 'The Symbolism of Poetry' (1900), reprinted from David Lodge ed., *Twentieth Century Literary Criticism: A Reader* London; Longman, 1972, pp.28–34 [28, 29, 32–33, 34].)

5.3 Henri Bergson, from *Creative Evolution* (1907)

The existence of which we are most assured and which we know best is unquestionably our own, for of every other object we have notions which may be considered external and superficial, whereas, of ourselves, our perception is internal and profound. What, then, do we find? In this privileged case, what is the precise meaning of the word 'exist'? Let us recall here briefly the conclusions of an earlier work.

I find, first of all, that I pass from state to state. I am warm or cold, I am merry or sad, I work or I do nothing. I look at what is around me or I think of something else. Sensations, feelings, volitions, ideas—such are the changes into which my existence is divided and which colour it in turns. I change, then, without ceasing. But this is not saying enough. Change is far more radical than we are at first inclined to suppose.

For I speak of each of my states as if it formed a block and were a separate whole. I say indeed that I change, but the change seems to me to reside in the passage from one state to the next; of each state, taken separately, I am apt to think that it remains the same during all the time that it prevails. Nevertheless, a slight effort of attention would reveal to me that there is no feeling, no idea, no volition which is not undergoing change every moment: if a mental state ceased to vary, its duration would cease to flow. Let us take the most stable of internal states, the visual perception of a motionless external object. The object may remain the same, I may look at it from the same side, at the same angle, in the same light; nevertheless the vision I now have of it differs from that which I have just had, even if only because the one is an instant older than the other. My memory is there, which conveys something of the past into the present. My mental state, as it advances on the road of time, is continually swelling with the duration which it accumulates: it goes on increasing—rolling upon itself as a snowball on the snow. Still more is this the case with states more deeply internal, such as sensations, feelings, desires, etc., which do not correspond, like a simple visual perception, to an unvarying external object. But it is expedient to disregard this uninterrupted change, and to notice it only when it becomes sufficient to impress a new attitude on the body, a new direction on the attention. Then, and then only, we find that our state has changed. The truth is that we change without ceasing, and that the state itself is nothing but change.

This amounts to saying that there is no essential difference between passing from one state to another and persisting in the same state. If the state which 'remains the same' is more varied than we think, on the other hand the passing from one state to another resembles, more than we imagine, a single state being prolonged; the transition is continuous. But, just because we close our eyes to the unceasing variation of every psychical state, we are obliged, when the change has become so considerable as to force itself on our attention, to speak as if a new state were placed alongside the previous one. Of this new state we assume that it remains unvarying in its turn, and so on endlessly. The apparent discontinuity of the psychical life is then due to our attention being fixed on it by a series of separate acts: actually there is only a gentle slope; but in following the broken line of our acts of attention, we think we perceive separate steps. True, our psychic life is full of the unforeseen. A thousand incidents arise, which seem to be cut off from those which precede them, and to be disconnected from those which follow. Discontinuous though they appear, however, in point of fact they stand out against the continuity of a background on which they are designed, and to which indeed they owe the intervals that separate them; they are the beats of the drum which break forth here and there in the symphony. Our attention fixes on them because they interest it more, but each of them is borne by the fluid mass of our whole psychical existence. Each is only the best illuminated point of a moving zone which comprises all that we feel or think or will—all, in short, that we are at any given moment. It is this entire zone which in reality makes up our state. Now, states thus defined cannot be regarded as distinct elements. They continue each other in an endless flow. [. . .]

There is, moreover, no stuff more resistant nor more substantial. For our duration is not merely one instant replacing another; if it were, there would never be anything but the present—no prolonging of the past into the actual, no evolution, no concrete duration. Duration is the continuous progress of the past which gnaws into the future and which swells as it advances. And as the past grows without ceasing, so also there is no limit to its preservation. Memory, as we have tried to prove, is not a faculty of putting away recollections in a drawer, or of inscribing them in a register. [. . .] In reality, the past is preserved by itself, automatically. In its entirety, probably, it follows us at every instant; all that we have felt, thought and willed from our earliest infancy is there, leaning over the present which is about to join it, pressing against the portals of consciousness that would fain leave it outside. [. . .]

From this survival of the past it follows that consciousness cannot go through the same state twice. The circumstances may still be the same, but they will act no longer on the same person, since they find him at a new moment of his history. Our personality, which is being built up each instant with its accumulated experience, changes without ceasing. By changing, it prevents any state, although superficially identical with another, from ever repeating it in its very depth. That is why our duration is irreversible. We could not live over again a single moment, for we should have to begin by effacing the memory of all that had followed. Even could we erase this memory from our intellect, we could not from our will.

Thus our personality shoots, grows and ripens without ceasing. Each of its moments is something new added to what was before. We may go further: it is not only something new, but something unforeseeable.

(Henri Bergson, *Creative Evolution* (1907), reprinted from Keith Ansell Pearson and John Mullarkey eds, *Henri Bergson: Key Writings* New York and London: Continuum, 2002, pp.171–72, 173–74.)

5.4 Sir James Frazer, from *The Golden Bough* (1890–1915; 1922)

a) From 'Sympathetic Magic'

The Principles of Magic.—If we analyse the principles of thought on which magic is based, they will probably be found to resolve themselves into two: first, that like produces like, or that an effect resembles its cause; and, second, that things which have once been in contact with each other continue to act on each other at a distance after the physical contact has been severed. The former principle may be called the Law of Similarity, the latter the Law of Contact or Contagion. From the first of these principles, namely the Law of Similarity, the magician infers that he can produce any effect he desires merely by imitating it: from the second he infers that whatever he does to a material object will affect equally the person with whom the object was once in contact, whether it formed part of his body or not. Charms based on the Law of Similarity may be called Homoeopathic or Imitative Magic. Charms based on the Law of Contact or Contagion may be called Contagious Magic. To denote the first of these branches of magic the term Homoeopathic is perhaps preferable, for the alternative term Imitative or Mimetic suggests, if it does not imply, a conscious agent who imitates, thereby limiting the scope of magic too narrowly. For the same principles which the magician applies in the practice of his art are implicitly believed by him to regulate the operations of inanimate nature; in other words, he tacitly assumes that the Laws of Similarity and Contact are of universal application and are not limited to human actions. In short, magic is a spurious system of natural law as well as a fallacious guide of conduct; it is a false science as well as an abortive art. Regarded as a system of natural law, that is, as a statement of the rules which determine the sequence of events throughout the world, it may be called Theoretical Magic: regarded as a set of precepts which human beings observe in order to compass their ends, it may be called Practical Magic. At the same time it is to be borne in mind that the primitive magician knows magic only on its practical side; he never analyses the mental processes on which his practice is based, never reflects on the abstract principles involved in his actions. With him, as with the vast majority of men, logic is implicit, not explicit: he reasons just as he digests his food in complete ignorance of the intellectual and physiological processes which are essential to the one operation and to the other. In short, to him magic is always an art, never a science; the very idea of science is lacking in his undeveloped mind. It is for the philosophic student to trace the train of thought which underlies the magician's practice; to draw out the few simple threads of which the tangled skein is composed; to disengage the abstract principles from their concrete applications; in short, to discern the spurious science behind the bastard art.

b) From 'The Corn-Mother and the Corn-Maiden in Northern Europe'

In Scotland, when the last corn was cut after Hallowmas, the female figure made out of it was sometimes called the Carlin or Carline, that is, the Old Woman. But if cut before Hallowmas, it was called the Maiden; if cut after sunset, it was called the Witch, being supposed to bring bad luck. Among the Highlanders of Scotland the last corn cut at harvest is known either as the Old Wife (*Cailleach*) or as the maiden; on the whole the former name seems to prevail in the western and the latter in the central and eastern districts. Of the Maiden we shall speak presently; here we are dealing with the Old Wife. The following general account of the custom is given by a careful and well-informed enquirer, the Rev. J.G. Campbell, minister of the remote Hebridean island of Tiree; 'The Harvest Old Wife (*a Chailleach*).—In harvest, there was a struggle to escape from being the last done with the shearing, and when tillage in common existed, instances were known of a ridge being left unshorn (no person would claim it) because of it being behind the rest. The fear entertained was that of having the "famine of the farm" (*gort a bhaile*), in the shape of an imaginary old woman (*cailleach*), to feed till next harvest. Much emulation and amusement arose from the fear of this old woman. . . . The first done made a doll of some blades of corn, which was called the "old wife", and sent it to his nearest neighbour. He in turn, when ready, passed it to another still less expeditious, and the person it last remained with had "the old woman" to keep for that year.' [. . .]

In some parts of the Highlands of Scotland the last handful of corn that is cut by the reapers on any particular farm is called the Maiden, or in Gaelic *Maidhdeanbuain*, literally 'the shorn Maiden'. Superstitions attach to the winning of the Maiden. If it is got by a young person, they think it an omen that he or she will be married before another harvest. For that or other reasons there is a strife between the reapers as to who shall get the Maiden, and they resort to various stratagems for the purpose of securing it. One of them, for example, will often leave a handful of corn uncut and cover it up with earth to hide it from the other reapers, till all the rest of the corn on the field is cut down. Several may try to play the same trick, and the one who is coolest and holds out longest obtains the coveted distinction. When it has been cut, the Maiden is dressed with ribbons into a sort of doll and affixed to a wall of the farmhouse. In the North of Scotland the Maiden is carefully preserved till Yule morning, when it is divided among the cattle 'to make them thrive all the year round'. In the neighbourhood of Balquhidder, Perthshire, the last handful of corn is cut by the youngest girl on the field and is made into the rude form of a female doll, clad in a paper dress and decked with ribbons. It is called the Maiden, and is kept in the farmhouse, generally above the chimney, for a good while, sometimes till the Maiden of the next year is brought in. [. . .] Now there are parts of Scotland in which both an Old Wife (*Cailleach*) and a Maiden are cut at harvest. The accounts of this custom are not quite clear and consistent, but the general rule seems to be that, where both a Maiden and an Old Wife (*Cailleach*) are fashioned out of the reaped corn at harvest, the Maiden is made out of the last stalks left standing, and is kept by the farmer on whose land it was cut; while the Old Wife is made out of other stalks, sometimes out of the first stalks cut, and is regularly passed on to a laggard farmer who happens to be still reaping after his brisker neighbour has cut all his corn. Thus while each farmer keeps his own Maiden, as the embodiment of the young and fruitful spirit of the corn, he passes on the Old Wife as soon as he can to a neighbour, and so the old lady may make the round of all the farms in the district before she finds a place in which to lay her venerable head. The farmer with whom she finally takes up her abode is of course the one who has been the last of all the countryside to finish reaping his crops, and thus the distinction of entertaining her is rather an invidious one. He is thought to be doomed to poverty or to be under the obligation of 'providing for the dearth of the township' in the ensuing season.

c) From 'The Fire-Festivals of Europe'

The Beltane Fires.—In the Central Highlands of Scotland bonfires, known as the Beltane fires, were formerly kindled with great ceremony on the first of May, and the traces of human sacrifices at them were particularly clear and unequivocal. The custom of lighting bonfires lasted in various places far into the eighteenth century, and the descriptions of the ceremony by writers of that period present such a curious and interesting picture of ancient heathendom surviving in our own country that I will reproduce them in the words of their authors. The fullest of the descriptions is the one bequeathed to us by John Ramsay, laird of Ochtertyre, near Crieff, the patron of Burns and the friend of Sir Walter Scott. He says: 'But the most considerable of the Druidical festivals is that of Beltane, or May-day, which was lately observed in some parts of the Highlands with extraordinary ceremonies. . . . Like the other public worship of the Druids, the Beltane feast seems to have been performed on hills or eminences. They thought it degrading to him whose temple is the universe, to suppose that he would dwell in any house made with hands. Their sacrifices were therefore offered in the open air, frequently upon the tops of hills, where they were presented with the grandest views of nature, and were nearest the seat of warmth and order. And, according to tradition, such was the manner of celebrating the festival in the Highlands within the last hundred years. But since the decline of superstition it has been celebrated by the people of each hamlet on some hill or rising ground around which their cattle were pasturing. Thither the young folks repaired in the morning, and cut a trench, on the summit of which a seat of turf was formed for the company. And in the middle a pile of wood or other fuel was placed, which of old they kindled with *tein-eigin*—i.e., forced-fire or *need-fire*. Although, for many years past, they have been contented with common fire, yet we shall now describe the process, because it will hereafter appear that recourse is still had to the *tein-eigin* upon extraordinary emergencies.

'The night before, all the fires in the country were carefully extinguished, and next morning the materials for exciting this sacrificial fire were prepared. The most primitive method seems to be that which was used in the islands of Skye, Mull, and Tiree. A well-seasoned plank of oak was procured, in the midst of which a hole was bored. A wimble of the same timber was then applied, the end of which they fitted to the hole. But in some part of the mainland the machinery was different. They used a frame of green wood, of a square form, in the centre of which was an axle-tree. In some places three times three persons, in others three times nine, were required for turning round by turns the axle-tree or wimble. If any of them had been guilty of murder, adultery, theft, or other atrocious crime, it was imagined either that the fire would not kindle, or that it would be devoid of its usual virtue. So soon as any sparks were emitted by means of the violent friction, they applied a species of agaric which grows on old birch-trees, and is very combustible. This fire had the appearance of being immediately derived from heaven, and manifold were the virtues ascribed to it. They esteemed it a preservative against witchcraft, and a sovereign remedy against malignant disease, both in the human species and in cattle; and by it the strongest poisons were supposed to have their nature changed.

'After kindling the bonfire with the *tein-eigin* the company prepared their victuals. And as soon as they had finished their meal they amused themselves a while in singing and dancing round the fire. Towards the close of the entertainment, the person who officiated as master of the feast produced a large cake baked with eggs and scalloped round the edge, called *am bonnach beal-tine*—i.e. the Beltane cake. It was divided into a number of pieces, and distributed in great form to the company. There was one particular piece which whoever got was called *cailleach beal-tine*—i.e. the Beltane *carline*, a term of great reproach. Upon his being known, part of the company laid hold of him and made a show of putting him into the fire; but the majority interposing, he was rescued. And in some places they laid him flat on the ground, making as if they would quarter him. Afterwards, he was pelted with egg-shells, and retained the odious appellation during the whole year. And while the feast was fresh in people's memory, they affected to speak of the *cailleach beal-tine* as dead.' [. . .]

The Hallowe'en Fires.—From the foregoing survey we may infer that among the heathen forefathers of the European peoples the most popular and widespread fire-festival of the year was the great celebration of Midsummer Eve or Midsummer Day. The coincidence of the festival with the summer solstice can hardly be accidental. Rather we must suppose that our pagan ancestors purposely timed the ceremony of fire on earth to coincide with the arrival of the sun at the highest point of his course in the sky. [. . .]

But while this may be regarded as fairly certain for what we may call the aborigines throughout a large part of the continent, it appears not to have been true of the Celtic peoples who inhabited the Land's End of Europe, the islands and promontories that stretch out into the Atlantic Ocean on the north-west. The principal fire-festivals of the Celts, which have survived, though in a restricted area and with diminished pomp, to modern times and even to our own day, were seemingly timed without any reference to the position of the sun in the heaven. They were two in number and fell at an interval of six months, one being celebrated on the eve of May Day and the other on Allhallow Even or Hallowe'en, as it is now commonly called, that is, on the thirty-first of October, the day preceding All Saints' or Allhallows' Day. These dates coincide with none of the four great hinges on which the solar year revolves, to wit, the solstices and the equinoxes. Nor do they agree with the principal seasons of the agricultural year, the sowing in spring and the reaping in autumn. For when May Day comes, the seed has long been committed to the earth; and when November opens, the harvest has long been reaped and garnered, the fields lie bare, the fruit-trees are stripped, and even the yellow leaves are fast fluttering to the ground. Yet the first of May and first of November mark turning-points of the year in Europe; the one ushers in the genial heat and the rich vegetation of summer, the other heralds, if it does not share, the cold and barrenness of winter. Now these particular points of the year, as has been well pointed out by a learned and ingenious writer, while they are of comparatively little moment to the European husbandman, do deeply concern the European herdsman; for it is on the approach of summer that he drives his cattle out into the open to crop the fresh grass, and it is on the approach of winter that he leads them back to the safety and shelter of the stall. Accordingly it seems not improbable that the Celtic bisection of the year into two halves at the beginning of May and the beginning of November dates from a time when the Celts were mainly a pastoral people, dependent for their subsistence on their herds, and when accordingly the great epochs of the year for them were the days on which the cattle went forth from the homestead in early summer and returned to it again in early winter. Even in Central Europe, remote from the region now occupied by the Celts, a similar bisection of the year may be clearly traced in the great popularity, on the one hand, of May Day and its Eve (Walpurgis Night) and, on the other hand, of the Feast of All Souls at the beginning of November, which under a thin Christian cloak conceals an ancient pagan festival of the dead. Hence we may conjecture that everywhere throughout Europe the celestial division of the year according to the solstices was preceded by what we may call a terrestrial division of the year according to the beginning of summer and the beginning of winter.

Be that as it may, the two great Celtic festivals of May Day and the first of November, or, to be more accurate, the Eves of these two days, closely resemble each other in the manner of their celebration and in the superstitions associated with them, and alike, by the antique character impressed upon both, betray a remote and purely pagan origin.

(Sir James Frazer, *The Golden Bough: A Study in Magic and Religion* (1890–1915); excerpts reprinted from the 1922 edition abridged by the author himself, London: Macmillan & Co., 1922, pp.11–12; 403, 407, 409–410; 617–18; 632–33.)

5.5 C.J. Jung, from 'On the Psychology of the Unconscious' (1917) and 'Definitions' (1921)

a) From 'On the Psychology of the Unconscious'

THE PERSONAL AND THE COLLECTIVE UNCONSCIOUS

Let us take as an example one of the greatest thoughts which the nineteenth century brought to birth: the idea of the conservation of energy. Robert Mayer, the real creator of this idea, was a physician, and not a physicist or natural philosopher, for whom the making of such an idea would have been more appropriate. But it is very important to realize that the idea was not, strictly speaking, 'made' by Mayer. Nor did it come into being through the fusion of ideas or scientific hypotheses then extant, but grew in its creator like a plant. [. . .]

The question now arises: Whence this new idea that thrusts itself upon consciousness with such elemental force? And whence did it derive the power that could so seize upon consciousness that it completely eclipsed the multitudinous impressions of a first voyage to the tropics? These questions are not so easy to answer. But if we apply our theory here, the explanation can only be this: the idea of energy and its conservation must be a primordial image that was dormant in the collective unconscious. Such a conclusion naturally obliges us to prove that a primordial image of this kind really did exist in the mental history of mankind, and was operative through the ages. As a matter of fact, this proof can be produced without much difficulty: the most primitive religions in the most widely separated parts of the earth are founded upon this image. These are the so-called dynamistic religions whose sole and determining thought is that there exists a universal magical power about which everything revolves. Tylor, the well-known English investigator, and Frazer likewise, misunderstood this idea as animism. In reality primitives do not mean, by their power-concept, souls or spirits at all, but something which the American investigator Lovejoy has appropriately termed 'primitive energetics.' This concept is equivalent to the idea of soul, spirit, God, health, bodily strength, fertility, magic, influence, power, prestige, medicine, as well as certain states of feeling which are characterized by the release of affects. [. . .]

So this idea has been stamped on the human brain for aeons. That is why it lies ready to hand in the unconscious of every man. Only, certain conditions are needed to cause it to appear. These conditions were evidently fulfilled in the case of Robert Mayer. The greatest and best thoughts of man shape themselves upon these primordial images as upon a blueprint. I have often been asked where the archetypes or primordial images come from. It seems to me that their origin can only be explained by assuming them to be deposits of the constantly repeated experiences of humanity. One of the commonest and at the same time most impressive experiences is the apparent movement of the sun every day. We certainly cannot discover anything of the kind in the unconscious, so far as the known physical process is concerned. What we do find, on the other hand, is the myth of the sun-hero in all its countless modifications. It is this myth, and not the physical process, that forms the sun archetype. The same can be said of the phases of the moon. The archetype is a kind of readiness to produce over and over again the same or similar mythical ideas. Hence it seems as though what is impressed upon the unconscious were exclusively the subjective fantasy-ideas aroused by the physical process. Therefore we may take it that archetypes are recurrent impressions made by subjective reactions. [. . .] Not only are the archetypes, apparently, impressions of ever-repeated typical experiences, but, at the same time, they behave empirically like agents that tend towards the repetition of these same experiences. For when an archetype appears in a dream, in a fantasy, or in life, it always brings with it a certain influence or power by virtue of which it either exercises a numinous or a fascinating effect, or impels to action.

b) From 'Definitions'

[*Soul as persona*]

This mask, i.e., the *ad hoc* adopted attitude, I have called the *persona*, which was the name for the masks worn by actors in antiquity. The man who identifies with this mask I would call 'personal' as opposed to 'individual'. [. . .]

[*Soul as anima*]

We can, therefore, speak of an inner personality with as much justification as, on the grounds of daily experience, we speak of an outer personality. The inner personality is the way one behaves in relation to one's inner psychic processes; it is the inner attitude, the characteristic face, that is turned towards the unconscious. I call the outer attitude, the outward face, the *persona*; the inner attitude, the inward face, I call the *anima*. [. . .]

As to the character of the anima, my experience confirms the rule that it is, by and large, *complementary* to the character of the persona. The anima usually contains all those common human qualities which the conscious attitude lacks. The tyrant tormented by bad dreams, gloomy forebodings, and inner fears is a typical figure. Outwardly ruthless, harsh, and unapproachable, he jumps inwardly at every shadow, is at the mercy of every mood, as though he were the feeblest and most impressionable of men. Thus his anima contains all those fallible human qualities his persona lacks. If the persona is intellectual, the anima will quite certainly be sentimental. The complementary character of the anima also affects the sexual character, as I have proved to myself beyond a doubt. A very feminine woman has a masculine soul, and a very masculine man has a feminine soul. This contrast is due to the fact that a man is not in all things wholly masculine, but also has certain feminine traits. The more masculine his outer attitude is, the more his feminine traits are obliterated: instead, they appear in his unconscious. This explains why it is just those very virile men who are most subject to characteristic weaknesses; their attitude to the unconscious has a womanish weakness and impressionability. Conversely, it is often just the most feminine women who, in their inner lives, display an intractability, an obstinacy, and a wilfulness that are to be found with comparable intensity only in a man's outer attitude. These are masculine traits which, excluded from the womanly outer attitude, have become qualities of her soul.

If, therefore, we speak of the *anima* of a man, we must logically speak of the *animus* of a woman, if we are to give the soul of a woman its right name. Whereas logic and objectivity are usually the predominant features of a man's outer attitude, or are at least regarded as ideals, in the case of a woman it is feeling. But in the soul it is the other way round: inwardly it is the man who feels, and the woman who reflects. Hence a man's greater liability to total despair, while a woman can always find comfort and hope; accordingly a man is more likely to put an end to himself than a woman. However much a victim of social circumstances a woman may be, as a prostitute for instance, a man is no less a victim of impulses from the unconscious, taking the form of alcoholism and other vices.

(C.J. Jung, 'On the Psychology of the Unconscious' (1917) and 'Definitions' (1921); reprinted from *Jung: Selected Writings*, selected and introduced by Anthony Storr, London: Fontana Paperbacks, 1983, pp.68–71; 98, 100–102.)

5.6 Virginia Woolf, from 'More Dostoevsky' (*Times Literary Supplement* February 1917)

Each time that Mrs Garnett adds another red volume to her admirable translation of the work of Dostoevsky we feel a little better able to measure what the existence of this great genius who is beginning to permeate our lives so curiously means to us. His books are now to be found on the shelves of the humblest English libraries; they have become an indestructable part of the furniture of our rooms, as they belong for good to the furniture of our minds. [. . .] Alone among writers Dostoevsky has the power of reconstructing those most swift and complicated states of mind, of rethinking the whole train of thought in all its speed, now as it flashes into light, now as it lapses into darkness; for he is able to follow not only the vivid streak of achieved thought, but to suggest the dim and populous underworld of the mind's consciousness where desires and impulses are moving blindly beneath the sod.

(Virginia Woolf, review of Dostoevsky's *The Eternal Husband*, translated by Constance Garnett, *Times Literary Supplement*, 22 February 1917, p.91.)

5.7 Ezra Pound, from 'A Retrospect' (1918)

There has been so much scribbling about a new fashion in poetry, that I may perhaps be pardoned this brief recapitulation and retrospect.

In the spring or early summer of 1912, 'H.D.', Richard Aldington and myself decided that we were agreed upon the three principles following:

1. Direct treatment of the 'thing' whether subjective or objective.

2. To use absolutely no word that does not contribute to the presentation.

3. As regarding rhythm: to compose in the sequence of the musical phrase, not in sequence of a metronome.

Upon many points of taste and of predilection we differed, but agreeing upon these three positions we thought we had as much right to a group name, at least as much right, as a number of French 'schools' proclaimed by Mr Flint in the August number of Harold Monro's magazine for 1911. [*Poetry Review*]

This school has since been 'joined' or 'followed' by numerous people who, whatever their merits, do not show any signs of agreeing with the second specification. Indeed *vers libre* has become as prolix and as verbose as any of the flaccid varieties that preceded it. It has brought faults of its own. The actual language and phrasing is often as bad as that of our elders without even the excuse that the words are shovelled in to fill a metric pattern or to complete the noise of a rhyme-sound. Whether or no the phrases followed by the followers are musical must be left to the reader's decision. At times I can find a marked metre in 'vers libres', as stale and hackneyed as any pseudo-Swinburnian, at times the writers seem to follow no musical structure whatever. But it is, on the whole, good that the field should be ploughed. Perhaps a few good poems have come from the new method, and if so it is justified. [. . .]

An 'Image' is that which presents an intellectual and emotional complex in an instant of time. [. . .]

It is the presentation of such a 'complex' instantaneously which gives that sense of sudden liberation; that sense of freedom from time limits and space limits; that sense of sudden growth, which we experience in the presence of the greatest works of art.

It is better to present one Image in a lifetime than to produce voluminous works.

(Ezra Pound, 'A Retrospect', reprinted from T.S. Eliot ed., *The Literary Essays of Ezra Pound* London: Faber, 1954, pp.3–14 [3, 4].)

5.8   Edward Moore [Edwin Muir], from *We Moderns* (1918)

a)   From 'The Old Age'

Modern Realism

How crude and shallow is the whole theory of modern realism: a theory of art by the average man for the average man! It makes art intelligible by simplifying or popularizing it; in short, as Nietzsche would say, by vulgarizing it. The average man perceives, for instance, that there is in great drama an element of representation. Come, he says, let us make the representation as 'thorough' as possible! Let every detail of the original be reproduced! Let us have life as it is lived! And when he has accomplished this, when representation has become reproduction, he is very well pleased and thinks how far he has advanced beyond the poor Greeks. But it is hardly so! For the Greeks did not aim at the reproduction but the interpretation of life, for which they would accept no symbol less noble than those *ideal* figures which move in the world of classic tragedy. To the Greeks, indeed, the world of art was precisely this world: not a paltry, sober and conscientious dexterity in the 'catching' of the aspects of existence (nothing so easy!), but a symbolizing of the deepest questions and enigmas of life—a thing infinitely more noble, profound and subtle than realistic art. The Greeks would have demanded of realism, Why do you exist? What noble end is served by the reproduction of ordinary existence? Are you not simply superfluous—and vilely smelling at that? And realism could have given no reply, for the truth is that realism is superfluous. It is without a *raison d'être*.

The average man, however, takes a second glance at classical tragedy and reaches a second discovery. There is something enigmatical, he finds, behind the Greek clearness of representation, something unexplained; in short a problem. This problem, however, is not sufficiently clear. Let us state our problems clearly, he cries! Let us have problems which can be recognized at a glance by every one! Let us write a play about 'the marriage question', or bad-housing, or the Labour Party! But, again, the theory of the Greeks, at least before Euripides, was altogether different. The 'problem' in their tragedies was precisely not a problem which could be stated in a syllogism or solved in a treatise: it was the eternal problem, and it was not stated to be 'solved'.

Thus the Moderns, in their attempt to simplify art, to understand it or misunderstand it—what does it matter which word is used?—have succeeded in destroying it. The realistic and the 'problem' drama alike are for the inartistic. The first is drama without a *raison d'être*, the second is a *raison d'être* without drama.

b) From 'What is Modern?'

Whither?

The fever of modern thought which burns in our veins, and from which we refuse to escape by reactionary backdoors—Christianity and the like—is not without its distinction: it is an 'honourable sickness', to use the phrase of Nietzsche. I speak of those who sincerely strive to seek an issue from this fever; to pass through it into a new health. Of the others to whom fever is the condition of existence, who make a profession of their maladies, the valetudinarians of the spirit, the dabblers in quack soul-remedies for their own sake, it is impossible to speak without disdain. Our duty is to exterminate them, by ridicule or any other means found effectual. But we are ourselves already too grievously harassed; we are caught in the whirlwind of modern thought, which contains as much dust as wind. We see outside our field of conflict a region of Christian calm, but never, never, never can we return there, for our instincts as well as our intellect are averse to it. The problem must have a different solution. And what, indeed, is the problem? To some of us it is still that of emancipation—that which confronted Goethe, Ibsen, Nietzsche, and the other great spirits of last century. It is an error to think that these men have yet been refuted or even understood; they have simply been buried beneath the corpses of later writers. And it is the worst intellectual weakness, and, therefore, crime, of our age that ideas are no longer disproved, but simply superseded by newer ideas. The latest is the true, and Time refutes everything! That is our modern superstition. We have still, then, to go back—or, rather, forward—to Goethe, Ibsen and Nietzsche. Our problem is still that of clearing a domain of freedom around us, of enlarging our field of choice, and so making destiny itself more spacious; and, then, having delivered ourselves from prejudice and superstition—and how many other things!—of setting an aim before us for the unflinching pursuit of which we make ourselves responsible. Greater freedom, and therefore greater responsibility, above all greater aims, an enlargement of life, not a whittling of it down to Christian standards—that is our problem still. [. . .]

Leisure and Productiveness

Granted the society which produces the highest goods in the greatest profusion is the best—let us not argue from this that society should be organized with the direct aim of producing goods. For what if goods be to society what happiness is said to be to men—things to be attained only by striving for something else? In all good things—whether it be in art, literature or philosophy—there is so much of the free, the perverse, the unique, the incalculable. In short, good things can only be produced by great men—and these are exceptions. The best we can do, then, is to inaugurate a society in which great men will find it possible to live, will be even encouraged to live. Can a society in which rights are affixed to functions serve for that? A function, in practice, in a democratic state—that will mean something which can be seen to be useful for to-day, but not for to-morrow, far less for any distant future. The more subtle, spiritual, posthumous the activity of a man the less it will be seen to be a function. Art and philosophy arise when leisure and not work is the ruling convention. It is true, artists and philosophers work, and at a higher tension than other men; but it is in leisure that they must *conceive* their works: what obvious function do they then fulfil? Even the most harassed of geniuses, even Burns would never have become immortal had he not had the leisure to ponder, dream and love. Idleness is as necessary for the production of a work of art as labour. And with some men perhaps whole years of idleness are needed. Artists must always be privileged creatures. It is privileges, and not rights, that they want. [. . .]

'Emancipation'

The rallying cry of the great writers of last century was 'emancipation'. Goethe, Heine and Ibsen alike professed as their task the emancipation of man; Nietzsche, their successor, elevated the freed man, the Superman, into an ideal, in the pursuit of which it was necessary meantime that men should discipline themselves. The later moderns, our own contemporaries, have belittled this freedom, seeing in it nothing but a negation, the freedom *from* some one thing or another. But Ibsen and Heine, these men of true genius, who believed most sincerely that they were 'brave soldiers in the war of the liberation of humanity' did not perhaps waste their powers in battling for a thing so trivial! It is barely possible that they meant by emancipation something much more profound; something spiritual and positive; indeed, nothing less than an enhancement of the powers of man! Certainly both poets looked forward to new 'developments' of man: Heine with his 'happier and more perfect generations, begot in free and voluntary embraces, blossoming forth in a religion of joy'; Ibsen with his perplexed figures painfully 'working their way out to Freedom'. It was the task of us in this generation, who should have been the heirs of this tradition, but are not, to supply the commentary to this noble vision, to carry forward this religion of hope further and further. But the *cult* of modernity has itself prevented this; the latest theory has always seized us and has invariably triumphed; and we have discarded the great work of last century before we understood it. Heine has been seized mainly by the decadents; his healthy and noble sensuousness, his desire to restore the harmony between the senses and the soul, *as a means* towards the emancipation of man, and as nothing else, has been perverted by them into worship of the senses for their own sake—a thing which to Heine would have seemed despicable. Ibsen has fallen among the realists and propagandists; all the spiritual value of his work has for this age been lost—and what a loss!—his battle to deliver man from his weakness and inward slavery has been reduced—it is no exaggeration—to a battle to deliver the women of the middle classes from their husbands. The old story of emanation has been again repeated, with the distinction that here there is no trace left of the original source except negative ones! Well, we have to turn back again, as Mr Chesterton is fond of saying; our task, second to none in grandeur, before which we may well feel abashed, is still the same as that of Goethe, Ibsen and Nietzsche, the task of emancipation. To restore dignity to literature, indeed, it would be necessary to create such a task if it did not already exist. [. . .]

Domination of the Present

To be modern in the accepted, intellectually fashionable sense: what is that? To propagate always the newest theory, whatever it be; to be the least possible distance behind the times, behind the latest second of the times, whether they be good or bad; and, of course, to assume one is 'in the circle' and to adopt the tone of the circle: in short, to make ideas a matter of fashion, to choose views as a well-to-do woman chooses dresses—to be intellectually without foundation, principles or taste. How did this convention arise? Perhaps out of lack of leisure: superficiality is bound to engulf a generation who abandon leisure. But to be enslaved to the present in this way is the most *dangerous* form of superficiality: it is to be ignorant of the very thing that makes Man significant, and with idiotic cheerfulness and unconcern to render his existence meaningless and trivial. In two ways can Man become sublime; by regarding himself as the heir of a great tradition; by making of himself a forerunner. Both ways are open to the true modern, and both must be followed by him. For the past and the future are greater than the present: the sense of continuity is necessary for human dignity.

The men of this age, however, are isolated—to use an electrical metaphor—from the current of Humanity; they have become almost entirely individuals, temporal units, 'men': what has been the outcome? Inevitably the loss of the concept Man, for Man is a concept which can be understood only through the contemplation on a grand scale of the history of mankind. Man ceases to be dramatic when there are no longer spectators for the drama of Humanity. The present generation have, therefore, no sentiment of the human sublime; they see that part of the grand tragedy which happens to pass before them, but without caring about what went before or what will come after, without a clue, however poor, to the mystery of existence. They know men only, the men of their time. They are provincial—that is, lacking the sentiment of Man.

How much decadence may not be traced to this! In Art, the conventions of Realism and Aestheticism have arisen. The first is just the portrayal of present-day men *as* present-day men; nothing more, therefore, than 'contemporary art'; an appendage of the present, a triviality. The second has as its creed enjoyment of the moment; and if it contemplates the past at all, it is with the eyes of the voluptuous antiquary—but a collector is not an heir. Art has in our time, both in theory and in practice, become deliberately more fleeting. In morality, there is Humanitarianism, or, in other words, the conviction that the suffering of to-day is the most important thing, coupled with the belief that there is nothing at present existing which can justify and redeem this suffering: therefore, unconditional pity, alleviation, 'the greatest happiness of the greatest number'. Modern pessimism, which springs from the same source, is the obverse of this belief.

It, also, regards only the present, and says, perhaps with truth, that *it*, at any rate, is not noble enough to deserve and demand the suffering necessary for its existence—consequently, *all life* is an error! All these theories, however, are breaks with the spiritual tradition of emancipation; they are founded on the magnification of the temporary—of that which only in a present continually carried forward seems to be important. This judgment of Life with the eyes of the present, this narrowest and most false of interpretations: how has it confused and finally stultified the finest talents of our time! The modern man is joyless; his joylessness has arisen out of his modernity; and now to find forgetfulness of it he plunges more madly than before—into modernity! For his own sake, as much as that of Humanity, it is our duty to free him from his wheel. One can live with dignity only if one have a sense of the tragedy of Man. It is the first task of the true modern to destroy the domination of the present. [. . .]

What is Modern?

It is time we erected a standard whereby to test what is modern. To be an adherent of all the latest movements—that is at most to be anarchistic, eclectic, inconsistent—call it what you will. Futurism, Realism, Feminism, Traditionalism may be all of them opposed or irrelevant to modernity. It is not sufficient that movements should be new—if they are ever new; the question is, To what end are they? If they are movements in the direction of emancipation, 'the elevation of the type Man', then they are modern; if they are not, then they are movements to be opposed or ignored by moderns. If modernism be a vital thing it must needs have roots in the past and be an essential expression of humanity, to be traced, therefore, in the history of humanity: in short, it can only be a tradition. The true modern is a continuator of tradition as much as the Christian or the conservative: the true fight between progress and stagnation is always a fight between antagonistic *traditions*. To battle against tradition *as such* is, therefore, not the task of the modern; but rather to enter the conflict—an eternal one—for his tradition against its opposite: Nietzsche found for this antithesis the symbolism of Dionysus and Apollo. Does such a tradition of modernity exist? Is there a 'modern spirit' not dependent upon time and place, and in all ages modern? If there is—and there is—the possession of it in some measure will alone entitle us to the name of moderns, give us dignity and make the history of Man once more dramatic and tragical. It is a pity that some historian has not yet traced, in its expression in events, the history of this conflict—a task requiring the deepest subtlety and insight. Meantime, for this tradition may be claimed with confidence such events as Greek Tragedy, the most of the Renaissance, and the emancipators of last century. These are triumphant expressions of 'the modern spirit', but that spirit is chiefly to be recognized as a principle, not always triumphant or easy of perception, constantly struggling, assuming many disguises and tirelessly creative. It is not, indeed, only a tradition of persons, of dogmas, or of sentiments: it is a principle of Life itself. This conception, it is true, is grand, and even terrifying—a disadvantage in this age. But is there any other which grants modernity more than the status of an accident of time and fashion?

c) From 'Art and Literature'

Dostoieffsky

Dostoieffsky depicted the subconscious as conscious; that was how he achieved his complex and great effects. For the subconscious is the sphere of all that is most primeval, mysterious and sublime in man; the very bed out of which springs the flower of tragedy. But did Dostoieffsky do well to lay bare that world previously so reverently hidden, and to bring the reader behind the scenes of tragedy? The artist will deny it—the artist who always demands as an ingredient in his highest effects mystery. For how can mystery be retained when the very realm of mystery, the subconscious, is surveyed and mapped? In Dostoieffsky's imperishable works the spirit of full tragedy is perhaps never evoked. What he provides in them, however, is such a criticism of tragedy as is nowhere else to be found. His genius was for criticism; the artist in him created these great figures in order that afterwards the psychologist might dissect them. And so well are they dissected, even down to the subconsciousness, that, to use a phrase of the critics, we know them better than the people we meet. Well, that is precisely what we object to—as lovers of art! [. . .]

Myth

The worst evil of our time is this, that there is nothing greater than the current average existence to which men can look; Religion has dried up, Art has decayed from an idealization of life into a reflection of it. In short, Art has become a passive thing, where once it was the 'great stimulus to Life'. The idealization and enchantment which the moderns have so carefully eliminated from it was precisely its *raison d'être*. And modern Art, which sets out to copy life, has forgotten Art altogether, its origin, its meaning and its end.

Against this mindless Realism we must oppose idealization, and especially that which is its highest expression, Myth. And let no one say that it is impossible at this stage in Man's history to resuscitate Myth. The past has certainly lost its mystery for us, and it was in the past, at the source of Humanity, that the old poets set their sublime fictions. But the future is still ours, and there, at Man's goal, our myths must be planted. And thither, indeed, has set the great literature of the last hundred years. Faust, Mephistopheles, Brand, Peer Gynt, Zarathustra—there were no greater figures in the literature of the last century—were all myths, and all forecasts of the future. The soil out of which literature grows, then, has not yet been exhausted! If we but break away from Realism, if we make Art symbolic, if we bring about a marriage between Art and Religion, Art will rise again. That this is possible, we who have faith in the future *must* believe.

d) From 'The Tragic View'

Nietzsche

What was Nietzsche, that subtlest of modern riddles? First, a great tragic poet: it was by a divine accident that he was at the same time a profound thinker and the deepest psychologist. But his tragic affirmative was the core of his work, of which thought and analysis were but outgrowths. Without it, his subtlety might have made him another Pascal. The Will to Power, which makes suffering integral in Life; the Order of Rank whereby the bulk of mankind are doomed to slavery; the Superman himself, that most sublime child of Tragedy; and the last affirmation, the Eternal Recurrence: these are the conceptions of a tragic poet. It is, indeed, by virtue of his tragic view of Life that Nietzsche is for us a force of such value. For only by means of it could modern existence, sunk in scepticism, pessimism and the greatest happiness of the greatest number, be re-created.

For the last two centuries Europe has been under the domination of the concept of Happiness as progress. Altruism, the ideology of the greatest happiness of the greatest number, altruism as a means of universalizing Happiness, was preached in the eighteenth century; until after a while it was seen by such clear-sighted observers as Voltaire that men did not obey this imperative of altruism; therefore they were condemned: the moral indignation of the eighteenth century, the century of censoriousness par excellence, was the result. First, an impossible morality was demanded, and for the attainment of an unattainable ideal; then Man was condemned because he failed to comply with it, because he was Man. Thus in the end the ideal of the greatest happiness worked out in pessimism: Life became hideous and, worst of all, immoral, to the utilitarian, when it was seen that altruism and happiness are alike impossible. Schopenhauer is here the heir of Voltaire: the moral condemnation of the one has become in the other a condemnation of Life itself, more profound, more poetical, more logical.

Altruism has in Schopenhauer deepened into pity; for Pity is altruism bereft of the illusion of Happiness.

How was Man to avoid now the almost inevitable bourne of Nihilism? By renouncing altogether Happiness as a value; by restoring a conception of Life in which happiness was neither a positive nor a negative standard, but something irrelevant, an accident: in short, by setting up a tragic conception of Life. This was the task of Nietzsche: in how far he succeeded how can we yet say?

Again

Nietzsche loved not goodness but greatness: the True, the *Great* and the Beautiful. Was not this the necessary corollary of his aesthetic evaluation of Life?

> (Edward Moore [Edwin Muir], *We Moderns: Enigmas and Guesses* London: George Allen & Unwin, 1918, pp.15–17; 91–93, 113–14, 120–22, 124–27, 128–30; 147–48, 172–74; 233–35.)

5.9   T.S. Eliot, from 'Tradition and the Individual Talent' (*Egoist* September 1919)

The progress of an artist is a continual self-sacrifice, a continual extinction of personality.

There remains to define this process of depersonalization and its relation to the sense of tradition: it is in this depersonalization that art may be said to approach the condition of science. I therefore invite you to consider, as a suggestive analogy the action which takes place when a bit of finely filiated platinum is introduced into a chamber containing oxygen and sulphur dioxide. [. . .]

The analogy was that of the catalyst. When the two gases previously mentioned are mixed in the presence of a filament of platinum, they form sulphurous acid. This combination takes place only if the platinum is present; nevertheless the newly formed acid contains no trace of platinum, and the platinum itself is apparently unaffected: has remained inert, neutral, and unchanged. The mind of the poet is the shred of platinum. It may partly or exclusively operate upon the experience of the man himself; but the more perfect the artist, the more completely separate in him will be the man who suffers and the mind which creates; the more perfectly will the mind digest and transmute the passions which are its material [. . .] for my meaning is, that the poet has, not a 'personality' to express, but a particular medium, which is only a medium and not a personality, in which impressions and experiences combine in peculiar and unexpected ways.

Impressions and experiences which are important for the man may take no place in the poetry, and those which become important in the poetry may play quite a negligible part in the man, the personality. [. . .] In fact, the bad poet is usually unconscious where he ought to be conscious, and conscious where he ought to be unconscious. Both errors tend to make him 'personal'. Poetry is not a turning loose of emotion, but an escape from emotion; it is not the expression of personality, but an escape from personality. [. . .] The emotion of art is impersonal. And the poet cannot reach this impersonality without surrendering himself wholly to the work to be done. And he is not likely to know what is to be done unless he lives in what is not merely the present, but the present moment of the past, unless he is conscious, not of what is dead, but of what is already living.

(T.S. Eliot, 'Tradition and the Individual Talent' (1919), reprinted from T.S. Eliot, *Selected Essays* London: Faber and Faber, 1951, pp.13–22 [17, 18, 19–20, 21, 22].)

5.10 T.S. Eliot, from 'The Metaphysical Poets' (*Times Literary Supplement* October 1921)

It is perhaps somewhat less fair, though very tempting (as both poets are concerned with the perpetuation of love by offspring), to compare with the stanzas already quoted from Lord Herbert's Ode the following from Tennyson. [. . .] The difference is not a simple difference of degree between poets. It is something which had happened to the mind of England between the time of Donne or Lord Herbert of Cherbury and the time of Tennyson and Browning; it is the difference between the intellectual poet and the reflective poet. Tennyson and Browning are poets, and they think; but they do not feel their thought as immediately as the odour of a rose. A thought to Donne was an experience; it modified his sensibility. When a poet's mind is perfectly equipped for its work, it is constantly amalgamating disparate experience; the ordinary man's experience is chaotic, irregular, fragmentary. The latter falls in love, or reads Spinoza, and these two experiences have nothing to do with each other, or with the noise of the typewriter or the smell of cooking; in the mind of the poet these experiences are always forming new wholes.

We may express the difference by the following theory: The poets of the seventeenth century, the successors of the dramatists of the sixteenth, possessed a mechanism of sensibility which could devour any kind of experience. They are simple, artificial, difficult, or fantastic, as their predecessors were; no less nor more than Dante, Guido Cavalcanti, Guinicelli, or Cino. In the seventeenth century a dissociation of sensibility set in, from which we have never recovered; and this dissociation, as is natural, was aggravated by the influence of the two most powerful poets of the century, Milton and Dryden. Each of these men performed certain poetic functions so magnificently well that the magnitude of the effect concealed the absence of others. The language went on and in some respects improved; the best verse of Collins, Gray, Johnson, and even Goldsmith satisfied some of our fastidious demands better than that of Donne or Marvell or King. But while the language became more refined, the feeling became more crude. The feeling, the sensibility, expressed in the *Country Churchyard* (to say nothing of Tennyson and Browning) is cruder than that in the *Coy Mistress*.

The second effect of the influence of Milton and Dryden followed from the first, and was therefore slow in manifestation. The sentimental age began early in the eighteenth century, and continued. The poets revolted against the ratiocinative, the descriptive; they thought and felt by fits, unbalanced; they reflected. In one or two passages of Shelley's *Triumph of Life*, in the second *Hyperion*, there are traces of a struggle toward unification of sensibility. But Keats and Shelley died, and Tennyson and Browning ruminated.

(T.S. Eliot, 'The Metaphysical Poets' (1921), reprinted from T.S. Eliot, *Selected Essays* (1951), pp.281–91 [287–88].)

5.11 Concerning Spengler: C.M. Grieve, from 'Causerie' (*Scottish Chapbook* March 1923)

Despite the chaos of conflicting opinion on every subject in the world to-day, there seems to be remarkable unanimity among intellectuals of the type who endeavour to form world-opinions in the view that Western civilisation is doomed. [. . .] Similar views have been expressed [. . .] by Herr Spengler, the German philosopher, who, in the *Downfall of the Western World* traced the causes of the decline of ancient civilisations and drew an analogy with the present. Spengler's central thesis has already— however ill understood—influenced the literature of every country in Europe: and has given rise to a literature already immense. Spengler is no pessimist: to translate the title of his book, *The Downfall of the Western World*, is to suggest a false idea of it. The idea he seeks to convey is rather 'fulfilment'—the end of one civilisation and the beginning of another—the emergence of a new order. Spengler considers the creative element in his writing to lie in the fact that he has proved by the test of concrete experience that universal history is not a universal succession of occurrences, but a group, so far numbering eight, of high civilisations whose life-histories, completely independent of one another, yet present themselves to us with a perfectly analogous development. It follows that he holds each of these civilisations to have an absolute standard, applicable to itself alone. Every vital idea—including Spengler's own, as he admits—belongs to its own age, its own civilisation, and in the course of history as a whole there are no false or true doctrines any more than there are false or true stages in the growth of a plant. For the man or nation with a true 'historic view' there are no past models to be imitated; there are only examples of the way in which this or that civilisation advanced to its appointed fulfilment. Everything depends upon the way in which men are fulfilling their destiny. [. . .] Western Europe, with America, has exhausted her creative energies as Greece, Rome, Assyria, Babylon, exhausted their energies before her. She can add nothing more to the sum of vitally new human knowledge, of fresh and adequate channels of self-expression. We must wait for the inevitable end or rather the new beginning which will come from a civilisation other than ours . . . And he asserts that already in Dostoevsky is to be found the first delineation of that new world.

Of the many antitheses out of which Herr Spengler builds up his thesis—which is destined to have an incalculable influence upon the future of human literature—that which predominates in every chapter is the distinction he draws between the 'Apollonian' or classical, and the 'Faustian' or modern type. The Appollonian type is dogmatic, unquestion-ing, instinctive, having no conception of infinity—in short, your average Englishman or German—and the Faustian mind, on the contrary, is dominated by the conception of infinity, of the unattainable, and hence is ever questioning, never satisfied, rationalistic in religion and politics, romantic in art and literature—a perfect expression of the Scottish race.

It was anticipated that Spengler, in his second book—which has just been published—would reveal the East as the source of the civilisation destined to replace our own, that of the declining West, . . . and in this connection it is well to remember in passing that we Scots are Oriental, the descendants of the lost tribes of Israel (sic). . . and so he does but only very briefly. [. . .]

The canny Scot tradition has been 'fulfilled' in the Spenglerian sense; and the future depends upon the freeing and development of that opposite tendency in our consciousness which runs counter to the conventional conceptions of what is Scottish. In other words, the slogan of a Scottish literary revival must be the Nietzschean 'Become what you are'.

(C.M. Grieve, 'Causerie', *Scottish Chapbook* 1:8 March 1923, pp.212–14.)

5.12 From 'Edwin Muir and F.G. Scott: A Conversation' (*Freeman* December 1923)

SCOTT: After the concert [at the Salzburg Festival] last night I was still not quite sure about that song-cycle of Schönberg's. It is perfect in what it attempts; and it is all sustained on one key, and that is not an easy thing to accomplish. A greater man would have found it impossible to remain for such a long time on the same key. He could have done it theoretically, for his power would have been sufficient. But he could not have done it in reality, because common sense, or the lyrical impulse, or whatever you call it, would have broken in and would have varied the mood. He would have asked himself, why am I doing this, this in particular and nothing else? and he would have widened the basis of his cycle.

MUIR: I believe you are right, F.G., though you must acknowledge that what you say goes against your preference for French literature. The French have poisoned us all with the itch for unity. I must confess—though it is shocking—that I have always found myself a little unconsciously ironical in reading *Madame Bovary*, marvellous work as it is and much as I admire it. I always feel that at any moment what you call common sense may break in and raise *Madame Bovary* to the first rank in literature, and disturb the inexorable tenor of the story, and destroy its unity of mood. What a relief that would be! As great a relief as seeing a rare vase splintered to pieces after years of anxiety lest it should be splintered to pieces. I have a gross suspicion F.G., about both you and myself. The thing which makes you not take Schönberg seriously, and what makes me not take *Madame Bovary* seriously, is a fundamental lack of reverence for art; for these are art, art distilled and concentrated, as it were, until there is nothing else left. We have an essential lack of reverence for art—a very rare quality in this age.

SCOTT: You have more reverence for art than you think, Muir. Why, you admire the Germans, who have always put reverence between them and art. You object to my liking for the French, but there is a very good reason why the French should be liked. They know what's what; and they know it not, like other races, in flashes but habitually. They are aware that art is one thing and life another, and they do not try to crush into art *das Ganze, das Geheimnis, die Seele, der Zeitgeist*, and on top of all that a *Weltanschauung*. They are too much in earnest to be reverential. You said last evening that you thought French writers must work far harder at their craft than English or German ones, seeing that their form is so much more inevitable and finished. But that is not it. They do not work harder than we do; think more closely. They always know what they are doing, and in art that is an uncommon thing. Flaubert's problem in *Madam Bovary* [sic] was to get a certain effect, and he took good care that he obtained it. He obtained other effects in *Salammbô* and *Bouvard et Pécuchet*. It was a matter purely of seeing his end concretely and using the best means for attaining it. When an artist reaches that stage he sees the whole problem too clearly to be capable of reverence; for it is impossible for a man to stand in awe of the effects he gets when he knows exactly how he produced them. French artists are behind the scenes the whole time—exactly where they should be; and they are more like actors than the artists of other nations. They know that art is *artificiel*, a word that in French, and quite rightly, has a far more respectable meaning than our 'artificial'. They know what to do to produce the phenomenon people call beauty, while they live among the means, which are themselves no more beautiful than the stage-properties seen from behind. They know this, simply because it is their business. It seems to me that French art is the most fundamentally irreverent art there is.

MUIR: Yes, F.G., I acknowledge that French art is irreverent, but it is not irreverent towards art. I can imagine a French poet regarding a really beautiful verse he has manufactured and smiling ironically, as Wordsworth could not have done, or Goethe either. But afterwards he will take art with enormous seriousness. He will acknowledge that it is a convention, but about this convention he will be more solemn than the most solemn German poet. German poetry has become much more serious since Stephen George [sic] began to Frenchify it; quite that solemnity it never had before. And then how much in earnest the French have taken the matter of form! They narrowed and conventionalised their whole literature for two centuries, and ours for one, by their deadly seriousness about form. They are doing so still, not in France only, but all over Europe. You can see the influence of France in Schönberg's adherence to one emotional key in his song-cycle. You can see it everywhere: in the conventionalisation of the novel in England, in the conventionalisation of the forms of unconventional verse, in the general blossoming of schools, which exist only for the sake of settling a form before it is practised and made alive. Is it not so? Well, all this I call taking art with intense and disproportionate seriousness. Our people, the artless Scots, thank God, could do nothing of the kind. Is it conceivable that any audience in London, in Dublin, or in Edinburgh, would stop a dramatic performance because the corresponding English word for *mouchoir* was used instead of the corresponding English word for *tissu*? No; our race, praise be to God, are not cursed with a sense of literary style.

('Edwin Muir and Francis George Scott: A Conversation', *Freeman* [USA] 8,
19 December 1923; reprinted from Maurice Lindsay, *Francis George Scott and the
Scottish Renaissance* Edinburgh: Paul Harris Publishing, 1980, pp.165–72 [165–66].)

5.13 Edwin Muir, from 'Friedrich Hölderlin' (*Scottish Nation* September 1923)

It was in 1916 that for the first time a complete collection of Hölderlin's poems appeared. The poet had died seventy years before, and the period in which he had written was past for more than a century. During that time he had had an acknowledged place among the lesser German poets; but the discovery of the new poems by Von Hellingrath changed at once his rank, and installed him in a position second only to Goethe's in the hierarchy of German poetry. He appeared now, by a happy chance, as not only the poet second in greatness to Goethe, but as the German poet most unlike Goethe, the poet who, in lacking most conspicuously the capacities which Goethe had, brought into German poetry a spirit and a vision which Goethe was prevented by the complexion of his genius from attaining. For Germany Hölderlin is in a sense the spiritual complement of Goethe, in a sense his spiritual antagonist, his salutary antithesis. Both seem to have felt during their lives an unspoken enmity. In Goethe's conversations there is, among encouraging comments on inferior writers, no mention at all of Hölderlin; and Hölderlin, in the long period of insanity which closed his life, pretended stubbornly, whenever the greatest of German writers was mentioned, that he did not know the name. Time has settled the quarrel; the genius of Hölderlin discovered in its fullness only a few years ago, has to-day a greater influence on the German spirit than that of Goethe, and in the next decade it may well become still more powerful. That part of the German spirit which was incarnated in Hölderlin is coming into the consciousness of German culture, now that the influence of Goethe has fructified and been for the moment exhausted.

To try to define what the genius of a great poet signifies in a specific culture is always a perilous task, and most perilous of all when it appears to be successful. But there are one or two broad points of difference between Goethe and Hölderlin which make clearer the essential contrast between their spirits. Goethe was a many-sided genius, all of whose sides were not equally great. He was great, supremely great, as a lyric and dramatic poet; he was great also, on a definitely lower plane, as a repository of practical wisdom on life, as, on the whole, the most unembarrassed liver and observer of life that the world has given us in modern times. His greatness as a poet was the greatness of absolute freedom; his greatness as a practical philosopher was the outcome of his calm recognition of the limitations of existence. There was a third Goethe, and probably a fourth and a fifth; there was, prominently exhibited, at any rate, the 'eingebildet' Goethe, the hero of self-culture who created himself in his own image so indefatigably and with such self-sacrifice; and this Goethe, it will be generally acknowledged now, was certainly less great than the natural Goethe out of whom he was hewn, the mighty spirit who imagined the last act in the first part of *Faust*, and who wrote the lyrics and ballads. But whether we admire it or not, we must admit that this was one of the sides of Goethe. He was, as Arnold saw, a naturalist in the great sense, a man who before every phenomenon accepted or despised by the human spirit, asked imperturbably, 'But is it so? Is it so to ME?' He was, as Emerson perceived, a prince of culture, a man who incarnated, or, at any rate, heroically strove to incarnate the highest normal life of humanity. He aspired to it, he essayed it; but when he essayed it he became at best didactic and at worst pedantic. Now Hölderlin is the chief mystical poet of German, as Goethe is its chief human poet. Goethe was greatest when he was pure artist; Hölderlin, when he was half-artist, half-prophet. To use very simple terms, Goethe was inspired by a vision of human life as it is eternally; whereas Hölderlin had his eyes fixed on the mystical goal towards which humanity is moving, and that chiefly inspired his genius. He was most truly himself when he described mankind not in its eternal normal state, but in its movement to a sanctified end. His landscapes are accordingly tremendous, and have the outline and the atmosphere of a gigantic dream; but their serenity is not that of rest, but of steady, celestial progress. He lived in this atmosphere, the atmosphere of humanity and of the gods, more permanently than any other modern poet except Blake. He lived with the gods, 'daring to bring the gods and men nearer together'. His problem was not, like Goethe's, to experience beautifully and normally the life given us by the earth, but to exist in a state of glory, in which the terrestrial and the celestial life were one, in which the terrestrial had become the celestial.

Even in his earliest poems he was haunted by the thought of the dual existence of the gods and of men. Why should they both exist, and why should there be an unbridgeable gulf between them? 'You wander up there in the light', he says in one of the most beautiful of his earlier lyrics, the 'Schicksalslied', 'on soft lawns, spiritual beings ... Fateless, like the sleeping child, breathe the heavenly ones. Chastely nourished in separate buds, the spirit blooms in them forever, and the spiritual eyes gaze in still, eternal clarity'. 'But to us', he cries,

> But to us is given
> In no state to rest;
> They vanish, they fall,
> The suffering mortals,
> Blindlings from one
> Hour to another,
> Like water from cliff
> To cliff flung downward
> Yearlong into the unknown below.

A profound sense of the irremediable division of life lies on all these early poems. [. . .]

Like Wordsworth, and with some striking differences, like his countryman, Nietzsche, Hölderlin was a mystic of the earth, of nature, and of man. He was concerned in his last poems with the gods only when they appeared on the earth, in history, and behind the forms of nature. He was no longer tortured by the dualism of a heavenly and a human life expressed so poignantly in his earlier poems; that was resolved for him in the end, he believed, in a form of being in which, while remaining human, he existed in a state of almost divine ecstasy. His task, as he accepted it, was, accordingly, 'to bring the gods and men nearer together'. This he regarded as a religious work, but where he differed from most of the religions which have fulfilled their mission in the world was in his belief that in order to exist as a seraphic being it was not necessary to deny the earth, but rather in a high sense to understand and be at one with it. He was a Pantheist, and his poems have no appeal to the weakness but only to the strength of mankind. They will attract perhaps no great number of men. But, however that may be, they have the power of ennobling those who live for a time in their atmosphere. That atmosphere is unlike anything else in German literature, and its nearest analogue is to be found in the music of Beethoven.

A great mystical poet, Hölderlin was also one of the masters of German poetic style. His sense of form, in a poetry which even at its greatest, even in Goethe, is distinguished chiefly by naturalness and spontaneity, was full-grown and sure. The masters of style, of style in the classical sense, in German poetry, are few. Outside Hölderlin there are only Platen, Hugo von Hofmannsthal, and Stefan George, but, fine as these were, Hölderlin was as a stylist, greater than them all. At his best he wrote in the grand style, in a style noble and large, which in its processional movement gave the simplest words and thoughts the significance and mystery which things take on when they are set apart, in an atmosphere inaccessible to common men. Like Milton he was not only noble, but conscious of the nobility which his theme imposed upon him, and it is this which gave his verse its majestic movement, its conscious, processional advance. He was neither so sure nor so magnificent a master of the grand style as Milton: there are whole tracts of his verse where the manner maintains an incongruous dignity far above the weak inspiration of the moment; there are poems, again, in which the expression and the thought are alike prosaic. But at his best, he wrote poetry which in elevation of utterance has not been equalled by any other German, and which has been surpassed by few except the very greatest poets.

(Edwin Muir, 'Friedrich Hölderlin', *Scottish Nation* 1:14, 11 September 1923, pp.6–7, 15 [6–7].)

5.14   C.M. Grieve, from 'William and Agnes M'Cance' (*Scottish Educational Journal* November 1925)

These names are still practically unknown in Scotland and only known in England to a very limited public and on the continent in certain advanced art-circles. But the existence of two such personalities—and their recent awakening, or return, to a sense of their distinctive potentialities as Scots and of the unique opportunities now offering themselves for a Scottish Renaissance—are unquestionably the most promising phenomena of contemporary Scotland in regard to art. If that divination of opportunity which five or six years ago led to what has since become known as the Scottish Renaissance movement, was well-founded—if, indeed, the psychological moment had arrived for a national awakening (and that was the preliminary assumption which has led to many of the subsequent activities and aspirations which I have been describing)—it was obvious that personalities of this very kind must speedily become active in Scottish art and so complement and confirm the manifestations of the new spirit already evident in literature, music, and other departments of our national life. This anticipation fulfils itself in Mr and Mrs M'Cance, and the lines along which they are now thinking and acting adumbrate the future of Scottish art—the effect of the Renaissance spirit in this sphere as it will be appreciated in retrospect. [. . .] Both Mr and Mrs M'Cance belong to the Glasgow district, and are in their early thirties. Prior to leaving Glasgow, Mr M'Cance gave a lecture to the young 'Society of Painters and Sculptors' on modern art which was received with a certain measure of hostility to say the least of it. They went to London, where he did a certain amount of illustrating and lecturing. At present he is art critic of the *Spectator*. In writing of their own work one is handicapped by the fact that probably none of one's readers have seen any of it. Exceptions may perhaps be made of Mr M'Cance's portrait of Mr William Brewer and of the fifty-foot panel he painted for the *Daily News*, which has been described as one of the best examples of progressive unity in modern painting. Both, however, are highly productive artists, concerned exclusively—and this is the measure of their artistic integrity—with the basic problems with which progressive artists everywhere are to-day preoccupied and not with the commercial application of established, that is to say effete, techniques. And they are necessarily approaching these problems, and resolving them, as Scots—that is to say that the psychological factor is so directly involved and dominant in work of this kind that the difference between the effects they are securing and the effects their French or German contemporaries are securing gives the precise measure of what is distinctively Scottish in this connection. [. . .] In the meantime their work is probably unintelligible to the great mass of those who look to find a 'likeness' in a portrait (and are at sea with a psychological criticism expressing itself in terms of the interrelationships of planes) or who demand of a picture that it reproduces a recognisable place or embodies a pleasing conception or 'points a moral or adorns a tale'. And the number of those in Scotland who have got beyond the stage of making such demands of any work of art with which they may be confronted is extremely small. Indeed the proportion which has yet been confronted with any work of art which does not conform to such preconceptions is extremely small.

The whole course of modern art in all its amazing and absorbing developments is a sealed book to all but a mere handful of the population of Scotland. [. . .] In Scotland—in art as in letters—we are still in precisely the same position as was Holland prior to the emergence of the 'De Stijl' Group in 1917—a country of pretentious and vigorous conservatism, 'constantly warming up the egg of the 80's', as Theo Van Doesburg has put it, although 'this celebrated movement only defended a tendency which had already lapsed in France'—a fight for the cast-off clothes of other nations.

But in the ideas of M'Cance and his wife and one or two others Scotland may soon acquire not only an equivalent to the 'De Stijl' development, but, thanks to the unparalleled strength of our engineering and dialectical aptitudes if these can be reoriented and applied in cultural directions, transcend it and at one step make good the long inhibition or subversion of our most distinctive powers and become the vanguard of the art of the future.

(C.M. Grieve, 'William and Agnes M'Cance', *Scottish Educational Journal* 20 November 1925, reprinted from Centenary re-issue, 1976, pp.58–59.)

5.15   C.M. Grieve, from 'Paul Valéry' (*New Age* 1927)

'*The intelligent man must finally reduce himself knowingly to an indefinite refusal to be anything whatsoever.*' Valéry.

The whole point of the neo-classical tendency which is increasingly manifesting itself in all the arts is being ludicrously missed by those who are confusing it with a return to any 'classical' formalism instead of to fundamental form and are welcoming the apparent volte-face of most of our advanced composers—e.g. Stravinsky, Bartok, Casella—as a repudiation of their 'wild oats' instead of a far more intensive cultivation of them.

The meaning of the effort to 'depersonalise' music—to rid it of its literary, personal and humanistic element, and to hail the time when all instrumental music will be played by mechanical reproducing instruments as a means to this end—is akin to that of Mallarmé when he said, 'Ce n'est pas avec des idées qu'on fait des vers, c'est avec des mots', or to Valéry's own call for a 'language machine'. All the arts must disencumber themselves completely of the moral and ethical clichés, the dreary literalism, the empty bombast, the democratic insistence on 'more meaning', the messianic illusion, by which they are presently confused and confounded. All kinds of eloquence are having their necks wrung with a thoroughness as unprecedented as it is vitally necessary. Let us regard all the arts altogether technically. Let us, in particular, disabuse ourselves of the idea that art becomes great in direct ratio to the number—and consequently relative ignorance—of those to whom it appeals. Let us get rid of all the solemn awestruck nonsense about genius, all the high-falution about 'poets being born, not made', and the like, and all the brainless rhodomontade about 'architecture being frozen music', music 'volatilised architecture', and the rest of the fatuous journalese. Let us acquire some such sane and self-respecting attitude to ourselves and our readers as Valéry's. 'M. Valéry would at once concede that neither in his choice of themes nor in his treatment of them is he concerned to stir the common heart of man.'

(C.M. Grieve, 'Paul Valéry', New Age 1 December 1927, p.54.)

5.16   Edwin Muir, from letter to Sydney Schiff (July 1929)

Crowborough
8 July, 1929

My dear Sydney, [. . .]

You ask me whether I have come across anything moving recently. By great good fortune I have. I don't know whether you have ever read Rilke's *Die Aufzeichnungen des Malte Laurids Brigge* and Franz Kafka's *Das Schloss*. I came across them both about the same time, and I was more moved than by anything I have come across for a long time. Rilke's poetry I really don't much care for, subtle and supremely skilful as it is, but this strange prose work certainly proves that he was a man of genius. The atmosphere is very curious, half Baudelairian, half Dostoevskyan, the psychology really subtle, and the style superbly brilliant and incisive. I was quite thrilled by the book, and I think you might like it. Kafka's book is still more strange in its atmosphere; it is a purely metaphysical and mystical dramatic novel; the ordinary moral judgments do not come in at all; everything happens on a mysterious spiritual plane which was obviously the supreme reality to the author; and yet in a curious way everything is given solidly and concretely. The book was left unfinished when Kafka died a few years ago. We are translating it for Secker. I don't know whether you would like it or not, but it appeals particularly to the part of me which wrote *The Marionette*. It is quite unique, and I think first class of its kind.

(Edwin Muir, letter to Sydney Schiff [the novelist Stephen Hudson] 8 July 1929, reprinted from P.H. Butter ed., Selected Letters of Edwin Muir London: Hogarth Press, 1974, p.67.)

5.17   From 'Book Reviews' (*Modern Scot* Summer 1930)

a) Mary Baird Aitken, from '*Marcel Proust: Sa Révélation Psychologique*'

Here is a book that, had the 'effort proustien' in life and letters, been less static and more dynamic, would have been a big book. Even so, the author, like Proust himself, under no illusion as to the shortcomings of his subject, and with something of Proust's own scientific detachment and charm, undertakes, with great suggestiveness, a somewhat technical psychological study of Proust's methods as author, posing inevitably the question of his 'insuffisance psychologique et morale'. The book is another of those fine critical studies by Frenchmen, such as Gide and Maurois, saying their say in the 'world debate' upon contemporary problems of science and art. Bergson, Freud, Frazer, and the French psychologists of the primitives are all called into service. [. . .]

M. Dandieu has interesting things to say abut the Proustian conception of Time. Time, on the one hand, had a tragic aspect for one so utterly dependant on memory (though such a marvellous one). But oftenest it is the Bergsonian conception of Time as that Duration or Flux which is the essence of Life, that is the Proustian one. In comparing him with the earlier novelists, M. Dandieu shows the poetic quality that results from Proust's never having pretended to be outside of time, controlling it: but rather, that he himself is in the flux, dependant on outside forces for his very materials. And again, in a fine passage, the critic shows the value of that same juxtaposition of past and present of which we have spoken, and which was largely lacking in the early romantic poets who did not perceive, 'que tout le secret de la réussite artistique réside dans la simulanéité du souvenir passé, et de la sensation présente', and who rather spent themselves in bewailing the flight of the past. [. . .]

Lasting impressions of the book, as of Proust's work, are of that strange new psychological reality whose larger air we breathe as we sit in the garden at Combray the long summer afternoon; an enlargement of the intuitive in man as an instrument of perception; a corresponding development of a wise, if passive, sympathy; an infinite, yet not sentimental, pity; a power, that Proust himself felt was his special gift to others, to enable them to 'lire en eux-memes'. These are the permanent gifts of Proust to art and life, but bought at a great price, and often, by the very tyranny of his memory, employed to evoke baser gods, rather as the ritualist than the artist.

b) Unsigned review of *James Joyce's* Ulysses: *A Study* by Stuart Gilbert

Until Valery Larbaud gave them the hint, how many of the young revolutionaries hailing James Joyce as master and falling over each other to imitate him thought to compare thoroughly the Irish *Ulysses* with its Greek prototype? Yet as M. Larbaud said, the 'key' to *Ulysses* is in its title, and unless the Homeric analogies in Joyce are appreciated the masterpiece loses half its meaning. The chief merit of Stuart Gilbert's volume is that it dissects *Ulysses* chapter by chapter and leaves (it is safe to say) not one Homeric reference unmarked, not one esoteric allusion fully [un?]explained. [. . .]

There is no criticism in Mr Gilbert's book as good as M. Larbaud's. But the author's aim is not to be critical but expository, and since his erudition is very considerable and he has had the help of Mr Joyce himself his book may be regarded as having a unique value. As Mr Gilbert says: 'The position of *Ulysses* is such that its commentator can claim a special dispensation. *Ulysses*, it cannot be gainsaid, *fait école*; hardly any of the younger generation of writers but has been influenced by Mr Joyce's work. And, if the structure and true import of *Ulysses* be misapprehended, its influence is apt to be misleading, not to say pernicious. For it seems at first sight a mere fantasia of the subconscious, the manifesto of those forces of disorder which riot in the back of the mind, a demonstration that indiscipline and anarchy can subserve creative achievement. One of the objects of this study is to assert the falsity of such a view. . . . In the seven years which Mr Joyce devoted to the construction of this monument of literature, he never once betrayed the authority of intellect to the hydra-headed rabble of the mental underworld. *Ulysses* is, in fact, a work essentially classical in spirit, composed and executed according to rules of design and discipline of almost scientific precision.'

c) 'De Mortuis. . .'

Transition, the international review published in Paris, the organ of James Joyce and his group, comes to an end with a huge Spring-Summer issue of some 400 pages (mercifully cut) containing some of the most valuable and interesting articles which have recently appeared in any periodical. During the three years of its active existence *Transition* has published large portions of Joyce's 'Work in Progress' as well as a considerable amount of articles and poetry by prominent French, English and American writers: Gertrude Stein, Tristan Tzara, Hart Crane, John Rodker, and Stuart Gilbert (whose study of Joyce's epic *Ulysses* we have reviewed in this issue) and has exerted an incalculable influence upon contemporary world thought and literature.

The most significant article in the last number of *Transition* is by Dr Jung, the eminent psychologist, establishing a direct relationship between psychology and poetry. This statement is by no means new, it had been made years before by Bergson and adopted by the Surréalistes as their creed; the interesting point is that the psychologist and the philosopher should have arrived independently at the same conclusions. The belief that 'man inherits the collected mythos of his race' was of course put into practice in *Ulysses* by Joyce with amazing results, though so far few of his disciples have been able to follow their master up the same precipitous path.

The importance of this creed is that it extends beyond literature; it is a positive religious belief in the fundamental value of man and the only belief which is truly consistent with our present knowledge and attitude to life. As in the 18th century religion was essentially concerned with ethics, in the 19th century with morals, so it will be in the 20th with psychology. The fact that all three attitudes: the ethical, the moral, and the psychological can exist side by side only superficially obscures the real issue.

The reader will find in this issue much matter concerning dream-psychology, which from the Joycian viewpoint is of considerable value. But there are other articles of more general interest, including a long study by S.M. Eisenstein, the Russian film régisseur on the Japanese culture and its influence on his own work, poems by Hart Crane, Kay Boyle, and the reproductions of paintings by Juan Gris, Picasso and Paul Klee. The British agents for the magazine are Messrs Neumayer, Charing Cross Road, London, and the price is 4/6.

('Book Reviews': *Marcel Proust: Sa Révélation Psychologique*, by Arnaud Dandieu; *James Joyce's* Ulysses: A Study by Stuart Gilbert; 'De Mortuis' [concerning *Transition*], *Modern Scot* 1:2, summer 1930, pp.45–6, 53–55.)

5.18 William McCance, from 'Idea in Art' (*Modern Scot* Summer 1930)

When we examine any movement in art as something isolated from either life or its own traditional trend, we can usually provide ourselves with a gargantuan sneer at its expense. It has become the fashion to dismiss the Art-for-art's sake movement as purely worthless and yet, when it is examined in the light of the welter of artistic naturalism which surrounded it, there lies in it a certain significance. Like most of the movements which followed later, it was a fumbling after dynamic values which had been thrown to the four winds, when painters had gone out to the wide open spaces of Nature in order to practise imitative verisimilitude. The art-for-art's sake painters saw that all kinds of matter extraneous to art had crept in like a canker to destroy the bloom of art, but all that they could substitute was a certain artificiality, which was admirably related to the affected mannerisms practised by these precious young men in their mode of life. The next movement, still prevalent to-day and overlapping into to-morrow, was towards an art-for-craft's sake attitude. The artist threw aside his wide-brimmed hat and became the real god-damned workman who handles tools. 'Don't talk about art or anything; just admire the magnificent brush—WORK.' 'By their work alone shall ye know them.' Work, work, always work and the dignity of labour.

Then there arrived on the scene a new foreman called Roger Fry whose ancestors had been marking oblong pieces of chocolate into four oblong sections, and he saw that art was not only brush work and vibration of colour, but also Design, while Mr Clive Bell kept to the clerical department and evolved an idea that it was not the milk in the cocoanut that counted, but the 'Significant form'. When you painted a chair, according to Mr Bell you had to get the 'chairness of the chair'. Since the Great War Bloomsbury has been sitting on comfortable divans surrounded by cushions, trying to discover the 'chairness' of chairs. The women have grown a little bit thin on it and have lost their breasts and their vitality. The young men are looking for the lost breasts on Guardsmen's tunics. This is what comes of the search after 'significant Form'.

Although very little design ever managed to appear on the canvases of the followers of Mr Fry, this emphasis on Design was not without its value, for, at least, it made clear that a work of art should have structure. Whistler had done his bit in this direction, although he confined himself to the making of flat pattern. Design differs from pattern in so far as it embraces relationships in space and three-dimensional organisation of forms. A further development towards pure design came with the Cubists. 'Subject matter does not matter' was virtually the slogan of the Cubists. 'What you do with it; how you re-arrange it' was their concern. The subject matter was merely a starting stimulus for the game of inventing a pattern which would be complete in itself and disassociated from life. While the Cubists always used the term 'design', strangely enough they seldom produced anything beyond flat two-dimensional pattern in their work. At best they accomplished at times a rather fine two and a half-dimensional effect—that is, a flat pattern which had a suggestion of spaciousness and was not merely a decoration. The Futurists attempted to ginger up the actual movement of design and were responsible to a great extent for the interesting experiments that have since been done with abstract movement on the Films.

As a reaction against what was looked upon as the cold intellectualism of the Cubist there arose 'Expressionism', which was primarily a German contribution although, in spirit at any rate, the work of the Frenchman, Matisse, can be so classified. The Expressionists talked themselves into ethereal and bloodless shadows about spontaneity of reaction to subject matter. To be an Expressionist it was essential to forget all you ever knew, work yourself up into a state of mind approaching that of a jelly-fish, hold the painting hand above the head until the blood left it; then you could proceed; the unconscious would do the trick. You would be allowed, however, to study child-art. Expressionism was an attempt to establish emotional values in Art. Its logical end was the monkey's paw. Yet here again was a movement that contributed something of value to modern art for, while it neglected structure, it brought a certain aesthetic sensuousness into Art.

All of these later developments bring a greater subjectivity to Art and *do* give recognition to the fact (in contrast to all the earlier talk about nature and naturalism) that man, as far as men are concerned, is the highest product of nature, *is* Nature.

Now let us see where we are. [. . .] Up-to-date, we have two chief streams of research which have a certain significance. Is it possible that a synthesis can be made from both which might create the lost element of art? Cubism symbolises art as cerebral organisation, or what is commonly confused with intellectualism, while Expressionism would attempt to create an externalised emotionalism. The former, in its crude state, leads to mechanisation. The latter is a mere hysterical gesture—the tame lion opening its mouth and letting its guts rumble at the sight of food. The fertilisation of the one by the other, however, may produce the real egg which may be hatched into that highest expression of man—Idea. The result would be a real imaginative intellectualism. It may well be, too, that from the opposite angle, Idea may act as a better stimulus to creative effort than any other subject matter. One might go further and say that a more dynamic form of Design would result from this source than from a purely conscious desire to create design as an end in itself. The desire to produce pure design may lead, and does lead, to a very manufactured article indeed, whereas the design which evolves from an idea has a quality of growth that the other lacks. One had only to go to the Primitive Italians who aimed at religious expression to confirm this. Here, at any rate, an idea did produce the goods, while the later Renaissance painters, more often than not, became banal and mechanical. Naturally every work of art must contain design. If the Idea does not produce Design then the mind that conceived it is just not that of an artist.

In my opinion Scotland is the great White Hope in the field of European Art. The black man can still create magnificent idols when left alone with his magic and not forced into a false position by the Western missionaries of the much misunderstood *Word*. In England, to have an idea beyond the mere technical and manipulatory branch of his art is counted a disgrace for an artist. Let him utter one word which reveals any mentality and he is suspect. Probably the critic is responsible for this state, for, being as he is, a thwarted creator, he gains his power through explaining the artist to the public; and he knows that he can do this with less fear of exposure if he can create the illusion of the artist as the magnificent naïve who doesn't know what he is talking about. When the Scot can purge himself of the illusion that Art is reserved for the sentimentalist and realise that he, the Scot, has a natural gift for construction, combined with a racial aptitude for metaphyiscal thought and a deep emotional nature, then out of this combination can arise an art which will be pregnant with Idea, and have within it the seed of greatness. Besides the awareness of this potentiality, however, the Scot must break through his narrow provincial barriers and gain a knowledge of what is actually taking place in the world around him before he can become master of himself and not merely the ideal slave of others.

(William McCance, 'Idea in Art', *Modern Scot* 1:2 summer 1930, pp.13–16.)

5.19 'Continental Literature' (*Modern Scot* Autumn 1932)

It is often forgotten that Scottish Nationalists are for the most part ardent Internationalists, and there are critics who would have that we wish to cut Scotland off from cultural and other contacts with Europe. On the contrary, we wish to strengthen these contacts, and aim at achieving direct contact, as a distinctive Scottish entity, with the continent, without waiting for Continental influences to percolate to Scotland through London. The Nationalists' ambition to deprovincialize Scotland is largely dependent on the re-establishment of Scotland's old contacts with the rest of Europe; this must be done, not in the manner of such bodies as the Franco-Scottish Society, which in its own sphere does excellent work, but by Scottish writers, artists, and all manner of creative thinkers.

With this thought in mind we intend publishing in *The Modern Scot* translations of works by contemporary foreign writers, and trust that their presence alongside the writings of Scottish authors will have stimulating results. In this issue we publish a portion of Paul Valéry's dialogue *Eupalinos*, and in the next issue hope to include a translation by Adam Kennedy of a short story by Hermann Hesse.

('Continental Literature', editorial statement, *Modern Scot* 2:3 autumn 1931, p.217.)

5.20 Edwin Muir, from letter to Hermann Broch (June 1932)

Crowborough
2 June, 1932

My dear Herr Broch,

I too must thank you for all your great kindness to us in Vienna, and for the pleasure of meeting one who, without knowing it, had done so much for us. I hope that, in trying to convey some of our gratitude, we did not tire or disturb you: human understanding is difficult as it is, but when the barrier of another language is added, the difficulty is unfairly intensified. I was sorry all the time I was in Vienna for my faltering German—we both used to speak it far better, indeed fairly well, years ago, when we stayed in Austria and Germany—and it was most unfortunate that it should fail us just when we particularly wanted to summon it.

I have been reading your *Pasenow* again, also part of *Esch*, for the essay I wish to write about you. I had been so immersed in your book for so long—during our translation of it—that I had begun to fear that I could no longer hope to feel and indicate what was unique in it, and so fail completely with what I wanted to say about it. But to my delight the re-reading of *Pasenow* and *Esch* brought all my first surprise back, all the first joy of discovery of something undreamed of. No, in spite of what you said in Vienna, I cannot think that your book will ever be forgotten; at any rate it will not be forgotten by me, for I really think it has given me the deepest experience I have ever had from an imaginative work, since the time, in my 'teens, when I discovered poetry. You have done something decisive for my generation—lost though it may be: so I can't help again expressing my thanks to you, even if they may seem importunate, though they are not intended to be.

(Edwin Muir, letter to Hermann Broch 1 June 1932, reprinted from Peter Butter ed., *Selected Letters of Edwin Muir*, p.76.)

5.21   From unsigned review ' "Breast to Breast with the Cosmos": *The Savage Pilgrimage: A Narrative of D.H. Lawrence* by Catherine Carswell' (*Modern Scot* Summer 1932)

The Savage Pilgrimage is not a full-dress biography of Lawrence; it is a collection of vivid reminiscences of him, interspersed with letters from him and quotations from his writings, and a diatribe against all who do not share her opinion of Lawrence, chiefly his 'betrayer', Middleton Murry. Fortunately, the figure of Lawrence does emerge clearly out of all the dust raised, and pending an adequate biography and competent critical survey of Lawrence's achievement, the book deserves to be widely read.

It is, it must be confessed, a gossipy book. At times the writer is too concerned with the reactions of literary London to Lawrence, and at one point one might think the book was written around the former editor of the *Adelphi*. There is a good deal of personal chatter, too, which admittedly tells us something about Lawrence, but something which could have been told in another and better way, not necessitating Mrs Carswell relating, for instance, how Lawrence objected to her coming downstairs partly undressed.

It is doubtful if Mrs Carswell realizes fully the implications of Lawrence's philosophy and relates it properly to the European tradition. She never compares him to other mystics (referring to him as a mystic in a footnote, as an after-thought), and while it is true that as she is not setting out to define carefully his thought but describe the man, it may not much matter, it does, however, affect her attitude to certain people's behaviour to

Lawrence. It is the nature of a society to protect itself (as it thinks) against a subversive influence like Lawrence, and although, as Rebecca West has pointed out, Lawrence suffered as a consequence, it could scarcely have been otherwise. It is inherent in a people not to like to be told that the principles that have animated their society for two thousand years are wrong, and the man who spurns society should not ask its favours: Lawrence himself did not. Lawrence was so obviously not as other men, that England as a whole cannot be blamed for its attitude to him, although Chelsea and Bloomsbury and literary London generally, because of their pretensions, can.

The Savage Pilgrimage would have gained by being shorter. It would have been much better if Mrs Carswell's reminiscences had been condensed into an essay comparable to Rebecca West's *D.H. Lawrence*, and if the details of Lawrence's movements, his business affairs, etc., had been sifted or published in appendices: then the book would have been a work of art. Still one must accept it gratefully as it is, for Mrs Carswell was one of Lawrence's most loyal friends, and even when she did not understand fully what he was driving at, she never deserted him, and enjoyed his confidences. She is a woman of deep intuition; one cannot listen to her speak even in public without realizing how 'quick' (in the Biblical sense) she is; and consequently she responded deeply to Lawrence's most vital teaching and communicates his fire. Her book has the merit of sending one back with fresh eyes and ears to Lawrence's own works, to *The Plumed Serpent*, for instance, which she regards as perhaps the peak of his achievement, *Women in Love*, *Mornings in Mexico*, and *Apocalypse*—the last Lawrence's final work, which has a magnificent close that might be called his creed:

. . . The dead may look after the afterwards. But the magnificent here and now in the flesh is ours, and ours alone, and ours only for a time. We ought to dance with rapture that we should be alive in the flesh, and part of the living, incarnate cosmos. I am part of the sun as my eye is part of me. That I am part of the earth my feet know perfectly, and my blood is part of the sea. My soul knows that I am part of the human race, my soul is an organic part of the great human soul, as my spirit is part of my nation. In my own very self I am part of my family. There is nothing of me that is alone and absolute except my mind, and we shall find that the mind has no existence by itself, it is only the glitter of the sun on the surface of the waters.

('Breast to Breast with the Cosmos', unsigned review of *The Savage Pilgrimage*: *A Narrative of D.H. Lawrence* by Catherine Carswell, *Modern Scot* 3:2 summer 1932, pp.163–65 [164–65].)

5.22 Lewis Grassic Gibbon, from 'Literary Lights' (1934)

Nearly every Scots writer of the past writing in orthodox English has been not only incurably second-rate, but incurably behind the times. The Scots discovery of photographic realism in novel-writing, for example—I refer to *Hatter's Castle*, not the very different *House with the Green Shutters*—post-dated the great French and English realists some thirty or forty years. But to the Scot Dr Cronin's work appeared a very new and terrifying and fascinating thing indeed; to the English public, astounded that anything faintly savouring of accuracy, photographic or otherwise, should come out of Scotland, it was equally amazing. At such rate of progress among the Anglo-Scots one may guess that in another fifty years or so a Scots Virginia Woolf will astound the Scottish scene, a Scots James Joyce electrify it. To expect contemporary experimentation from the Anglo-Scots themselves appears equivalent to expecting a Central African savage in possession of a Birmingham kite to prove capable of inventing a helicopter.

Consciousness of this inferiority of cultural position within the English tradition is a very definite thing among the younger generation of Anglo-Scots writers of to-day. Their most characteristic organ, *The Modern Scot*, is a constant reiteration of protest. Owned and edited by one of those genial Englishmen in search of a revolution who have added to the gaiety of nations from Ireland to Uganda, *The Modern Scot* has set itself, strictly within the English tradition, to out-English the English. As one who on a lonely road doth walk with fear and dread, very conscious of the frightful fiend who close behind doth tread, it marches always a full yard ahead of extremist English opinion—casting the while an anxious backward glance. It decries the children of 'naturalism' with a praiseworthy but unnatural passion, championing in their place, with a commendable care for pathology, the idiot offspring begat on the modern literary scene in such numbers from the incestuous unions of Strindberg and Dr Freud. It is eclectic to quite an obscure degree, is incapable of an article that does not quote either Proust or Paul Einzig, and raises an approving voice in praise of the joyous, if infantile tauromachic obsessions of Mr Roy Campbell. Its motif-note, indeed, is literary Fascism—to the unimpassioned, if astounded, eye it would seem as if all the Fascist undergraduates of Scotland these days were hastening, in pimples and a passion for sophistication, to relieve themselves of a diarrhoetic Johnsonese in the appropriate privy of *The Modern Scot*. The entire being of the periodical, however, is rather an exhibitory, or sanitary exercise, than a contributing factor towards authentic experimentation.

(Lewis Grassic Gibbon, 'Literary Lights', *Scottish Scene or The Intelligent Man's Guide to Albyn*, pp.194–207 [197–98].)

5.23 Hugh MacDiarmid, from 'Rainer Maria Rilke' (*New Britain* February 1934)

When Rainer Maria Rilke died in 1927 there were no paragraphs in the British newspapers announcing the fact. The death of a great poet—the birth of a great masterpiece of human expression—has no 'news value'. Most people have been so debauched that they need to keep themselves posted in the tittle-tattle of all the ends of the earth—the crimes, the divorces, superficial and generally erroneous gossip about political and social tendencies; and one who disavows any interest in such matters is regarded as a queer chap, a narrow-minded crank. So is anyone who takes—and ventures to suggest that most people ought to take—any interest in current foreign philosophy and literature and art and music. We remain in all important matters hopelessly insular.

All this notwithstanding, Rilke is receiving attention much more quickly and adequately in British literary circles than is usually the fortune of foreign contemporaries. How much of Blok, for example, is yet available in English translation, though Blok died in 1921? How much of Boris Pasternak? Only a few translations in advance-guard American reviews. How much of Stefan George—next to Rilke the greatest of modern German poets? Carl Spitteler, the Swiss poet had to wait a long time for English translation and discussion. Paul Valéry has fared better; several of his works have been excellently translated. And Valéry, like George and Pasternak, is still alive. An enormous literature in most of the languages of Europe has grown up about Rilke since he died, and though what is yet available about him in English is a mere moiety of what is to be had in the other leading languages, it is clear that he is going to be the subject of a very great deal of interest in English too. [. . .]

The earliest translations of Rilke poems in English were those of Jethro Bithell in his *Contemporary German Poetry* in 1911. A sumptuously produced translation of the ten Duino elegies was published by the Hogarth Press in 1932, the translators being V. and Edward Sackville West. But as Dr Otto Schlapp and other German authorities and Rilke enthusiasts pointed out these were extremely bad translations. The translators themselves said they were only a 'crib'; but their method of 'literal accuracy' was inapplicable to Rilke of all writers, for his usage of German is extremely novel and difficult, and literal translation simply lands one in a mass of ludicrous misreadings. In this untranslatable usage of German, Rilke is, of course, in line with advanced literary artists in all European languages today. [. . .]

Rilke is in many superlatively important directions by far 'the furthest point yet' of human consciousness and expressive power—a lone scout far away in No Man's Land, whither willy-nilly mankind must follow him, or abandon the extension of human consciousness.

(C.M. Grieve, 'Rainer Maria Rilke', New Britain 28 February 1934, p.450.)

6

Women on Women: Gendering the Renaissance

6.1 Willa Muir, from 'A Woman in Prague' [1922]

Prague is a city of extremes, where the civilisation of the West sweeping across Europe meets the civilisation of the East with a shock. Electric trams of the best continental model run rapidly through narrow cobbled streets full of dirt and palaces: women in Turkey red peasant costumes with shawls on their heads sit in the stalls of the National Theatre: in the magnificently upholstered banks one must dawdle three hours to have a cheque cashed; and in every dish of one's exquisitely cooked dinner there are caraway seeds! One does not know whether to laugh or lose one's temper over the fact that there is only one hotel in Prague with a modern bathroom—in Prague, where baroque palaces crowd and shoulder each other in every street, and where it is almost impossible to find a lodging free from bugs. The city, it is true, tries to cope with the bug problem by forbidding wallpaper in even private houses; but the bugs survive this deprivation with apparent ease.

This anomaly, the existence of two currents of civilisation which flow side by side without blending can be most clearly perceived in the lives of the women. Outside Prague, in the country, there is no anomaly, for Western civilisation has penetrated only into the big towns. From the windows of the Vienna express as it thunders across Czechoslovakia one can see a woman and an ox yoked together as a plough team, driven, most probably, by the woman's husband. Women exist only to work for their men, and to work hard. Even in Prague, however, this attitude towards women is still the fundamental one; but it is bewilderingly overlaid by French fashions, the Y.W.C.A., and women's suffrage—at least among the educated classes.

For example, all the unskilled heavy labour of the town is provided by women. It is not considered a man's job to carry hods of bricks, or to deliver a ton of coal up three flights of stairs. When the coal cart stops in front of a house the shawled and barefooted women sitting on the back climb down and stand patiently in the gutter while the man in charge shovels the brown coal into the enormous baskets which they carry on their backs. The weight of these baskets is incredible; I have seen a Scot straining himself to lift one without budging it an inch from the ground. Every woman of the lower classes carries one as a matter of course if she goes out; full of firewood, or laundry or furniture, towering so high above her head that in the distance she is barely discernible beneath it. The weight of the basket is partly borne by the hips, but it must pull terribly on the shoulders: and it does not conduce to a graceful carriage. The women in Italy who balance enormous loads on their heads walk beautifully, but in Prague the women plod in a bowed, stolid shovel-footed way.

When a coal-carrier gets too old for her job she becomes a street cleaner, in company with superannuated men who are out of work. They drift through the streets in gangs of about six, painfully collecting in their aprons the scattered refuse which the dust-carts have left, and sweeping up the leaves and sticks. This organisation, as might be expected, breaks down completely in face of a thaw following weeks of heavy snow; and the streets of Prague in that condition must be seen to be believed. However, I believe that in this respect the old régime is giving place to the new; for the corporation of Prague is procuring mechanical street-sweepers in the best New York style.

A domestic servant in a Prague flat works like a slave. She sleeps in the kitchen on a shake-down, gets up every morning at five (the children must be in school by seven o'clock), earns very little, and kisses her mistress's hand devoutly morning and evening. And yet the mistresses grumble: for during the war the girls learned the 'freedom' of factory life, and there are many rebels who refuse to carry coal from the cellar and to do the family washing and ironing without extra pay.

In Prague society one must steel oneself to hand-kissing. All married ladies have their hands kissed on every occasion, either in fact or in words. Before one is used to it, it is very embarrassing at a reception to stretch out a handclasp and find it suddenly transformed into a handkiss and bow. These receptions are hearty affairs. The invitation says 'Come to tea'. But the woman who takes the invitation literally is lost. She will be confronted by a buffet of liqueurs, tables heaped with sandwiches and cakes, jellies and custards, mayonnaise and trifle. Tea also, of course; but the tea-party lasts from five till eleven, helped out by music and dancing; and she will be expected to eat continuously . . . And on the way home, if it is a frosty night, one stops to eat hot sausages from one of the shining sausage-engines at the street corner. 'Horky parky!' That is the Czech for 'hot sausages'. It is a wonderful language. Before the war German was the language of high society; Czech was despised as a 'kitchen language'. But even then the Czech patriots, who were working passionately for the rehabilitation of their nation, were endeavouring to restore the social prestige of their old language. They argued truly that patriotic political associations might be sufficient for men, but that the movement would never flourish unless the women were enlisted; and that the first thing to do was to establish a really fashionable social function at which Czech would be spoken. So a great ball was given, at which the Czech national dance, the Beseda, was given the place of honour. The Austrian authorities could not solemnly forbid a sentimental celebration of the Beseda: and it became an annual event of the utmost importance to the national movement. Now, of course, Czech is the official language; but the women in Prague can still speak German, and usually French and English as well. This is something to be thankful for, in a city where every public notice in the streets, the post-offices, and the railway stations is unintelligible except to Slavs. (When the virulence of Czech nationalism triumphant has worn off a little, perhaps they will be so kind as to put up a few French or English phrases in the post-office, at least. It will then be possible for the bewildered foreigner to buy stamps.) The Czech language consists of consonants, and those odd signs one sees scattered about on a typewriter. There are a few vowels, but they are seldom taken out for an airing. Yet some of the words are very expressive; I am particularly fond of 'krk', which means neck, and of 'mlc' (pronounced 'mltch') which means 'shut up'.

As it was once the ambition of every woman in Scotland to see her son 'a minister of the Kirk', so it is certainly the ambition of every Czech woman to see her son in a bank. To be in a bank is to have some subtle prestige, some social cachet which a merely academic or commercial career fails to provide. The competition for vacancies in the Prague banks is so fierce that only distinguished doctors of law or of economics stand a chance of getting in. When you ask a University research student 'Why are you doing this particular bit of work?' he will answer, 'Oh, it will be useful for a bank . . .'. One is certainly impressed by the superiority of the bank clerks; the common man waits humbly with his hat off for one hour, two, three, until his cheque has been scrutinised by six or seven aristocrats in private rooms. The Czechs think nothing of waiting. They wait for hours in the parcel offices, in the banks, in a stamp or theatre queue, in a café. All the young men who have not attained to the splendour of a bank sit in the cafés and wait for drinks or a turn at the diminutive billiard table. Of course, one never sees the women so magnificently unoccupied: they are at work.

(Willa Muir, 'A Woman in Prague', typescript article, Willa Muir Archive, University of St Andrews Library, pp.1–4.)

6.2   Catherine Carswell, from 'Proust's Women' (1923)

The literature of imagination has always been rich in autobiography, confessed and unconfessed. It is in its essence, perhaps one should say in its impulse, largely an affair of passionate reminiscence. [. . .] *A la Recherche du Temps Perdu*—Proust was not the first, nor will he be the last, to choose it as a theme. [. . .] But to come to the women.

A man of particular sincerity once said to me that after twenty years of married life he understood his wife no better than on the day he married her. He had of course become familiar with her modes of thought and action which served as knowledge for practical daily purposes. But familiarity had never bred understanding. Her underlying motives, the ultimate significance of her looks and words, remained hidden.

This, I think, is Proust's position, more especially when the woman happens to affect him powerfully. In every case we can *see* his women, and thus far they are the reverse of shadowy. Grandmother, mother, aunts, and servant—the women that surround his childhood; Mlle Vinteuil and the Duchesse de Guermantes—female figures that shock or thrill his boyish imagination; Odette—the mature cocotte that stands throughout his youth for feminine mystery and glamour; Odette's daughter Gilberte, and later Albertine—the young girls, minxes both, with whom he falls in love; Madame Verdurin and her circle—the social climbers who call forth his most delicate adult irony as well as his most rancid contempt—these, simply as pictures, leap out at us complete. Nothing could be more objective than their presentation to the eye and the ear of the reader. We feel with each one as if we had met her in the flesh—as one has met a casual acquaintance. The mother's submissive wifeliness; the almost masculine incorruptibility of the grandmother; the raciness of the servant; the neurosis of Aunt Léonie; the half-hearted viciousness of the music-master's daughter; the slightly comic social splendour of the duchesse; the unmeaning melancholy of Odette's eyes; the unredeemed vulgarity of Madame Verdurin; the domineering girlishness of Gilberte, by turns frank and secretive, appealing and repellent; the smile with which Albertine, at once innocent and wanton, receives the youth in her bedroom—in depicting these Proust never trespasses beyond natural as compared with literary experience. We all know with what liveliness in conversation any man with the gifts of observation and wit can create an image for us of some female 'character' met with in his childhood or his travels. But let that same man come to speak out of his emotions of some woman who has moved him deeply, then his heart will cloud his brain, his tongue will falter or run away with him, and he will no longer be capable of outlining a portrait. As listeners our impressions of his subject will be gained, not from what he says, but independently from what we perceive that he feels, which may well be in direct conflict with his words. In life, that is to say, the more important a character is to us the more we are thrown back for our ultimate knowledge on the emotions aroused by that character in ourselves. In fiction it is usually the other way about. It is his central figures whom the novelist pretends to know best. Proust, however, has recognised this discrepancy with scientific clearness. He devotes himself, therefore, where his important women are concerned—aside from the very minimum of detached, objective observations—to a presentment of the effect they have upon the men that love them.

So his women set us wondering and supposing and coming to our own conclusions exactly as we do in life, either when an individual of our own sex is described for us by one of the other sex, or when we are emotionally affected by some one of the other sex.

For this is important. When it comes to his male characters, Proust takes a different tone. Here he finds himself able, quite consistently with his philosophy, for far more positive assertion. In various ways he can allow them to reveal and expound themselves, and even each other, as when Bergotte speaks of the married Swann as a man who 'has to swallow a hundred serpents every day'. The point of view, the intellectual outfit which all males have in common—these give the male novelist a certain tract of solid ground when dealing with characters of his own sex. A man's fellow-feeling for other men is very strong. It has but a faint and imperfect parallel as between woman and woman. Proust, accordingly, without any sacrifice of conscience, can, 'by his belief', endow Swann with a soul. But— marvellous and highly characteristic creation as he is—Swann may be put in the same category with other male characters by other male novelists. Odette, Gilberte, Albertine, are in a category by themselves. Outside of Proust's book they are only to be met with in life.

It is in this differential treatment of his women that we perceive how rigorously Proust applies his artistic method. He never seeks to transcend his own personality. In him, the observer, the whole of creation lives and moves and has its being. Men are creatures made in his own image. He can faithfully follow his own emotions, and 'by his belief' can conscientiously endow his men with souls. But women are in a different case. He has no inner guide to assure him that they are anything more than the phantoms they seem. Strictly speaking, this should imply no more than a negative attitude. In fact, however, Proust goes further. Because he has no grounds for belief he passes into unbelief. In his philosophy *esse est percipi*, therefore, the souls of women for him have no existence. Herein it is likely that he has borne out the unavowed experience of most men. Whether or no, he certainly has expressed the truth of his own experience with a purity that few, even among great writers, can rival.

One thing more. There is Proust's mother.

No doubt the avenging eagerness with which I reintroduce her for my conclusion is due in part of my being myself of the soulless sex. But quite apart from any such feelings, to speak of this novelist's women without reckoning especially with his mother would be inexcusable. That he adored her in childhood he makes manifest. Further, that throughout his life this adoration effectively debarred him from profound emotion where other women were concerned becomes clear enough to the reader. It hardly appears, however, that Proust was himself wholly conscious of this. True, there is a passage in the *Combray* section in which he speaks of 'that untroubled peace which no mistress, in later years, has ever been able to give me, since one has doubts of them at the moment when one believes in them, and never can possess their hearts as I used to receive, in her kiss, the heart of my mother, complete, without scruple or reservation, unburdened by any liability save to myself'. But this is the only place where he seems to allow that the love he bore his mother was even comparable in kind with the love aroused by other women later in his life. Indeed, though he repeatedly speaks of the anguish with which in his childhood he longed for his mother's good-night kiss, the ecstasy with which he received it, as if it were the Host in an act of communion, conveying to him 'her real presence and with it the power to sleep'; though he tells how, for that 'frail and precious kiss', he prepared himself in advance so as to 'consecrate' the whole minute of contact; though he dreaded to prolong or repeat the kiss lest a look of displeasure should cross those beautiful features with the slight, beloved blemish under one of the eyes; yet he describes himself at this time as one 'into whose life Love had not yet entered', as one whose emotion, failing love and as yet awaiting it, happened to be at the disposal of 'filial piety'. No wonder if, when temporary 'loves' came, he compared with them as unconsciously as unfavourably this good and gracious mother—so admiringly timid as a wife, so gentle towards strangers, so perfect socially, so full of stern solicitude as a parent ('she never allowed herself to go to any length of tenderness with me')—and found them merely exciting to the senses. He had already, so far as woman was concerned, given his heart away.

Yet, after all, perhaps he knew it well enough and merely takes his own way of saying it. He tells us little enough of his mother, though probably he tells as much as he knows. What her own real thoughts and feelings were we are left to guess. But 'never again', he says, after describing one very special visit of hers to the boy's bedroom—'never again will such hours be possible for me. But of late I have been increasingly able to catch, if I listen attentively, the sound of the sobs . . . which broke out only when I found myself alone with Mamma. Actually their echo has never ceased.'

(Catherine Carswell, 'Proust's Women', *Marcel Proust: An English Tribute*, collected by C.K. Moncrieff, London: Chatto & Windus, 1923, pp.66–77 [66–7, 71–7].)

6.3 Willa Muir, from *Women: An Inquiry* (1925)

Yet, if motherhood can be defined, rightly or wrongly, as the sole function of women, it must be a function which in some degree expresses the quality of womanhood as distinct from manhood. Even in this artificially narrowed field of activity one should be able to find some clue to the essential nature of women. It is therefore advisable first of all to compare motherhood and fatherhood.

Fatherhood seems the more casual relationship of the two. It cannot be proved with the same certainty as motherhood. [. . .] A man can be a parent without knowing it: a woman cannot.

Motherhood is also a greater tax on vital energy than fatherhood, even if we take motherhood merely as a physical function. The process of bearing a child culminates in a crisis which exhausts a woman's energy: to such an extent, indeed, that women often die of it. Moreover, it is a process which, once initiated, is not under conscious control, so that the reserve of energy drawn upon is not deliberately assigned to this purpose by its owner. It is not at her free disposal to grant or to withhold it; it cannot be exhausted by an act depending on conscious volition. The race in this respect is stronger than the individual. [. . .] As far as the race is concerned, all women are potential mothers, and must have the necessary reserve of energy for this function whether they intend to become mothers or not. They cannot waste it even if they would. Thus men have more energy to waste on their own individual purposes than women: that is to say, men have more energy at their conscious disposal. [. . .]

The implications of this hypothesis must be considered. It is attractive because it establishes an essential difference between men and women which makes them complementary to each other. There can be no question of absolute domination of one sex by the other when the strength of each lies in a different direction. If man's energy is diverted more into conscious life, woman's energy is diverted more into unconscious life, and one is not more important than the other. It is a relative, not an absolute difference; both men and women are human beings, and all that concerns human beings is their joint affair. But it means, as will be seen, a difference in the kind of creative work done by each: they will tackle the same things from a different point of view, and with different results. On this basis men and women would each have an equal right, the right of the creative spirit to do its work without let or hindrance.

Conscious life implies rational thinking. In thinking about things we arrange them in patterns, we give them form and system. But we do not give them content; conscious life modifies or seizes upon things which it does not originate. Growth is a process which is already well advanced before it enters consciousness at all. [. . .] Consciousness is thus the shaper of form, which is one aspect of life, and its work tends to a permanence beyond the vicissitudes of living. But its vitality depends upon its communion with the unconscious. [. . .] The unconscious is concerned with growth rather than form; it is essentially emotional, spontaneous, and irrational. As far as we know, it is concrete in its thinking and not abstract;

it creates living agents and systems of thought. Thus, while conscious processes supply form and permanence in our world, unconscious processes supply growing vitality and change. [. . .] Unconscious life creates, for example, human beings; conscious life creates, for example, philosophy. If men are stronger in conscious life, and women in unconscious life, their creative powers must express their strength. Men should excel in translating life into conscious forms, women in fostering the growth of life itself. Men will create systems of philosophy or government, while women are creating individual human beings. [. . .]

The facts of human life tend to confirm this theory. Starting again from the fundamental relationship of a mother to her child, we can see that owing to the peculiar position of the human race, the physical act of motherhood is only the merest beginning of motherhood as a function. Man, because he is destined for a more complex life than the other animals, is born more helpless than any of them, and takes a longer time to come to maturity. [. . .] He is terribly at the mercy of his mother. She can ruin or strengthen that harmony between the conscious and the unconscious which is a necessary condition of full human development. In short, she must create not only a human body, but a human being, if she is to fulfil her function as a mother. But if it is her business to foster growth in her children, it must be equally her business to foster growth in all the people with whom she is intimate. If she is a specialist in the needs of the growing human spirit, her peculiar knowledge must be of service to men and women of all ages who are still capable of growth. And what is true in this respect of mothers must be true for all women: a special equipment for motherhood does not descend suddenly by the grace of Heaven upon the individual. All girls are potential mothers, and whatever gifts of intuition are necessary for the creative work of motherhood must be accessible to all women. If the full content of motherhood is thus recognized, it must inevitably be recognized as a special application of the creative power of women. Therefore the concept 'superfluous women' can only arise in a society which denies the real functions of motherhood and which consequently prevents women from free expression and ignores the creative power of womanhood. Creative power of any kind is, of course, the obverse of an equal power for destruction. [. . .] Woman's power of fostering growth in human life implies, therefore, an equal power of hindering it. [. . .] If the average man sees woman alternately as an angel and a devil, it is because she exercises both a creative and a destructive influence upon his inner life. He would neither fear nor reverence her so intensely if she were merely an inferior counterpart of himself.

(Willa Muir, *Women: An Inquiry* London: Hogarth Press, 1925, reprinted from *Willa Muir: Imagined Selves* Edinburgh: Canongate Classics, 1996, pp.1–30 [5–10].)

6.4 Willa Muir, from letter to F. Marian McNeill (January [1926])

My dear Floss:

You are a dear: you have lifted a weight off my mind. I have not been able to write to anybody for some time, & I had visions of wrathful friends. We have had a trying time—you will realise why, when I tell you that shortly after I came home I proceeded to have a bad miscarriage—think of it! I had no idea that I was pregnant (I thought I had got a chill, & when I was sick I thought it was caused by lumbago) and then we were worried by a debt which suddenly cropped up—very worried—and then I had the miscarriage, to my own shock & surprise. No wonder I was brooding over the bearing of children! I was, and am, disgusted. The doctor said it was a two months foetus, or thereabouts. However, it is established that there is no displacement, & I may live in hope that it may be all right next time. Why I have had no conceptions until now neither he nor anyone can tell me. It is so far good that it encourages me to believe in a 'next time'. Well, the whole affair was nauseating, & upset me terribly; I am now beginning to feel all right, but I was nervy for a good time. The next trial was a fit of appendicitis for Edwin, with the threat of an operation—happily avoided. He is only now recovering—out of bed yesterday for the first time. I don't know when we shall proceed to France: but as soon as possible. My poor mother has had a bad time with us!

We have been fortunate in other respects: the contract for translating another German book has been signed, & we have got an advance on it of £40, & so all is well. Edwin's book of essays is nearly finished: it would have been sent off by this time if he had not been smitten in the appendix: however it is to be quite a good book. I must attack the translation & won't have much time for anything else till it is finished—it must be finished by May. [. . .]

My old essay has fallen very flat. I don't think people realise its implications—perhaps because of the purposely moderate & reasonable tone. *The Nation* said it was as unexciting as boiled rice. *Time & Tide* has not reviewed it at all! I thought women's societies & associations would have been interested. However—I shall launch bombs next time!

I shall let you know when we come down.

Much love
Willa

(Willa Muir, letter to F. Marian McNeill 26 January [1926],
National Library of Scotland MS 26194, 98.)

6.5 Catherine Carswell, from correspondence with F. Marian McNeill (April 1928)

a) From letter of 24 April 1928

My dear Flos,

I wrote a long letter to you and next day decided not to send it, as I felt the matter could not be helpfully thrashed out in letters. [. . .]

I'm determined for your sake as well as for my own, not to write at length today! Must however say one or two things as briefly as possible.

I would never dream of suggesting that my way (or Joanna's which is not identical with mine except in certain respects) should be indicated as your way . . . or as you put it 'Everybody's'. My truth is only valuable in that it is mine. The only point is that Joanna does fashion or find out *some* way for herself and *some* truth. Whereas —— remains vague and without a clear impulse.

I'm sure your trouble is (and it sticks out in your letter and in your phraseology and in your habits of thought) that you are too much given over to *ideas* which have not sprung straight from your own experience but have been imported from without by reading, etc. and always through the intellect first. This is all very well for the undergraduate stage. Such expressions as 'wild love', 'bitter virginity', 'children for the sake of children', and all the heredity business or the explanation of one's difficulties by reason of one's heredity are essentially adolescent expressions. The time should come when experience and personal, individual emotion breaks through and transmutes and crystallises the whole thing. Till that comes, as I see, there can be no sense of creation. It is all floundering in a morass of ready-made ideas which have life only in so far as they are handled and re-created afresh by each new soul. Each soul must cut some time or other, the umbilical cord and stand up in its essential integrity, knowing that there is a birth independent of heredity, nation, accident and all else. And if there is not there is no creative soul. There are no valid excuses or explanations. Every individual has enough hereditary difficulties, repulses, etc.—some more than others—and it is not always the most happily dowered who succeed in the necessary rebirth, the breaking free, the proud arising of the new naked soul from the morass with the declaration—'here I am'.

You are sincere, but it is not enough. More important is it to find one's own truth. [. . .]

To intellectualise is the temptation and the disaster. You stay dallying with ideas and not once does the clear urgency and emotion break through.

Have to go now. Shall write another time. All news then,

Love from Cathie.

b) From letter of 30 April 1928

Dearest Flos,

Just got home today—and after a day of it feel *dead* tired. I'm delighted to hear you are coming up. It will make a break for you. This apart from our looking forward to seeing you. And I do hope we shall have a chance of a talk. I'm afraid till we have had a talk we shall only plunge deeper in by putting things in writing. To take a single instance I can see we have a different notion of what I mean by 'intellectualising'. The *essentially* intellectual being does not 'intellectualise', as it is natural and therefore right for him (if he exists!) to deal with life through the intellect. But for a woman or any being whose nature it is to live through the emotions, clarity of mind can only be got by taking the natural order. And I do think many of us thinking and educated women of this age—go against our natures by striving to *force* ourselves to deal first through the intellect, living too much with ideas and not sufficiently trusting ourselves to the truths that would come to us through the deeper sensual and emotional channels. So we get confused, uncreative, and 'pathological'. [. . .]

To *think* for me is entirely different from to 'intellectualise'. One can and should *think* with all one's being—*thought* to be real must be linked up with the stream of the blood. The intellectualising business uses *other people's* experience and borrowed stuff and is a sort of cutting off and cowardice. But perhaps you will feel this is twisting words [. . .]

Love from Cathie.

(Catherine Carswell, letters to F. Marian McNeill of 24 and 30 April 1928, reprinted from John Carswell ed., *Catherine Carswell: Lying Awake: An Unfinished Autobiography* (1950), Edinburgh: Canongate Classics, 1997, pp.198–200.)

6.6 Lorna Moon, from letter to David Laurance Chambers (January 1929)

Dear Laurance Chambers,

As I wired you a minute ago I'm trying to get comments for the jacket, I don't know what you will think of this, but anyhow—I like very much the part of the blurb which catalogues the things in it. I mean the part which says: 'Here are so and so a brothel worthy of Hogarth, a Tongueless man' etc.—this seems to me good sales talk—it gives the reader images—the things I don't like are dead words like 'strength, delicacy, beauty', they are over-used till they have lost the small savor they had, all books bear them. They convey nothing to the reader.

I don't like the part which says she belongs to the Scottish heroines of literature and that Scott, Stevenson, Barrie would have understood her—

because they *wouldn't*—(Thank God!) and a comment like that relegates the book to the musty old shelves where women wore rats in their hair and became 'fallen'. Nancy is 1929. [. . .] If you add anything to the edited jacket following the line: 'But this is Nancy's story and not to be broken on the wheel of comment'—say something about her being—Oh don't you see that she has all the romance and poetry of bygone heroines, but with it she has the clear thinking bravery of 1929 girlhood. You know, that is what all this is leading us to—sin will cease to be a nasty baster—there won't be a 'fallen woman' anymore than there are 'fallen men'. It is revolting to me that in a civilized world a woman's virtue rests entirely upon her hymen.

Excuse me I always get worked up over this. [. . .]

L.

(Lorna Moon [Nora Wilson Low], letter to David Laurance Chambers, Bobbs-Merrill publishers, about her novel *Dark Star* (1929), 5 or 6 January 1929, quoted in *The Collected Works of Lorna Moon*, pp.267–8.)

6.7 Elizabeth Kyle, 'Modern Women Authors' (*Scots Observer* June 1931)

a) Nan Shepherd

In 1928 the reading public were made aware of a new personality in the world of letters, by the publication of *The Quarry Wood*, a novel which one critic has hailed as being alongside of Naomi Mitchison's *Cloud Cuckooland*, one of the two best Scots novels of our generation. *The Quarry Wood* shows an interesting parallel with *The Mill on the Floss*, being as thoroughly Scots as that is English, but the central theme and the temper of mind are much the same, and both books show the same vigour, humour and grip on the underlying philosophical values. Those who were hoping for a real renaissance in Scots letters felt, with its appearance, that their hope had not been in vain and that, granted another writer or two of the same power and originality as that possessed by Nan Shepherd, its author, Scotland might yet make her mark upon the world of literature and art which is too often prone to leave her in the rear.

It is a significant fact, however, that *The Quarry Wood*, conforming as little as it did to the accepted ideas of what a Scots novel should be, was refused by thirteen publishers who did not know quite what to make of it, before being finally accepted by Messrs Constable, who were rewarded for their insight in the book's instantaneous success. The publishers' readers who dealt with it were evidently bewildered by the impossibility of fitting it into the hitherto known categories of Kailyardism, Scott Romanticism and House-With-Green-Shutterism, which too often make up the only lines along which the general public imagines all Scots novels should run.

Miss Shepherd herself feels strongly on the subject of the modern tendency of shoving an author's work into one category and leaving it there. 'All categories are absurd where art is concerned', she said. 'I don't believe in categories, but in individualities. It's just the slack thinking that is one of the curses of our hurried and mass-producing age that makes lazy people love to label things and think they have understood them. Mental inertia makes one flick a book into a category and then suppose that is all there is to it. Whereas what there is to it is an individual mind, a mode of experience, a whole universe, one unique vision of truth. Or should be. Though, of course, the odd thousand among the thousand and one books of the day fail just there—that they really do seem to be mass-produced to the formula of the American training-school, or the psychoanalyst, or whatever authority they find to offer them a formula. Magic word, formula.

'By which you may gather something of my attitude to present-day fiction. As a matter of fact, I read few novels. They bore me. I never wanted or intended to write one myself, and I can't tell you why I did it. All novels don't bore me, though. Some excite me tremendously. That's when I find what I tried to indicate—the raw material of life as we all know it, transfigured and irradiated and given significance by the impact of a mind. Fiction without imagination, no matter how clever, how witty, how "true to life" (in the misleading cliché) leaves me cold. I like irony too—say, as in Montagu's *Right Off the Map*. That's imagination working through irony, and magnificent stuff. Or Neil Gunn shows the quality I mean in some of the tales in *Hidden Doors*—notably in the conclusion to the tale that ends by the picture of an old man frozen dead as he sat staring out over the unbroken moorland he had been attempting to reclaim. The individual figure becomes greater than itself—becomes a symbol of the whole long bitter fight between man and the pitiless forces of nature. It is fine.' [. . .]

Two years after publishing *The Quarry Wood*, Miss Shepherd published *The Weatherhouse*. Both books contain fine landscape painting which, incidentally, betrays the countryside to which she herself belongs—Aberdeenshire. She was born and has lived most of her life within five miles of Aberdeen, in a house with one of the loveliest views that could be found—all up and down Deeside and across to the Mearns of the Weatherhouse. The Quarry Wood is within half a mile of the house. In appearance, she is tall, of typically nor'east stock, with thick auburn plaited hair and hazel eyes. An Aberdeen High School girl and an Aberdeen graduate, since she left the university she has been on the English staff of Aberdeen Training Centre, and has been head of it for some years now. She is a brilliant teacher and enormously popular with her pupils. How well she knows the country woman student is visible enough in the character of Martha Ironside of *The Quarry Wood*. She speaks the Doric as well as she writes it, which is saying a good deal, and has a keen sense of humour.

Also, she is a very out-of-doors person, as anyone could tell who has read her books, and a very keen gardener with a beautiful garden; and she keeps hens. Above all other recreations, she loves long walks out on the open hillside. 'I love tramping in open country', she says, 'as I love few things on earth. Indeed a great deal of material is worked out and wrought into shape while I am on the tramp. As for my other interests; well, I have my garden and like delphiniums and scilla and crocuses and things—but who cares about that? So, I dare say, do a thousand other people. And anyhow, I love hills more than any garden.'

b) Dot Allan

As the green car travelled along Great Western Road, I found myself wondering what sort of personality lay behind the signature, 'Dot Allan', seen so frequently in periodicals as well as on the backs of one or two of the most stimulating, modern novels of the day. It was suitable and fitting, as I thought, that the author of *The Syrens* which was published some years ago should still live within sound of the Clyde, for, as J.J. Bell said once of her, she was the first novelist to write of Glasgow as a port.

I had left the car by now and was skirting the pleasant oasis of the Botanic Gardens. Round in a curve to the right, past the Queen Margaret College, and there, facing me, was a row of tall grey houses with gardens laid out before them. Entering one of them, I found Miss Allan in a room whose proportions pointed to its having been built at a date when people required, and were given enough space to live in; a room full of charming things, flowers, shaded lamps, and comfortable cushions. There was nothing in this room to suggest that Bohemian, half masculine creature, the 'lady novelist' in fiction.

Nor did its occupant look the part; small and dainty, with grey eyes looking at one from under black, arched brows, she seemed to protest against being debarred, in the public imagination a least, from the feminine delights of life.

In spite of the fact that Miss Allan is best known as a 'Glasgow' writer, she was not born in the city, but in Stirlingshire. 'I certainly have written a good deal about Glasgow', she said, 'but I have written about other places too. I don't believe in the localisation of a writer's talent. One ought to take the world for one's field if one wants to. There are no boundaries to art. That's why I am not altogether in sympathy with the Scots Renaissance movement and other allied movements, which, in my opinion, tend to cut us off from the rest of the world, instead of making us one with it. I think in fact, that a United States of Europe wouldn't be at all a bad idea, and there doesn't seem to me to be any reason why it shouldn't work!'

Although Miss Allan attended classes at Glasgow University for a time, her education was somewhat spasmodic, owing to winter migrations to the South of France, where she had lessons from a very interesting and original Frenchwoman, a protegée of the Empress Eugenie, whose villa was nearby, and one who had had the privilege of teaching Queen Ena of Spain. Such travel, however, together with frequent change of surroundings, probably stood her in much better stead during her after-career than a hide-bound curriculum faithfully carried out. Later she went to school at Leamington Spa in Warwickshire, a school where M.P. Willocks, the Devonshire novelist, was at that time English mistress.

'What was my first piece of writing? I think it was a poem, written at the age of ten.' She smiled at the remembrance. 'I called it a sonnet, and dispatched it hopefully to the *Glasgow Citizen*. In due course it came back with a letter from the editor, in which he pointed out that a sonnet does not usually have twenty-eight lines in it!

'Much later, though still in my callow youth, I became stage-struck as so many young girls do, and was desperately anxious to meet Sarah Bernhardt, who, old and frail, was paying a visit to Glasgow. The only way I could think of doing so was just to ask for an interview, which she granted. She was kindness itself, listened to my halting French, and answered me with sympathy and courtesy. But I had an awful job selling that article afterwards! The newspapers all said they had had enough of Sarah Bernhardt at the moment; but the *Evening Times* published it in the end.

'Then I wrote *Snowdrifts*, which was the first new repertory play ever to be presented in a music-hall. My second play, *Yellow Fever*, which came out at the Repertory Theatre a few months later was produced by Lewis Casson, the husband of Sybil Thorndike, who was at that time the producer for the old Repertory Theatre in Glasgow. He is an extraordinarily interesting man, quite apart from the theatre. I believe he invented the first poison gas projector to be used on the Somme. I was then, and always have been, very interested in theatre-production.

My first novel, *The Syrens* was published in 1922, and dealt with Glasgow and its shipping interests. It was published simultaneously in this country and in America; while it also was translated into Dutch, and ran as a serial in a leading Dutch paper. Critics have accused me, in *The Syrens*, of making mistakes in nautical matters, but as a matter of fact there really couldn't be any, because Captain David Bono vetted the book for me, so that I shouldn't go astray. Later on, I published *Makeshift*, and my last novel to appear was *The Deans*, which Jarrolds published.'

'What kinds of books interest you most?', I asked, rising to leave.

She thought a little before replying, 'Almost every kind. I'm a very catholic reader. If I were stuck in a country hotel and had forgotten to bring my own choice of books with me, I believe I could read through every battered novel and pamphlet left behind by previous guests, with at least a certain amount of pleasure, rather than not read anything!

'I particularly enjoy such writers as Wells and Aldous Huxley, however; and I admire the novels of Tennyson Jesse enormously. As for Scots writers, George Blake's book *Paths to Glory* which dealt with Gallipoli, seemed so much better than most of the war books that have been boosted lately, that I can't think why the general public didn't hear more about it. It seems to me very important for a novelist to read all the new works of fiction he or she can lay hands on, for by doing so one can learn both what to avoid and what to emulate!'

(Elizabeth Kyle, 'Modern Women Authors', interviews with Nan Shepherd and Dot Allan, *Scots Observer* 18 June 1931, p.4, and 25 June 1931, p.4.)

6.8 Willa Muir, from letter to F. Marian McNeill (July 1931)

Tel. Crowborough 448   The Nook
Blackness Road
21 July, 1931   Crowborough

My dear Flos,

Your letter took my breath away and I am only beginning to recover it. What a peculiar agitation it rouses in me to find people who have been moved by my novel! Peculiar, for, of course, to move people in some way is obviously the purpose of a novel, so I should be prepared for such an effect: but I am much less serene than you think my book is and commendation from people I know puts me in a painful flutter, just as disparagement from people I know makes me resentful, whereas disparagement from strangers leaves me cold. So I assure you that I was incapable of replying by return! And yet I am very glad that the book moved you to a positive feeling—that was what it was meant to do; but apparently, some brains are needed for the understanding of my work, since there have been so many utterly stupid comments, stupid both in praise and in blame.

Let me finish off just what I have to say about *Imagined Corners*: you object to my letting Elise leave Scotland. Well, my dear, it was supposed to be 1913, when there was little Nationalism: also, I was thinking more of Elise, when I followed her, than of national sentiment: and Elise would not have stayed in Calderwick, however it might have benefited from her presence—which I don't deny. I was not describing what *ought* to be in

Scotland, but what actually would have happened there in 1913 to the characters in my book: and I think I am right in conceiving that Elise & Hector were bound to leave it. Elizabeth was almost equally bound to come back: but all that I left to the imagination of the reader, being more concerned to present an illumination of life in Scotland than a reformation of it. Anyone who has really felt the thoughts I expressed in it will be all the fitter to reform Scotland, but it is indirect, not direct propaganda that literature provides. I am proposing to write another novel about Calderwick, but you needn't look for Nationalism with a big N in it. None the less, I think I shall be 'doing my bit' for Scotland. Some people can talk and fight and work politically: probably I *could* do one of the three quite well: but what I want to do more than anything else is to write a great book, and if I succeed I shall have served Scotland too. [. . .]

We are busy on the *Sleepwalkers*, and Edwin is doing bits to his next novel, and Gavin is growing large and strong. I must confess that I have been ailing, and it now comes out that when Gavin was born I got so badly torn up that I should have been sewn together: but I wasn't, and so my inside has been going all squee-gee for the past three years and must now be sewn up as soon as possible. When we finish this translation therefore I am going into the Crowborough Hospital for a fortnight to be tacked together again and have my organs restored to their proper places. The doctor thinks it won't mean more than a fortnight off. So that will be my holiday this summer. [. . .]

Are you coming down? There's always a spare bed here, mind that.

Much love from Willa.
Edwin sends his love too.

(Willa Muir, letter to F. Marian McNeill, 21 July 1931, National Library of Scotland
MS 26195, 24–27.)

6.9   Naomi Mitchison, from 'Pages from a Russian Diary' (*Modern Scot* Autumn 1932)

On the Ship to Leningrad

I wonder what we all think we shall get in Russia, apart from technical things; I talked to ——, the architect, for a time, and I think he hopes to find what I hope for—that people will look at one differently, that there will be real happiness and freedom—not, presumably, political freedom, but a real *liberté des moeurs*. M——, I think, wants the same. O—— has been before. I don't know in detail what it will be like; I can't imagine it, less than I can any other country. At present I am just feeling happy at having nothing to do, at being able to sit in the sun; there are NO MORE PROOFS. I would feel guilty if I didn't think I deserved a holiday. And yet I don't know that I have done anything. Is this book I have finished really valuable? Was it, anyhow, real work? I enjoyed it. Does that count? Is it praxis? Mirsky seems to think it might be. Why do I feel that his opinion is valuable? Is it just that the strict doctrine of his Communism is so attractive—and is valuable here? Mirsky says that I am in the half-way stage that one always goes through before getting to Communism, that I am still thinking in terms of dope-emotions. The underground things, Lawrenceism, the group sense, the pattern of happiness that is outside reason—opium for the people. But how can one intellectualize every-thing?—even put everything into words; we have only been using words for forty or fifty thousand years, if that.

Yet this doesn't answer my question of whether I, personally, deserve a holiday, whether I'm not being an individualist. Why should I have got this good position? Am I—is anyone—sufficiently valuable to get the things I've got? What about the sea[she?]-sailor? Would I like Lois to do that, be that, have that much praxis? Why should I want to insist that my children should have these other values, be in high-brow professions that make them feel as timid and valueless as I do? Does the she-sailor feel herself valuable? She looked as if she might. I suppose at any rate that having children is praxis: it is the work of the body though rather an odd kind, because it can't be only proletarian, yet it is completely untheoretical. It is this unfortunate universality of it that makes J—— not think it valuable, not think it practical. Does it make it valueless to have children if one has them in comfort, with doctors and chloroform? I suspect people who say that of anti-feminism; I suspect them of not knowing anything about it. Or am I such a physical coward that I cannot face praxis? I know I shouldn't like now to be a she-sailor myself.

Will this be answered in Russia? Shall I still find the strict doctrine of Communism so attractive, so pulling, so like a super-Catholicism? Or shall I be a Protestant? . . . [. . .]

On the Black Sea

I went down to the cabin to get some more typing paper, and there found one of the Russian girls, who began to talk to me. I offered her chocolate, which she much liked. Then two others came in, and before I knew where I was, I was sitting on the floor, trying to understand and answer their questions. They always want to know first what one does. I explained and asked them; they are all working in Sovtorgflot at Rostov and are coming to the Sanatorium to rest. They are surprised to see a single tourist about by itself. The next thing to explain is politics. They are satisfied with me as a Socialist and Dick as a 'Socialist candidate', which I suspect means something rather different to them. I produce photos of the children—such as I still have; they are delighted, especially when I explain that I also work.

None of them have children and seem to think rather ill of husbands; I am asked in expressive pantomime if my husband loves me—if I nursed the babies myself—whether I have a nurse. I interrupt to make tea on the spirit-lamp, my malinko samovar; the first woman produces bannocks of white flour filled with cheese—very good—made by her mother. Somehow or another we discuss London theatres and the length of hair. I find I have given the impression that Socialists have long hair and linen dresses, Capitalists short hair and silk dresses, but I just can't explain it all again! . . . [. . .]

On the Way Home [. . .]

There is one thing which I have left out so far, though I think it is very important, and this is the question of men and women. I feel they have solved, or nearly solved, the sex question which has preoccupied us for so many years, simply by giving women complete economic freedom and equality.

It remains to be seen what will happen when a higher standard is possible, whether with the return of silk stockings there will be a return of sex appeal and complexes. But just now there is wonderfully little work for the psychiatrist in the U.S.S.R. At present I have certain criticisms, which I would express in practical terms by saying: why no anaesthetics for child-birth or abortion? I believe the answer really is that this part of the equality business, having babies (or not having them) is a woman's job, just as she might have a job in a factory or just as a man might. She ought to be able to do her job herself, with the minimum of outside assistance, if she is a competent worker. I believe women now refuse to have the anaesthetics which would probably be good for them, just to prove that they are competent workers and the equals of men on this highly specialized job. I feel that this is a temporary attitude which will pass, as the general standard of hardship is lowered.

I also feel that Lawrence's criticism may apply—that men and women must be polarized, that if they are always doing things together it is no good to anyone, and the great exchange which is life-giving to both can never happen. If this criticism is valid, it may mean that men and women, boys and girls, should play together less, spend their leisure less together, when they are really being men and women in the fullest and most functional sense; but I do not think that it need in any way interfere with their working together, since in working hours they are functioning not as 'men' and 'women' but as fellow-workers. At present no doubt the overcrowding makes it particularly difficult to have any kind of segregation, especially what I think may be perhaps even more important than the segregation of the sexes, namely, the segregation of parents and children. But this again is a temporary condition.

At any rate in the U.S.S.R. there is no gossip, no sexual shame or slander, none of the strain and pain which is caused in other countries partly by marriage and divorce laws, partly by economic circumstance, and partly by the traditional upbringing of children in regard to sexual matters. The citizens of the Soviet Union are done with 'morality' and can put it away in a museum of horrors, where it properly belongs.

Thus far on the boat, slightly interrupted by a ship's officer who said I was in the way. . . .

(Naomi Mitchison, 'Pages from a Russian Diary', *Modern Scot* 3:3 autumn 1932, pp.229–36 [229–30, 232–33, 235–36].)

6.10 Willa Muir, from letter to Marion Lochhead (March 1933)

Hampstead 1280

7 Downshire Hill
London N.W.3.
3d March 1933

Dear M.C. Lochhead:

Every woman her own biographer—wouldn't that bring out some highly-coloured histories! You tempt me, you know, to give my imagination full reign, and to lead you to believe that never was there a woman so cultured, so clever, so handsome, so beloved as myself. Well, well! The facts are very sober, on the other hand, and almost incredibly heavy reading. I don't envy you your job of compiling an article about me. Incidentally, I must apologise for keeping you waiting: you are quite right. I am very busy and also very desperate, for I cannot, no I cannot get my novel finished, and until it is finished I shall be scarcely human; so that is why I did not answer your letter. Your postcard, however, reads like an S.O.S. and so I sit down to fling you a few scraps of information in my present sub-human manner. [. . .]

How do we live? Translating from the German, reading German books for publishers, doing anything that turns up.

How do we want to live? On the proceeds of our own creative work. Apparently quite impossible.

My own publications—apart from translations—are very few.

Women, an Enquiry [sic]—an essay published by the Hogarth Press in 1924 [sic].

Imagined Corners—a novel published by Secker 1931.

But I am finishing *Mrs Ritchie* of which I have some hopes. It is—or will be—much better than my first novel. However, I think my best piece of work is Gavin—a large, well-made, healthy clever boy!

I have become terribly interested in the motive power of *symbolism* in all our thoughts & actions, & this, I think, is to some extent worked out in *Mrs Ritchie*. There is much work that I could still do in this direction. [. . .]

Photographs I have none of which I am not ashamed, except snapshots. Perhaps some day I will be photographed satisfactorily. The difficulty lies in the fact that I have naturally a grave, heavy horse-like face, but that it is a mobile face when I am speaking and creates the illusion of good looks, which no photograph ever confirms! Consequently I dislike photographs of myself, and I don't want to send you one.

I really do know something about Latin & Greek.

Ditto, ditto about German.

I know a little about education & psychology.

I have a smattering of music and can play the ocarina and make a loud noise in a chorus.

I am a very bad housekeeper, but a good cook.

I smoke and I drink and in my youth I played cards a lot.

I like fun and high spirits, and I like a serious argument, but in between these two extremes I am not very competent socially.

Altogether: I do not see how you are to write that article at all!

Perhaps it could be summarised by describing me as half a 'stickit' scholar, with scholarly and intellectual leanings, and half a temperamental woman: if I were whole-heartedly one or the other life would be much easier for me. I drive too many incompatible horses in my team. As a scholar, a writer, a psychologist, I have a conscience: but when I feel daft I have no conscience at all. The only helpful thing about me is that I am more civilised now than I was at twenty; and with increasing age I may become completely civilised.

Yours sincerely,
Willa Muir.

(Willa Muir, letter to Marion Lochhead 3 March 1933, National Library of Scotland MS 26190, ff.95–97 [95, 97].)

6.11 Nannie K. Wells, from 'Woman and the New World' (*Free Man* July 1933)

A new weekly has appeared, which wants more than a passing glance from readers of *The Free Man*. It was inspired by a Scot, whose wireless talks on 'Freedom in the Modern World' woke such a response that some medium, some channel, had to be formed to store and use the moral force generated. Its aims are, as stated in every number, as follows:—It has strong Douglasite sympathies; it has published articles on 'The New Scotland' and 'The New Wales', which show a measure of understanding denied to the old petrified visions of better-known journals. The mind behind it, with its emphasis on integrity—or really, on freedom—on the 'perfection of the individual', is pure Scots. It needs not the McMurray [sic] label to tell us this. And it takes more than mere courage to challenge Professor MacMurray on his own hearth. Bearding the lion is a trifle to it! But when he writes for 'Women in the New Revolution', and declares that the family as we have known it must cease to function as the social unit, and further opens the lists for the tilting, he must bear with challengers. [. . .]

Professor MacMurray's problem is 'to keep individualisation compatible with social unity'. With all respect to Professor MacMurray, this has been woman's problem since the beginning of time. It is the real reason why Eve gave our first forefather the apple; the true meaning of his inward compulsion to eat. Women ever since have had to reconcile somehow the right of their men to be individual with the merciless encroachment of the social system upon their liberty of character and conduct. (Incidentally, women know that irresponsible fatherhood is not likely to make for a higher type of male, and that mere economic responsibility on the Russian Plan is not enough.)

But I take leave to disagree with Professor MacMurray when he implies that the increasing individuation of women is primarily a revolt against the family. Woman in the process of her individuation will carry the family and the home in some shape with her. Her revolt is rather against standardisation, against mass-treatment of her mate and her off-spring, either as cannon-fodder or business-fodder; against centralisation, rationalisation, monopoly, anything which denies her men their proper individuation.

It is true that she also must be individuated, must realise herself, but for a great number of women 'gouverner les hommes' is the realisation of herself she most desires, and for the others the experience, continuously expansive as it is of the family, is an essential of development.

Let us face a simple elementary fact. In *normal circumstances a woman's children will outlive her.* Where and when would Professor MacMurray have the relation cease? In its present form it could with advantage to both sides be pruned and purified. Mere money considerations, i.e. dependence or independence of the child, does not dispose of the relationship with all its varied exchange of feeling and experience and its source of love and power and beauty. The family in this sense should not cease to function, although it may evolve new forms.

It is perhaps just as well that I have no definite pattern of social unit to offer to Professor MacMurray; these do not lie about ready-made. Individuals here and there make, at deep cost to themselves, their own patterns. But threads there are out of which a common pattern may be woven, and three women of my acquaintance have furnished me with threads:

214

Willa Muir (I quote from a conversation): 'We must give the life of the emotions its proper prestige. Up till now we have reckoned too much with mind only as the source of distinction.' In this connection it is obvious that when women are economically independent of men they will evolve—have to evolve—a new technique of the emotions, more delicate, more noble. The cash-nexus is destructive of just that prestige, that distinction and delicate independence which should mark the new social unit.

Catherine Carsewell [sic], with her interpretations and vindication of D.H. Lawrence and his gospel: 'I was surprised to find him pilloried as a false prophet in *New Britain* recently.'

Naomi Mitcheson [sic], who threw out in the *Modern Scot* a hint which, as far as I know, she has never amplified, about 'a steading civilisation', presumably a modern agricultural community which might provide a framework for Professor MacMurray's suggested integration of two or more families with a life in common.

Is it mere chance that all three are Scotswomen? I think not. For the Scotswoman has always been encouraged, both by Scots law and by custom, to 'individuate' herself, to take responsibility, to hold her own views, and make her beliefs felt. And yet in Scotland the family plays a bigger part than in England; our children stay in the home to be educated, while English children go to 'prep' and 'public' schools.

It is up to women to go on individually modifying and recasting the present forms of the social unit, in such ways as they feel to be real and sincere. But they must leave the common solution to grow out of the experience of the community. Psychologically, it is our business to combat mass management, standardisation, and the indifferentism which results from these. These things injure our integrity, they damage the delicate new growth of the 'prestige of the emotions'. A woman who bears a child to the man she loves, who has experienced 'the divine visitation', *dare not tolerate mass psychology*: it is a denial of the divine in man, and must be resisted with her last breath.

(N.K.W. [Nannie K. Wells], 'Woman and the New World', *Free Man*
2:26, 29 July 1933, p.6.)

6.12 Willa Muir, 'Women in Scotland' (*Left Review* November 1936)

Scotland, taken by and large, is, I suppose, a Socialist country. Yet it is difficult to speak of women's movements in Scotland, since most Scottish working-class women—and men, too, are dominated by the belief that outside the home men should have all 'the say'. In Scotland, again taking it by and large, a woman's place is still considered to be the actual home. A Scotswoman at a mixed public meeting or on a mixed committee feels that it is not her 'place' to let her voice be heard, and she will not risk speaking up unless she has something very urgent to say. In consequence, the ordinary women of Scotland, petty bourgeois and proletarian alike, in the rural districts and in the industrial towns, are untrained in public life, almost unrepresented, relatively unorganised and largely inarticulate outside the home. Even in purely feminine movements, such as the Women's Rural Institutes and Women's Citizen Associations, the ordinary working women let themselves be run by 'the county'. In other organisations they let themselves be run by their own menfolk, or by the Kirk, except when it comes to staging a bazaar or a social function. Ordinary Scotswomen, politically speaking, are as difficult to tempt into the open as the occupants of a Hindu zenana. The ratio of men to women contributors in this Scottish number of the *Left Review* is a fair reflection of what happens in Scottish public life.

Inside the home, of course, the tables are apt to be turned. A Scotswoman who is too timid to utter a word in public may tongue-lash her family in private with great efficiency. Inside the home she may have plenty of 'say', since her husband and her children are entirely dependent on her services. A Scotswoman at home can be a formidable figure; she is essentially a mother rather than a wife and comrade; she provides meals, darned socks and other comforts to the whole family, and from her point of view a husband is often enough only a more exacting child among the other children. It would be a mistake to assume that the 'missis' is a cypher merely because she keeps silent or goes off to wash the dishes whenever the menfolk argue about politics or religion. Her authority is rather a different kind of authority from her husband's; his is the concentrated authority of an individual, hers is the more diffuse, pervasive atmospheric authority of an environment. And like other atmospheric conditions it can cause profound electrical disturbances.

This is an old pattern of domestic life. The mother as environment for her family is, so to speak, the basic diagram of womanhood. It is a pattern that survives from a world immeasurably older than our monetary civilisation in which we are caught up to-day, and you would recognise it, with local variations, in many parts of the world at different stages of history. It sounds a reasonable enough partnership: the man, as an individual, emerging from the home circle to dominate the alien world outside; the woman, as an environment, dominating the home circle. But it remains a reasonable partnership only when there is a fair balance between the prestige and rights of the partners, and the progress of our economic system has destroyed that balance. To-day, at the present stage of capitalistic development, the circle of environmental authority within which a mother stands has both shrunk in area and dwindled in relative importance. Artificially created environments such as the State, the Big Business Monopoly, the factory, have encroached upon it and are steadily encroaching upon it.

These rival environments have economic status, while a mother has none. They interfere with and determine the education, the scale of nutrition, the medical treatment, the employment, the leisure recreations and personal loyalties of a woman's children. Unlike other mothers, the human mother cannot go out nowadays and forage independently for her youngsters' needs; she is hedged in by the bars of our monetary civilisation as if she were in a zoo; she must 'make do' with what she happens to get. That greater environment, the State, also has to 'make do', in theory, with what it can get from individual tax-payers, but it possesses compulsive powers and can control the amount of its levies. A mother has similar responsibilities on a smaller scale but no comparable rights. In theory, the father of the family is the conduit-pipe through which money flows into the house; in theory, the mother gets all she needs and administers it to the family, remaining outside the competitive economic market, preserving among the money values of the world an intact island of simple human values. It is a pretty theory. It has survived for so long simply because a woman nursing her own babies does not behave like a Milk Marketing Board. But in fact, in the world of to-day, the non-economic environmental services of women are horribly exploited. The monetary system by this time has encroached upon every corner of the home, and the simple human nucleus that makes a mother's world has shrunk almost to a pin-point. Her elemental needs, food, clothing and shelter for her children, are all prescribed by outside economic agencies over which she has no control.

The husband, of course, is equally a victim of economic circumstances, but his place is not considered to be exclusively the home; he has a certain economic status, but he is in direct communication with the outside world, he is active politically and can make his voice heard in public. That is what makes the position of working-class women in Scotland so ambiguous to-day; they are confined to the home, and the home is shrinking visibly around them. They are still living by a tradition which modern economic life is hammering to pieces.

And the results? A startlingly high maternal mortality rate, a high infant death-rate, a general increase of unfitness, a rapid fall of the population. These are all signs showing not only the effects of economic depression but the profound, if inarticulate, discouragement of the women.

What is to be done about it? You can, of course, assume that in a new state of society private home environments will vanish completely. A mother would then rank as an individual, as a paid breeding-machine; she could park her children in State crèches, schools and institutes, and exercise her maternal gifts in administering the food, clothing and housing of a nation rather than a family. This system might possibly produce more hygienic human beings than come out of the industrial slums where over-driven mothers are trying to cope with family life on the Means Test, but nobody really believes it is humanly possible. The alternative policy is to create a right balance between the home environment and the outside world. That means a fifty-fifty partnership between men and their wives. It means that a mother should become also a political comrade, with an economic status of her own and a 'say' in public affairs. I suggest that Scotsmen accustom themselves to this idea, and do their utmost to enlarge the environmental circle within which their women are cramped. With a right balance between environment and individual, the family can be a solid basis for national life. A nation made up of such families would survive the disappearance of any State. Moreover, such a national ideal would appeal to the discouraged women of Scotland. Scotland as a nation has been so long a 'puir auld mither' that Scottish mothers are likely to have a fellow-feeling for her. And if this fellow-feeling is not to be exploited by monopoly capital behind a barrage of Nationalist slogans, it must be used now as a means of enlightening Scotswomen. For they need to be shown where they stand, and I suspect that they are waiting for a lead.

Scotsmen, co-opt your women!

(Willa Muir, 'Women in Scotland', *Left Review* 2:14 November 1936, pp.768–70.)

6.13 Naomi Mitchison, from *Among You Taking Notes* (3 September 1939)

I listened to the 9 o'ck news, realising fairly clearly what the next was to be. The others were mostly not down, but I had not slept well. Valentine went off to Mains to look after the Glasgow children; Dick and I discussed what was to be done about the education of Avrion and Valentine; the latter can go to school here for a term, but the former would learn nothing. Tony said I'll start this war clean and went to wash her hair; a little later I did the same; it wasn't quite dry by 11.15. As we listened to Chamberlain speaking, sounding like a very old man, I kept wondering what the old Kaiser was thinking, whether he was old enough to see it all fully. The boys looked pale and worried, though Robin was laughing a little. At the end Joan said How could he ask God to bless us? . . . As God Save the King started Denny turned it off and someone said Thank you.

The maids hadn't wanted to come through; I told Annie who was wonderfully cheerful and said she remembered the Boer War, and Bella who said Isn't that heartbreaking. After a bit she began to cry, a saucepan in her hands, said Think of all our men going, then to me Of course you've got boys too. Dick said Think of the women in Germany all saying that too, but there was no response. Then she asked When will they send our men over? But none of us had much idea.

In the drawing room the big boys were writing and reading; I think perhaps writing poetry. I was feeling sick, and so were Stewart and Hank and I went over to Mains, but the teachers had just left—we followed them. Valentine had brought the Glasgow children over; they were talking happily but looked very white and thin and small. The village was empty; most people at church. It began to rain hard and we took shelter at the Galbraiths. [. . .]

I got back to the house, changed and dried my hair while the boys talked, taking in this gulf we have stepped over. Robin said 'All my tastes are pre-war!' And they all began saying things were pre-war; there was a certain amount of genuine laughter: *pourvu que ça dure*. Denny went on with his anatomy. Then Denny and I took the groceries round to the woman at Portrigh and I talked to her soothingly. She and the others are Glasgow slum prolet; one of the other mothers had a boy of sixteen in a territorial pipe band; I said I was sure he wouldn't be taken overseas. Another had a daughter unemployed.

The Mains children had been having a grand time dressing up and were very cheerful. After tea we had the 6 o'ck news; three of the maids came for the King's speech. I talked to the boys and to Dick, whose application to the Treasury Solicitor has been refused. I advise him not to rush off for the moment. The storm has broken a lot of the beautiful gladiolus and brought down some apples; at least it is a natural thing. . . .

(Naomi Mitchison, *Among You Taking Notes: The Wartime Diary of Naomi Mitchison*, edited by Dorothy Sheridan, London: Gollancz, 1985, 3 September 1933, pp.35–37.)

WHITHER SCOTLAND?

As discussed in the Introduction, one of the defining characteristics of the interwar literary revival was its insistence that any cultural revival in Scotland must be part of the regeneration of the nation as a whole: for the writers involved, the arts could not be kept separate from the country's social, economic, religious and political life. While in the early to mid-1920s the renewal debate focused significantly on literary identity and the challenging and reshaping of literary traditions, from the late 1920s and throughout most of the 1930s, the condition of Scotland, 'that distressed nation', as George Malcolm Thomson characterised it, became the dominant concern, accompanied by argument and debate between ideological positions offering perceived remedies for the crisis.

'Whither Scotland?' is itself divided into three sections, although as with 'Towards a Scottish Literary Renaissance', there is a certain overlap between them. 'The Condition of Scotland' deals predominantly with social and economic conditions, and with perceptions of loss of identity and decision-making power. 'Celtic Connections and the Situation of the Highlands' reflects the interwar interest in rediscovering Scotland's Celtic heritage and its links with Celtic Ireland and Irish culture: a vision which might seem to be at odds with the complaints about Irish immigration in the previous section. Yet, for the writers of the time, and with Eire as an example, Celtic identity could be seen as a symbol for both artistic and political and social/economic regeneration. Very importantly, however, this section also reflects the actual everyday concerns about emigration, loss of language and general social and economic decay in the Gaelic-speaking Scottish Highlands, with participants debating in a practical way sources of decline and possible ways forward. The final section 'Competing Ideologies' reflects the diversity and complexity of the ideological positions of the time. Nationalism is, as might be expected, a dominant position here, but there are also attempts to define more precisely what exactly is meant by 'nationalism' and to explore its implications, while there is a recurrent insistence, variously expressed, that it is a position complementary with, not oppositional to, internationalism. Similarly, the nationalist debate both engages with and departs from socialism and communism as instruments of renewal. In this respect, some of the private correspondence between writers in the late 1930s, when war was again threatening, is of especial interest in relation to their political views and actions at this time.

7

The Condition of Scotland

7.1 'The Church and the Slums' (*Scots Observer* October 1926)

At its August meeting the Glasgow Presbytery received a deputation from the Slum Abolition League, and it was remitted to a small committee to report on the activities of the League. In presenting the report of this committee at the Presbytery meeting on Wednesday, the Rev. Dr David Watson (St Clement's) referred to the commission on housing appointed by the Presbytery nearly 40 years ago. Much had been done, yet to-day they had 13,000 houses condemned as unfit for human habitation and yet occupied, 125,000 citizens for whom home meant one room, and 250,000 people living in overcrowded conditions. The physical, social, and moral results of such conditions were a challenge to the Church and to the Christian conscience. The Government was alive to the evil. The corporation of Glasgow was grappling earnestly with a gigantic task. It was working on right lines, re-housing as fast as it was dis-housing.

No New Slums

'I have visited the areas where the transferred slum-dwellers now reside', said Dr Watson, and I have seen some of the people, whom I knew before, in their new houses and new surroundings, and I wish to say here that they have responded nobly to their new environment. They have *not* made slums of their houses. There are, no doubt, some inevitable failures—about 10 per cent. There will always be a residuum of incorrigibles in all ranks of society. But if 90 per cent are doing well, keeping their houses clean and taking a pride in them, then this Glasgow experiment in slum clearance is abundantly justified.' (*Cheers*)

Much remained to be done. Only 700 of the 13,000 condemned houses had been demolished. The Slum Abolition League proposed to help matters by following the example of the Workmen's Dwellings Company, formed in 1890 on the suggestion of the Presbytery Housing Commission. If they could get shareholders who would be content with 2½ per cent, they would be able to build houses that could be let at 6s per week. Referring to the proposals of the League, he moved that the Presbytery express its willingness to take part in any conference arranged by the Churches, and its approval of the suggestion that the subject of housing and slum clearance be brought before all the congregations on an agreed Sunday.

The resolution was seconded by Rev. W.M. Wightman (St Enoch's Hogganfield), and was unanimously adopted.

('The Church and the Slums', unsigned report of the August meeting of the
Glasgow Presbytery, Scots Observer 1:1, 2 October 1926, p.1.)

7.2   George Malcolm Thomson, from *Caledonia or The Future of the Scots* [1927]

a) Concerning Scottish myths

Up and down the world, in his various scrubby and subaltern positions—golf professional, sub-editor, ship's engineer, chartered accountant, etc.—the Scotsman has revenged himself on his mediocre circumstances by inventing and disseminating a myth about Scotsmen which has reached gigantic proportions and gained a world-wide credence, with the most gratifying perquisites of reflected glory for its manufacturers.

In this legend the Scot strides the earth a Colossus, carving out a kingdom for himself in the lands of lesser peoples who acknowledge his superiority and accept his leadership with sulky gratitude. Hard-headed, practical, and energetic, he shapes the policies, orders the industries, or directs the commerce of the country of his crowned exile; silent, stubborn, and successful, he surveys an earth prostrate beneath his dominion, and editors of newspapers, immigration officials, politicians, and captains of industry unite to praise him.

Many an over-worked, under-paid little Scots invoice clerk living in Clapham is, with the aid of this myth, able to see his conscripted emigration as a glorious adventure (which is as if a man ignominiously kicked out of a fourth floor window were to represent himself to the crowd on the pavement as the martyr of a personal investigation into the laws of aeronautics), and tries to look 'dour' and 'canny', and laughs complacently when Englishmen tell him the story of the Scotsman who came to London and met 'only the heids of Departments'. He struts punctually to his stool as to a throne and, with the glamour still over him, proceeds for another day to live up to the national motto of middling through.

But the matter does not end there.

Out of the harmless and consoling legend of the conquering Scot, composed like other legends out of a vast number of half-truths, has emerged, as a natural corollary, a singular and universal belief about the country of his origin. It is shared by the grouse-shooters who know Scotland only as a battue and a Ben and the tourists who think that the Trossachs are the Highlands, as well as by the greater number whose notions of Scotland are quarried from the sugar strata of Ian Maclaren. The inhabitants of Scotland themselves would be shocked by the merest hint that it might not, after all, be the true view of the case.

The truth is that no one—and least of all a Scotsman—ever troubles to think about Scotland at all, but, if pressed for an opinion, the average man would probably divulge a vague complex of generalizations crystallizing out somewhat as follows:

Scotland is a comparatively poor country, plain down one side of the map and jagged down the other, inhabited by a ferociously independent race whose surnames mostly begin with Mac. It is democratically and efficiently governed; its industries and commerce display the enterprise and shrewdness for which the nation is renowned. It is economically developed to the highest pitch. Its educational institutions are one of the wonders of the modern world. The people is notoriously one of the best educated on earth. An extraordinary amount of intellectual activity ferments among them; the love of good literature and high thinking is widespread, but is balanced by a strain of harsh practical wisdom. The first is reflected in the austere standards of its newspapers, the vigour of its mental life and the academic glories of its universities. From the second derive the prosperity and security which mark the peaceable, well-ordered life of the community. The people are further distinguished for their stalwart patriotism. They cherish jealously their national idiom, their national religion, their time-hallowed customs, and all the traditions with which their long history has endowed them.

A pretty picture, seeming to relate to some comfortable mid-nineteenth century of the world rather than to these flustered, disillusioned, unscrupulous, and out-at-elbows 1920s. It does not relate to the 1920s. It is, in fact, only a beautiful picture in a beautiful golden frame, a well-nurtured misconception, a whole mythology rather than a single myth.

b) Concerning immigration and emigration

The first fact about the Scot is that he is a man eclipsed. The Scots are a dying people. They are being replaced in their own country by a people alien in race, temperament, and religion, at a speed which is without parallel in history outside the era of the barbarian invasions. Certainly there is nothing in modern times to compare with the ousting of one population by another which has been taking place in Scotland during the last sixty or seventy years and which is going on with undiminished momentum at the present time.

To-day every fifth baby born in Scotland is a little Irish Catholic. In Glasgow in 1924, 28½ per cent of the children born saw the world through the windows of an Irish Catholic home. And, most sinister and significant of all, one-third of the crimes committed in Scotland are the work of Irishmen.

It is as well to make it plain at once that Catholic and Irish are for all practical purposes interchangeable terms in Scotland. True, there has always been a small native Roman Catholic population in Scotland centred mainly in Inverness-shire and Dumfriesshire. In Inverness it numbers about one-seventh, and in Dumfries about one-twenty-fifth of the total inhabitants of the county, proportions which have remained stationary for centuries. Nor has proselytism had any appreciable part in the revolutionary change in Scotland's religious complexion. The Kirk has lost its hold over many Scots, but it has not relinquished it to the Church. The Covenant's deserters have not been Rome's recruits.

The problem of dividing the responsibility for the continued increase in the Irish population between immigrants from Ireland and the greater fertility of the Irish already settled is a ticklish one. The Roman Catholic priesthood in Scotland has naturally been quick to claim the growth of the Irish community as a victory for the superior domestic virtues of their flocks, and, in especial, their freedom from what a recent Pastoral Letter of the Roman Catholic Bishops of Scotland described as 'a grave sin, separating us from the friendship of God, and rendering us liable to eternal punishment'—Birth Control.

It is gravely to be doubted, however, whether there is much to choose between the Irish and the Scottish working classes in this respect. The Scots workman has always taken his marital relations simply and realistically. The creed which still provides much of his moral environment gives him, moreover, copious examples among the Hebrew patriarchs and the Reformers, as persuasive as any precepts of an infallible church. Direct evidence on the question is not lacking. In one populous mining district where comparisons were made, the Scottish birth-rate was in 1922 higher than the Irish. Aberdeen, a purely Scots city, has a slightly higher birth-rate than Dundee, which is one-fifth Irish.

It is impossible to do more than guess at the average annual Irish immigration into Scotland as there are no figures which give the information. This extraordinary absence of data characterizes almost every branch of social and economic enquiry in Scotland, in itself an illuminating comment on the national mentality. That immigration continues, and in large volume, may be inferred from a comparison of the numbers of Irish and Scottish school-children in Glasgow, Lanarkshire, Renfrew, Dumbarton, Dundee, and Edinburgh, during the post-war period. Had the two populations remained in the same proportions, the natural change in the numbers at the end of this period as compared with the beginning would have shown a loss of 620 Scots and 335 Irish. The actual results reveal a Scots loss of 6,300 and an Irish gain of 5,540. [. . .]

Those who have been brought up to the great Scottish legend will naturally be prone to find in this immense influx the portent of an economic development that has outstripped the natural growth of the Scottish people. But unfortunately it coincides with an emigration of Scots from Scotland which begins to assume the aspect of a rout. A liner drops anchor in a quiet Highland loch and strips an island or two as berry-pickers a hill-side. It is not the surplus of adventurous youth that goes: a whole stock is uprooted. Since the war over 300,000 Scots have gone abroad never to return, and by 1936 it is likely that one million will have left the country since the beginning of the twentieth century. It is this that gives its peculiarly sinister aspect to the Irish inundation.

But, to a foreigner, educated by his newspapers to believe in the jealously nationalist Scot who is always fighting his Bannockburns over again, the strangest thing about all this is that events which would have caused a race war in America and a pogrom in most European countries are not even a minor political issue in Scotland. If it had not been that a religious as well as a racial revolution was taking place the very existence of the Irish invasion would have only been vaguely suspected. As it is, the Assembly of the Church of Scotland alone has exhibited the slightest concern over what is the gravest race problem confronting any nation in Europe to-day. And the public spirit of the Church is suspect. They think of congregation rather than of nation; and the sincerity of their new-found zeal is largely discounted by the fact that they never ventured to condemn the greed for cheap labour which is the root of the trouble. The Scottish Churches propose to control the immigration by act of Parliament. It can be safely assumed, however, that there is not the slightest chance of anything happening so long as it remains a Scottish problem. When England is menaced, swift action will follow.

Nor is Ireland the only source from which the conquering Scot is being pushed out of his own country. Since the war a strong tide of English immigration has flowed. There are now more Englishmen living in Glasgow than there are Scots in that prostrate Scottish dependency, London. English shops and stores have trebled since 1918. 'Everywhere', laments one observer, 'is the English professional man and shopkeeper and the Irish labourer.'

c) Concerning the slums

Slums are to Scotsmen a commonplace, and to Englishmen who have not visited them a wild exaggeration. 'We have as bad in London', they will say. They have not. There is nothing in Europe to compare for vastness and vileness with the slums in Scottish cities.

Once, in a train in Scotland, I met a wealthy English manufacturer who had been lured by his curiosity to visit one of Glasgow's slum districts. His horror was highly diverting. 'I emptied my pockets of money', he said, 'and went back to my hotel for more. What else could one do? These children were like animals.'

But in Scotland there is no horror, and if, occasionally there is despair, the most prevalent attitude is apathy and a vehement desire to say and think as little as possible about an unsavoury topic. The only book on Scottish slums with any imaginative power and passion in it is the work of an Englishman. The ringleaders in the revolt against the Clydebank housing conditions which culminated in the famous rent strike were English settlers. These are truths with which the more persistent kind of Scottish social nuisance can be confronted with the most excellent results.

Nor are the slums a local ailment. They are a malignant disease affecting the whole body of the nation. Two million people live more than two in a room. It is ludicrous to pretend, as the vast majority of Scotsmen do, that their country is at the same level of prosperity and civilization as England's, so long as forty-five per cent of Scotsmen live more than two in a room as compared with 9.6 per cent of Englishmen. The gulf between the countries is not that dividing poor and rich relations but rather that between coolies and their white exploiters. Of the inhabitants of Wishaw and Coatbridge, two towns in the Lanarkshire industrial region, twenty-three per cent live in one-room houses, the corresponding figure for all England and Wales being 1.7 per cent.

But figures selected from a vast mass of statistics only draw the outline of this monster: a visit to one of those dwellings is needed to fill in the colours. There, in a backland (a tenement built on what was originally the drying green behind an older tenement), a family of eight people sleep in one bed in a room into which the daylight never penetrates. An unspeakably foul odour permeates everything—the famous slum smell, to the making of which centuries of filth, damp, soot, bad air, and decay have gone. Over the door there may be a small label with a number. This signifies that the house is 'ticketed', i.e. liable to entrance and search at any time of the day or night by the sanitary officials. [. . .] Half Scotland is slum-poisoned. The taint of the slum is in the nation's blood; its taint in their minds has given birth to a new race of barbarians. Rickets and other infantile diseases, tuberculosis, venereal disease and various disgusting blood disorders abound in an appalling degree. The standard of height and physical development is low. The slum is to be regarded not so much as an area of bad housing but as a deadly plague. The annual death-rate of adult males living in one-roomed houses is 27 per thousand compared with 12 per thousand among those living in four-roomed houses.

There is one street in Glasgow where there is not a pane of glass in the windows and where women give birth to children on a newspaper spread out on the two inches of fine coal-dust that covers the floor. Dundee, which to the slum adds the further monstrosity of a proportion of female factory labour four times as high as in Glasgow, boasts of the highest infantile mortality in Great Britain, and the word 'boasts' is not ironically used. A Dundee doctor once said to me, voicing the local complacency, 'We kill off the weak ones, so those that are left can stand anything'. But those that are left do not present to the impartial observer such an appearance of health or beauty as would lead him to share this cheerfulness. [. . .]

It will occur to the reader that the Scottish slum problem is somewhat difficult to reconcile with the Scotsman's famous ability to manage his own country—and anyone else's—on a civilized level of decency and efficiency. Confronted by this dilemma, the shrewd, hard-headed, middle-class trades-men who run the domestic affairs of the country will agree that the slums are deplorable, but suggest that they are not so big after all, and that their population is a 'submerged tenth', whose fate is their fault. The answer to which is that one half of the population lives below the not too exacting standard of the Ministry of Health, that to make Glasgow fit for human beings to live in would cost sixty millions, and that even if the money could be raised, no one can see how the rents of the new houses could possibly be paid.

d) The decline of Scottish industry

There is not a single important industry in Scotland which, viewed in the light of the world's increase in consuming capacity, does not show a decline, all the more alarming because it cannot be attributed to temporary causes alone. This general shrinking of production is eloquently reflected in the present state of Scottish seaports. In Leith, the second seaport of the country, huge docks stand empty and desolate, grass grows on the once busy streets leading to the dock-gates, and 4,000 unemployed make the port the blackest spot on the Ministry of Labour's map. To visit Leith is to remember Bruges.

And, in spite of the fact that the leading Scottish industries are in a state of manifest decay, there is no sign of determined efforts to replace them by new enterprises. There is nothing of that swift reaction to the first symptoms of adversity which one would expect to find in a vigorous commercial people, no ingenious adaptations of technique, no fierce search for new avenues. The scent of death which Cunninghame Graham found in the Scottish countryside thirty years ago has drifted into the cities, and commerce grows feeble, rigid and cowardly in its miasma. The only hopeful symptom is the programme of electrical unification which is to be carried out during the next ten years under the direction of a Board sitting in London. But this is not a national scheme for utilizing the hydro-electric resources of the country but only a re-organization of the existing power plants in the industrial area. It has nothing to say about Highland water-power and the part it might play in a resurrected rural economy. It is only an attempt to bolster up the tottering machine industries of Scotland.

Not only is Scottish industry decaying, it is steadily ceasing to be Scottish. Four out of eight banks have been affiliated to English banks on terms which, while leaving them much local freedom, will tend to make them increasingly the slaves of the needs and emergencies of the London money market. Money will be liable to sudden recall from Scotland to meet the wants of the predominant English partners. Already there have been rumours that the local knowledge of branch managers, in which so much trust used to be placed, is no longer being allowed its former liberty to meet local needs. There seems also some danger that the jealously guarded note-issuing power of the Scottish banks, which nurtured Scotland's industrial growth, will be lost as a result of these new entanglements. A century ago when such a proposal was made, Sir Walter Scott talked darkly of claymores and the Government dropped the idea. To-day there are no Scotts, and the Scots will probably congratulate themselves on the removal of an 'anomaly'.

Scottish railways are now directed from London. Local repair shops have been transferred to England, the lack of locomotives has been the subject of many complaints, but the most dangerous aspect of the amalgamation to a commercial community is the absence of officials with authority to make immediate decisions.

However, the capture by English capital of banks and railways are only two instances of a general process of removing the control of Scottish administration, commerce, and industry four hundred miles further South. The Scottish business man shows a self-effacing readiness to be absorbed by large combines and multiple-unit concerns. Examples are numerous.

The head offices of shipping companies which once were crowded together in Glasgow no longer fly their house-flags in St Vincent Street. They are mostly transferred South of the Border to London or Liverpool. The important chemical and dyeing industries are now controlled from England. The Scottish branch of the Ministry of Pensions, though more economically administered than any of the other branches, was closed, and at present a bill is before Parliament to replace the Scottish Board of Agriculture, the Board of Health, and the Prison Commissioners by departments in Whitehall. It will, of course, become law, although it is opposed by a majority of Scottish members.

One immediate result of this tendency is to give increased impetus to a form of emigration from the country which, though numerically unimportant, is as serious and deplorable as the artisan exodus—the drain of the educated, intelligent, and energetic middle-class youth who would normally become the leaders of the commercial, political, and intellectual life of the country.

e) Universities, religion and the press

Being cheap and easily come by, Scottish education has been the subject of much undiscriminating adulation from people who ought to know better. It is perfectly true that the proportion of students at Scottish Universities to the population is about four times England's, but no number of half-wits will make an educated nation, though they be decked out in a veritable rainbow of degree-hoods and can marshall whole alphabets after their names.

At a recent Scottish University dinner, the speaker of the evening said: 'There is this about our universities which distinguishes them from English seats of learning: they enable the student who passes through them to earn his living and pursue his career with greater chance of success.' A sentiment which was received with prolonged applause by the company. At an Aberdeen University function lately, Sir J.A. Thomson said: 'The Aberdeen student has a distinguishing characteristic, a quiet, dogged determination to get there.' (*Applause*.) It may be assumed that for most of the speaker's audience 'there' had a meaning bank-managers would understand. The expectation that everyone will declare a dividend on his education at once separates Scotland from countries where education—higher and especially University education, at least—is assumed to have a cultural intention. It goes far to explain why Scottish Universities have sunk to the level of technical schools, and why none of their students ever looks back on his university days with the pleasure which even vulgar and insensitive people can derive from Oxford reminiscences. [. . .]

The cheapness of the Universities brings with it huge classes—a class of 300 is not unknown—and a loss of that personal contact between teacher and undergraduate which might mitigate the worst evils of utilitarian education. And in the Arts faculties which ought to be her citadels, a plague of embryo teachers harries Culture, the fair deserted maid, without the walls. [. . .] To them, knowledge is a series of 'subjects', to be carefully written down in note-books, swotted up for examinations, and eventually passed out of and obliterated. They have made examinations and marks the main pillars of Scottish University education. [. . .]

The Scottish Reformation was the single-handed work of a man with a taste for French logic, French wines, the society of women, and convivial supper parties on Sunday evenings. It was an intellectual feat. It pinned God, in a slightly abridged form, within *The Shorter Catechism*.

From the days of Knox, however, no intellectual development has taken place in Scottish religion. To-day, its best products are men of the missionary type, expounding a rough-and-ready banjo Christianity to the natives of Central Africa. It has no one capable of teaching a philosophic theology that would not be instantly rejected by the minds of educated people. The very vocabulary of its preachers, plentifully interlarded with unctuous tags, disgusts and estranges the younger generation to whose Freud- and Shaw-tinctured minds threadbare doctrines are not any more recommended because they are clothed in a phraseology borrowed from some minor prophet. It has no parallel to Inge in England. Its St Pauls are apostles to the genteel, preaching in their ugly, comfortable, suburban churches a vague and sickly creed of benevolence in which a nebulous Redeemer presides over a pleasant drawing-room game of doing good to others. [. . .]

Turning from the pulpit to the press, we find that the newspaper with the highest circulation in Scotland is one of the five English-owned journals published in the country; the newspaper whose circulation comes next is the *Daily Mail*. Scottish newspapers are, at their best, good provincial sheets and no more. There is no national newspaper looking to Scotland first and at the rest of the world through Scottish eyes. Not one of them has shown even the ambition to transcend its provincial status and to become a national organ as the *Manchester Guardian* has done. The greatest condemnation of the Scottish press is that not once has there appeared in a Scottish newspaper an article devoted to an intelligent scrutiny and investigation of a Scottish problem. It is in such ways that the people have grown up in the incredible ignorance of their own country's state which has already been noticed, and in the illusion that their problems and difficulties were identical with those of England.

A Scottish editor's vital cord is the telegraph wire uniting him with his London office. In his relations to his political party he is *plus royaliste que le roi*, betraying an absence of independent criticism which an intelligent foreigner would have no hesitation in ascribing to bribery. But the Scottish press has not even this excuse.

(George Malcolm Thomson, *Caledonia or The Future of the Scots* London: Kegan Paul, Trench, Trubner & Co., [1927], pp.5–9; 10–13, 14–17; 18–22; 40–44; 47–51, 55–59.)

7.3 From unsigned review of *Rip Van Scotland* by William Bell (*Modern Scot* Spring 1930)

Mr William Bell in *Rip Van Scotland* has little to say about modern Scotland that has not already been said by Mr C.M. Grieve in one form or another; but his book is a highly commendable summing up of our present position, and is important inasmuch as it excellently combines constructive with destructive criticism.

No Scotsman of the slightest intelligence and integrity can regard the plight of his country to-day with anything but profound disquietude. He sees what was once a nation rapidly becoming more and more a mere backwater of England; he sees the Scottish Renaissance, a concern of a select few, endangered by the most pernicious provincialism; on every hand he sees the counterpart of Scotland's cultural decadence in its economic decline. These things are patent to all, and Mr Bell in writing as trenchantly as he does about them expresses the thoughts of thousands of his fellow-countrymen.

If it consisted entirely of a description of how Scotland lags behind England, of our unemployment problem, distressing housing conditions and comparative cultural sterility, *Rip Van Scotland* would only take a place alongside *Caledonia*. Mr Bell, however, goes much further than hurling vituperation at those who neglect the evils obvious to the half civilised. He aligns himself with those working for Scottish Nationalism, and not only shows again the utter hopelessness of Scotland's expecting any remedy for her wrongs at Westminster, but joins Mr C.M. Grieve in urging a thoroughly radical approach to the whole problem.

There is widespread agreement now that the most Scotland can hope from Westminster is the consideration meted out to one of the more remote English shires. The present problems of Scotland are for a large part distinctively Scottish ones, and centralisation of government is anyhow pernicious. Scotland will never be a nation again so long as its M.P.s sit in London: we must have a Parliament in Edinburgh. Not only that, Mr Bell points out—our entire notions of what Governments can and cannot do must be changed if we are to escape the economic disaster at the moment threatening the whole of Britain. He urges Scotland to sponsor the most far-seeing changes in orthodox economics.

The Scottish M.P.s are obviously powerless to act as Scotsmen at Westminster, and in turn the whole Westminster Parliament is helpless in the hands of the financiers. [. . .] The economic salvation of Britain, not to mention the whole of the industrialised world, lies in a wholesale reform of the financial system, along the lines laid down by Major C.H. Douglas; and the chief importance of Mr Bell's *Rip Van Scotland* is in its making 'Douglasism' part and parcel of Scottish Nationalism. [. . .]

'Without a complete reorganisation of credit control along the lines of the Douglas analysis', writes Mr Bell, 'I believe there is small hope of trade revival for the Scottish people whether the administration be at Westminster or Edinburgh. Merely to establish the Parliament in Edinburgh, but to leave the power to issue credit in control of the Bank of England, is but to quibble with the meaning of self-government. Any Westminster parliament, no matter what party forms the administration there, is to-day governed by the

Bank of England. Despite the "safest" working majority over all other parties, any "government" is only in political office, never in financial power. The "hidden hand" behind any democratically-elected administration is always the privately elected government personified in High Finance.'

Major Douglas is a Scotsman, and in Scotland if anywhere he should be recognised as the very important world-figure he is. Mr Bell very properly devotes almost half of *Rip Van Scotland* to his economic theories, and one cannot help agreeing with him when he says, apropos the long list of Scotsmen who have won fame as economists—'The advent of Major Douglas at this precise moment in history is a significant portent economically for Scotland as it is for the whole world. For now arises the question whether the destiny of Scottish genius may be to drain the economic morass in which the first-class nations of civilisation are floundering. It may be that the Scottish people shall be the first to express in terms of economic action that celebrated equation first enunciated by her latest son of economic genius'.

The pedant more concerned with form than matter may say *Rip Van Scotland* is carelessly written, and truth to tell it is obviously hurriedly written. That, however, is a matter of no moment compared with the fact that the author, besides being one of the many Scots wishing to destroy, is also one of the few who know how to build, quickly and surely.

(Unsigned review of *Rip Van Scotland* by William Bell, *Modern Scot* 1:1 spring 1930, pp.43–46.)

7.4   Andrew Dewar Gibb, from *Scotland in Eclipse* (1930)

a) From 'The Irish Immigration'

It is idle to suggest that emigration is and has always been a necessity for Scotland, since during a great part of the period when emigration has been in full swing, the immigration of Irishmen into Scotland has kept pace with it. The only other conclusion is that this exchange was necessary because the immigrants were persons willing to accept a poorer and lower standard of living than the emigrants, and that only this lower standard was available. But it seems questionable whether this is true, since the mode of life usual amongst the Highlanders was hard and comfortless. At any rate it can be said that if in truth the country required to shed its surplus population in thousands and hundreds of thousands, the benefit of so doing must have been completely lost by reason of the simultaneous process of replacement. Viewed in any light the great Irish trek to Scotland is a national problem and a national evil of the first importance. There has been much desultory and some serious writing on the subject. No book which pretends to deal with the running sores from which Scotland suffers can be absolved from giving some independent view of the matter.

If Scotland is conscious of no other grievance; if all that English bureaucratic insolence has been able to do for her has left her supine and indifferent, at least she is conscious and very angrily conscious of the Irish question. Year after year and generation after generation a steady stream of low-grade immigrants of the labouring class has set from the wilds of Kerry and Limerick and from the slums of Cork and Dublin to the West Coast of Scotland. From there the immigrants have spread to the Lanarkshire coal-fields, to the coal-fields of Fife and the Lothians and to Dundee. As a rule quite unprosperous, they have in some places displayed special abilities. Thus in Glasgow they are fast developing a monopoly of the priesthood, the pawnshops and the public-houses. They form an appreciable proportion of the population of Scotland, breeding as they do not merely unchecked, but actually encouraged by their own medicine-men. An eminent geographer has recently stated the matter thus: 'A large foreign population, chiefly Irish, is taking possession, ousting Scotsmen and doing by peaceful penetration what no previous invaders were ever able to do by force.' They are responsible for most of the crime committed in Scotland, which otherwise would be the most law-abiding country in the world. Wheresoever knives and razors are used, wheresoever sneak thefts and mean pilfering are easy and safe, wheresoever dirty acts of sexual baseness are committed, there you will find the Irishman in Scotland with all but a monopoly of the business. Glasgow is cursed with gangs of young loafers who prowl about the East End in Bridgeton and Calton, attacking one another and often attacking the police and strangers. Their names, as the newspaper reports show, are Irish to the extent of at least ninety per cent. [. . .] Thus in the heart of a dwindling though virile and intelligent race there is growing up another people, immeasurably inferior in every way, but cohesive and solid, refusing obstinately, at the behest of obscurantist magic-men, to mingle with the people whose land they are usurping; unaware of, or if aware, disloyal to all the finest ideals and ambitions of the Scottish race: distinguished by a veritable will to squalor which is mainly responsible for Scottish slumdom; squatting and breeding in such numbers as to threaten in another hundred years to gain actual predominance in the country. In the years 1921–1926 some 300,000 people emigrated from Scotland, and it has not been suggested that the population has declined by anything like that number. But speculation on this point does not affect the main problem, which is the proper disposal and treatment of the deplorable Irish colony in Scotland. No amount of anti-immigration legislation can prevent Irish labourers from having families of twelve nor Irish priests from telling them that to attend a birth-control clinic is a deadly sin. To this problem modern Scotland is thoroughly awake. It is on the way to becoming a question of practical politics. Questions are asked in Parliament about it. Resolutions urging Government to deal with it are passed at political gatherings, principally of the Conservative party. The Assembly of the Church of Scotland solemnly appoints committees to see what can be done about it. Dean Inge makes a sympathetic reference to it in an article published by the *Evening Standard*. London papers touch on it, with of course very humorous asides about the Scottish invasion of England. It may indeed be pointed to as the one question exclusively of interest to Scotland which has aroused Scotsmen of all classes and parties to a sense of danger threatening, not the British Empire, but *Scotland*, their common country.

b) From 'Modern Tendencies in Commercial Scotland'

Scotland is to-day, ten years after the War which played havoc with the prosperity of both, very much less prosperous than England. Her greatest centre of population lies in her 'industrial belt', and it is the industries which in former times made that belt prosperous that are now most severely depressed. This depression is affecting similar industries in England, but England possesses other resources in a measure that Scotland does not, and England is nearer the Continent of Europe at a time when markets are won or lost by narrow margins, and when the cost of transport is a serious burden. Over all, then, Scotland suffers more than England. The proportion of persons unemployed in Scotland is consistently higher than it is in England. This fact cannot, of course, be ascribed wholly to the debit side of England's account, yet it seems incontestably true that in her efforts to regain something of her former prosperity Scotland is writhing in the stranglehold that England is putting upon her. [. . .] What then is the outstanding feature of the 'rehabilitation' of trade in Scotland during the past ten years? The only possible answer is that as a result of the search for economy and the consequent application of new ideas in technique and in finance there has been a process of absorption and amalgamation which has meant to Scotland a stark loss of invaluable industrial assets. That tendency was apparent before the war, but the abnormal conditions caused by the war pressing with especial force upon Scotland have terribly accentuated it. Great commercial concerns have flitted their offices, lock, stock and barrel to London or elsewhere in England. The reason apparently alleged is that they must be near the centre of things if they are to compete with their rivals. Yet concerns equally impressive have not taken this step; foreign concerns never take it, however closely their interests may be bound up with those of London, and it is amazing that it should be necessary at a time of day when people can communicate with one another over long distances more easily than ever before. The proceeding is a dubious one and is probably as much prompted by the familiar Scottish megalomania as by any more weighty reasons. The result, however, is serious—the enrichment of England and a corresponding loss to Scotland. [. . .] Instances of total closure are to be found in the shipyards, in the chemical and sugar-refining industries, in agriculture, in the railway workshops, in the textile trade. [. . .] Scottish newspapers and road transport enterprises disappear into English maws. The Scottish-owned theatre or cinema is a *rara avis*. More and more of the great shops and stores pass under English control. They, too, run the risk of being ruthlessly scrapped the moment their English directors think they can do better by concentrating on their southern concerns. Every step in these disastrous processes means more unemployment, more misery and more emigration for Scotsmen.

c) From 'Scots Humanities'

The central fact in the situation is that modern Scotland has no capital. 'The metropolis' means not Edinburgh but London, and when that well-meaning paper the *Scots Observer* headed a column 'News from the Metropolis', it was always with a slight start of amusement that the reader discovered himself reading chatty church news from Edinburgh. 'Metropolis'—mother-city—the city to which the country looks for its spiritual and intellectual nourishment, as a child to its mother. 'The children cry out and are not fed'—it is long since those withered paps gave generous nurture to any living thing. No stranger arriving in Edinburgh to-day would readily suspect that he was in a capital town. Save for a few brass plates on terrace doors denoting the occupancy of some sub-branch of government, there is no indication that Edinburgh is other than a large though beautiful provincial town. Arrived in a metropolis, the intelligent stranger will want to hear the music of the town, to see the theatres, the pictures and the beautiful buildings of the town, and in hearing and seeing all this to take in an epitome of the culture of the country. What music is he going to hear in Edinburgh? Once a week for a very short season, an excellent orchestra, which is for ever sitting on the edge of a financial precipice. Music in Scotland, after centuries of discouragement, requires support from the State. If State support for music in Great Britain ever came, and it has recently been refused, it would come to the metropolis, to London and not to Edinburgh. There is no musical focus in Edinburgh. There is no musician of European repute settled there. Small continental capitals seem to have sufficient attractions to hold even first-class players. The nearest possible destination of a gifted Scottish musician is London. [. . .] Where is Scottish music to be fostered and encouraged and directed if the capital can do no more than this? All that can be said by way of answer is that Glasgow has meantime cut in to found The Scottish National Academy of Music. This, however, is unlikely ever to take the place of a real metropolitan school of music.

If Edinburgh is a musical desert what is to be said of the drama there? What famous theatre should an intelligent visitor make a point of seeing? Would he have time in the course of a short stay to form a fair conception of Scottish drama and test the quality of the first-rate Scottish actors in the world's great plays? A question which does not admit of an answer 'yes' or 'no'. To understand the reason, consider this, a complete list of the plays staged in Edinburgh in Assembly week in May 1928, at a time when the city was full of strangers from all over Scotland and from all over the world. At the Lyceum Theatre, *The Sign of the Cross*; at the King's Theatre, 'the famous farcical comedy', *The Whole Town's Talking*; at the Theatre Royal, a variety programme without a single well-known name. As in music, so in the drama. Edinburgh fails utterly in its function of giving a lead to Scotland. The most notable efforts in the last generation have been made by Glasgow, first, with its Repertory Theatre, and then with the Scottish National Players, the former now extinct and the latter holding on bravely in the face of odds. [. . .] It is interesting to speculate on the results for Edinburgh, and for Scotland, had it been possible for a man like Sir James Barrie to see his work produced in a theatre manned by even a few of the Scottish actors who have proved their worth on the London stage. Most Scotsmen would dismiss this idea with a smile of contempt for the dreamer. Probably Barrie himself would join in the laugh. But the example of Dublin with her Abbey Theatre stands ready to give the lie to the scoffers, and the reason why Dublin, itself then also a capital *pour rire*, did what Edinburgh cannot do is because Ireland then, as ever, though with far less reason than Scotland, felt herself to be a nation and kept steadily before herself the need of independence and was determined to have it. The practical and realist nature of Irish sentiment enabled Dublin to hold for herself the devoted and invaluable services of the distinguished men she was producing.

As in the theatre and in music, so in journalism and literature Edinburgh plays and is content to play a provincial part. Here certainly it was not always so. In the late days of the eighteenth and the early days of the nineteenth century her name was known throughout the civilized world as a focus of culture. Her publishing houses were famous. Many reviews were published, some of them indeed short lived, but others running on for long periods. [. . .] The Edinburgh of to-day harks back to them constantly, but makes no attempt to be worthy of them or to imitate them. Most of the great publishing houses have migrated to London, and nothing but their printing presses, if even so much, remains in Edinburgh. [. . .] The one 'magazine' which Scotland produces is published in Glasgow. With the exception of the admirable Porpoise Press in Edinburgh the only publishers likely to give sympathetic attention to the works of young Scots writers are small folks in Glasgow, Stirling, Paisley, Aberdeen, who honourably attempt the task that is shirked in Edinburgh.

The great journalistic enterprise of Edinburgh is the *Scotsman*, which goes hand in hand with the *Glasgow Herald* in its self-appointed task of keeping Scotland submissive to the yoke that lies upon her. They are openly hostile to everything resembling a claim for Scottish independence, whether in the realm of action or ideas, and, upon the emergence of such a claim, they either ignore it wholly or they seek to club it to death, their leader columns glowing hotly with hatred of the 'fanatical few' and 'a narrow parochialism', while lofty appeal is made to 'the dictates of a wider patriotism'. [. . .] Between the *Scotsman* and the *Glasgow Herald* there is nothing to choose. Neither adequately represents Scottish opinion, for the man in the street is, to his credit, not quite satisfied about the affairs of Scotland to-day. No attempt is made, as even English papers have attempted, to deal sympathetically with this feeling of dissatisfaction, to measure its extent, nor to probe into its causes. On all occasions these journals strike loud and clear the keynote of modern Scottish sentiment, respectful subservience to the views and desires of England.

The outstanding importance of the *Glasgow Herald* is symbolical of the pre-eminence of Glasgow in the Scotland of to-day. Glasgow *is* Scotland. For the outside world all the significance of Scotland is summed up in the word 'Glasgow'. It may or may not be as hateful as its many critics hold it is, but it cannot be overlooked. It is one of the great cities of the world. Intensely alive, immensely important even yet, by reason of its manufactures, its commerce and its ships; notorious for its rain and its slums and the wild political creed of its swarming half-Irish proletariat, Glasgow occupies foreign eyes to the exclusion of All Scotland outside its boundaries. And this helps to throw Edinburgh further into the background and in effect to reduce it to the status of a museum town. Between the two there exists a foolish yet not wholly unnatural jealousy, which is still more detrimental to Edinburgh's metropolitan repute. [. . .]

In the realm of fiction and *belles-lettres* the provincial spirit has probably been responsible for the oft-denounced writers of the Kail-yard School. They have certainly not seen Scotland whole. They have represented, truly enough, certain aspects—rather maudlin aspects—of Scottish life. For that they are not to blame, since to each man his theme. But by tiresome iteration they gave the world to understand that these trivialities and emotional delights constituted the very life of Scotland. It is essentially a provincial *genre*, fatally misleading unless counterbalanced by other styles. It is a disconcerting step from the romantic warriors of Scott and the pirates of Stevenson to the village moron loafing about the streets of Tillywhan. The people of Scotland remained unportrayed. It was not worth while to write about the workers of the towns, about the rich swarming life of classes in the towns. All this had been done in England and really the two were indistinguishable. A recoil of course came, usually associated with *The House with the Green Shutters*, a savage indictment of Scottish life in a small town, which unduly tipped the scales in the opposite direction. Hence the rise of the 'Stinking-fish' School, which has been responsible for such outbursts as the recent onslaught on Scotland contained in Mr Thomson's *Caledonia*, Mr Carswell's *Brother Scots*, and Mr Muir's *John Knox*, all able works though perhaps rather smart than serious. But the threat to the culture of Scotland which is implicit in her loss of nationality is a far more serious thing than mere over-insistence on sentiment. In strictness, a Kail-yard School should be able to exist and play its part and carry the day or be laughed out of court without imperilling the native reputation. It is not the choice of subject that makes or mars art, literary or pictorial. Scotland produces quite sufficient men of distinction or greatness in art and letters to counterbalance her less creditable writers, were those men consciously contributing to a Scottish culture as distinct from a British, or an English culture. All that is written by Scotsmen to-day should go to build up and adorn the humanities of Scotland. So far is this from being true that there are many distinguished names in the world of letters which few know to have been borne by Scotsmen at all.

(Andrew Dewar Gibb, *Scotland in Eclipse* London: Humphrey Toulmin, 1930, pp.53–58; 65–69; 140–48,164–66.)

7.5 Edwin Muir, from letter to James Whyte (September 1931)

Crowborough
10 September 1931

Dear Whyte,

Many thanks for your letter. I did not think that there was much immediate hope of an economically self-supporting Scottish literature—and it may be that there isn't ever any ultimate hope of it. You are on the spot, and far more in touch with things than I am; and your findings—with which I can do nothing but agree—are pretty hopeless. But if there is no ultimate hope of such a consummation—or even no hope of it in our life-time—I think I am clear too on this further point; that Scottish literature as such will disappear, and that London will become quite literally the capital of the British Isles in a sense that it has never yet quite been; that, in other words, it will become our national capital in just as real a sense as it is the capital of an ordinary English man to-day. How long it will take for this to happen it is impossible to say—a few centuries, or only one, what does it matter? 'Hugh MacDiarmid' will become a figure like Burns—an exceptional case, that is to say—an arbitrary apparition of the national genius, robbed of his legitimate effect because there will be no literary tradition to perpetuate it. Scottish literature will continue to be sporadic— and being sporadic, it will be denied the name of a literature, and it seems to me rightly so. But for myself I feel so detached, when I look at this possibility objectively, that I cannot even quite exclude the thought that this resolution of the Scottish spirit, its disappearance finally into a larger spiritual group, to which it would inevitably contribute much, may be a consummation to be hoped for. At any rate, all things seem to me to be working for it: the fact that Scottish energy has gone mainly into international forms of activity, finance, industry, engineering, philosophy, science—forms of activity where one's nationality is irrelevant; the fact that Scotsmen have helped to shape the industries of so many other countries and neglected their own; their almost complete blindness or indifference to the forms of activity in which the spirit of a nation most essentially expresses itself—poetry, literature, art in general: all this, looked at from outside might almost make us imagine that Scotland's historical destiny is to eliminate itself in reality, as it has already wellnigh eliminated itself from history and literature—the forms in which a nation survives. But the really awful phase is the present one: we are neither really quite alive nor quite dead; we are neither quite Scottish (we can't be, for there's no Scotland in the same sense that there is an England and a France), nor are we quite delivered from our Scottishness, and free to integrate ourselves in a culture of our choice. It was some such dim feeling as this that made me take up the question. The very words 'A Scottish writer' have a slightly unconvincing ring to me: what they come down to (I except Grieve, who is an exception to all rules) is a writer of Scottish birth. But when we talk of an English writer we do not think of a writer of English birth: we hardly think of such things at all. A Scottish writer is in a false position, because Scotland is in a false position. Yes that's what it comes down to; and now that I think of it, that is what fills me with such a strong desire to see Scottish Literature visibly integrated in a Scottish group living in Scotland for that would make the position unequivocal, or at least would be a first step towards doing it; it would not merely be a gesture, or an expedient, but a definite act, and therefore with a symbolical value. England can't digest us at the present stage, and besides one does not want to be digested—it is a shameful process—one wants to be there. And there is no there for Scotsmen. And the idea that there might be is, I feel sure, a dream. Like Scottish nationalism and the great digestive act, Scotland will probably linger in limbo as long as the British Empire lasts. It seems inevitable. [. . .]

(Edwin Muir, letter to James Whyte 10 September 1931; reprinted from *Selected Letters of Edwin Muir*, pp.70–72 [70–71].)

7.6 From first editorial of *The Free Man: A Journal of Independent Thought* (February 1932)

The Free Man by its title indicates its main purpose. We are living in an age when mass education, mass propaganda, and mass control threaten to destroy the possessions of personality and to prevent the exercise of that individual freedom without which no civilisation has any real value. Because we believe that Scotland still retains a vital spark of the spirit of individualism *The Free Man* has been brought forth to give expression to that spirit and to endeavour to focus the aspirations and the action of those who know that eternal vigilance is the price of Freedom. It is our purpose also to discover whether there are in Scotland to-day men prepared and able to act as leaders, having a goal towards which the whole nation may be led with sincerity and confidence to a fuller and richer national life. We seek to know, too, whether the people of Scotland are truly anxious to realise to the full their social, economic and cultural heritage. We do not know what the answer to these questions will be, but we believe passionately that Scotland can and ought to play a notable part in world affairs. *The Free Man* is the earnest of our intention to promote increasing and intelligent interest in our own country first, and to strive along with all who are aware that 'the fault is not in our stars, but in ourselves that we are underlings'.

Gumption

Scotland was never more in need of this excellent quality than it is now. Those who possess any of it should give it plenty of exercise, and the pages of *The Free Man* are open to all who have something to say pertinent to the times, and can say it with pith and purpose. Romantic appeals to the past or sentimental havers about the present are specially requested to be sent elsewhere. We have been told by certain eminent Scots that a new paper has no chance unless it is backed by tons of money and has as its contributors the well-known popular Scottish writers of the day. Well, we think otherwise, for we have neither the money nor the popular writers. Anyway, most of us know just what most popular writers are likely to say on most subjects. We would rather give opportunity to unknown writers to express themselves. We are confident there are many fine intellects in our land awaiting such an opportunity, and whether by article, verse, or story we will welcome their contributions. We should, however, state that meantime no contributions can be paid for.

Our Airt

While we shall be concerned with all that concerns Scotland, it should be noted that we are attached to no party, nor are we thirled to any particular policy. We fully recognise the importance of these, but we wish to deal not only with all the cultural aspects of life in Scotland, but also to relate these to the world as a whole. What, if anything, has Scotland to offer to the world without which the world would be poorer? Despite all the talk that has gone on and goes on, despite all the articles that have been written and are being written, we have no sure evidence yet that Scotland is anxious to realise what she, as a nation, stands for, or means to stand for. Indeed, it is somewhat doubtful if Scotland is to any considerable extent aware of her desperate need for self-expression in keeping with her heritage, tradition, and capacities. We shall aid and encourage anyone and anything that will enlarge the awareness of that need in every direction, not only from the national standpoint, but from the wider aspect of world relationship. Always in the background, however, must be our own national interests, for only a virile nationalism can create and maintain a vital internationalism.

(Editorial, *The Free Man: A Journal of Independent Thought* 1:1, 6 February 1932, p.1.)

7.7 J. Gibson, from 'A Scheme for Assisting Scottish Unemployed: The Provision of Allotments' (*Free Man* February 1932)

The Scottish National Union of Allotment-Holders and the Society of Friends are jointly responsible for the appeal for £3,000, which has recently appeared in the Press. This sum of money is to be used for the purpose of enabling the unemployed in Scotland to secure and cultivate allotment gardens.

At the outset it may be well to show the degree of success which has already attended this praiseworthy effort; at the same time it cannot be too strongly emphasised that, if the scheme is to be extended to the full number of unemployed men desiring allotments, there is little time to lose, because the planting season will soon be upon us.

On Saturday last, the 13th February, the annual conference of The Scottish National Union of Allotment-Holders was held at Dundee, and in his address the Secretary and Treasurer stated that there was a sum of £1,170 in hand, received from 200 subscribers—this amount included a grant of £750 from the Pilgrim Trust, which had already so generously supported a similar scheme, initiated for the benefit of the English unemployed.

With this sum the Committee, representing the two bodies concerned in this appeal, have felt justified in pressing on with the actual work of organising assistance, and already the Honorary Secretaries of the Local Associations affiliated to the National Union are in possession of the papers enabling them to put the machinery into working order. It is by using the voluntary organisation already in existence that costs of administration are practically eliminated.

The allotment-holder is to be provided with half the cost of seed, manures, and tools, and, where absolutely necessary, assistance with the rent will be considered. The quota of the expenses falling on the holder will be paid back in small weekly instalments, and it may be stated here that last year in England of £17,000 due from holders almost the whole was punctually received. It is estimated that for an outlay of 14/- from the fund a man may be provided with about 300 square yards of land, which is capable of producing upwards of £8 worth of fresh vegetables, at a cost to himself of about 6d per week, including rent. In England 64,000 men were assisted, and the Committee in Scotland are confidently hoping that fully 6,000 men in this country will receive the same benefit. While the money value of the foodstuffs produced is considerable, of even greater value is the increased health, both mental and physical, accruing to the allotment-holder and his family.

We think our readers will agree with us when we say that here, in these days when so much is said and written about the desirability of helping our unemployed, we have a scheme which is simple and effective, and one which has already been proved elsewhere to be eminently successful. This is practical help, and it has the great merit of helping men to help themselves—something is given, but the men give more—in time, effort, and planning, and out of their meagre resources they *pay* part of the cost also.

(J. Gibson, 'A Scheme for Assisting Scottish Unemployed', *Free Man* 1:3, 20 February 1932, p.6)

7.8 J. Alexander, 'The Call of Scotland' (*Free Man* March 1932)

Scottish youth of to-day and to-morrow would appear to have little reason for saying that 'there is nothing worth while left to do'. Particularly so, if it finds itself in agreement with Compton McKenzie's [sic] statement that Scotland must go back on herself, consolidate her position and then go forward to take her rightful place among the nations of the world. Looking around to-day, it is amazing to find how few Scots really 'think Scots'; not in the sense of 'Wha's like us?' but from the viewpoint of making Scotland their focus point for world events. Everything would seem to be considered first in the light of John Bull's approval. The task lying before internationally-minded nationalist youth in Scotland is of a magnitude which ought to make all eager to play their part and of sufficient importance to give endless satisfaction in the performance. War days may or may not be over, but there is a chance of a peacetime fight which should appeal to the dour strain supposed to be part of the 'make-up' of the Scot.

There is a choice of a battle-ground for all trades, professions and opinions. For the financially-minded, there are chain cinemas, chain stores, banks, railways and other transport services to be brought back under Scottish control. Developments in the utilisation of water-power may completely alter the rural economy of many parts of the Highlands and it lies with Scotland to make sure that the control of such important sources of cheap power remains in the hands of her own people. Aviation has arrived and will in time consolidate Scotland to a degree never before known, but as yet, both from the point of view of construction and application, Scotland is still asleep. It is not easy to reconcile the possibilities of aircraft construction in a country said to possess some of the finest engineering craftsmen in the world, with the actual position found to-day. For the architect, the evolution and application of structural types suitable for Scottish climatic and landscape conditions offers vast scope, while in the field of scientific town planing, the surface has not yet been scratched.

An urgent need exists for economists who still study, on the spot, the economic development and possibilities of Scotland. In mining, fishing, the heavy industries, farming, distribution and social conditions, there is a wealth of material lying untouched. The statistician again will have his chance of working on practically virgin soil; both trade and agricultural statistics in Scotland are probably the most inadequate of any country in the world. Scottish year-books, statistical bulletins and research services are needed, but are not available. Scotland must be the only country in the world which does not know her balance of trade!

For the agriculturist, there is a sufficiency of scope in maintaining Scotland's world-wide reputation for superior breeds of livestock; in evolving efficient co-operative marketing; in reducing the climate handicap by the continued breeding of specially selected strains of cereals, roots and grasses; extending the peat reclamation work now in progress in the Hebrides and settling the small-holder under the conditions which ensure maximum success. Scottish afforestation and the creation of forest holdings are still in their infancy.

There would appear to be scope for juvenile publications dealing with home and world affairs from the Scottish view-point. Scottish magazines, news films, educational films and books originating in Scotland are urgently needed. For the historian, novelist, artist, teacher, thinker and poet there is wealth of material and unbounded opportunities for service.

(J. Alexander, 'The Call of Scotland', *Free Man* 1:5, 5 March 1932, p.5.)

7.9 From interview: 'C.M. Grieve Speaks Out' (*Free Man* April 1932)

'SCOTLAND CAN GIVE ME NOTHING.'
'MISCHIEVOUS AND MINDLESS' SCOTS.
OUTSPOKEN AUTOBIOGRAPHY PROMISED.

In a special interview with *The Freeman* [sic], Mr C.M. Grieve ('Hugh MacDiarmid') said that he wished to make it clear, since his name had been so largely associated with these bodies, that he had resigned from the Scottish Centre of the P.E.N., of which he was the founder, and requested his name should no longer be used on notepaper, etc., in that or any other capacity; and that under the constitution of the National Party of Scotland, he was no longer eligible for membership.

Old Deadheads

Continuing, Mr Grieve said that he was entirely in opposition to the Scottish National Development Council and the Scottish Watch. He had no use and no time for non-political, non-party organisations of any kind. The Development Council was founded on the impossible basis of trying to help Scottish commerce and industry by carefully avoiding any of the fundamental financial, economic, and political factors. It had been carefully 'rigged' from the outset—not in the interests of Scotland, but as a 'newspaper stunt', and most of the people associated were demonstrably hopeless. Their past records showed that. Not only so, but all efforts to put the Movement on better lines and give it the benefit of experience gained in similar enterprises, had been baulked in deference to a futile 'Couéism', a parrot-like cry that if we got all together Scotland would improve. It wouldn't. It was significant that all the old dead-heads who for decades had been responsible for Scotland's decadence had hastened to join it. Not one of them understood—or wanted to understand—Douglasism; the only real contribution Scotland had made to the problems in question.

The Scottish Watch

As for the Scottish Watch, it was the same old thing under a new name. 'Give the people circuses'. When the idea was first conceived a militant youth organisation was contemplated. This was speedily abandoned in favour of the line of least resistance. And all the old gang again hastened to give it their benediction. What on earth could be expected of any organisation with which duds like Rosslyn Mitchell and Hugh Roberton had to do? He was sorry some of his own friends had been misled—people like Dr Insh and Wendy Wood ought to have known better.

Return to Scotland Impossible

Asked about his own work and whether he would ever return to Scotland, Mr Grieve replied that he was so completely at variance with practically everything that was thought and believed in Scotland to-day (even by those who imagined they were promoting a National Movement) that he thought any question of his returning was impossible. 'Besides', he added, 'I must live and nobody would give me a job. They daren't even print my stuff.' As to his work, Mr Grieve said two new very long poems of his were appearing shortly, both in English periodicals—the 'Second Hymn to Lenin' in the *Criterion*, and 'The Oon Olympian' in the *New English Weekly*. Both were in Scots, and parts of his huge poem, 'Clann Albainn'. He had lots of others on the stocks. 'I expect no recognition from Scotland', he added, 'and who is there in Scotland whose opinion is worth a damn beside that of T.S. Eliot and A.R. Orage? So long as they like my work I am not concerned over the opinion of anybody in Scotland.'

Under No Delusions

'Scotland will—and can give me nothing', added Mr Grieve. 'I will continue to give Scotland all I can. I know lots of young people in Scotland are following me closely—they are right. I am under no delusion as to my powers, but I am the only person who counts or can count with them. None of the rest have a spark of creative ability.'

(Interview report, 'C.M. Grieve Speaks Out', *Free Man* 1:13, 30 April 1932, p.4.)

7.10 From 'At the Mercat Cross': readers' responses to 'C.M. Grieve Speaks Out' (*Free Man* May 1932)

a) Glasgow, 2/5/32

Sir,—What with the sad tale of 'Iolaire' [previous contributor on the National Party of Scotland], and the dramatic declamations of Mr C.M. Grieve, it is all too plain there is no hope for Scotland! I wonder? Doesn't the existence of *The Free Man* suggest that all is not lost? That Scotland has lost Mr Grieve is in truth a thing to deplore, yet Scotland may survive even that. She has known worse misfortunes.

Yours,
Young Scot.

b) 'Our Cultural Decay': Glasgow, 2/5/32

Sir,—The attitude of C.M. Grieve—which is one that has obviously been forced upon him—is one more indication of the moral and intellectual decay of Scotland. We are, alas, not so richly furnished with genius that we can afford to drive it furth of Scotland. Mr Grieve ranks high in the realm of European letters, yet, as he so truly says, we have nothing to give him. Scotland's industrial decay is a thing of widespread concern—even if the causes are but little understood—but there is, I fear, little even being thought about our cultural decay. On this equally grave condition much might be written, but there could be no more significant commentary than the callous manner in which we have exiled one of our most brilliant sons.

Yours,
Kirrie

c) 'Mr C.M. Grieve': Glasgow, 5/5/32

Sir,—It is truly a sad reflection upon the intellectual decline of Scotland when a writer of the calibre of Mr C.M. Grieve cannot find a living in the land of his birth. There is much, very much, in the style and the opinions of this author which I do not like, but that does not make me blind to his undoubted ability. He has definitely the creative vision, and that covers a multitude of sins. Nothing, however, can excuse the sin of Scotland's treatment of this son of hers.

Yours,
W. Cameron.

('At the Mercat Cross': letters to the *Free Man* 7 May 1932, p.8, and 14 May 1932, p.6.)

7.11 From *Scotland in Quest of her Youth: A Scrutiny* (1932)

a) David Cleghorn Thomson, from editor's 'Introduction'

'Scotland begins to be talked up in the world a little', wrote Daniel Defoe, at a time when the *Union of Parliaments* was being hotly discussed in the first decade of the eighteenth century; and now that a very virile young political party is growing up in our midst, calling for independence and separate status in the third decade of the twentieth century, the problem of Scottish survival or renaissance has again come into journalistic prominence, and books and articles about her welfare and estate are once more in vogue. The emergence of the Scottish Nationalist Party as a significant force in politics has coincided with the return to Scotland of a group of Scots writers from the south, and with the development of regional broadcasting policy, which has provided an increasingly valuable platform for the views of those who, whether Nationalist in politics or not, are vitally interested in the future of Scotland as a cultural entity.

For a little over five years it has been my privilege, as a returned Scot, to observe the trend of matters cultural, artistic and educational here, from a rather unusual coign of vantage, and to keep in touch with most of the vital movements which have been stirring during those years—the National Theatre, the project for a Little Theatre, the foundation of the Scottish Branches of the British Institute of Adult Education and the Travel Association, the competitive Festival Movement, and the efforts to establish a National Orchestra and an annual exhibition of modernist art.

The majority of the contributors to this book have been participants in one or other of the series of broadcast talks given during the last five years, arranged with a view to concentrating public attention on the main problems of Modern Scotland, under the general titles 'Scotland To-day'; 'What is wrong with Scotland?'; 'Building Scotland'; and 'New Lamps for Old'. All the contributors have been actively engaged in one way or another in the general movement which has brought about the sudden revival of interest in Scotland's destiny, referred to above; only a few of them are Nationalist in politics. [. . .]

There is a popular belief that Scotsmen are born to be administrators, bank managers, accountants and 'prancing proconsuls', but are seldom imaginative creators. Our national art has suffered from this hard-dying myth and its attendant curse of practical-mindedness. For decades most Scotsmen have come to art and aesthetic experience with tired, closed, sentimental minds, suspicious of such things as unpractical and non-dividend-bearing. They have underestimated the value and importance of dreaming. Every picture must tell a story or depict a memory; every piece of music must have 'a tune'; every play must be a sermon. Any number of Scotsmen in and out of Scotland have been guilty of saying that it will be time enough to worry about the lack of a Repertory Theatre, a National Orchestra and a Literary Weekly in the country when the Scottish National Development Council has restored industrial prosperity. 'Seek ye first the Kingdom of Success and all these things shall be added unto you'. But prosperity cannot come without imaginative leadership; and the only people who can provide that leadership will neither stay in, nor return to, Scotland if it is devoid of all the real accompaniments of modern civilisation—theatres, restaurants and opportunities of aesthetic experience.

And why the title? someone may ask.

It was chosen for various reasons. Scotland for years has been breeding for export and fostering 'lads o' pairts' to become heads of other people's departments. For economic reasons this export has ceased, and the youth of Scotland is kept within her own shores for a time; and it is demanding a greater share in the control of her destiny. It is tired of the prevalence of what might be termed the death-bedside manner, and lives in hope that the twilight of the 'buddies' is at hand.

The cuckoo was defined by a Scots schoolboy as 'a bird which laid other birds' eggs in its own nest, and vivâ voce'. This definition is devastatingly suitable to Scotland in its national attitude to its own prophets and to many other national phenomena as well. Like the cuckoo, Scotland has separated the generative and the maternal instincts in the most extraordinary way. She not only prefers laying her eggs in other birds' nests, but welcomes unduly other birds' eggs in her own.

A paradox in Scotland which has long been famous is its combination of a quixotic, generous spirit on the one hand and an infuriating cautiousness and timidity of heart on the other. More causes have been nobly lost in Scotland than in most other European countries. Frequently, they have been lost on account of parochial bourgeois faint-heartedness which it would be difficult to equal elsewhere. Just now when, almost in spite of itself, a flame of Scottish National consciousness is flickering to life, there are more people within Scotland eager to souse that flame by pouring on cold water than there are outside it. Authority is very firmly entrenched in respectability in Edinburgh, and as someone said the other day, in reference to the row over the Library site, the triumph of the advocates over public opinion in this matter is only another example of that wall of active apathy which seems to lie between the real people of Scotland and the vital minds that wish to do something for them, to weld a new feeling of national unity to some dignified and suitable purpose.

It is the hope and belief of the present writer that a new day is dawning for Scotland, and that largely because a mobilisation of her youth is succeeding in breaking down some of the traditional barriers to imaginative expression and emancipation.

b) George Scott Moncrieff, from 'Balmorality'

To-day the dawn finds Scotland an extraordinary muddle. First she was free in body, romantic, cultured, and uncivilised, till her government was taken over by a usurious Kirk, wielding power through superstition. The boor for a century, she was repopularised by Scott, adopted as plaything by a foreign queen, suffered worse than any nation in the industrial upheaval, and finally left an abortive carcase rotting somewhere to the North of England.

In Edinburgh to-day what have we? Beautiful old houses, stately streets, fine buildings, incomparable vistas. Stand on the crest of the Mound and see two things, breathe two atmospheres: both dead. To the left the Castle, of which too much has already been said: below, the Colossus of nastiness, the giant wart of the North British Hotel, echoed at the West End by the pink scab of the Caledonian Hotel (North British, Caledonian, it is all they stand for). Two atmospheres, both dead. The Old Town with a rich history, a thing of the past, but, in death, manure to fertilise the future. The word BALMORAL, flaunted in vast gilt letters opposite, standing with a million other things for the dead Victorian era that lingers on, re-kilted with tawdry tartans, retold in glossy guide-books.

Through Princes Street we pass; in the shops are tartan booklets of sayings from Scott, Songs from Burns, Carlyle's Wisdom; there are boxes of tablet and Edinburgh rock decked out in tartans, with photographs of Edinburgh on their covers. The Scott Memorial looms bleakly. Kirks, many hideous, blacken streets like mourners. George Street is lovely save for a fantastic horror, the Scottish Co-operative Society's store, gawky on pillars. Everywhere there is a chaos as a man might see waking from a beautiful dream in an ugly room, confusing the foundered chair and the washstand with the grottoes he has left.

Now walk down the respectable grey streets of the residential quarters. The houses are nice, pre-eminently respectable, rather monotonous. But in the Old Town, in the poorer quarters, or down by the *backs* of these respectable houses, the stone is rough-hewn and the houses achieve beauty. So, although much has been said, and with justice, about the sterile state of Edinburgh's aristocracy with its remarkable lack of culture, justice has not been paid to the man in the Edinburgh street. In towns people lose to a large extent their friendliness and civility. Londoners are intolerably rude, and so are the townsfolk of the English Midlands. But the man of Edinburgh is civil, intelligent, friendly. It is no mere chance that the Edinburgh pubs are so preferable to the London: they are made for easy converse, for comfort and companionship. In London the wealthy have taken the queer houses of charm and beauty and fine views and occupied them. In Edinburgh the upper classes prefer their dull respectability and spurn the Dean Village and the Old Town. But the poor man in the picturesque places will often be found to appreciate his home—when it has not been reduced to an overcrowded slum.

Glasgow is more alive than Edinburgh: one feels a pulsating, one hears a sound of machinery, action. But Glasgow has yet to attain gracefulness. She has suffered a deal from being a secondary town—to London, not to Edinburgh, which is too different to be a rival. And Glasgow's backlands are a disgrace to any nation. Apropos of the Irish 'problem': it seems to be generally forgotten that there was a similar inrush of Irishmen to London a hundred years ago, and these have settled down equably, as at that model of what a dockland quarter should be, Wapping—exclusively Irish. Like the Edinburgh man, although he is very different, the Glaswegian has good manners and friendliness.

In the country districts there are peoples of a culture of a much higher standard than, for example, the southern English peasant. There is an instinctive kindliness that even the worst influences of the Kirk have failed to stifle (at least on six days of the week) though they have produced a gloom that is noticeably absent in Roman Catholic districts.

Victoria is dead; the Industrial Age has crashed in flames. Scotland is free again. For too long she has tried to live as Scotland in these bones and ashes and gone for everything else to England. Now she has awoken to the sound of the world's chaos.

251

She may well have shuddered in horror at the state she has found herself in, with her Religion, her Art, her agriculture, fisheries, manufactures: over everything the deadening slime of Balmorality, a glutinous compound of hypocrisy, false sentiment, industrialism, ugliness and clammy pseudo-Calvinism; a slime that has made her forget that she is a country and regard herself as a suburb. But it is time to stop shuddering and to welcome the glorious difficulties of rebuilding.

c) From 'Letters' [responses to the editor's request for a commentary on the state of contemporary Scottish literature]

All the tolerance commonly extended to adolescence and its enthusiasms is required of those who would know the reason and meaning of all this pother about a 'Scottish Renaissance'. We are very young and very ambitious, and most of our geese are swans, and we are altogether terribly self-conscious about ourselves as literary forces. A man just can't produce a thriller with his tongue in his cheek, but we will insist on measuring his achievement by the highest critical standards.

It is all quite natural. A 'consciousness of Scottishness' came to us all after the War. We began to see—or believed we saw—that the Scottish spirit had been misrepresented in literature by kailyard pawkiness on the one hand, and whaup-and-heather romance on the other. We took *The House with the Green Shutters* to represent us most adequately in fiction, and the poets turned violently away from Burns in the direction of Dunbar. New horizons seemed to open out before us. There was a stirring.

Then somebody, the wish being father to his thought, called it a 'Renaissance'. A fatal hour! A renaissance of the will to live more fully and of the will to express Scottish life more truthfully there undoubtedly was, but the use of that unhappy word led to the assumption that the actual products of the movement were numerous and substantial. Whereas they were, and are, not; and that with all respect to the Book Society. We have a very long way to go. The talk was useful in its day, but now we await the work.

It is being done. Scottish novels—to accept fiction as a convenient criterion of activity—keep appearing at the flat rate of one a week. *E pur, si muove.* It may mean that Scotland is going to enjoy a fruitful renaissance. On the other hand, it may not. All that has still to be seen. Certainly we have reached a point when the talk is so much waste of time and only the hard darg of production matters.

GEORGE BLAKE

I admire your suggestion that recent Scottish literature may be summed up in a short note. Sufficient space should thus be left for you to deal at length with more vital matters such as transport. Scotland cannot go in quest of her youth without adequate transport. In fact, you might take Transport as a symbol for the whole body politic and easily prove that we need expect no literature of any consequence until the national joints begin to creak consciously and properly. History would bear you out, even if the literary critics would bear you down. But then you know the critics in their various kinds. There is one kind for whom even I dare to have a grave sympathy. I refer to the delightful fellow who discovers a great writer and risks his immortal reputation with a laurel wreath. But alas! observe how his higher-flying mates descend upon the wretch and pluck him (to the tune of blooms that blight in their spring, you know)—all in the interests of our splendid and austere tradition of Scottish Criticism. Nor would I entertain for a moment the idea that the simple fellow, being both childlike and bland, has any more than a child's interest in flying kites—or getting kites to fly.

So far, then, as our criticism is concerned, it is watchful and sound, and that, when all is written and done, is what really matters—together with transport, of course.

For the rest, there are tentative shoots, and half a century may see a harvest. I believe it will. But that (with a bow in the right direction) is faith for, more terrible than our climate, than our transport, than our criticisms even, is the present state of our belief in what, with the genuflexions of a godfather, you so bravely call Scotland.

NEIL M. GUNN

The books that are being written are right enough. The only question is who is reading them? There are established and delicate prose-writers, like Rachel Annand Taylor or Agnes Mure Mackenzie, who are sure of their audience—in London. Neil Gunn's success is a London success; Catherine Carswell seems more in contact with Lawrence than with Burns. Even those who use the Lowland dialects are not much read north of the Border; Violet Jacob will have little sale in Fife, and Hugh McDiarmid, far the most exciting poet which Scotland has produced for generations, is perhaps read by a few high-brows in Edinburgh and Glasgow; but what Ayrshire Socialists have read his *First Hymn to Lenin*? And what happens to young writers with no reputation? If they use the Gaelic, as they must if they feel and think in it, London is puzzled and made uncomfortable, and Edinburgh is little better. Take, for instance, one of the most definitely national books which have been published lately—Fionn MacColla's *The Albannach*—who is going to read it? It ought to be read by the people it was written about. But it won't be, not yet at any rate.

This is of course mainly economic; the people who matter in Scotland, the workers by hand and brain, can't afford 7s 6d books, and if books are not bought they are not published in cheap editions. This might be different with a reorganised society, but even so, Scotland must learn not to be ashamed of its own youth and vigour. The elders who attacked Catherine Carswell are still the people with power, but the real muse of Scotland, from Dunbar to Burns and beyond, was always crude, vigorous, unashamed of speech and of acts, a dweller in cold mists whose veins had need to be filled with hot, quick fire. Her touch is on young Scotland now, and should be.

NAOMI MITCHISON

(Scotland in Quest of her Youth: A Scrutiny, edited by David Cleghorn Thomson,
Edinburgh: Oliver & Boyd, 1932, pp.1–2, 6–8; 83–86; 158–59, 163–64, 170–71.)

7.12 Edwin Muir, 'The Functionlessness of Scotland' (*Free Man* February 1933)

Christopher Grieve sent me a letter a little while ago asking me to write something about the function of Scotland in the modern world. I replied saying that I could not imagine what Scotland's function could be, but that I would like to investigate the difficulty: perhaps it would be a way of coming to closer grips with the subject. This article is the result.

That nations have some historical function in the general development of civilisation—a function that changes with changing circumstances, it is true, but yet is operative in some way at every moment of their existence—is, I think obviously true, however difficult it may be to determine what that function is. And it does not matter how small the nation may be: Austria, in spite of the lamentable size to which it has shrunk, has still a function; Latvia, though small and new, has a function. A nation that is effectively a nation, that has, in other words, some independent central organ directing and symbolising its life, has necessarily an objective importance, even if it is by mere virtue of its geographical situation. It affects and is affected by the other organic units surrounding it, and consequently influences, in a greater or lesser degree, the general course of civilisation. But there also exist hypothetical units, units which remain in a condition of unchanging suspended potentiality (which fail to achieve a crystallisation and create a central organ), and these remain in a sort of limbo, half within the world of life and half outside it: a melancholy, unsatisfied, blindly aspiring state which romanticism is always ready to exploit, and for which the only cure is an active realism. Scotland is at present one of these hypothetical units.

And being that, it has no functions. It has no calculable effect, as an entity, on the development of civilisation, though individual Scotsmen and Scotswomen, wrested from their context, may have in a very small way some such effect. If Scotland were really capable of merging with England, there would be no difficulty at all, and the hypothetical nation north of the Tweed would vanish, and the inhabitants of what was once Scotland be freed from the curse of a hypothetical existence and become active and genuine members of an organic civilisation. But even Scotsmen who are against the idea of nationalism will deny, with a heat they do not understand, that that is possible. Scotland has not become a real part of England, nor has it succeeded in remaining a separate and independent entity. That is its problem. All that effectively remains of it, therefore, is a name and an aspiration which, until very recently has never seriously wished to be fulfilled. The result is an emptiness and unreality quite peculiar to Scotland, and that only becomes intensified when such adjectives as Scottish or Celtic have to be employed, for the words themselves evoke a disquieting sense of the merely contingent reality of the things they stand for. Into this semi-vacuum the population of Scotland are born, imaginary citizens of an imaginary country; and it is not surprising that so many should leave it. The only remedy for this state of things is either for the whole Scottish people to become English, or for Scotland to become a nation. The first has proved impossible.

A nation without a central organ to give it unity, a merely discarnate nation such as Scotland, is far more defenceless against the mechanical and purely materialistic forces of civilisation than any integral group could be. All that it can oppose to those forces is a floating tradition; and a tradition that has no concrete symbol to embody it soon fades, and presently there is nothing between the isolated individual and the operation of mechanical forces but a name or a memory. That has not yet happened to Scotland, but it has been happening for the last hundred years; and it probably helps to explain why so many Scotsmen have excelled in engineering and business, and so few have done anything remarkable in the humane arts. Having a nation only in name, they inevitably become servants of pure undifferentiated 'progress' at its most impersonal and its least humanly significant, servants of a thing that acknowledges no national boundaries, even one's own, that indeed scarcely acknowledges humanity, though created to serve it. So Scotland has earned the reputation of being a nation of engineers, servants of the machine. In other words, it has suffered more from the development of industrialism, from the effects of the industrial revolution, than any other part of the British Isles. It has suffered more, and both physically and spiritually, because against the rage of that revolution it could oppose nothing but the mere idea of a nation, an imagination that could do nothing to shield it.

It is this that makes a more human ideal necessary for Scotland now. An ideal for a people must to-day be a national ideal. All the evil of the world seems to be becoming more and more supernational and sub-national. Consequently any assertion of national independence now is far more essentially a challenge to that evil than to any other that may be accidentally connected with it. There are two main streams in the development of civilisation at present. One is in the direction of supernationalism; the other in that of nationalism. The first is essentially hostile to the old, complete human tradition; the second, in spite of the excesses and crimes of Chauvinism, is friendly to it. The ultimate aim of the first is uniformity, or, as it is correctly termed, standardisation; the second demands diversity as well. It is possible to fight for either ideal from the highest motives. But every one must make a choice, one way or the other.

(Edwin Muir, 'The Functionlessness of Scotland', *Free Man* 2:2, 11 February 1933, p.6.)

7.13 Edwin Muir, from *Scottish Journey* (1935)

a) From 'Edinburgh'

In spite of its proud display, then, Edinburgh cannot hide away its unemployed or its poor. Yet as it is a city which must keep up appearances, there are certain rules which it does not like to see broken. It accepts the unemployed groups in the Canongate without visible annoyance; but when about a year ago a procession of the unemployed stopped in the town on their way to London, and slept for the night in Princes Street gardens, there was general indignation, in the tea-rooms, the tram-cars and the columns of the local newspapers; for people's sense of propriety was outraged. [. . .] There are streets in Edinburgh which correspond exactly to the drawing-room and the servants' hall. The people one meets in the first are quite different from the people one meets in the second. The crowds that walk along Princes Street, for instance, are a different race, different in their manners, their ideas, their feelings, their language, from the one in the Canongate. The distance between the two streets is trifling; the difference between the crowds enormous. And it is a constant and permanent difference. You never by chance find the Princes Street crowd in the Canongate, or the Canongate crowd in Princes Street; and without a revolution such a universal American Post is inconceivable. The entire existence of Edinburgh as a respectable bourgeois city depends on that fact. Nothing more than a convention is involved, but the conventions on which a society rests easily become sacred; and so a wholesale invasion of Princes Street by the poor would be felt not only as an offence against good taste, but as a blasphemy. That is why the temporary presence of the unemployed there was so deeply resented and feared.

But one does not need to go so far as the Canongate to see this curious principle in full operation. Within a stone's throw of one end of Princes Street begins a promenade quite different in character. This is Leith Street and its continuation Leith Walk, a long spacious boulevard containing some fine old houses, which have with time sunk to the status of working-class tenements. Here, instead of the cosy tea-rooms and luxurious hotel lounges of Princes Street, one suddenly finds oneself among ice-cream and fish-and-chip bars and pubs. At one point the two different streams of promenaders are brought within a few yards of each other; yet they scarcely ever mingle, so strong is the sense of social distinction bred by city life. They turn back when they reach this invisible barrier, apparently without thought or desire, as if they were stalking in a dream; and if, through necessity or whim, an occasional pedestrian should trespass for a little on enemy ground, he is soon frightened and scurries back as fast as he can. The prostitutes are the sole class who rise superior to this inhibition. They live, as members of the proletariat, in the poorer districts, but their main beat is Princes Street, and it has in their eyes the prestige and familiarity of a business address. But their occupation seems to be the sole remaining one in modern society which acts as a general dissolvent of all social distinctions; and that in reality is because they are tacitly outlawed by all society, in which the principle of class distinction is constantly operative. The ordinary crowds, not possessing this classless power, turn back at a certain point. The upper and lower middle classes, the men about town, clerks, commercial travellers, students, patrol Princes Street, because, without being conscious of it, they look upon that walk as a preserve where they can be at their complete ease, and where nobody will ever intrude upon them. And this calculation is justified. Their seclusion is as perfect as if they were behind locked doors.

b) From 'Glasgow'

The squalor of the slum-dwellers' lives in Glasgow is one reason for the respectable attitudes which I have tried to describe. A stronger reason is their open publication of their degradation, which springs partly from their hopelessness and partly from a feeling that it is wrong that misery and vice such as theirs should be ignored. This public flaunting of degradation is one of the things which distinguish the Scottish from the English slums. Probably it arises from a last-ditch sentiment of justice. To publish one's degradation is a moral protest. The London slums are dreary; but the Glasgow slums always hold a sense of possible menace; they take their revenge on the respectable and the rich if in nothing else in compelling them to grow a still thicker hide of insensibility and suppression. That revenge may appear small, but its effects are beyond computation. There can be hardly any decent Glaswegian but has seen some sight in passing through the slums which he afterwards wanted to erase from his memory. Such memories should be kept open, not hidden away in places where they fester, for that is the only hope both for those who suppress them and for the eventual health of society. But it is easier to say this than to do it. For the life of an average member of the respectable classes in Glasgow is a direct fight against the slums, and in that fight suppression and insensibility are invaluable weapons, and as long as society continues to be competitive they will be used. Thus the existence of the slums and of poverty in general poisons the life of a community in all sorts of hidden ways. It is this settled almost comfortable poisoned state which I have tried to give some idea of. It is the generic state of Industrialism. [. . .]

One's impressions of a people are bound to be incomplete and biassed, that is, determined by what one looks for in them; and to correct my own view I am going to take the liberty of quoting Mr George Blake's brief analysis of the Glasgow people in his excellent book, *The Heart of Scotland*. 'It may be confidently maintained,' he says, 'that here is the liveliest community in Scotland. This fantastic mixture of racial strains, this collection of survivors from one of the most exacting of social processes, is a dynamo of confident, ruthless, literal energy. The Glasgow man is downright, unpolished, direct, and immediate. He may seem to compare in that respect with the Aberdonian, but in him there is none of that queer Teutonic reserve, which is so apt to affect human intercourse with the native of Buchan. That he is a mighty man with his hands, the world knows and acknowledges; that he is nearer the poet than his brothers in the other cities is less obvious, but equally true. He has the "furious" quality of the Scot in its most extreme form. He can be terribly dangerous in revolt and as terribly strong in defence of his own conception of order. He hates pretence, ceremonial, form—and is at the same time capable of the most abysmal sentimentality. He is grave—and one of the world's most devastating humorists.'

Mr Blake adds that these observations apply mainly to the Glasgow working man. They give a different picture of him from the one I have tried to give. If the two pictures could be combined, the result might be a more or less objective portrait of the Glasgow workman. 'Downright, unpolished, direct, and immediate' certainly describes one side of him very well. Whether he is 'nearer the poet' than any other workmen, I could not say. He is certainly a mighty man with his hands, or was at one time. But I do not think that, singly or collectively, he is 'a dynamo of confident, ruthless, literal energy', nor that it would be a good thing if he were. [. . .] There are certainly a great number of people in Glasgow with ruthless energy, but they are mainly to be found, I think, among the climbing middle classes and the men who have risen to wealth 'by their own efforts', as the popular but misleading saying goes.

c) From 'The Highlands'

One can feel the enchantment of the Highlands by taking a few steps out of Glasgow to the north or the north-west; and that seems at first one of the strangest things about it. The natural explanation is that Glasgow is only the extreme fringe of a whole sea of grime and dirt extending east-wards almost to within sight of Edinburgh. To the north-west of Glasgow this sea washes against the hills and in between them until it is spent.

But it was to the east that I had to go now, between pocked fields through which iron-coloured brooks sluggishly oozed, and where stringy gutta-percha bushes rose from sward that looked as if it had been dis-honoured by some recondite infamy. I noticed that as I drove through the defaced and suffering patches of country which still persist between Glasgow and Hamilton and Airdrie and Motherwell, no scents from the hedges and fields streamed into the open car. They had borne me company on my journey almost all the way to Glasgow; they rose to meet me again as soon as I was past the industrial belt, refreshing and sweetening the air. But it was as if in this region nature no longer breathed, or gave out at most the chill dank mineral breath of coal and iron. The air itself had a synthetic taste, the taste of a food substitute, and seemed to be merely an up-to-date by-product of local industry. The forlorn villages looked like dismembered parts of towns brutally hacked off, and with the raw edges left nakedly exposed. The towns themselves, on the other hand, were like villages on a nightmare scale, which after endless building had never managed to produce what looked like a street, and had no centre of any kind. One could not say that these places were flying asunder, for there was no visible sign of anything holding them together [. . .] They were merely a great number of houses jumbled together in a wilderness of grime, coal-dust and brick, under a blackish-grey synthetic sky. [. . .]

A little beyond Motherwell I came upon the tiny village of Carfin with its Grotto, which I had been told to look out for. This place of pilgrimage was created some years ago by the Roman Catholic Church in honour of Sister Thérèse of the Child Jesus, a young French girl of great piety who died of consumption in 1897. The Grotto covers a good deal of ground and contains a heterogeneous collection of rock-gardens, lawns, shrines, images of Christ and the Virgin, which are rather confusing to one's eye on a hot summer's day. The greater part of the actual labour on this shrine, apart from the planning and the statuary, was done voluntarily by miners and railwaymen. I have heard people who know more than I do about plastic art criticising its arrangement; nevertheless, it appeared to me the only palpable assertion of humanity that I came across in the midst of that blasted region. Father Taylor, who was largely instrumental in having the sanctuary begun and completed, and now watches over it, deserves to be honoured by the people of these towns. I could vouch from my own experience that the place, with its green lawns, its flowers, its little streams winding through their rocky mazes, its shrines and statues, had a power of communicating peace which is extraordinarily rare in the modern world. There were very few visitors to it when I was there, that was in the late forenoon of a very hot summer's day;

and the only people I spoke to were two old Irish women who asked me some question or other about the Grotto which I could not answer. They rattled on cheerfully about Glasgow, where they lived, hoping for a time that I was Irish too, but finally arriving at the fact that I was not. Thereupon they sympathised with me, poured a few pious but kindly blessings over me, and left me to myself. The last I saw of them they were kneeling side by side on the warm grass before one of the many statues. [. . .]

Now to turn to Carfin itself. In July, 1920, a group from Carfin took part in the Scottish pilgrimage to Lourdes, and decided on returning to erect a small grotto on some ground opposite the church. Carfin is a mining village. It is a bleak and ugly enough little place, but its name, which Father Taylor says is of Gaelic origin, apparently means 'beautiful residence'. The great majority of the population is Irish, with an admixture of Lithuanian. The village is quite a small one, and the fact that a knoll close by contains the ruins of an ancient sanctuary does not seem an adequate explanation for the erection of a new one in such an unlikely place. Cardinal Bourne, in an address given at the Grotto in 1924, asked in his usual rhetorical style 'Why Carfin?' and went on, 'Why Nazareth?' Father Taylor is more reasonable on this point. 'Perhaps one may ascribe the choice, in part at least,' he says, 'to the faith of the three hundred volunteers who have toiled at the shrine.' But then he continues, less reasonably, perhaps: 'We must reckon, too, with the promise from the nuns of the Carmel of Lisieux, from the surviving sisters of St Thérèse, that the Little Flower would multiply the pilgrims to Carfin, and so prove her passionate love for Mary, the mother of Christ. Intercession is also made for it in Uganda, in India, in China; at Loreto and Genazzano; in ancient Chartres, at Notre Dame des Victoires, and by special command of its Bishop—the Grotto of Lourdes itself; as well as in countless centres of devotion nearer home.'

If some of these quotations should sound ironical to a Protestant reader, it is without any intention of mine; for the Grotto is too interesting as a piece of contemporary history, and too clearly the creation of a sincere faith, to be treated with superficial sarcasm. The Grotto was opened in October, 1922. By next year water from its well had begun to be carried away for the use of the sick.

(Edwin Muir, *Scottish Journey*, pp.10–13; 122–23; 158–60; 167–74.)

7.14   Dane McNeil [Neil M. Gunn], from 'Doom in the Moray Firth' (*Scots Magazine* October 1935)

On a recent fine morning, the quays of Wick were enlivened by as ardent a piece of discussion as has been heard there for many a day. Indeed 'discussion' is a polite term for the epithets that flew about with the vehemence incidental to an older and happier age. There in the selling mart it was almost as if Wick had come alive again, as if the independent spirit of the daring seamen of past generations was once more raising its face, bloody perhaps, but still unbowed!

The storm arose through an action taken by the recently constituted Herring Industry Board, an action that might have had its ironic humour were it not fraught with such misfortune for so many fishermen on the Moray Firth coast. And here let it be said at once that every consideration is extended to the Board in their admittedly difficult task of regulating a national industry fallen on evil times. It is only too easy to crab the efforts of a constructive body. In any form of reorganisation or rationalisation, someone it seems is bound to suffer. No one realises this better than your clear-headed northern fisherman. But any sort of reorganisation or national control that inflicts needless hardship on the very people whom it is pre- sumably designed to relieve or assist must expect an outcry and damaging criticism. And this is precisely what happened.

First let it be explained that in the old days the summer herring fishing, from such ports or creeks as Wick, Lybster, Dunbeath, and Helmsdale, ran from about the last week in July to the end of October. It was from the inshore herring caught and locally cured in September and October that the surrounding countryside procured its full barrels and half barrels for winter use—'the tattie herring'. They did not wish herring caught and cured earlier in the season. A herring, like any other fish, does not improve the longer it is kept in brine. Anyway, such has been the traditional practice. Again, as September approaches, the herring come inshore and may be caught in the drift nets of the new type of motor boat (just under forty feet) which these last few years has been making a valiant effort to bring the decayed northern harbours to life again. This lively sea-boat, with its equipment of seine net, cod net, and herring net, is of an ideal size for Moray Firth fishing because it can cover the local fishing grounds adequately and because its overhead or running expenses are negligible compared with those of the large drifter. But when it comes to competition in deep sea fishing with the large drifter, which carries a crew of ten men and a fleet of a hundred and twenty nets, the local motor boat is at a grave disadvantage. This was completely exemplified during the herring fishing season in Wick this summer. The large drifters went fifty to sixty miles to sea to meet the herring shoals, returning to port with their catches for immediate sale and cure. The motor boats of Helmsdale, Dunbeath, and Lybster, could not follow them there and accordingly had a very thin time. They did not complain about that. The battle is still to the swift and the money to the rich. And in this case let it be clear that the majority of the drifters engaged were from the south, owned to a considerable extent by large English syndicates—a factory system that runs completely counter to the old Scottish ideal of the skipper-owner. In Wick, once the greatest fishing port of the north, counting its boats by hundreds, there are now six drifters and less than six motor boats. But, as I say, there was no complaint on the score of an English invasion, no outcry against big financial interests raiding the home fishing banks. The drifters scooped such pool as there was, and then duly prepared to depart to other waters where shoals were forming. By the first week in September they were gone, the herring had come inshore, and the motor boats from the creeks were getting good catches of excellent quality. Their season had at last arrived and haste must be made if outstanding debts were to be met and the winter was to be looked forward to with anything but dark misgivings.

With shots varying up to thirty crans, local boats arrived at Wick—*to find that no curer could legally buy their fish*. The Herring Board had caused to be published a day or so before a Notice prohibiting the cure of herring on the East Coast of Scotland between the 2nd day of September and the 31st day of October, 1935. The Board was wired to the London address given on the Notice. Could not the herring be cured locally for local consumption? No. The herring could not be cured by anyone for any purpose whatsoever!

But this seemed absurd. Had not each boat its new licence from that very Board permitting the catching of herring up until the end of September? True. They were not debarred from *catching* them during September; they could even sell them for freshing or kippering; but—they *must not have them cured.*

After the consternation, the discussion, as has been said, became more forceful than polite. The tragedy of the fishing decline on this coast ensured that only a few boats were actually concerned, which made the principle at stake all the more important, for there is wrapped up in it the question of profit which alone makes general revival possible. What could be sold was sold in small quantities to local carts for cadging about the country-side, and a few crans were sent to Aberdeen as samples, it was understood, for tinning purposes. But the biggest catch of all had to be held by the skipper, who would have accepted an offer of roughly half of what had been the ruling price a few days before. He decided to defy the new powers and to cure the herring whatever came of it. To do that, it was pointed out, would possibly call down upon him severe measures, including even the suspension by the Board of his fishing licence. The retort came to the effect that nothing could be severer or more desperate than the position in which the honourable craft of deep-sea fishing had already landed him! Whereupon he procured barrels and salt and set about curing his catch on the quay-wall in front of his own boat.

And there, at the moment of writing, the position rests. Strong representations have been made from the fishing ports named above, but so far the Board have declined to move. In Helmsdale the writer found that two crews of women had actually been engaged (on the strength of the licence to fish during September) to deal with the September catch for cure and subsequent local sale. And now not only will loss be entailed by the fishing community there, but the surrounding country of crofters and others will be done out of their winter herrings—or, at least, they will be compelled to buy herring cured earlier (which they don't want) at the big ports at a bigger price. [. . .]

But the real tragedy of this business lies in the blow struck at the strong local endeavour of recent years to revive the fishing creeks of the coast. [. . .] If this recent Order is typical of what may follow, then our coastal fishermen may be justified in their growing belief that it would have been better for them if the Herring Industry Board, complete with London address, had never been spawned.

(Dane McNeil [Neil M. Gunn], 'Doom in the Moray Firth', *Scots Magazine* 24:1 October 1935, pp.24–27.)

7.15   Edwin Muir, review of *Scotland: That Distressed Area* by George Malcolm Thomson (*Criterion* January 1936)

This is one of the best books that have been written about the Scottish question: indeed, probably the best. It gives briefly and clearly the results of a careful enquiry into the economic development of Scotland from 1907 until the beginning of the slump, with a short note on the state of things since. That development is described mainly by statistics; many of these statistics were not publicly available until Mr Thomson got hold of them; and as he uses them they provide for the first time a means of definite comparison between the economic state of Scotland and of England as well as of six or seven European countries, such as Norway, Finland, Holland and Denmark, which have roughly the same population as Scotland.

There is no space in a review like this to give Mr Thomson's actual figures, and the best way to show what he has proved about the state of Scotland will be to summarize his conclusions. Between 1913 and 1930, then, that is before the slump affected the question seriously:

1) The population of Scotland declined, while the population of England and of nine European countries resembling Scotland in size increased.

2) Unemployment was very much higher than in England or in those small countries. This in spite of a far heavier drain by emigration on the Scottish industrial population.

3) Scotland's national income fell, 'so that the average Scotsman who started the century as rich as the average Englishman is now only two-thirds as rich'.

4) 'The volume of *industrial production* in Scotland, which was still rising during the years 1907 to 1913, has since then fallen, so that in both 1929 (pre-slump) and 1930 it was not merely lower than in 1913 but actually lower than in 1907.' During the same time production in England as well as in all western European countries except Germany increased, the increase in some cases being spectacular.

5) Scotland's basic industries have fallen off, and she has failed to get hold of new secondary industries.

These facts speak for themselves, but a few figures may help to bring them home more vividly. From statistics compiled by the Institut für Konjunkturforschung, Berlin, Mr Thomson has extracted the following figures, showing the indices of production in several countries in the years 1913 and 1930. (I give only a few of the countries.) Going on these indices production in Norway rose from 57 in 1913 to 112 in 1930, in Finland from 44 to 83, in Denmark from 72 to 116, in France from 79 to 110. During the same time production fell in Scotland from 116 to 94. And Mr Thomson says: '*Scotland is the only one of these European countries which shows an actual fall in production in the period between the start of the War and the start of the slump*'; for even Germany's production was slightly higher in 1928 than in 1913 (though it sank again in 1930) while Scotland's production had fallen even in 1928 by 16 points. The post-slump figures which Mr Thomson gives are just as disturbing. During 1933 and 1934, 1,075 new factories were opened in England and Wales and 510 shut—a net gain of 565. During the same time 34 new factories were opened in Scotland and 65 shut—a net loss of 31. As for unemployment, Scotland had in 1931, 'the year when the British Government extended official recognition to the world crisis, a mass of unemployment three-quarters of the total of workless in six countries whose aggregate population is six times as great as her own.'

The point of this book is that it defines clearly for the first time the economic state of Scotland; and it is the state of a country slowly dying without having wakened to the fact. For, as Mr Thomson says: 'The character of the Scottish problem is that of stealth, of a gradual attrition of physical and economic resources, of a decline in strength which is only perceptible over comparatively long periods and which therefore displays itself in outward signs not to the eye but to the memory.' But even where it is openly displayed it is accepted as the natural state of things. Mr Thomson quotes a letter to the *Scotsman* by the Rev. T.M. Murchison, a Church of Scotland minister: 'Many Highland parishes are becoming inhabited almost entirely by the aged, school rolls dwindling, churches becoming derelict because there are so few left to worship, ministers officiating at ten funerals for every one marriage or baptism.' If we were to read such things in past history we should recognize them at once as clear evidence of organic decay. But they are happening at present; Mr Murchison's letter was written in June this year.

Mr Thomson merely states the facts about Scotland without attempting any systematic explanation of them; and in this he is right, for any explanation would have weakened the overwhelming impression which his book produces. He is of the opinion, however, that the economic decline of Scotland is partly due to the centralization of finance in London; and indeed that decline may be merely one of the results of a general process within Capitalism, the transition from the phase of industrial capital to that of financial capital. But whatever may be its cause, for Scotland it is a national and domestic problem as well as an economic one. In this book Mr Thomson has tried to rouse Scotland to a realization of its state. But his book should also be of interest to England, if she takes the Union seriously or thinks of it at all. The attitude of the average educated Englishman to the Scottish question is pained surprise at any hint that Scotland might wish to dissolve the Union, combined with a total lack of interest in Scotland as a part of the United Kingdom. Mr Thomson is convinced that Scotland would be better off now without the partnership than with it, and indeed the comparisons he has drawn between Scotland and such small countries as Norway and Denmark justify him in his belief. It is clear that Home Rule should in any case be freely granted by England now, both for her own sake and for the sake of Scotland; otherwise she may find that a still important part of her kingdom will have sunk past hope and past recovery.

(Edwin Muir, review of *Scotland: That Distressed Area* (1935) by George Malcolm Thomson, *Criterion* 15:59 January 1936, pp.330–32.)

7.16   Neil M. Gunn, from 'The Family Boat: Its Future in Scottish Fishing' (*Scots Magazine* June 1937)

No more certain indication of the desperate condition of the herring-fishing industry could be found than in the recent insidious press campaign against the Scottish system of family-owned boats. Responsible fishing opinion in Scotland is satisfied that the campaign was officially inspired, though direct evidence is naturally difficult to obtain. This may be a political point and therefore not to be pursued here, though there are so many parallels to precisely this sort of attack in Scotland's economic history that at least Northern opinion may be forgiven its apparent assumption of official inspiration. The truly insidious nature of the attack lies in this: it is known that the Scottish boats are heavily in debt; if to this fact could be added the idea that the Scottish system is uneconomic compared with the English, then not only a Government department, but banks, ships' chandlers, and private individuals would hesitate to finance such a system and its ruin would be inevitable. Discredit a man or a system in so subtle a way and his or its doom is written, economic collapse being hastened by the very despair that overtakes the human factors involved. Evidence of this truth may all too readily be found in practically every port on the east coast of Scotland at the present moment.

The Scottish Herring Producers' Association resisted this attack strongly in letters to the Ministry of Fisheries, the Secretary for Scotland, and the Fishery Board for Scotland, and produced facts and figures designed to show that the Scottish system of individual ownership compared favourably with the English company system. If the Scottish boats made a smaller number of landings per boat during the English fishing season, it was because, unlike the English boats, they did not go to sea on Sundays. And if the average shot was smaller, this again had to be offset against the fact that in the given period (6 October–28 November 1936) the English boats had fished on Sundays during October and on Saturday and Sunday nights during November; and accordingly must have landed considerable quantities of overday's and salted herrings. 'The present system of individual ownership in Scotland is not doomed to extinction', declares the Association, 'and will never be replaced by company ownership.'

It is a valiant declaration, but even in the moment of making it the Association is aware that 'the English boats are backed by capitalists, who may keep on making losses, hoping to recoup themselves later on by the extinction of some of the individual Scottish owners, whose capital is tied up in his boat and gear'.

And therein lies the real danger. 'The cold truth is that from 1931 to 1934 herring boat-owners, both Scottish and English, made considerable losses. There was an improvement in 1935, and again in 1936, but the English-owned boats have no more surmounted their difficulties than have the Scottish.' True; but being 'backed by capitalists', they are more likely to surmount them, because they are better able to last the desperate pace.

The large company can always smash the small individual in any sphere of industrial effort from the local multiple shop to the foreign market. Moreover, when it comes to any such test of endurance, many factors other than the purely financial automatically align themselves in favour of 'big business'. Let me illustrate with a simple instance. There is more than one fishing port on the Moray Firth where fishermen's houses were condemned because they did not comply with local bye-laws regarding sanitation and cubic airspace. The humane local authority accordingly proceeds to build 'council houses' for those affected. The fishermen move in, but find that now they have no lofts and outside sheds for storing gear, painting buoy, or mending nets, as they had in the old homes. Result—they have to pay for storing their gear and for having it mended or repaired.

It may be protested that surely such a position could have been foreseen. I suggest that it might be an interesting exercise among the factors that manipulate our local authorities to discover why it never is.

Or take the case of the men who have cut their losses and gone in for the motor-engined boat and seine-netting for whitefish—an individual enterprise. I have talked to the best of them on both sides of the Firth and already they foresee the end. The slaughter of immature fish has been enormous. The grounds are getting less and less fruitful. Drag after drag often produces nothing of value. They are naturally tempted to poach within the three-mile limit. Many of them are already prepared for any workable system of restriction or regulation that would ensure a reasonable future for the catching of 'flats' and other white fish. But all they actually see in front of them are foreign trawlers in the firth (where British trawlers are prohibited) swinging round on a three-mile radius and systematically cleaning the grounds. They have no feeling of security; no conviction that the Government will ever interfere to protect their interests against state-subsidised foreign boats or attempt in any way to assist them with grants or wise organisation. When the Government votes 1,500 million pounds for the defence programme it forgets about the drifters and trawlers, though the Admiralty used over 2,100 of them in the war. All that colossal sum for destruction, yet not one penny for the solitary part of the defence arm that in peace time is productive! It is reckoned that the Buckie fleet in the last fifteen years has lost over a million sterling. And to-day Buckie fishermen, the majority of whom are unemployed from November to June, have the pleasure of watching Danes landing fish at their home port.

Perhaps the basic trouble is that in Britain the fishing industry is not sufficiently organised—in England of not sufficient value—to be of importance in the political game. If Scotland had to deal with her own affairs, her fishing industry would at once be of major importance in her economy, and she would very soon be compelled to give it the attention that the Germans, Danes, Swedes and Norwegians give to theirs. Consider how energetically the Scandinavian countries, for instance, deal with the foreign trawler! But as things are, trouble on the London buses takes precedence in the minds of our Westminster legislators. Though that is less than the truth, for I have been unable to trace any Parliamentary discussion of the fishing industry throughout the life of the present government. And as for the Herring Industry Board's plans for the reconstruction of the herring fleet, these 'moneylender's terms', as they have been aptly called, it is difficult not to agree with the fish-curer who suggested that their terms were meant not for restriction but for destruction. [. . .]

I suggest that the answer may be found in some system of co-operation similar to that which has proved so successful in Scandinavian countries. Co-operation implies duties and restrictions, but such duties and restrictions would be imposed by the fishermen themselves for their own good and not in the interests either of shore capitalism or of state control. If this were done on an inclusive scale, then they would find themselves in a superior position to the English combines for two reasons: 1) they would not have to provide profits for a capitalist organisation ashore, and 2) they would continue in their own interests to look after their own gear in a way that no driven wage-hand ever does. [. . .]

Co-operation in this way would be merely an enlargement, to meet modern conditions, of the old communal way of running affairs that is at the root of Scottish institutional life. Once they got their system properly organised and functioning, it would be extremely formidable. If Orkney can make three times her agricultural rental out of her own co-operative way of selling eggs, is it beyond hope that the Scottish fishermen, with their great traditions and renowned fishing grounds could make shift to get out of debt? Co-operatively organised, Scottish fisheries would overcome English capitalism, and with a Government prepared to fair play on the international market, they would not need to fear even the state-subsidies of foreign countries.

(Neil M. Gunn, 'The Family Boat: Its Future in Scottish Fishing', *Scots Magazine* 27:3, June 1937, pp.169–74 [169–71, 174].)

7.17 George Blake, Note to the Second Edition of *The Heart of Scotland* (1938)

This essay on Scotland and the Scots was written during a period of desolating 'slump' in industry, when a man might be forgiven for taking short, dark views of his native country. Revising it for a second edition, however, and that in a 'boom' period, I have found very little that I would alter. The generalisations of 1934 seem to me to hold good for 1938. The Scottish problem, for it amounts to that, has merely had its angularities sharpened within the period.

The economic shadows over the Highlands grow darker and darker. The Caledonian Power scheme, designed to impound the waters of western Inverness-shire to supply power for a carbide factory at Corpach, near Fort William, has been three times thrown out by the House of Commons in three years. That there was always a majority of Scottish members *for* the Bill perhaps does not signify. The Highlanders themselves were fatally divided. The staple fishing industry is nearly in rack and ruin.

On the other hand, the dominant heavy industries have recovered brilliantly from Depression, and did so in the first place without the sinister aid of rearmament. The inauguration of this year's Empire Exhibition has brought industrialists and artists and writers into belated collaboration. The 'consciousness of Scottishness' finds more and more vivid expression through such bodies as the National Trust for Scotland, fighting for amenity and the preservation of the really good old things.

The bones are stirring, indeed, and much more cheerfully than in 1934. But the essential questions raised in this essay remain, grimmer than ever.

Are Scotland's fortunes, and her soul and heart, tied ineluctably to the vagaries of heavy industry? Does an identifiable Scottish tradition remain, or do we desert the glens and islands and go down the helter-skelter with the rest, saluting the New Age with a glad and unanimous *Ja!*?

(George Blake, *The Heart of Scotland*, London: Batsford, 1934, 'Note to the Second Edition' 15 July, 1938, p.xi.)

8

Celtic Connections and the Situation of the Highlands

8.1 C.M. Grieve, from 'A Scotsman Looks at His World' (*Dunfermline Press* April 1923)

[V]arious significant elements emerging in contemporary Scottish literature may be briefly described as a quest for Continental affiliations, and a more or less conscious repudiation of the dominance of English influence; deliberate efforts to go back upon well-established tendencies in Scottish history which caused the desuetude of the Doric and of Gaelic and to 'denationalise' the teaching of history and literature in our schools, and even thus belatedly, to act as if these had never been, and to supply now the sort of literature in Gaelic and Doric that would have existed had the contrary tendencies never developed.

(C.M. Grieve, 'A Scotsman Looks at his World', *Dunfermline Press*, 14 April 1923, p.6.)

8.2 Daniel Corkery, from *The Hidden Ireland* (1924)

a) From 'Introduction'

It has to be insisted upon that Renaissance standards are not Greek standards. Greek standards in their own time and place were standards arrived at by the Greek nation; they were national standards. Caught up at second-hand into the art-mind of Europe—thus becoming international, their effect was naturally to whiten the youthfully tender national cultures of Europe. That is, the standards of a dead nation killed in other nations those aptitudes through which they themselves had become memorable. Since the Renaissance there have been, strictly speaking, no self-contained national cultures in Europe. The antithesis of Renaissance art in this regard is national art. To some it must seem as if the Renaissance has justified itself in thus introducing a common strain in the art-consciousness of all

European countries. That common strain was certainly brilliant, shapely, worldly-wise, strong, if not indeed gigantic, over-abounding in energy, in life! Yet all the time there was a latent weakness in it, a strain, a sham strength, an uneasy energy, a death in life. It always protested too much. Dissembling always, it was never simple-hearted enough to speak plainly, and so, intensely. It therefore dazzles us rather than moves us. [. . .]

The Renaissance, artificial from the start, rootless, had sometime to die. Dead, what could succeed it except a return to national standards? Whether or not we feel that every literature in Europe is doing this may be a question of knowledge. But it is not necessary to take them in turn and observe their courses. Let us rather ask ourselves: what language in Europe since the French Revolution—which outburst, for all its Classicism, really meant the overthrow of the Renaissance—has done the greatest work in literature? The answer is the Russian. That literature, born too late to share deeply in the wares of the Renaissance, is at once the most national and the most significant of all modern literatures. A memorable and comforting fact—pointing out the way of light and freedom.

Note again, the influence that other late comers in the field of world-literatures, such as Danish, Norwegian, Swedish, are having on the world of letters. It is the literatures of these countries that are really the path-finders of to-day. Note again, how impossible it would have been for America to make any progress in literature if Whitman had not arisen to slay the New Englanders. Still further observe the huge extent to which dialect is entering into the stuff of modern literature in almost all countries. Imagine what Racine would say to Eugene O'Neill! Dialect is the language of the common people; in literature it denotes an almost overweening attempt to express the here and now, that, in its principle is anti-Renaissance.

b) From 'The Hidden Ireland'

The facts here gathered are the commonplaces of the social history of eighteenth century Ireland; and the political history of the period explains the causes of the whole frightful disorder: [. . .] Living from hand to mouth, with no reserves, the cottier was at the mercy not only of winds and rains, but of every change, and even threat of change, in the body politic, the body economic. It happened that just as the Industrial Revolution had begun to open up new avenues of wealth to the big landowners in England, to woo them into the ways of commerce, disease on a large scale broke out among the herds of cattle in England; and the remedy shows the new direction that men's thoughts had taken: Ireland began to be envisaged as England's feeding ground of the future. A beginning was made by the raising of the embargo on Irish cattle, whereupon vast herds of Irish bullocks were set upon the roads towards the Irish ports. Then followed huge clearances: the landlords became suddenly aware that continuous cropping impoverishes the soil; moreover, no tithes needed to be paid on pasture: in what way they justified their grabbing of the commons is not very clear: the result of all was that herds of dispossessed human beings, as well as the herds of beasts, began to darken the roads. To know with any sufficiency what it meant one must take up some such book as MacKenzie's *Highland Clearances*.

c) From 'The Aisling'

The word *Aisling* means vision; and the vision the poet always sees is the spirit of Ireland as a majestic and radiant maiden. This really is the essential feature in the *Aisling*. Of course, before the *Aisling* became recognised as a distinct genre, there were vision-poems in the language—many of them—in which the self-same spirit of Ireland appears and utters her distress and her hopes. [. . .] The use of the word in the new technical sense may date from Aodhagán Ó Rathaille's poem beginning, 'Aisling ghéar do dhearcas féin am leabaidh is mé go lagbhríoghach' (circ. 1700).

It was this poet, Aodhagán Ó Rathaille, who first makes the vision, the *Spéir-bhean* (literally, sky-woman), bewail the exile of the Pretender; it was this poet who, we may say, bound up the *aisling* type of poem with the Jacobite cause. The *Aisling* proper is Jacobite poetry; and a typical example would run somewhat like this: The poet, weak with thinking on the woe that has overtaken the Gael, falls into a deep slumber. In his dreaming a figure of radiant beauty draws near. She is so bright, so stately, the poet imagines her one of the immortals. Is she Deirdre? or Gearnait? or is she Helen? or Venus? He questions her, and learns that she is Erin; and her sorrow, he is told, is for her true mate who is in exile beyond the seas. This true mate is, according to the date of the composition, either the Old or the Young Pretender; and the poem ends with a promise of speedy redemption on the return of the King's son. [. . .]

Comparing these Jacobite *aisling* poems with the Jacobite poetry written elsewhere, mostly in Scotland, the differences we notice throw us back on the two worlds in which the poems flourished. The Scottish poems are simple, homely, direct; and if they have life in them to this day, as many of them have, it is because they were written to and about a living man on whom living eyes had rested with affection. Warm affection is the note of them. [. . .]

The *aisling* poems had no such close inspiration. The Irish Gaels [. . .] were a people with no leader. [. . .] And of this they were not unconscious: 'Gan triath ach Dia na Glóire' ('Without leader save the God of Glory') is a commonplace in their verse. [. . .]

What is imperative in these songs in the art of the singer. [. . .] A beautiful thing is being wrought out before our eyes, and it is through the beauty of it we are moved, or not at all. Indeed their own beauty, not Prince Charlie, is their theme; whereas, in the Scottish poems, to leave out the 'bonnie bird' is to leave all out. It is curious how little else except warm affection for the Prince himself is in these Scottish songs—the poet has but scant thought for anything else, little for Scotland, not much for the Cause. On the other hand, Ireland is in all the *aisling* poems; and the only lines in them that strike fire from us are those of her sorrows,—her princes dead, her strongholds broken, her lands in the possession of churls, her children scattered across the seas [. . .]

The place that the Stuarts themselves occupy in the Scottish poems is occupied in the Irish poems by Ireland herself. So that, in spite of their theme, we get from them the feeling that their writers were playing with a far-off woe when the Stuarts are in question, but with a living sorrow when Ireland is their vision.

(Daniel Corkery, *The Hidden Ireland* (1924); reprinted Dublin: Gill and Macmillan, 1967, pp.12–15; 36, 38; 128–33.)

8.3 William Sharp, from Introduction to *Lyra Celtica* (1896: 1924)

It is not yet thirty years ago since Matthew Arnold published his memorable and beautiful essay on Celtic Literature, so superficial in its knowledge, it is true, but informed by so keen and fine an interpretative spirit; yet already, since 1868, the writings of Celtic specialists constitute quite a library.

Of recent years we have had many works of the greatest value in Celtic ethnology, philology, history, archaeology, art, legendary ballads and romances, folk-lore, and literature. Of all the Celtic literatures, that which was least known, when Arnold wrote, was the Scoto-Gaelic; but now with books such as Skene's *Celtic Scotland*, Campbell's *Popular Tales of the West Highlands*, with its invaluable supplementary matter, Dr Cameron's *Reliquiae Celticae*, and many others, there is no difficulty for the would-be student. Again, it is impossible to overrate the value of popular books at once so able, so trustworthy, and so readily attainable, as Professor Rhys's *Celtic Britain*, or Dr Douglas Hyde's *Story of Early Gaelic Literature*; while Breton literature, ancient or modern, has found almost as many, and certainly as able and enthusiastic, exponents as that of Wales or that of Ireland. [. . .]

The Celtic Renascence, of which so much has been written of late—that is, the re-birth of the Celtic genius in the brain of Anglo-Celtic poets and the brotherhood of dreamers—is, fundamentally, the outcome of 'Ossian', and, immediately, of the rising of the sap in the Irish nation. [. . .]

Of living poets who write in Gaelic, there are more in Scotland than in Ireland. The Hebrides have been a nest of singers, since Mary Macleod down to the youngest of the Uist poets to-day; and though there is not at present any Alexander Macdonald or Duncan Bàn Macintyre, there are many singers who have a sweet and fine note, and many writers whose poems have beauty, grace, and distinction. [. . .] In the *Celtic Monthly*, and other periodicals, much good Gaelic verse is to be found, and it is no exaggeration to say that at this moment there are more than a hundred Gaelic singers in Western Scotland whose poetry is as fresh and winsome, and, in point of form as well as substance, as beautiful, as any that is being produced throughout the rest of the realm. The Gaelic Muse has also found a home in Canada, and it is interesting to note that one of the longest of recent Gaelic poems was written by a Highlander in far-away Burmah.

'The Highlander' (and in this and the following passage I quote the words of Professor Mackinnon, from his Inaugural Address on his succession to the Celtic Chair at Edinburgh University) 'The Highlander may be truly described as the child of music and song. For many a long year his language is the language, for the most part, of the uneducated classes. And yet, amid surroundings which too often are but mean and wretched, without the advantages of education beyond what his native glen supplied, he has contrived to enliven his lot by the cultivation of such literature as the local bards, the traditions of the clan, and the popular tales of the district supplied. He has attempted, not unsuccessfully, to live not the day and hour alone, but, in a true sense, to live the life of the spirit! He has produced a mass of lyric poetry which, in rhythmical flow, purity of sentiment, and beauty of expression, can compare favourably with the literature of more powerful and more highly-civilised communities.

'In the highest efforts of Gaelic literature, in the prose of Norman Macleod, in the masterpieces of the lyric poets, in the *Sean Dàna* of Dr Smith, and above all, in the poems of Ossian, whether composed by James Macpherson or the son of Fingal, the intellect of the Scottish Celt, in its various moods and qualities, finds its deepest and fullest expression. Here we have humour, pathos, passion, vehemence, a rush of feeling and emotion not always under restraint, and apt to run into exaggeration and hyperbole—characteristics which enter largely into the mental and spiritual organisation of the people. But above and beneath all these, there is a touch of melancholy, a "cry of the weary", pervading the spirit of the Celt. Ossian gives expression to this sentiment in the touching line which Matthew Arnold, the most sympathetic and penetrating critic of the Celtic imagination, with the true instinct of genius, prefixes to his charming volume, *On the Study of Celtic Literature*:

"They went forth to the war, but they always fell".'

[. . .] And of all races, none has so worshipped the 'Rose of the world' as has the Celt.

'No other human tribe', says Renan, 'has carried so much mystery into love. No other has conceived with more delicacy the ideal of woman, nor been more dominated by her. It is a kind of intoxication, a madness, a giddiness'. [. . .]

Let me conclude, then, in the words of the most recent of those many eager young Celtic writers whose songs and romances are charming the now intent mind of the Anglo-Saxon. 'A doomed and passing race. Yes, but not wholly so. The Celt has at last reached his horizon. There is no shore beyond. He knows it. This has been the burden of his song since Malvina led the blind Oisìn to his grave by the sea. "Even the Children of Light must go down into darkness." But this apparition of a passing race is no more than the fulfilment of a glorious resurrection before our very eyes. For the genius of the Celtic race stands out now with averted torch, and the light of it is a glory before the eyes, and the flame of it is blown into the hearts of the mightier conquering people. The Celt falls, but his spirit rises in the heart and the brain of the Anglo-Celtic peoples, with whom are the destinies of the generations to come.'

(William Sharp, 'Introduction', *Lyra Celtica: An Anthology of Representative Celtic Poetry* (1896); reprinted Edinburgh: John Grant, 1924, pp.xx–xxi; xli–xliii; xlvii; li.)

8.4   Donald A. Mackenzie, from 'A Celt's Protest' (*Scottish Educational Journal* January 1926)

Sir,—I think it is about time that a mere Celt, with a name as 'tartan' as mine, entered a protest against the gross libels on his people and their literature which have of late appeared in your correspondence columns. H. Brown, who is assisting Mr C.M. Grieve to decide how future literary geniuses must think, feel and write, alleged recently that the Teutons had 'tougher' minds than the Celts. I don't pretend to know what a 'tough mind' is, but I hope it has no connection with what my old schoolmaster used to call a 'wooden head'. Perhaps, however, H. Brown wanted to flatter the non-Celts. Now, R.L. Cassie (his surname sounds as Celtic as the one translated 'Brown') grows lyrical over 'the direct and virile Germanic speech', which helps 'to infuse more of action and achievement into the Celtic contemplation and dreaminess'. He goes on to allege that 'the Celtic tongues have always been misty and elusive, while the Germanic languages combine a rich under-current of poetry with lucidity of expression, rigid word-economy, and pitiless common sense'. [. . .]

When the Celts raided Rome and 'held up' the citadel garrison, their language was not in the least 'misty'. They made themselves perfectly well understood, and they set an example to their descendants (not forgotten in the Scottish Education Department in our own day) of making a collection of valuable Roman coins. The Celts in Italy, who terrorised the Romans for a few centuries, those who fought for Carthage, for Pyrrhus etc., those who plundered Delphi, those who held a great part of Europe and part of Asia Minor in tribute (as a Greek writer reminds us), those who fought against Caesar in Gaul, and those of ancient Britain, from whom so many of us are descended, had never any difficulty in making themselves understood, and they were fairly 'tough'. According to Julius Caesar, the Gaulish Celts were much more cultured and had a higher standard of living than the Germans. The Celts are quite respectable in history.

Celtic literature is not 'misty', and it is certainly not 'elusive' and it is less 'dreamy' than many suppose. The old Gaelic bards dearly loved a satire— one that (as they said) 'raised blisters', and many modern Highlanders are very satirical fellows and are not lacking in 'pitiless common sense'. One of the literary needs of our time is, I think, a little satire in the typical Gaelic manner. [. . .]

It was a Celt who acted as tutor to Julius Caesar and taught him much, including Greek, which resembles the Celtic languages in several respects. The Celts were not all soldiers.

As for the mental equipment and practical tendencies of modern Celts, I need say little. A few names from my own native county (all of Black Isle stock or birth) may, however, convey much to my readers. These are Hugh Miller and Sir Roderick Murchison, the geologists; Sir Hector Macdonald, the military genius; Sir George Mackenzie, the statesman; Sir Thomas Urquhart, the great translator; and Alexander Mackenzie, the renowned explorer, whose surname is printed across a large area in Northern Canada. They were all able and resolute Celts and not dreamers of misty dreams with minds in a complicated state like Fiona Macleod's curious folk.

During the late war many Highlanders proved that they had inherited the valour and dourness of their Caledonian and Gaulish ancestors. My mother's clan, the Mackays (known to Caesar as the Aedui in Gaul) showed up well among other Celts.

The Celts of Scotland are neither weak-kneed nor weak-minded, and their literature reflects their innate characteristics—their modes of thought based on their modes of life. If Teutonised dreamers like H. Brown and R.L. Cassie would only read some translations of genuine Gaelic literature, they would be less inclined to write about a large section of the inhabitants of Scotland with as little knowledge as if they were dealing with the inhabitants of China or Timbuctoo. [. . .]

The nineteenth century nonsense about the 'Celtic temperament', the 'Celtic gloom' and 'Celtic dreamers' should be flung into the nearest ash-bin with other rubbish.

(Donald A. Mackenzie, 'A Celt's Protest', letter to the Editor, *Scottish Educational Journal* 15 January 1926, pp.77–8.)

8.5 From inaugural editorial, *Pictish Review* (November 1927)

It is customary for the undertakers of new periodicals to vouchsafe some brief explanation touching the ends proposed to them; and to this useful convention we are agreeable to conform. As its name implies, the *Pictish Review* has been set on foot in order to present a Pictish view of things in general; to re-elucidate the values implicit, and explicit, in Pictish history and civilisation; and, further, to impart a turn to current affairs, and the interpretation of them, which shall be conformable to the genius and inherited tendencies of the Pictish nation. In fine, we propose to restore the name of Pict to the politico-cultural map of Scotland, from which it has been banished, for no good reason apparent to us.

The two nations of the Picts and Scots have now been too long joined to be separated; and we would be opposed to their separation were their separation desirable or practicable; but then neither of these alternatives is either. At the same time, we see no good reason why, so far as history and the common usage of speech are concerned, the Pict should have been taken, and the Scot alone left. The first element is at least as important as the last: comparisons are notoriously odious, and we have no intention of indulging them; but this at least may be urged with perfect propriety in behalf of the Pict, that this land was his, and the civilisation he set up in it, long before any Scot struck foot on Pictish soil. That truth, and its corollaries in truth, in time, and circumstance, we propose to demonstrate; aye, and to apply, so far as the application of them to current conditions may be judged desirable and practicable *Dia'na thoiseach*.

(Hon. R. Erskine of Marr, editor, *Pictish Review* 1:1 November 1927, p.1.)

8.6 Dane McNeil [Neil M. Gunn], 'The Gael will Come Again' (*Scots Magazine* February 1931)

That Mr Alexander Urquhart in his article on 'Celt and Norseman' has unjustly overstated his case against the Highland Gael does not, as he may feel it would—or even should—rouse that picturesque figure of his fancy to immediate fiery wrath.

The dignity 'frequently indistinguishable from the silliest form of vanity', may, when it exists (and where doesn't it?) be affected. That is about all. Why? Just because of that element of truth underlying the trenchancies of Mr Urquhart's charge, an element seen by the true Gael himself more than by any other. This is not a matter for sweeping comparisons and violent accusations. One may be down at heel and yet not a fool. In the world of affairs it is a commonplace that the predatory instinct triumphs over the spirit. Nor need we slip on platitudes. For what has long happened to the north-west of Scotland is now perceived as happening to Scotland as a whole. There has been an insidious process of decline, throwing up the usual symptoms, which Mr Urquhart observes in the case of the dreamer with his 'humbug', but may miss in the case of the Scot with his haggis. It might be interesting to diagnose these symptoms, but it would probably land us in the wide region of national life and affairs, where the external simplicities of Mr Urquhart's observations would neither explain nor reveal very much.

His comparisons with the Norse may be, for example, entirely mis-leading. It is possible that on one of his islands a thousand miles north of the Hebrides a colony of Gaels might thrive (and so repeat history), and that on St Kilda, because of those very contacts with 'civilisation', a colony of the hardiest Norsemen might in a generation or two ask a beneficent government to help them 'to conquer fortune' (a fine phrase!) by removing them to the mainland. Any Saxon business man whom I have met would indeed consider such a move for such a purpose a natural and wise one. So that when Mr Urquhart is being ashamed over the St Kildan exodus, I feel that his shame is really not so much for Celt or Norseman as for human nature. And we all have our share of that.

Perhaps that is why Mr Urquhart cannot find the cause of the 'lethargy and slackness' of the west, though he is satisfied that it lies not in race but in the language, nurture, and tradition of the people. That is about as vague a statement as even a dreamer could make! It is, more unfortunately, an illogical one. For as Mr Urquhart asserts, at one time St Kilda carried a population of 200, who throve on the results of their own labour. I make no doubt they throve as well as did any contemporary Norse settlement similarly placed. They were also, according to travellers, given to the social arts of singing and dancing. And of that self-supporting colony, a remnant of 86 was evacuated recently and the island abandoned. Yet it was the same language, an unbroken tradition; and, in the same environment, there were presumably the same potentialities for nurture. The 'slackness and lethargy' cannot therefore be implicit in these three factors. The cause must be searched for elsewhere.

Nor is St Kilda the solitary example. The mainland was also in time past inhabited by a self-supporting people, who gave a good account of them-selves not only in social life and the creative arts of poetry and music, but also in the matter of personal daring and courage. They not only fought with distinction in the wars of Europe, but took a hand in making history at home—and if they had then developed, in place of their marked individuality, this new art, which Mr Urquhart observes, of 'leaning' on each other, it is possible that that hand would have been a decisive one. But in those days there was, alas! less 'leaning' amongst them than amongst their enemies, the Saxons, who also, of course, had numberless more shoulders for the purpose.

The language, tradition, and nurture of the Gael sufficed in those days, and would have sufficed in these, if they had not been interfered with from outside. I am not now referring to tourists' tips nor charity's tinned meats, though these may be all that trouble the facile minds of travellers to-day. The root-cause is deeper and more desperate. It struck at language, at honour, at livelihood, at tradition, at their arts and amusements, in a way that for stark brutality is without parallel in modern Christendom (Ireland not excepted, that other home of the Gael). There is no space here for the petty details, though their tone might be given by quoting from the oath which a Highlander had to take after the '45. It refers to the charming matter of the pattern of the tweed he wore. This is what the Sheriff asked him to repeat:

. . . and never to use tartan, plaid, or any part of the Highland garb; and if I do, may I be cursed in my undertaking, family, and property—may I never see my wife and children, father, mother, relations—may I be killed in battle as a coward, and be without Christian burial in a strange land, far from the graves of my forebears and kindred; and may this come across me if I break my oath.

The people were not only 'cleared' out of the glens, hunted and dragooned, or shipped abroad like cattle, but those who remained, after being cowed into a mood of utter subjection, were by the most subtle and insidious means, religious and educational, made to despise their language and tradition (nurture now barely arising).

From such a gruelling onset, pursued in various guises through generations, a people does not recover all at once. It takes time. 'Lethargy and slackness' are not perhaps unnatural. Even 'dirt and squalor' might be expected. Tinned jellies are acceptable, and a little Celtic-twilight is imported for sleep.

I would pray Mr Urquhart not be intolerant and, before the Gael has quite come to himself, threaten him once more with a Norse invasion.

Also I would ask him, when he finds so certainly that the Gael's 'affinity to poetry and beauty' is 'all humbug', to enquire into the matter beyond the personal chance encounter. He would not, I presume, call the glorious record of English literature 'all humbug'—after spending a day in Clapham.

Gaelic poetry and music are no myths. There were dialectal differences all over Gaeldom, but scholar's Gaelic was common currency in Scotland and Ireland until the seventeenth century. Gaelic literature was in its flower centuries before the beginnings of English literature. Dr Johnson was revealingly ignorant when he said that there was no Gaelic MS over 100 years old. There is indeed such a wealth of Gaelic MSS in existence that one savant suggests it will take 200 years for Gaelic scholarship to deal with them. And as a Gaelic poet of to-day says of this literature as a whole: 'Its poetry is sunbred; twilight for it is just the tremulous smoke of one day's fire. Not with dreams but with fire in the mind . . .'

There might well be then the 'lethargy and slackness', but what has been is passing before the slow but sure uprising of a new confidence. As for Sir Archibald Geikie's 'squalor, dirt and laziness', I can but suggest that any foreign visitor would be unfortunate who got his idea of the Lowlands from the Cowgate or the Cowcaddens. But Gaelic history is proverbially the comment of the outsider. Lecky found conditions a thousand times worse in the Ireland of his day—even if, incidentally, he failed to find at the same time the existence of the 'Courts of Poetry'. The Gael under the pale was certainly at his social lowest. He had lost heart, and was living in conditions utterly appalling. But he lived through that infamous time and to-day is running his own affairs in a Free State that is financially about the only one in Europe approaching complete solvency.

In my experience of the west I may have been more fortunate in missing the 'squalor, dirt and laziness', and finding instead hundreds of homes, humble enough materially, but at least with the graces of hospitality and a natural courtesy. The exception occurs everywhere—and here need hardly be a concern for our scorn in the face of history.

Finally, Mr Urquhart's preoccupation with his Saxon ideal of the go-getter is interesting as a personal expression but not conclusive as a way of life. It has hardly, for example, landed the world in a golden age completely devoid of poverty and squalor. In the midst of plenty (called over-production), we suffer the grisly spectacle of famine. Against the tyranny of the machine and the predatory instincts of the go-getter, new conceptions of life and work are needed. The Gael in Scotland may have had 'inferiority' drummed into him, but he will come again—only, in his own way, which may not be the way, however admirable, of the 'humdrum Saxon', nor, perhaps, will the world lose by the distinction.

('Dane McNeil' [Neil M. Gunn], 'The Gael Will Come Again', *Scots Magazine* 14:5 February 1931, pp.324–27.)

8.7 C.M. Grieve, from 'English Ascendancy in British Literature' (*Criterion* July 1931)

The Consultative Committee of the Board of Education has just published a report on 'The Primary School' in which there is a passage stressing the need to realise that there are many varieties of English; that it is not the function of schools to decry any special or local peculiarities of speech; and that a racy native turn of speech is better than any stilted phraseology, especially for literary purposes.

This is excellently said and represents a departure or suggested departure in Departmental attitude which, it is to be hoped, may be speedily followed up in the schools themselves, relieving the children of tomorrow from a subtle but far-reaching psychological outrage which has been inflicted on many generations of pupils and seriously affected the quality and direction of those of them who had literary inclinations. The passage may be commended in particular to the attention of the B.B.C. and to such typical spokesmen of the contrary spirit as Sir John Squire, who thinks that Burns might just as well have written in English, and Mr St John Ervine, who declares that 'we are resolved to use language for its purpose, the understanding of each other, and not the preservation of quaintnesses or the indulgence of literary idiosyncrasies'. [. . .] The problem of the British Isles is the problem of the English Ascendancy. Ireland, after a protracted struggle, has won a considerable measure of autonomy; Scotland and Wales may succeed in doing the same; but what is of importance to my point in the meantime is that, in breaking free (or fairly free) politically, Ireland not only experienced the Literary Revival associated with the names of Yeats, 'A.E.', Synge and the others, but has during the past half century recovered almost entirely her ancient Gaelic literature. Dr Douglas Hyde tells us that in his early days highly-educated Irishmen were incapable of conceiving that in this whole corpus there was anything worth recovering, let alone an entire classical tradition, with its own elaborate technique, its own very different but (if only because incomparable) not inferior values which maintained itself intact— in active intercourse with all contemporary European developments, but unadulterated by them in the integrity of its own modes—for at least two thousand years, and has (as has Icelandic literature) an alternative value of prime consequence when set against the Greek and Roman literatures which are all that most of us mean when we speak of 'the Classics'. One may well speculate what the results to-day would have been if this great literature, instead of being virtually proscribed by the 'English Ascendancy' policy and practically forgotten, had been concurrently maintained with the development of 'English Literature'. Would such a synthesis or duality of creative output (each element of it so very different that they could have complemented and 'corrected' each other in a unique and invaluable fashion) not have been infinitely better than the sorry imperialism which has thrust Gaelic and dialect literatures outwith the pale [. . .] To recognise and utilise these, instead of excluding them, could only make for its enrichment. It is absurd that intelligent readers of English, who would be ashamed not to know something (if only the leading names, and roughly, what they stand for) of most Continental literatures, are content to ignore Scottish Gaelic, Irish, and Welsh literatures, and Scots Vernacular literature. Surely the latter are nearer to them than the former, and the language difficulty no greater. These Gaelic and Scots dialect poets were products of substantially the same environment, and concerned for the most part with the same political, psychological, and practical issues, the same traditions and tendencies, the same landscapes, as poets in English to whom, properly regarded, they are not only valuably complementary, but (in view of their linguistic, technical and other divergencies) corrective. [. . .] To institute certain comparisons in English literature one has to compare the present with the past. But if one takes in Gaelic literature, the ancient technique, even the tone, is practically unchanged; the comparison is with the changed English present and the unchanged Gaelic present. The point need not be pursued.

It is time, so far as Scottish literature in particular is concerned, to do as the Irish have done in their case, and reverse the attitude that has hitherto prevailed—exemplified by the late Professor J.H. Millar, who began his *Literary History of Scotland* with the disconcerting remark: 'With the Celtic literature of the Highlands we have here no concern. Our business is with the literature of the English-speaking Scots.' The phases of Scottish poetry—the lets and hindrances of its evolution—cannot be properly understood if the fact that great poets like Alasdair MacMhaigstir Alasdair, Duncan Ban MacIntyre, and Iain Lom wrote gloriously of Scotland and Scottish matters in a language of which the great majority of Scottish people know nothing, but against which they are still deeply prejudiced, is not taken into consideration [. . .]

The third point is the necessity to bridge the gulf between Gaelic and Scots. Both have been tremendously handicapped by circumstances, and yet in their evolution, thus miserably attenuated and driven underground by external factors, they have continued to complement and correct each other in the most remarkable way. I am not going to make use of the terms 'Romantic' and 'Classical', although these dubious counters do roughly correspond to the Scots and Gaelic traditions in poetry respectively. But the failing of the former in modern times has been formlessness, while the latter has been choked by an excessive formalism. They have a great deal to learn from each other.

In addition to their equal and opposite needs (and they have so profound a bearing on the position of literature as a whole today, in its search for 'a new classicism', that if Scottish poetry could effectively bridge this Gaelic–Scots gulf it might well lead the way in the great new movement in poetry which is everywhere being sought for) both Gaelic and Scots poetry have this in common—the need for a prolonged and exhaustive pre-occupation with their own languages. 'What Gaelic needs', says Donald Sinclair, 'is a tremendous recovery of idiom. A great deal of the language has gone dead through disuse. It must be revived.' The problem in Scots is precisely the same. The language has been allowed to disintegrate into dialects and these have gradually lost all the qualities befitting them for major expressive purposes rather than for homely, local uses.

If, to this intensive concern with the problems of the two languages, can be joined a dignified concern with making a creative contribution worthy of Scotland, the conditions of a real Renaissance will perhaps be available.

(C.M. Grieve, from 'English Ascendancy in British Literature', *Criterion* 10:41
July 1931, pp.593–613 [593–94, 595–96, 600–601, 606–607].)

8.8 C.M. Grieve, from 'The Caledonian Antisyzygy and the Gaelic Idea' (*Modern Scot* Summer/Winter 1931)

I cite these Russian names and use these Russian quotations advisedly. We in Scotland are at the opposite side of Europe. The old balance of Europe—between North and South—has been disrupted by the emergence of Russia. How is a quadrilateral of forces to be established? England partakes too much of Teutonic and Mediterranean influences; it is a composite—not a 'thing-in-itself'. Only in Gaeldom can there be the necessary counter-idea to the Russian idea—one that does not run wholly counter to it, but supplements, corrects, challenges, and qualifies it. Soviet economics are confronted with the Gaelic system with its repudiation of usury which finds its modern expression in Douglas economics. The dictatorship of the proletariat is confronted by the Gaelic commonwealth with its aristocratic culture—the high place it gave to its poets and scholars. And so on. It does not matter a rap whether the whole conception of this Gaelic idea is as far-fetched as Dostoevsky's Russian Idea—in which he pictured Russia as the sick man possessed of devils but who would yet 'sit at the feet of Jesus'. The point is that Dostoevsky's was a great creative idea—a dynamic myth—and in no way devalued by the difference of the actual happenings in Russia from any Dostoevsky dreamed or desired. So we in Scotland (in association with the other Gaelic elements with whose aid we may reduce England to a subordinate role in the economy of these islands) need not care how future events belie our anticipations so long as we polarize Russia effectively—proclaim that relationship between freedom and genius, between freedom and thought, which Russia is denying—help to rebalance Europe in accordance with our distinctive genius—rediscover and manifest anew our dynamic spirit as a nation. This Gaelic idea has nothing in common with the activities of An Comunn Gaidhealach, no relationship whatever with the Celtic Twilight. It would not matter so far as positing it is concerned whether there had never been any Gaelic language or literature, not to mention clans and tartans, at all. It is an intellectual conception designed to offset the Russian Idea: and neither it, nor my anti-English spirit, is any new thing though the call for its apt embodiment in works of genius is today crucial. It calls us to a redefinition and extension of our national principle of freedom on the plane of world-affairs, and in an abandonment alike of our monstrous neglect and ignorance of Gaelic and of the barren conservatism and loss of the creative spirit on the part of those professedly Gaelic and concerned with its maintenance and development.

The essential point is that all fixed opinions—all ideas that are not entertained just provisionally and experimentally—every attempt to regard any view as permanent—every identification of Scottish genius with any particular religion or political doctrine—every denial of the relativity and transience of all thought, any failure to 'play with' ideas—and above all the stupid (since self-stulfifying) idea that ideas are not of prime consequence in their qualitative ratio and that it is possible to be over-intellectual—are anti-Scottish—opposed to our national genius which is capable of countless manifestations at absolute variance with each other, yet confined within the 'limited infinity' of the adjective 'Scottish'. [. . .]

I have said that, from the point of view of the Gaelic idea, knowledge of, or indeed even the existence of, Gaelic is immaterial. It is not for nothing that Mrs [Rachel Annand] Taylor cries:

> It is unfair that I have not the Gaelic although I be a Gael
> And to the sweet and intricate inflexions that prevail
> In that proud language dances my heart,

and that William Power and others who 'have not the Gaelic', with a few who had it not but have since acquired it, have led the way in insisting upon its major importance to creative Scottish endeavour, while almost all the Gaelic speakers have been hopelessly false or unequal to their trust.

It is along these lines that we must discover this god of our own—that we must, in consonance with our natural genius, meet the Russian Idea at every point. [. . .] The importance of the fact that we are a Gaelic people, that Scottish anti-Irishness is a profound mistake, that we ought to be anti-English, and that we ought to play our part in a three-to-one policy of Scotland, Ireland, and Wales against England to reduce that 'predominant partner' to its proper subordinate role in our internal and imperial affairs and our international relationships (not to go further for the moment and think of a Gaelic West of Europe as essential to complement the Russian idea which has destroyed the old European balance of north and south and produced a continental disequilibrium which is threatening European civilization, and, behind that, white supremacy) are among the important practical considerations which would follow from the acceptance of *Blutsgefül* in Scotland.

(C.M. Grieve, 'The Caledonian Antisyzygy and the Gaelic Idea', *Modern Scot* 2:2/2:4 Summer/Winter 1931; reprinted from Duncan Glen ed., *Selected Essays of Hugh MacDiarmid* London: Cape, 1969, pp.56–74 [67–69, 71].)

8.9 Neil M. Gunn, from 'Highland Games' (*Scots Magazine* September 1931)

There is an odd persistence about Highland customs and institutions. We are always doing something to keep them alive, as though they came out of a social past which we cannot let die—or dare not. Searching among the underlying reasons we come on something not so much sentimental as quixotic. There is that air of holding to a tradition of manners which was natural to the knight of La Mancha—and is perhaps not altogether unnatural now to many leaders of the Gaelic 'causes'? Or should one use the more general term and say 'Scottish causes'? Anyway, has not Bernard Shaw said of Cunninghame-Graham that when not in his company he believes the man a myth? When young John MacCormick is holding forth on our parlous state, or Mr Angus Robertson is rounding a period to the honour of the ancient tongue, might not the spectacle appeal to a Scottish Cervantes—with the irony to appreciate what they are tilting at? And if that may seem amusing to the rest of us, it may be as well to remember that his master was sometimes amusing to Sancho Panza, for those of us who dare not lead are proverbially wise.

Well, of all our institutions, Sancho Panza has got complete control of one, namely our Highland Games. No idealism, false or otherwise, is allowed to intrude there. The race is to the swift and the battle to the strong—for cash. No nonsense about it; a free field and no favour. And so we have our two or three heavy and light athletes travelling from village to village, games to games, and collecting the money that local endeavour is able to gather for them. In a word, it has become for the most part a commercial business. This has disgusted those who have a mind above what they consider professional sport of the worst kind, who still believe in games as a field of local rivalry and disciplined effort with thrilling uncertainty as its climax, and who in their beliefs, quixotic or unconscious, derive from an age anterior to the time of Christ. For the Highland Games go far back into Gaelic legend, and at least we know of one Boy Corps that competed in friendly rivalry in all field sports, in honour and chivalry, of whose splendid company, Cuchulainn, that small dark man, was one. Against such a conception, Sancho Panza and his travelling 'weights' of many kinds, do not make an impressive show. The more the pity, for there has persisted—there persists still—in our Highland Games an elusive semblance of its ancient meaning. [. . .]

Assuming, then, that the Highland Games have got their distinctive note from the perpetuation of an old tradition, it would seem reasonable, if it is desired that the unique note be kept, to continue as far as possible the spirit of that tradition. Now, as I see it, that means concentration on the local aspect of the event. The whole endeavour should be to stimulate Highland music, athletics, and dancing within the district where the Games are held. The reasons are clear. Country life, particularly in these days of intense emigration of the finest stock and the consequent creation of an atmosphere of defeat and decay, needs all the healthy stimulation it can get. Athletics, music, and dancing breed sound bodies, active minds, and a distinct social sense. All that grows sour and inferior in the action of hopelessness gets routed out of the system by a fine rivalry. The schoolboy hopes someday to emulate the athletic deeds of his elder whom (and this is the significant part) he meets, and talks to and secretly admires, and whom he may see any night 'having a practice'; or if his mind runs to music, then he has countless opportunities of listening to the local champion and gaining for his own use by imperceptible degrees that appreciation of the finer shades of execution which is about all that technique means. It is impossible to overestimate the importance of this. It gets at the core not merely of the Games, but of the whole conception of communal life. It shows us the real value of tradition, shows us growing and blossoming from our own roots. (The old Gaelic heroes were of the people, doing the day's tasks about steading or shore.) Without this tradition we may live, but season by season we throw less of the flower and finally become fruitless and settling into inevitable decay.

Now there are two direct ways of looking at that local aspect. One can say frankly that one does not believe in it; or believing in it, that it is no longer possible to achieve.

If one does not believe in it, then let us by all means have our perambulating professionals lifting the local cash. And let *piobaireachd* (though why perpetuate so exclusively Highland a musical form?) be set to competition in bowler hats. Only, to be logical, one should drop the description 'Highland Games' and get an apter label. [. . .]

If, alternatively, one does not bow to this 'open' logic, yet believes it impossible to achieve the local aims, then possibly the only honest thing to do is to let the whole sorry business go by the board.

There is, however, the middle way, the way of compromise [. . .]

Lay all the emphasis and organisation on local effort, spend most of the money that can be raised on providing attractive local prizes, let there be cups or medals or badges for distinction or honour, let the whole affair be fostered again from however simple if true beginnings, let communal pride enter in from parents to school children, and there would arise a new and more healthy interest in our ancient Highland Games. What is needed is not a blind acceptance of bad conditions, but the initiative to work out new conditions. [. . .]

Now it may be considered that there has been shown here no appreciation of the prowess of what we have called the 'visiting professional'. This is entirely to misconstrue my contention. I consider on the contrary that it would be a good thing for the local men to see the man who is the champion of his class. But this could easily be arranged by simply inviting him at a fee to attend to 'give an exhibition'. And while this might be advisable on the athletic side, I should say that it would be essential on the piping and dancing side. To have a master of *ceòl mór* play at a given time would be the local way of honouring the master and the occasion. There would be no feeling of the local men competing against him. You would thus obtain the 'draw' that the secretary desires and at the same time let the local aspirant see the highest development of his secret dream. As for the 'masters', they would themselves compete in the two or three great national gatherings (such as 'The Northern Meetings' in Inverness) where their claims to leadership could be openly settled.

In some such way the evils of an insidious professionalism might be combated and renewed life and interest given to the local Games.

(Neil M. Gunn, 'Highland Games', *Scots Magazine* 15:5 September 1931, pp.412–16.)

8.10 From unsigned review of Hon. R. Erskine of Marr's *Changing Scotland* (*Modern Scot* Winter 1931)

Mr Erskine's latest collection of papers constitutes an examination of early Scottish history and a plea, in the light of his reading of that, for the restoration of Scotland to the position of a Celtic state. He takes the case for Scottish autonomy practically as proved, and confines his attention chiefly to urging, as against any conception of nationalism that allows room for cultural diversity within Scotland, the establishment of a completely Gaelic-speaking nation north of the Border. [. . .]

Mr Erskine is fully aware of the wide divergence between that conception of Scottish Nationalism and the views of the majority of people calling themselves Scottish Nationalists. For our part, we disagree with him on several important points. In the first place, it is not correct to say that the case for Scottish Nationalism depends on the fostering of a language distinct from English (whether the Doric or Gaelic), any more than it is contingent upon the possession of a distinctive religion or a population racially differentiated. These things may be ancillary to the presence of a national consciousness, but it is dependent on none of them. It is precisely that national consciousness (robbed of political expression by the ruling parties at Westminster) with which Mr Erskine never comes to grips: for quite apart from the fact that when comparing the advantages of the use of the Doric, English and Gaelic in Scotland he is comparing incomparables, the only possible basis for a just and practical comparison—the nation's equal facility in the use of all three—being lacking, apart from such considerations as whether there is truth in the widespread belief that cultural debility might result from Scotland's retirement into a milieu through which no breath of European civilization has blown for several decades, Mr Erskine is blind to the fact that the important thing about a tradition is its *continuity*, and that the national consciousness he would seek to direct is the national consciousness as it exists now.

An English reviewer put his finger on the weakness of Mr Erskine's schemes for changing Scotland when he pointed out that he painted a glowing picture of the fine flower of Scottish Celticism that would result if he had his way, but failed to indicate how the young plant was to be protected in its infancy from the storm of contemporary Scottish antipathy.

It is not as if Mr Erskine, countering Scottish politics, were holding firm to, say, a philosophical idea, which he refused to adulterate to suit everyday political requirements: a philosophical absolute is an absolute, and on the plane of the ideal an unyielding dogmatism is proper. Politics, on the other hand, far from dealing with things on that plane, deals with things as they are and are becoming, and Mr Erskine's ideal of a Celtic polity is not a philosophical but a social and political one. [. . .] To achieve a political end a political weapon is necessary, and that Mr Erskine has not found: nor will he look for it, since the present is the politician's *point de départ*, and the past from 1603 onwards is 'so little venerable' to him that he will not examine it closely enough to find out what elements exist *today* in the national consciousness. It is absurd, for instance, to talk as if Scotland were in the grip of the feudalism of David the First.

If the author of *Changing Scotland* had not disdained to consider 'how and why Celtic culture fell in Ireland, Wales, Gaul and elsewhere', he might have found how national cultural movements are initiated and grow. Signor Mussolini is a type of national leader who is in no doubt about the process, and there is a lesson for Scotsmen in the evolution of Fascism. At the outset of his career, Signor Mussolini found that he could not win Italy for Socialism, because Socialism tended to sever class from class, and left out of account elements in Italian national thought that have existed and have been added to since the time of the Caesars. He accordingly based the doctrines of Fascism on his revised conception of the national mythos, thus taking account, as the politician must, of the contemporary forces he wanted to mould. The Scottish Nationalists have still to evolve a Scottish counterpart of Fascism, and hence the number of Nationalists at sixes and sevens. One thing is certain, the Celtic myth is quite inadequate for national purposes, since it is capable of uniting only a handful of Scotsmen.

His failure to realize the fact of continuity in human history and to think politically gives Mr Erskine's papers an air of unreality. A couple of years or so ago, on the score of the many sound things the author says here and there, we might have welcomed his book as 'stimulating'; but Scotland is now past the stage of needing the merely 'stimulating'. We now require a leader.

(Unsigned review of *Changing Scotland* by the Hon. R. Erskine of Marr, *Modern Scot* 2:4 winter 1931, pp.345–47.)

8.11 'The Irish Situation' (*Free Man* April 1932)

The action of De Valera in regard to the Oath and the payment of annuities has brought Irish affairs into the foreground again. As a result there are many and varied efforts being made to explain the situation. One section of the press favours the idea that the decision of De Valera has been brought about by a desire to placate the Republican Army, but the latest news from Ireland suggests that the Republicans don't care more than two hoots for the Oath and Annuities. They want complete separation, and it should be obvious that such a cute politician as De Valera must have been clearly aware of the fact. Another section of the press has been suggesting that Ireland is suffering from a sort of dementia which drives them to a passionate belief in a Gaelic kingdom, living within itself and unto itself, uncaring for and despising the world outside. Irishmen are much too shrewd to indulge in such conceptions. It is undoubted that there is an intense Irish patriotism concerned with retaining something of Ireland's individuality in a world which is threatened with a drab uniformity, and none can deny that Irishmen are entitled to hold fast to everything in their heritage which has proved of value. They do not ask the rest of the world to follow the Irish pattern. Nor will they accept the pattern of the world. This does seem so reasonable that one wonders at feeble attempts that are made to twist it into something else. It is distressing to read in the British press the veiled threats of what may happen to Ireland if she withdraws from all connection with the British Empire. It would be more honest to give some space to considering what might happen to Great Britain, but of that not a word is said. Yet, there are those who think that Great Britain has more to fear and lose. After all, Ireland does lie between Britain and America, and trouble with the latter country is not outwith the bounds of possibility, nor of probability either. In such an event—well, it is hardly necessary to emphasise the point, for it is plain enough—and should certainly not be lost sight of.

('The Irish Situation', from a correspondent, *Free Man* 1:9, 2 April 1932, p.2.)

8.12 'A Song-Drama of the Gael' (*Free Man* May 1932)

A Festival of Commemoration and Renewal, designed by Arthur Geddes, will be presented in the Music Hall, Edinburgh, on 3rd and 4th June. The 'Spirit of the Tartan', is in four acts—'The Making of the Tartan'; 'The Wearing of the Tartan'; 'The Forbidding of the Tartan'; and, lastly, 'Mourning and Renewal'. In each act the Gaelic songs, all given in English, and many of them translated afresh, are strung together in their natural order of usage, custom and history.

The first act opens with the singing of the 'Herding Croon' to the accompaniment of the Celtic harp. Then the curtain rises on a picturesque group of women and girls spinning and carding wool, and singing as they work. The 'waulking' of the tartan follows and its 'waulking' songs, and the scene closes with the beautiful 'Consecration of the Cloth'.

In the second act, the 'Wearing of the Tartan', bridal songs are sung, and a bridal party dances, but the gaiety of the singers is suddenly checked by the warning note of the pipes playing 'The Gathering of the Clans'—a call to rise for Prince Charlie, followed by a foreboding lament.

Then follows Act III, the 'Forbidding of the Tartan', where a poignantly dramatic note is struck in the part of a Highlander, who, sorely against his will, takes the historic oath, forswearing the tartan, prescribed by King George's Government. The wearing of the Tartan being forbidden to all save soldiers, this scene is followed by that in which a recruiting sergeant, by the gaiety and guile of his songs, enlists lads for the Highland Regiments, falling back at last on force, as the old song of a conscript attested: 'My grief to be wearing King George's Red Cothing!'

In the last act, by the 'Song of the Kertch', a sentry remembers his Bridal Day on the eve of his death in battle, and the lullaby of the mother is stifled by the news of her soldier husband's death. The grief almost of despair is finely expressed, yet the dialogue closes on a note of faith with the ancient 'Rune of the World's Light'.

('A Song-Drama of the Gael', unsigned report, *Free Man* 1:17, May 28 1932, p.5.)

8.13 Fionn MacColla, 'Scots Put to Shame' (*Free Man* January 1933)

The emotional type of Gaelic enthusiast—and the type is usually emotional in proportion as it is mentally lazy—is accustomed to point to the very large area over which Gaelic is still spoken in order to support the claim that the language is quite safe from any danger of extinction. Such evidence is superficial and worthless and no evidence. It ignores the factor of continued decrease of population within that area. And it ignores a further factor—by far the most serious and disquieting aspect of the situation— namely, the rapid disintegration of the language from within. To one who does not understand it, Gaelic may sound very much the same in the mouth of any speaker. Emphatically this is not the case. The spoken language to-day is far from being a' ae 'oo'. An ever-widening gulf exists between the speech of the older and younger generations. The latter commonly speak a kind of slovenly and illiterate Gaelic, from which many of the characteristic sounds which made Scottish Gaelic the most melodious language in Europe have disappeared, as has also a great part of a once peculiarly rich and varied vocabulary, which loss has been partially made up by the adoption of large numbers of mispronounced English words. So much is this so that the younger generation of Gaelic speakers to-day are for the most part incapable of maintaining a conversation in Gaelic of any degree of purity on any subject not rustic and trivial. The overwhelming majority of Gaelic speakers born within this century speak only—because they know only—a colourless, impure and impoverished form of the language. That is to say, that the richer, purer, more idiomatic older Gaelic is only spoken now by individuals who in the natural course of events will be dead within the next twenty years. A priceless heritage will die with them, for there are so far no signs of any steps being taken on the part of any Scottish agency to counteract the effects of two centuries of criminal neglect.

But what we have not known how to cherish, others have appreciated. Foreign names were most notable among the leaders of the revival of Celtic studies of sixty or so years ago, and now a Russian has successfully carried out on his own account a part of the task of which Scots themselves have proved unworthy.

'The present dictionary' [A Pronouncing Dictionary of Scottish Gaelic by Henry Cyril Dieckhoff] says Father Dieckhoff, in his preface, 'owes its existence to the desire of the author to contribute his mite towards the preservation of the traditional pronunciation of a melodious and expressive language which he learned to appreciate during his long residence in the Highlands of Scotland.'

Father Dieckhoff has taken one of the mainland dialects which have been least corrupted by foreign influence—that of Glengarry—and made a phonetic record of the words composing it on the basis of the pronunciation of natives of the district born before the second half of last century. For such a task no one could be better equipped, for, in addition to being a scholar and philologist of standing and repute, Father Dieckhoff himself speaks perfect Gaelic. The present work is characterised by the thoroughness and accuracy we are entitled to expect from such an author, and is to be heartily recommended to learner and scholar alike. It would be asking too much of a Scottish public totally ignorant of its own language and traditions—even contemptuous of them—to wish the book the success its excellence deserves, but Father Dieckhoff can be assured at least of the gratitude and admiration of those few Scots who have preserved a Scottish sense in so Anglicised a Scotland.

There is a lesson, of course, in the nationality of the author, but I doubt if the majority of my fellow-countrymen can read it. An invasion of Russians or Germans would doubtless save the Gaelic language from extinction; it begins to seem rather late in the day to expect the Scots to awaken to a sense of responsibility in the matter.

(Fionn MacColla, 'Scots Put to Shame', review article on A Pronouncing Dictionary of Scottish Gaelic by Henry Cyril Dieckhoff, O.S.B., Free Man 1:49, 7 January 1933, p.2.)

8.14 Fionn MacColla, 'Welshing the Scottish Race' (Free Man March 1933)

The B.B.C. recently accepted a recommendation from its Central Council for School Broadcasting that two special courses in Welsh be given for the benefit of Welsh schools.

Commenting on this in a recent issue the *Daily Record* says: We may now expect our Gaelic enthusiasts to demand a similar experiment in Scotland, but it must be remembered, of course, that there is no use broadcasting Gaelic lessons if the schools don't want them. Welsh is still very much a living language in Wales, and is quite a normal school subject.

I forbear to do more than point out in passing what the *Daily Record*'s myopic Anglicism has failed to perceive, namely, the relation (of cause and effect) in which the two parts of the last sentence stand to each other, the fact that Welsh is still very much a living language in Wales just BECAUSE it is a normal school subject. I make only passing protest also against the indiscriminate use of the term 'Gaelic enthusiast' with its impertinent suggestion in this connection that a belief in the usefulness of Gaelic as a school subject can of necessity only be based upon irrational enthusiasm, and cannot be compatible with cool judgment. But I should like, as far as space permits, to make one or two observations anent the statement that Gaelic should not be broadcast to schools 'IF THE SCHOOLS DON'T WANT IT'.

I do so not because I think it worth anyone's while to try to set the *Daily Record* right—unless I am mistaken its point of view renders it permanently incapable of seeing in true perspective any aspect of Scottish affairs—but because it happens to have expressed here an attitude commonly maintained by members of the public, whose minds, doubtless, have been somewhat coloured by excessive reading of the *Record* and like papers.

I should object at the outset to the use of the figure of speech in the phrase 'if the schools don't want it', because, intentionally or not on the part of the paragraph-writer, the impression is conveyed that we have here to do with an impartial selective agent—'the school'—fully informed of all aspects of the case, and whose decision is not to be questioned or appealed against as it is infallibly in accord with realities and principles. I should object that a school is not a person, endowed with intellect and will, and so capable of choice or judgment, a school is not even an organism, with a centre of consciousness, and therefore cannot strictly be said to 'want' anything at all.

It may be objected that the point is a small one, not worth mentioning, but just how important it is can be seen by the complete change in the aspect of the case when the figure is removed and the question stated in plain terms. 'It is no use giving Gaelic lessons if school teachers and school children don't want them.' That alters matters. The infallible selective agent guarding entry to the curriculum vanishes away, and in its place we perceive only an uncertain number of fallible individuals whose opinions, like our own, are capable of being affected by bias and imperfect knowledge, just as their 'wants' are capable of being suggested to them from outside—

as they are being suggested in this very instance, may I point out, by the Anglophile and pseudo-Scottish *Daily Record*.

But even that is not the most serious of the insinuations in a particularly offensive paragraph. Let us immediately put the whole question on a clearer footing and enquire: Can 'the schools' be said to 'want' the subjects which already appear on the curriculum? Because if they can not it is no use carrying the discussion farther on the basis of the (*Daily Record*'s) assumption that the completest unanimity exists as to the desirability of the subjects already laid down to be taught. It is now that we come to the truth of the matter. For the fact is that 'the schools' have nothing to do with it, they were never consulted. The teachers are paid to teach, just as the children for their own comfort are well advised to learn, subjects which they did not choose, but which were laid down for them from above. So that if we restate the question in terms that have most correspondence with the truth, it boils down to this—Gaelic will not be accorded a place on the curriculum of Scottish schools, will not become 'quite a normal school subject', unless the Education Department—and behind them their masters, the Government of England—consent thereto. That looks to me pretty much like letting a particularly kenspeckle cat out of the bag! Anyway, now we know where we are. . . .

Now, with the intrinsic merits of the case we are not at the moment concerned, but as the question of Gaelic teaching in Scottish schools is certain to be pushed more and more to the front in the near future it would be as well for us to consider in advance what would be the results of such a change in educational policy from the point of view of those who at present control it. That will account for their attitude to the whole question, and any steps they may take in connection with it, whether they appear less disinterested or not, will at least be comprehensible.

This much can be said right away; a generation of Scots for whom their national history had been illuminated by a knowledge of the old national language and of the submerged traditions associated therewith, would be infinitely less docile and tractable, infinitely less hospitable to influences of Anglicisation than the present generation of Scots whose knowledge—if the term can be used in such a connection—of their national history is falsified from the start by the Anglophile assumptions with which they were taught to approach such limited aspects of it as were disclosed for their study. Admit Gaelic into the schools and you commence the destruction of the whole English-ascendancy ideology which our rulers have been at such pains—largely through the agency of those same schools—to build up. Naturally that is the LAST thing they would encourage. The emergence of an independent, SCOTTISH Scotland would be a menace to English hegemony in these islands and within the British Commonwealth of Nations, and a menace to English security among the peoples of Europe. The 'British' Government has a life-and-death interest in keeping things as they are.

So far as Gaelic in the schools is concerned, this means that the question stands not an earthly chance of being discussed on its merits. It means, in fact, that everything will be done to prevent reasonable consideration of it—too much hangs upon the issue. We can with perfect certainty predict, therefore, that as soon as the question becomes a live one all the agencies of mass-suggestion will be set furiously to work by the financial-governmental interests to stir up such a state of prejuduce—of hysteria, if necessary—as will ensure that reason will never be brought effectively to bear on the matter.

In particular the Press will be busy. It will be suggested in a thousand subtle ways that as the majority of Scots are Teutons, with heads of a surpassing squareness, Gaelic is a foreign and not merely a forgotten language, that it is a rude and barbarous language, that 'the schools' don't want it—readers of the *Daily Record* please note—that the man in the street doesn't want it, and above all and in particular—the same old hoary trick: it still seems to work—that to revive Gaelic would be to 'put back the hands of the clock' and therefore contrary to modern progress!

Is it too much to hope that the Scottish people have been cheated once too often and this time will refuse to be taken in by this kind of 'progress', which is merely denationalisation under a thin disguise.

(Fionn MacColla, 'Welshing the Scottish Race', *Free Man* 2:5, 4 March 1933, p.7.)

8.15   The Hon. R. Erskine of Marr, from 'The National Tongue and the Ascendancy' (*Free Man* March 1933)

It is natural that Scots who are children of the ascendancy should speak the language of their captivity. One does not expect figs from thorns or understanding from half-wits; but it is disappointing that persons professing national principles should on occasions speak as glibly as the others this same language of ascendancy. Some one remarked in this journal the other day that if you are a true Communist you are necessarily such in all things. This truth is so obvious that to state it were unnecessary, one would think; but that there is need to affirm it is proved by the fact that 'Communists' there are who are such but in part, and therefore are not whole or true Communists.

The National Party of Scotland 'spoke' the language of ascendancy when it resolved to seek a footing on 'the floor of the House'. That footing it has yet to gain; but though far may be the cry from it to the N.P.S. still the extent of the distance is no excuse in respect of that of the blunder. Imagine men who rose with Charlie, or appeared in arms for his father James, tolerating for a moment any so flagrant breach of elementary national tactics and principle!

Others there are, too, who speak ascendancy with regard to the Gaelic language, though they, as the others here glanced at, profess national principles. Indeed, at one time there was a definite 'school' formed of these whimsical eclectics. This cult or 'school' of letters was called the 'Anglo-Celtic' and for a time it had quite a lively vogue. It is disappeared now; but I mention it the rather since some of the ideas that moved the band are still current among us.

The Anglo-Celtic great idea was to use the English language to serve Celtic literary ends. The Gaelic, they said in effect, is dying. In a few years' time probably it will be extinct. Besides, it is an archaic form of speech. Why fash about it? Still, in the Gaelic language and literature are embedded certain beauties of word and phrase, of idea and myth and legend whose spirit should not be allowed to perish. We Celts who write English should seek out these manifold beauties and popularise and perpetuate them by means of our art and the English tongue, which latter, after all, is now the vernacular of all of us save a sorry and decaying remnant. [. . .]

The Anglo-Celtic 'school' reasoned as it did largely because it was mentally lazy. Neither collectively nor individually would it be at the pains to learn Gaelic. Most languages need much pains to learn them properly; but, in order to the same end, Gaelic needs well-nigh an infinity of them. I speak here, of course, more as a writer than from the point of view of a conversationalist.

So the Anglo-Celts being mentally lazy, and the Gaelic language hard to gain, they came to speak ascendancy about it, vowing that it must soon perish, and that though it might have some good literature in the past of long ago, yet now it was become archaic most evidently. Once the dog has been cursed to perdition any stick or stone should serve his better beating; and once sloth has overcome us, no matter what and how sorry the excuse, it will serve fine to cloak our mental inactivity.

But I repeat that though the 'school' named is dead as mutton to the world of letters, yet it continues to speak ascendancy through the lips of divers others. For example, are there not modern Scots who say: 'The language of the Gael is spoken by too small a remnant of our people to allow of its being made the common language of the Renaissance'; others who affirm that 'modern thought is not represented in such Gaelic literature as appears nowadays: therefore we can have none of it'; and yet others who cry: 'What we need to-day is one clean, clear cut with all tradition, be it Gaelic or Braid Scots. We cannot go back, culturally, to either. We must move forward, even as the hands of the clock do so'?

So, from sloth of mind, from inability or reluctance to brace themselves to learn Gaelic, do these last, as was the case with the first, come to speak ascendancy; and how true is it that often one damned thing leads on to yet another, till the last stage of the inept and the unreasoning resembles that into which the true children of ascendancy have been born, and pass their whole miserable existence!

(The Hon. R. Erskine of Marr, 'The National Tongue and the Ascendancy', *Free Man* 2:8, 25 March 1933, p.4.)

8.16 Earra-Ghaidheal, from 'The Truth About An Comunn Gaidhealach' (*Free Man* September 1933)

A great flourish of trumpets and columns of newspaper puff proclaimed the opening of the thirty-seventh Annual National Mod of An Comunn Gaidhealach in Glasgow on Tuesday. It will last till Friday, by which time the promoters, having relieved the over-burdened Glasgow taxpayers of the second instalment of their municipal rates, will return to the Celtic Twilight taking with them the Language and any other odds and ends of the National Culture they can lay hands on. And they have managed to wangle a civic reception too, where the miscellaneous tribe of enterprising nobodies will accidentally meet the benevolent somebodies who can assist to position and favours. It will all be camouflaged with Celtic glamour, but, truth to tell, it seems a very shabby way of working the confidence trick on the unsuspecting Lowlander.

Let us now consider the credentials of An Comunn. Founded in Oban forty-two years ago, it arrogated to itself 'National Status' five years later. Its objects are briefly to propagate the Gaelic language and encourage native industries in the Highlands of Scotland. The results are illuminating. In 1901 the Gaelic-speaking population numbered some 230,000, while in 1931 it had fallen to little over 130,000. The statistics for Argyllshire—to take one instance only—are positively shocking. During the lifetime of An Comunn the percentage of Gaelic-speakers has fallen from 60 to 33 per cent and is still falling rapidly. By a curious coincidence in the very number of *An Gaidheal* (An Comunn's monthly magazine), where this distressing information is recorded, the president, Dr Neil Ross, has a snappy little editorial on Hunting—dogs, however, not men; and in his 'Annual Survey' (1931–2) he naively remarks, 'It is encouraging to see how the cause is quietly gaining its way'. The Rev. Dr, who appears to have a sinecure of the presidential office, is likely to be the officiating clergyman at the funeral of the national tongue.

The term 'National Mod' is really a misnomer. No attempt has ever been made to treat the Gaelic as a national question. A 'corner' has been made of the Gaelic movement by a coterie of Highland lairds, parsons and schoolmasters, with an odd ghillie thrown in to give the usual democratic flavour to the conspiracy. Lowlanders, including Aberdonians, are regarded as 'Sassenachs', i.e., Englishmen minus the 'Damn' if there are ladies in the company. And, of course, to attempt to interest such unregenerates in the Gaelic would be like casting pearls before swine!

But unpleasant questions might be asked about the Gaidhealtachd, i.e., the Highlands. For instance, what about the rising generation? The venerable lie is annually trotted out, of some 300 schools where Gaelic is taught—but like any other foreign language. There are no Gaelic text-books on Arithmetic, Geography, History, Mathematics, &c. Frankly, this so-called Gaelic teaching is a barefaced swindle. An Comunn (Annual Report, 1932–3, page 5) admits that 'No Gaelic is being taught in the day-schools of Perthshire', and this is the net results of forty years of 'intensive' propaganda!

Turn now to industry. Fisheries, Agriculture, Afforestation, not to speak of the land problem, have been burning questions for Highlanders during the last generation, but what has An Comunn done in the matter? Nothing. Some years ago it got a few rugs made. Of these sixteen remain unsold, and according to the 42nd Annual Report (1932–3), 'The Art and Industries Committee is continuing to do all that is possible to expedite their disposal. No further rugs are in process meantime.' Meantime, of course, the poor natives can either emigrate to the slums of Glasgow or Edinburgh, or gather solemnly on the slopes of the Coolins and quietly perish to the ghostly wails of Fin MacCool and other defunct heroes. In no case must anything be done to embarrass the Government. For did not Mr Neville Chamberlain make some exceedingly flattering remarks concerning An Comunn at Kinlochleven, and does not the President himself, Dr Ross, remark feelingly in his Annual Survey (1932–3), 'the Fort-William Mod of 1932 was an outstanding success. It will be notable as the first occasion on which the Mod had the honour of a visit from a British Prime Minister.' Mr Ramsay Macdonald is the Prime Minister in question, and doubtless the Rev. Neil found his chance visit remarkably convenient with a view to future possibilities.

Gentle reader, the Gaelic is dying, and dying rapidly, and its assassin is An Comunn. The Mod is merely a gigantic piece of bluff to gull the public into thinking that all is well with the language. So thoroughly has this institution done its damnable work that Gaelic is regarded as a sign of social degradation, only to be used when money can be made out of it. Dr Ross himself says in his defeatist way, 'English is inevitable' (see Mod Supplement, *Daily Record* 26/9/33). But worse still falls to be recorded. The *Daily Express* correspondent reports (26/9/33) as follows on a visit he made to the children who have come to compete at the Mod, 'From Portree, from Oban, from Carradale they have come, these bright-eyed, excited, soft-spoken Children of the Mist. But it was not the Gaelic they were speaking as they chattered among themselves. They only do that, it seems, when they are performing.' After this there is only one conclusion the unbiassed reader can come to, and that is that the Gaelic is in its death throes. It will soon be dead and damned.

(Earra-Ghaidheal, 'The Truth about An Comunn Gaidhealach', *Free Man* 2:35,
30 September 1933, p.6.)

8.17 Iain Ruadh, 'A Gaelic Revival in Reality' (*Free Man* October and November 1933)

Before this article is published another Gaelic Mod will have been held, this time in an important Lowland city, and will be doubtlessly hailed as another success, financially as well as linguistically. The evening concerts will be presided over by four eminent chairmen, of whom perhaps one is able to speak the Gaelic language intelligibly; a large proportion of the singers will have repeated patriotic songs in a tongue which they would certainly otherwise never utter; and the number of speeches made in English about Gaelic will certainly vastly outnumber all the Gaelic speeches that are made about anything.

Nevertheless, it is not the intention of this article to animadvert upon the Mod, which is by now an institution of some venerability and no small social importance. It is rather to consider what effect forty odd years of Gaelic Revivalism have had upon the daily lives of the Gaelic-speaking Highlanders themselves, who are, after all, the most important people concerned in the matter.

In their case the results can be summed up quite briefly; Highland children are no longer punished for speaking their native language on the school playground, and Gaelic has received tardy admission into the school curriculum as an optional subject alternative to French, to be studied as a dead language through the medium of English. Beyond this, the efforts of an Comunn Gaidhealach, its friends and supporters, have had next to no effect upon the generality of Gaelic speakers. Its monthly magazine, *An Gaidheal* which could be, if made popular, a most excellent vehicle for propaganda, the more so as it is at present without a competitor in the field of Gaelic journalism in Scotland, remains largely given over to amateur literary efforts (unpaid), occasional scholarly articles, and branch reports (nearly always written in English); the very existence of this magazine is practically unknown to the real Gaelic world, while at large it has scarcely any circulation, and is rarely, if ever, seen on any Highland bookstall.

In fact, Scottish Gaelic is continuing to decline, with a persistence which makes it clear that the remedies brought forward so far to alleviate its decay have not been either sufficiently thorough or comprehensive to be effective. The reason for this is not difficult to discover. From all discussion of the revival of Gaelic the political aspect has up till now been rigorously excluded, with the result that the question has hitherto been considered on an academic basis alone. It is the purpose of this article to consider it upon a practical one.

I am at present living in an island off the west of Scotland which is entirely Gaelic-speaking. That is to say that everyone who is a native of the place can understand Gaelic, and nearly everyone speaks it habitually. Some old people, and nearly all the children under school age, know no other language. In short, one might consider that this place was as thoroughly Highland as any part of Scotland could possibly be.

And yet an English-speaking foreigner visiting the island could well be excused if he failed to observe that the inhabitants had anything to distinguish them from those of any English country district, except for a slight accent on their English speech; and he might think that some were either a little deaf or a little slow of understanding before he discovered that the English which he saw used everywhere in writing was not in fact the native language of the people at all, but a foreign idiom forced upon them by a standardised anglicising education and the exclusion of their own tongue from every public use. In fact, our individuality must run underground; in daily life it can have no place. English in our shops, English in our post-offices, English notices on the steamer that takes us to and from the mainland; not a single word of Gaelic anywhere. In school the children are taught through the medium of English from the earliest possible moment; there are no text-books printed in Gaelic, not because it would be more expensive to print Gaelic text-books than to use the ones that do in Edinburgh (though this pretext would probably be pleaded today if the question of printing Gaelic text-books was brought up), but because we are, though many of us have become habituated to it, a conquered country to be assimilated by every means to the language and the customs of our conquerors. And since Gaelic is entirely barred from public life, and given no official recognition, no Gael can now make a career for himself even within his own country using only his own language, so that the monoglot Gaelic speakers are today nearly eliminated and the vitality of the Gaelic language, and its power to assimilate borrowings are enormously impaired.

These are conditions which would eventually undermine the attachment of any people to their language. Sentimental outsiders often accuse the Highlanders of apathy and indifference to the fate of their tongue; in fact, the wonder is that Gaelic has lived so long, robbed as it has been of nearly every chance of development. If it is to survive these conditions will have to be radically altered. Mods and songs and prize novels and plays are all very well in their way; what is needed is a background where Gaelic can exist as a living language, not as a proscribed patois. It is intolerable in these days, when the rights and languages of minorities all over Europe are safeguarded and guaranteed by treaties to which Great Britain is a party, the Highlands should continue to be the victim of a policy of assimilation no less rigorous than that Alsace suffered under German rule from 1871 to 1918. No one who is genuinely concerned with the preservation of what today is one of the most characteristic and individual features of Scottish life can ask for less than that Gaelic should have within the Highlands the same status that French enjoys in Quebec or Afrikaans in South Africa. This necessitates political measures of an obvious nature. Demands of the following kind must be formulated, and, once formulated, never abandoned.

1. Official recognition of the Gaelic language within the Highlands. The proper Gaelic names of towns, villages, etc., to be restored; all public notices, wherever and however displayed in the Highlands, to be in Gaelic as well as in English.

2. All elementary education in the Gaelic-speaking districts to be given through the medium of Gaelic only. English is to be taught as a special subject when a good knowledge of Gaelic is achieved.

3. Gaelic to be a compulsory subject in every Highland school.

4. A knowledge of Gaelic to be an indispensable qualification for all persons holding public appointments of any kind whatever in any Gaelic-speaking district. (This would apply chiefly to school teachers, post-office employees, policemen, school inspectors, and all other Government employees.)

In asking for what many citizens of the British Empire already enjoy, in point of view of recognition of their own language, we would be doing nothing unusual or outrageous. No friend of the Gaelic who wishes its survival can do less. Those who are content with half-measures and palliatives are amongst its worst enemies. A little inconvenience may be caused to those who would prefer a standardised anglicised Scotland; but if the Highlands are worth their traditional pride they should not let that consideration deter them from guarding their own.

'A Gaelic Revival in Reality'—Part II

The policy proposed for the regeneration of Gaelic life in the first article under this title (*Free Man*, October 7th) had nothing actually original about it, being fundamentally the same as that proposed by the Free State Commission to the Gaeltacht, whose report, a document of great interest, has been most curiously neglected by Gaelic revivalists in Scotland; which is a pity, because it could teach them a great deal.

The implications of this policy remain to be discussed, and likewise some of the difficulties which would be involved in enforcing it; the policy would have to be thorough in its aim but gradual in its application because—

1. It would be essential that the sound teaching of English to Gaelic-speaking children should not be compromised, so long as many of them will have later to seek work in places where Gaelic is not understood.

2. It is essential that such a policy should not compromise efficient public services in the Highlands.

In the opinion of the writer, both these difficulties can be overcome. The thesis of the Nationalist Gaelic Revival should be a) that it is not necessary to anglicise the Highlands in order to teach the Highlanders to speak English, and b) that it should not be necessary for a Highlander who lives all his life in the Highlands to use any language except his own. English as a special subject would retain an important status in education.

Elementary education in other subjects would be carried out through the medium of Gaelic. Later, higher grades would be carried out through the medium of Gaelic, the keystone of the education arch being the creation of a Gaelic University at a date when education through the medium of Gaelic has progressed to such a point that the teaching of advanced subjects through Gaelic was practicable, AND NOT BEFORE.

In the case of Gaelic being a necessary qualification for public appointments in the Highlands, existing appointments would not be disturbed, apart from possible exchanges; but from a given date a knowledge of Gaelic would become an indispensable qualification for all such appointments, even if exceptions had to be tolerated at first.

It is extremely odd that the vast majority of Highlanders have always taken a crassly utilitarian view of their language and have never realised that under a nationalist regime Gaelic would have a monopoly value in the Highlands that could be turned to excellent account. Once a knowledge of Gaelic was made essential to anyone aspiring to occupy a public position in the Highlands, the idea of Gaelic as an accomplishment of, to say the most, no more than sentimental value would be completely overthrown, and the base conception of the value of their tongue, to which the Gaels have been forced to surrender, would be banished for ever.

There remains to be discussed another equally important aspect of the real Gaelic revival; the creation of a centre for Gaelic life, a neutral meeting-place such as the Delphic Oracle was to the Greeks or the Tree of Guernica (Gernikako Arbola) is to the Basques. At present far too many Gaelic activities centre in Glasgow, miles away from the Gaidhealtachd. It is necessary to find a spot, as accessible as possible from all parts of the Highlands, where Gaelic activities can be concentrated and carried on against a Highland background. This could be a real centre to Highland life and in the future become the home of the Gaelic University. As long as the centre of the Highland circle is outside its circumference Gaelic activities will be under a foreign and disintegrating influence. Since Gaelic Ireland ceased long ago to be the centre of the higher studies of the Scottish Gaels, a centre must be made in Scotland itself.

(Iain Ruadh, 'A Gaelic Revival in Reality' *Free Man* 2:40, 7 October 1933, p.4, and 2:41, 11 November 1933, p.6.)

8.18 William Power, from *Literature and Oatmeal* (1935)

In 1922 there was published that monumental and indispensable volume *Early Sources of Scottish History*, by Dr Allan Orr Anderson. A novel feature of it was the prominence given to Irish authorities on early periods about which, we used to be told, there was nothing really known, and in any case nothing worth knowing, since they were the periods of the Celtic tribes, who were merely savages. Civilization and authenticity came in with the Anglo-Normans! So far as cultural history down to well within the fourteenth century is concerned, we can discover a great deal more about Gaeldom than about the small Anglo-Normanized portion of Scotland. On dynastic, religious, and military matters in the early Celtic period, the information is so plentiful that, as Miss Grant has shown in her *Lordship of the Isles*, we can work back, with a fair amount of confidence, to Irish events about the beginning of the Christian era. But Irish events and authorities were regarded as barely serious or respectable; the Irish origins of Scotland were better forgotten; and, anyhow, despite the example of Skene, a Scots historian was not supposed to dip much into Gaelic matters.

The blame for the extraordinary neglect of Scotland's Gaelic history and culture rests with the Scots Gaels themselves. They failed to preserve and cultivate the national heritage of which they were the natural custodians. Largely owing to a decadent clan system and irrelevant religious sectarianisms, they became parochial in their outlook. Their literary sense decayed. They became unable, apparently, to discriminate between the mediocre work of modern hymn-writers and the classic work of the seventeenth and eighteenth centuries. The old men from whom Dr Carmichael took down a beautiful version of the *Deirdre* story, and a fine *Lay of the Sons of Uisnach*, had left no successors. Though An Comunn has helped to improve the taste of the younger folk who think it worth while to retain their Gaelic, the important work of Scots-Gaelic collectors and scholars has had little reflex in the Highlands generally. But even Dunoon must have been rather interested to learn than an Inverness scholar, Dr D.J. Macleod, H.M.I.S., had been made a Doctor of Letters of the University of Rennes for a masterly French thesis on the poems of Duncan Bàn Macintyre. Strange, that a foreign university should attach such importance to a language that enlightened Argyll was throwing away like a pair of old shoes!

Work like that of Dr Macleod will begin to tell in the long run. Also, Lowland interest in Professor Watson's scholarly book on Gaelic place-names, and the inclusion of many of these in guide-books, may have caused some searchings of heart even in that despicable type of Gael who thinks it clever not to know the tongue of his ancestors. The easy infection of the Scots Gaeldom with third-rate Lowland fashions and standards—for a people who abandon their own culture cannot absorb the best elements of another culture—is one of Scotland's mysteries. It must be due to the adjacency of big industrial populations to whom there is something risible in the idea of a language and a way of life different from their own. Had the coalfields and tinplate works been just outside the Welsh border instead of well within it, Welsh culture might not have proved so finely resistant.

(William Power, *Literature and Oatmeal: What Literature Has Meant To Scotland*
London: Routledge, 1935, pp.186–88.)

8.19 Edwin Muir, from *Scottish Journey* (1935)

The hotel dining-room, like most of the others I was to find in the Highlands, had its walls covered with pictures of all sorts of wild game, living or in the various postures of death that are produced by sport. Between the pictures the walls were alert with the stuffed heads of deer, furnished with antlers of every degree of magnificence. A friend of mine has a theory that these pictures of dying birds and wounded beasts are intended to whet the diner's appetite, and perhaps they did in the more lusty age of Victoria; but I found they had the opposite effect on me, and I had to keep my eyes from straying too often to them. In one particular hotel this idea was carried out with such thoroughness that the walls of its dining-room looked like a shambles, they presented such an overwhelming array of bleeding birds, beasts and fishes. To find these abominations on the walls of Highland hotels, among a people of such delicacy in other things, is peculiarly revolting, and rubs in with superfluous force that this is a land whose main contemporary industry is the shooting down of wild creatures; not production of any kind but wholesale destruction. This state of things is not the fault of the Highlanders, but of the people who have bought their country and come to it chiefly to kill various forms of life. These intruders do not understand or regret the corrupting effect this must have on a race forced to accept this abnormal life as a vocation. Such a life is natural enough in nomad tribes who have never known the arts of civilisation; but in a civilised people it is so unnatural that it gives one a feeling of perversity.

The history of the clearances in the Highlands over a century ago is well known, so I shall not say much about them. Thousands of crofters' families were evicted and their farms turned into sheep-runs, on the principle that sheep were more profitable than human beings. Crofters who protested or even begged for a few days' delay had their houses burned over their heads. Many died of exposure and starvation: the more fortunate escaped overseas to a life of exile. The chief excuse for this barbarous treatment of a helpless people was first of all economic: to turn their crofts into sheep-runs seemed more productive, and so the enlightened opinion of the day held it to be desirable. Mrs Beecher Stowe, who could not have been an inhuman woman, was actually angry with the Highlanders for complaining of losing their homes.

Another excuse was that the crofters were lazy and improvident, and that their farms were so poor that they lived in a state of semi-starvation. That they were very near starvation some winters cannot be denied: but nevertheless they produced a race of men who were the admiration of Europe. There is a very interesting passage about them in Eckermann's conversations with Goethe. Talking about the people of Paris, Eckermann said that he had once seen in Napoleon's time an infantry battalion made up of Parisians, but all of them looked so small and thin that he could not conceive what they could have done in a battle. 'Wellington's Scottish Highlanders,' Goethe replied, 'were a different set of heroes, from all accounts.' Eckermann replied: 'I saw them in Brussels a year before the battle of Waterloo. They were men! All strong, nimble and free as if they had come straight from the hand of God. They carried their heads so freely and gaily and marched so lightly, swinging along with their bare knees, that you would have thought they had never heard of original sin or the primal curse.' That does not look like the picture of a lazy or starving race. Yet these men were brought up in the Highlands, many of them on those very crofts that excited the Duke of Sutherland's appalled consternation; and a great proportion of them returned after the Napoleonic wars, to be evicted along with their kindred. The sheep-runs which replaced their homes were not so profitable as the Duke of Sutherland had foreseen; so that even economically the change did not justify itself. In the long run it has proved disastrous in every way. The glens from which the crofters were driven a century ago still lie waste. I have passed through them. Their soil is very like that of the Orkney islands, and the Orkneys are now the most prosperous farming community in Scotland. A century ago they were probably as poor as the region that the Duke of Sutherland turned into a wilderness. The progress in the science of cultivation has since made them a happy and productive community, and it might quite well have done the same for the wide glens of Sutherlandshire.

(Edwin Muir, 'The Highlands', *Scottish Journey*, pp.195–98.)

8.20 'Will Highlands Become Like This—Or This? Warning to Scots to Save Themselves' (*Bulletin* October 1936)

Will the Scottish Highlands through time become the playground of the rich and Highlanders neglect their own industries to become a race of Swiss hotel-keepers?

The dangers of such a transformation were hinted at by Sir William Goodchild when speaking to Glasgow Publicity Club yesterday on 'The Paradox of the Highlands—National Asset and National Problem'.

The mass of the population of the Highlands, said Sir William, benefited but little from grouse moors, fishing, and other types of sport. The season was a short one.

It did seem to him doubtful whether the Highlands could, or should, look forward to an existence primarily based on a traffic of visitors, as though they should aim at becoming a race of Swiss hotel-keepers. Catering for tourists was a useful adjunct of national economy, but it was not an end in itself.

Sir William was emphatic that the Scottish Highlands had much more to offer than sport and pleasure. Among the resources of that vast area there was unlimited water power, peat, stone, and minerals, as well as kelp, tweed making, and other rural industries.

There was also timber. But afforestation, while most valuable as a means of ultimately enriching the country, unfortunately did not provide a large measure of employment.

'It has been well said that the best product of the Highlands is the Highlander', declared Sir William. 'Surely, then, it is only right that all methods should be considered for removing the obstacles which stand in the way of Highland progress before abandoning those people with their great traditions to dispersal and decay.'

The Economic Committee of the Scottish Development Council did not entertain any such defeatist view. He had no hesitation in saying that that Committee meant to get right down to the job. Colonel John Colville had given an assurance that the Committee had full support from the Government Departments, and had already benefited by their assistance in its preliminary work.

The Committee earnestly wished to enlist the assistance of all thinking Scots who had the interests of the Highlands at heart, and especially of all Scottish organisations which had that end in view.

It was premature to predict the outcome, said Sir William, and it would also be foolish to talk of success at the start, but no effort would be spared.

('Will Highlands Become Like This—Or This? Warning to Scots to Save Themselves', unsigned report, *Bulletin* 17 October 1936, p.9.)

8.21   Neil M. Gunn, from '"Gentlemen—The Tourist!"': The New Highland Toast' (*Scots Magazine* March 1937)

Tourist traffic is becoming a matter of importance in the affairs of most nations, and generally there is a department or semi-official body ready to hand out pamphlets to allure the traveller. Even the intricate matter of money exchange may to a slight extent be manipulated in favour of the visitor as anyone contemplating a tour in Germany should know. The underlying idea is the apparently simple one that money brought into a country and spent there adds to the wealth of that country.

Apparently simple—because this business of the wealth of a country is in reality extremely complex. I got my first lesson here when as a lad I read *Progress and Poverty*—and learned that in proportion as the wealth of a nation increased so did poverty amidst the workers of that nation. It seemed a mad paradox, but facts proved it true. With this phenomenon most of our modern economists have been concerned, whether of the orthodox kind that rule our banks or of the revolutionary kind like Douglas and Marx. The increase in recent years in unemployment in this country has been accompanied by an increase in the national wealth and by an incalculable increase in the potential national wealth. And the reason for this is simple enough: the perfecting of machinery by invention and scientific discovery at once increases production and displaces labour. The fact is now generally admitted, and the political fight is concentrated on the nature of the remedy required. We are not concerned here with the nature of the remedy, but we are concerned with the underlying facts.

For in the Highlands at the moment a fight is going on over the question of whether or not a limited liability company should be given statutory powers to use the waters of a certain area of a county for the production, by hydro-electricity, of a commercial commodity within that county. The inevitable questions of local rights or jealousies do not concern us here. What is pertinent to our purpose is that prominent opponents of this water-power scheme base their general opposition on two points: 1) they do not desire to see the water power of the Highlands used in creating private industry, and 2) they consider that the tourist traffic should solve all the economic ills of the Highlands.

Now this is a matter of grave, perhaps of crucial, importance to the Highlands at this particular moment in time. For the decline in every phase of Highland life is becoming alarming. It is easy to quote census figures showing a progressive depopulation of the Highland counties, but it is not so easy to grasp precisely what that implies by way of emigration of the youthful best, and the leaving behind of an ever-preponderating number of the aged and unfit. The old croft is no longer a self-supporting unit. The sea-fisheries are in desperate straits. There have been more economic tragedies on the Moray Firth coast in recent years than should last a whole sea-faring nation for a century. The distribution of national or public relief has been constantly increasing, until at last a problem has arisen, particularly in the Outer Isles, that the Department of Health is finding it difficult to solve: the problem of the 'manufacture' of work by men and women, so that, within the meaning of the Act, they may get thirty stamps affixed to a card and so qualify for the dole. The suggestion that one should 'blame' them for this is merely a piece of insufferable moralism. But there is the picture. All vital statistics of the Highlands point the same way. And not least those of insanity.

A correspondent in these pages last month referred to the increase in the inmates of the Inverness District Asylum, which serves the counties of Inverness, Ross, Sutherland, Moray and Nairn. Not only is the pauper lunacy rate for this area far higher than for any other part of Scotland, but it is more than twice as high as that for the congested industrial towns of Lanark, where conditions amongst the vast mass of the poor have been and are surely dreadful enough. The General Board of Control in its report on pauper lunacy in Scotland states: 'At the top of the list stands without a break the whole Highland and insular region of Scotland.'

And the Scottish Committee of the British Medical Association, in its Memorandum of Evidence, comments thus: 'One causative factor is depopulation, which has drained the Highlands and Islands of much good stock, leaving behind weaker and older people who are unable to stand up to the strain of daily life on the sea coast or among the hills. Nothing has been done by way of a really serious attempt to preserve the fine type of people, mentally and physically, which the Highlands and Islands have hitherto possessed and produced.'

But the decline of what we call our Highland heritage is even more marked on—if I may be allowed the phrase—the cultural side. We may have the finest folk music in the world, and, in the Gaelic, one of the finest folk literatures. Is any music being created today, or any literature of the slightest significance? And what about Gaelic itself? Dying steadily.

Now, painting this negative side is not pleasant. None of us likes evidence of 'gloom'. The Highlander, despite all writing to the contrary, is a cheerful fellow. But then so is the consumptive. In short, whether we are made uncomfortable or not, whether our pride is hurt or not, we must face up to facts so long as we are truly concerned about the future of our land. If we are no longer so concerned, then nothing matters but the self-induced warmth of make-believe until the feast or the famine is over and the bones left for the inevitable antiquary.

Taking the Highlands as we know them today, can the tourist industry in fact restore the economic life of the people, can it revive what have so long been its whole way of living, namely crofting and sea-fishing?

First, let us revert to our opening remarks. Tourists who come to this country do spend money. That money, let us say, increases national wealth. But how far does this tourist money as spent in the Highlands increase the wealth of the working Highlander? Could we, as in *Progress and Poverty*, have an increase of apparent wealth floating about the Highlands coincident with an actual impoverishment of the crofter and fisherman? In short: 1) how does the tourist traffic directly affect the general industries of crofting and sea-fishing, and 2) in how far are the hotels which tourists patronise dependent on the products of Highland labour?

Let me take a certain wide area of the Caithness coast which I visited a few weeks ago. Many townships are there; many scores of crofts. There is a harbour that in its heyday had over a hundred fishing boats sailing from it and now has five motor boats. There is the usual hotel, though not a sporting one. Most of the folk I know personally. The highway to John o' Groats passes through this region. I went into the matter closely. In this whole area there are two families that benefit, to a certain degree, from the tourist traffic: the family that runs the hotel and the family that runs the garage. No other families benefit. The tourist traffic has not given rise even to one small standing order for fish or for croft produce. That is the fact, and I could analyse it out into minute detail, if space permitted. I could show, for example, what precisely sea-fishing means in the way of capital costs, gear, catches, contracts, and markets, and how tourism cannot even begin to affect it. All through the winter months these boats have been seine-netting for flat fish or haddock—one of their main seasons, when tourists are as remote as swallows. I was there in January, when the recent gales were at their height. For two days and nights the fishermen had not been to bed; they had been standing by their boats, waiting to do what they could, should the next sea tear all the moorings before it. The condition of the inadequate harbour was an unspeakable disgrace to the authorities concerned. And now in the mad seas the old breakwater was going, and already wooden piles could be seen heeling over in the white surf of the bay.

While waiting there, word came to us of a boat having been smashed in a neighbouring creek. Almost certainly it would not have been insured, as insurance rates are prohibitively high to these men struggling so magnificently to make simple ends meet. The scene was unforgettable. I remember leaving the harbour once in the half-dark, and, on coming to the main road, the wind whistling in my ears, having to leap for the ditch as a magnificent saloon car swept by, bearing the motto: 'Monte Carlo Rally'. It may have been a moment for ironic comment. It is sufficient for my purpose to suggest that the incident adequately illustrates the effect of Highland tourist traffic on the deep-sea fishing of our coastal creeks and ports.

And as with that Caithness region so with nearly all the rest of the truly crofting and sea-fishing areas of the Highlands. Individual houses here and there may be encountered along the great main roads where a night's accommodation can be obtained, and in a few special areas, as in Badenoch, there is a regular house-letting business, run for the most part by women who otherwise have only slender means of support. But I am concerned here with the true crofting and fishing areas, with the crofter and fisherman who have their own homes and their own families, and my experience satisfies me that the three months' tourist season does not affect one per cent of them to the value of one pound sterling.

Now for the hotels, particularly as we know them in the West, complete with sporting privileges. I suggest that the food for these hotels is purchased not from local shops or other local source, but direct from the great city stores, wholesale or retail. In fact, in view of the table that has to be provided for high-paying guests, this must be done. The hotel proprietor has no option. Such fresh foods as milk or vegetables he generally takes care to provide from his own byre or garden. And as for sea fish, he keeps in touch with the nearest town or provides it himself. Last year a friend of mine, staying in a West Coast hotel, went for a day's sea-fishing in the hotel boat and helped to swell a very considerable catch. For this privilege he was charged thirty shillings.

These hotels, in the season, give employment to some maid servants and gillies, and wages got in this way over a month or two may affect the economy of a few fishing or crofting families. But I suggest the effect over all is negligible. Most of the money drawn at the hotels goes to pay Southern stores, and the profit retained by the hotel-keeper finds profitable investment neither in crofting nor in sea-fishing. Tourist traffic, then, as we know it at present, offers no solution of the land and sea problems of the Highlands. Nor can I see how it ever will. [. . .]

Yes, it is easy to dream dreams and to draw up schemes; to see the harbours rebuilt, new boats purchased, cheap transport, co-operative marketing, Government action against trawlers and Government co-ordination of the whole industry, with control of seine and ring netting and care for spawning grounds. It is easy to launch out, in imagination, on increased afforestation, local industries such as fish-freezing, fish-canning, cloth-weaving, kelp-burning, eggs and honey; to assist crofting, with all the power supplied by small hydro-electric plants—on the basis, say, of one plant to one glen, so that there would be no more jealousies! I myself have been turning over that dream for a generation. And at least it is a decent dream that might well perpetuate and make creative once more the Highland spirit.

But alas! I see no slightest sign of such a dream ever being realised. The Government at Westminster cares nothing for it; is overwhelmed in any case by economic distress on a vaster scale elsewhere. And as for our local authorities—such a conception of things does not appear to have come even within their dreams. The best the Inverness Town Council could suggest the other night at a public meeting was tourism as the solution of all our ills, and the Highlands no longer as a brain or a heart or a creative force but as 'a lung'—a lung freed from all taint of industrialism, so that folk from south of the Highland line could clamber into its emptiness to breathe.

Well, it is not enough. In face of the realities of the situation I find it impossible, for example, to blame the Lochaber men who want work and believe they can find it in the proposed factories of the Caledonian power scheme. This may be remote from the ideal—but who in authority is going to bother about the ideal in their lifetime? If I were an unemployed man in the Highlands, a broken fisherman, a three-months gillie, I should prefer to work in a factory in the Highlands rather than one in Lanarkshire, South Wales or the Midlands of England. The folk who object to the scheme because it is to be run for private profit would not impress me, because each one of them runs his own business for private profit. Even their objection on the basis that it would destroy the tourist traffic I should see to be specious, inasmuch as countries like Switzerland, Norway, and Sweden, with hydro-electric works all over them, have an immense tourist traffic; and even in the Irish Free State, since the erection of the Shannon scheme (in the most lovely part of the country), with its pylons marching across the breadth of Ireland, tourism has increased enormously.

But tourism one way or the other wouldn't matter. I should demand a man's work, and I should demand it in my own land. I might hate the forces, national or local, that had so misgoverned and impoverished the Highlands as to compel me away from my fishing and crofting and into a factory. But better a factory than starvation; better a self-respecting worker in my own trade union than a half-sycophant depending on the whims of a passing tourist. For I should know that so long as Highlandmen are employed in the Highlands, so long as they constitute the mass of the workers there, then there is hope for the Highlands. In virile life, however employed, there is a future, because free men will not bear indefinitely the evils of our present industrial system. But when this virile life is absent, then not all the deserving old women attending to the tourists of the world and prattling of the scenic beauty of empty glens can save the ancient heritage from decay and death.

(Neil M. Gunn, ' "Gentlemen—The Tourist!": The New Highland Toast', *Scots Magazine* 26:6 March 1937, pp.410–15.)

8.22 Neil M. Gunn, from 'The Ferry of the Dead' (*Scots Magazine* October 1937)

'In the main the Celts, after advancing to the West of Europe, retreated in the same direction. If we look carefully at the map we shall see that the districts where they are found are refuges. The Celts came to a stop there at the sea, clinging to the rocks. Beyond the sea was their next world. They stayed on the shore, waiting for the ferry, like the dead in Procopios. . . . What now remains of the Celts, in the west of their ancient dominion, was driven there and confined there by other peoples arriving or growing up behind them. This general movement of expansion and contraction taking the Celts to the west and confining them there may be called the law of Celticism. It must be studied as a capital fact of European history.' [Henri Hubert, *The Rise of the Celts*]

Is it possible, by a careful analysis of the existing conditions of the Gaelic people of Scotland, to dispute the continuing validity of this 'law of Celticism'? Can we suggest that the long historical process, like a ninth wave, has reached not an ultimate shore where it breaks and dies but an ultimate rock of endurance which, taking the force of the wave, sends it backward?

It might be pleasant to think that we could, not merely for the sake of the Highlands but for what might be added to the diminishing goodwill of the world. For if we take such a manifestation of the Celtic spirit as our annual Mod we find there social and spiritual values that could be of a deep and regenerating potency. It is essentially a festival of the folk and calls into being the true communal virtues: hospitality, gaiety, singing, colour, dancing, in an atmosphere of goodfellowship where, for the time being, worldliness with its greedy gains and losses is forgotten. And it is founded on a historical reality: the ceilidh-house, the house where folk met and discussed the affairs of the day, of yesterday, and of legendary times, and illustrated their friendliness by epic or epigram, song or weird story, for the common interest or laughter: a clearing-house not of banknotes or cheques but of those imponderable debts of the spirit that humanity still owes itself but is forgetting how to pay.

Of the reality of this Celtic attitude to life there can be little doubt. What actuates the Mod is the ancient profound spirit of fellowship, of communism, a desire for human warmth and entertainment and instruction in a circle of social equality. So much was this the case in the past that the privacy of the home never became 'the castle' (that hangover of feudalism in whose irony the common Englishman is smothered). Privacy was all the more delicately respected and misfortune assisted because the front door of hospitality was never locked. It was all a way of living, of life. And the Mod is a festival we have based on it.

And so we arrive at the point where we have to ask ourselves a few questions and endeavour to answer them honestly.

Is this way of life still a reality? Is the old order of crofting and sea-fishing still fruitfully continuing or is it 'clinging to the rocks . . . waiting for the ferry . . .'? Has it lost its self-sufficiency, its independence, and how now does it diminishingly continue to survive, on what substance of charities or doles? What sort of spirit actuates it? How fares it with its language?

Is the law of Celticism working here with a cumulative inevitability, a final swiftness, visible to us almost from month to month? And if it is, what in essence is this Mod? A pure manifestation of nostalgia? A bath of sentimentality? Something of which the sensitive Gael, who believes he knows the true native conditions, may be a little shy and ashamed when he has not the toughness to enjoy the merry-go-round while it lasts and then forget it?

For many recent weeks I have been wandering around the West and North. For a generation I have known the conditions of life in this region fairly intimately and have been able therefore, perhaps, to assess the value of official statistics giving the figures of decline in population and in Gaelic-speaking, coincident with an increase in lunacy and public or State assist-ance. One can, for example, discuss with a schoolmaster, minister, priest, or other well-informed resident, the chances of survival of a specific crofting area or fishing creek and arrive at fairly sound conclusions. Where a township is inhabited by the old, by bachelors or spinsters; and the young who, in the ordinary course of nature, should have inherited the crofts and reared families have departed for the cities or emigrated; then, in the absence of claimants for the land from outside crofting areas, what is going to happen is quite clear; for the very same processes have already been at work in other townships, where the land has gone out of cultivation and become part of a sheep farm or of a sporting estate (for I discovered a process going on of large estates in the West getting broken up into small estates, whose owners, wanting their land for sporting purposes, get rid of the sheep-farmer, who, as a tenant with none of the rights of the crofter, must on due notice sell out and go).

Again in the fishing creeks one finds a similar sort of process going on. In these columns last month I mentioned some of my experiences with fishermen or those interested in sea-fishing as an industry. Here the matter is directly affected by outside agencies like trawlers and foreign markets, and there is little good in blinking the fact that for the most part the western Gael is making no effort to hold his own at sea. Trawler-men think of him not as a sea-fighter or even a land-fighter but as a mouth-fighter. 'Another Highland grouse.' 'He wants money for nothing.' They are ironic, sarcastic. [. . .]

While writing this, one particular island in the far West came to mind. It is a small island, yet a generation ago had no less than thirty fishing boats sailing from its bay. Today it has none. Now the population has not declined—an unusual fact, I recognise. Fishing for and dry-curing ling was the important or money part of its sea industry, though, of course, herring and most kinds of white fish were caught in their season. Fish and oil from fish livers were part of a diet, simple, perhaps, but at least now known to contain all the essential vitamins.

Well, there is an old seaman in that bay who has a good boat and would like to start fishing again. With him will die the knowledge of where the fishing banks lie and he would like to pass on that knowledge before it is too late. A man from that district, who is making money in a professional career elsewhere, offered as a gift to fit out the boat with everything necessary in the way of gear if the old man could get a crew of young fellows to go to sea with him. And the old man tried—but without success. Why? Because the young fellows were on the dole or qualifying for the dole and would not lose the certainties thereof for the uncertainties of the sea. They would not even 'give it a trial' lest their neighbours should 'tell on them'. Yet there is a home market for white fish in that particular part of the world that never existed in the old days.

I have satisfied myself that this is not only a true story but that it is more or less typical. It is now a saying that the Islesman knows the Unemployment Insurance Acts better than his Bible, and there is a joke in Lewis to the effect that a man of a certain district will not go to a funeral unless he gets an insurance stamp. The number of cases that have to be officially investigated of what is called 'faked employment' is beginning to present a real problem to the Departments concerned. This is now so widely known that commercial travellers out West while away an evening hour in relating the more ingenious methods of gathering insurance stamps as a new kind of smoke-room story.

It would be easy to give in detail typical instances of employment deliberately constructed to pass the test of being insurable work within the meaning of the Unemployment Insurance Acts, but that would take up too much space; and, in any case, I am more anxious to consider criticism, aired in the press, which has made use of terms like moral degradation. For the kernel of the trouble lies in this, that these Acts were designed for industrial areas and not for the Highlands and Islands, and that accordingly the Highlander finds himself naturally impelled so to reconstruct his circumstances as to bring them within the scope of the Acts. Occasional employment outside the croft has always been a feature of life either for himself or one or more of his family. Take the case of a man who has had several months of continuous or intermittent road work and at the end of it finds himself with twenty stamps on his card. These stamps represent lost money to him—unless he can within two years increase their total to thirty, when he will be in a position to claim unemployment insurance benefit and, in due course, the benefits that follow on. (And public assistance is now losing the old dreadful stigma of parish pauperdom.) In that man's position I naturally should make every effort to get my thirty stamps. If therefore, a few of us could arrange a scheme of work to meet our needs and in the process enter into such contracts of service with one another as would satisfy the Acts, what official or other person has the right to inquire into the necessity for the work or raise any moral issue whatsoever? Because a man is an Old Age Pensioner, that does not preclude his becoming an employer of labour. [. . .]

Now I do not wish all this to be understood as a complete picture of life in Scottish Gaeldom. Far from it. There are folk who work hard and never draw the dole, just as there are crofting areas vastly overcrowded, while the ancient ways of courtesy and independence are still to be found. But the decline in crofting and sea-fishing and the increase in State aid are facts that must be realised, for they indicate a change in every feature of the social scene, from the use of tinned foods to cheap finery, that is surely taking place and that will presently make the Mod about as meaningful and pleasant a piece of pageantry as dancing round the maypole. [. . .]

But even this business of direct State aid must in time decrease, as the old die, the population continues to decline, and even the opportunities for constructing employment within the meaning of the Acts grow inevitably fewer. In a recent annual report, the Medical Officer of Health for the whole county of Ross stated that the population was becoming increasingly old and that the age distribution had left the normal. The death rate was over 16 per 1,000, the birth rate 14, while there had been an increase of 2 per cent in those over 65 in the last census period.

So it would seem that in fact M. Hubert's 'law of Celticism' is duly working itself out. The busiest ferry on the West is the ferry to Iona and those who use it go to commune with the dead.

That is the broad aspect of things as I see them. But we are masters of our destiny to some degree. It is bad legislation to apply Acts designed for one sphere of social activity to quite another kind of sphere. Trawling can be stopped. Fishing could be made lucrative for the fishermen. Proper transport, co-operative marketing, controlled prices, and other constructive features discussed by us all *ad nauseam*, are not beyond human realisation. But I am not concerned with the constructive aspect for the moment. I am concerned only with the realities, with trying to see clearly and objectively things as they are. And when I turn to the Mod and try to see what it is doing for Gaeldom, I find it difficult to be impressed. Despite its concern with the things of the spirit, it is essentially neither a creative body nor an inspiration towards creation. At the core, it stands for the remembrance of things past, and does not envisage a future in terms of that past. Its most notable leaders or publicists deprecate action of any kind.

I remember a talk with one of them who had made a magnificent rhetorical speech on the glories of Gaeldom to an admiring audience. But when, later, we tried to get him, in face of the material realities, to formulate some scheme of action whereby the glories might continue to be fed and housed, and thereby naturally perpetuated in the future, his reply was that he would have nothing to do with politics. The Mod must remain pure and undefiled. Actually he feared realist action. He was too pleased with things as they are. For in this show he was a figure. His personal prestige was warmed by his own rhetoric, and, for the rest, his sons had got the right English accent. Someone mentioned what Ireland had done. He walked away. Ireland, indeed. We, who had made the British Empire!

And that is why no real Gael, in his heart, believes in the Mod. And when he is a decent man he is troubled, because here in truth are precious things of the spirit, and he knows that the life that bred them is dying.

(Neil M. Gunn, 'The Ferry of the Dead', *Scots Magazine* 28:1 October 1937, pp.13–20.)

8.23 Hugh MacDiarmid, from *The Islands of Scotland* (1939)

The Muse with whom I am concerned in this book—since it deals not only with the Hebrides but with the Scottish Islands as a whole—is not Deirdre, but (one of the greatest, yet least-known, women in Scottish History) Audh, the 'deep-minded', wife and mother of chieftains, Gaelic and Scandinavian, who, at the end, left the Hebrides and voyaged, via the Faroes, where she landed to see some of her grandchildren, to Iceland, where she died and lies buried in one of its cold *jokulls*.

These stray facts must not be allowed to obscure the picture as a whole, however. If Scotland is on the march, she has a very long way to go; as Mr Malcolm MacDonald recently said, it must not be imagined that under even the most sympathetic Government the Highlands and Islands could be rehabilitated except as the final outcome of a long-term policy, carrying us perhaps into the beginning of next century. And whatever the promising beginnings may be that are now being made in this direction or that, it is essential to remember that the islands are (as Mr David Keir recently showed with a devastating marshalling of really incredible facts and figures in his pamphlet, *Desolation of the Highlands*) part of a 'distressed area'—and actually the most distressed of them all. At Stornoway, the chief town in the Western Isles division of Ross and Cromarty, 65.4 per cent of the insured population were unemployed on 14th March 1938, as compared with 56.4 per cent for the whole of Ross and Cromarty, 25.5 for Glamorgan, 1.5 for Cumberland, 21.3 for Monmouth, 18.6 for Durham. In Lerwick in the Shetland Isles at the same date the percentage of insured persons unemployed was 38.4—a percentage exceeded only by Maryport in Cumberland, Merthyr-Tydfil in Glamorgan, and Blaina in Monmouthshire (and, of course, as just mentioned, Stornoway). Again, 'in Ardnamurchan, Argyll, it is estimated that about 35 per cent of the district has been rendered useless by bracken, but that is only one example. Thousands and thousands of acres of fertile sheep land have been rendered useless on this account in most Highland districts, and the curse is spreading steadily year by year. Bracken-clearing is a form of occupation which can readily be allied with other work, with afforestation, for example. But it needs a large-scale attack.' Since 1891, the seven Highland counties have lost 70,000 of their population—a frightening decline for an area with an aggregate population now of less than 700,000. The Shetlands had 28,711 in 1891 and only 21,410 in 1931. Even the relatively flourishing and progressive Orkneys declined from 30,453 in 1891 to 22,075 in 1931. Decrease percentages of 8.4 in Orkney and 16.1 in Shetland were recorded at the 1931 census.

During the past twenty years there has been an ever-increasing stream of books and pamphlets on the subject of the present position and prospects of Scotland. A good select bibliography of these would list upwards of fifty separate publications. [. . .] These facts and figures involve the area with which this book is concerned, the Islands of Scotland, in the most crucial way. But I do not propose to traverse the ground already covered by these publications. I would rather have it said that, observant, vigorous, sympathetic and knowledgeable as my chapters may be, these qualities are yet not the core of my book, which is rather a certain philosophical insight into the real as distinguished from the obvious dangers of our epoch—and the chiefest of these (so far as Scotland is concerned—and the same thing is true of almost all other civilised countries) is the shameful, the catastrophic, neglect by Scotsmen of their own country. We have come to regard the country as a site for development or a recreation for the towns, and against this poison I protest with all my might. My passion is for the reunion between Scotland and Scotsmen, and that can only be achieved by the restoration of the land not as a series of beauty spots but as a soil for growing things. Above all, whatever the limitations and difficulties of Scotland may be, it is necessary to insist that our great trouble (and the source of all our other troubles) is not on the material but on the spiritual plane, and that unless our idea of Scotland is deeply and truly enough laid, superficial efforts after rehabilitation can only register minor and relatively negligible successes. In Scotland—mainland and islands alike—it is this king-pin that is lacking and must be replaced.

(Hugh MacDiarmid, 'Introductory', *The Islands of Scotland* London: Batsford, 1939, pp.41–44.)

9

Competing Ideologies

9.1 C.M. Grieve, from 'Programme for a Scottish Fascism' (*Scottish Nation* June 1923)

Scotland is not Italy and the political, social, and industrial traditions and conditions of the people of Scotland, and their psychology differ entirely from those of Italy. Nevertheless there is need for a Scottish Fascism just as there was need for an Italian Fascism—and the first plank in the programme of the former would be precisely the same as the first plank in the latter— 'Scotland First' for us as it was 'Italy First' for them. There is no sense in Scottish constituencies sending members to the Parliament at Westminster simply to be outvoted on all matters that vitally affect Scotland by English majorities. There is no sense in a majority of Scottish town councils period-ically passing resolutions in favour of Home Rule for Scotland—and tamely submitting to the Prime Minister's refusal to consider the question, or as in former Parliaments, to the defeat of successive Scottish Home Rule Bills by English majorities. There is a grotesque anomaly in the great Scottish Churches deploring the menace to Scottish national traditions—and not taking such effective measures as their memberships, which comprise the majority of the Scottish people, would readily enable them to do to conserve them. In Housing—in Education—in Agriculture there is the same tale of ignominy and powerlessness. Can efforts to render effective the declared desires of the great Scottish Churches—to grant the 'hardy annual' demands of the majority of Scottish Local Authorities, the Scottish Trades Union Congress, and other bodies—to rescue the chosen representatives of the Scottish people from the intolerable predicament which robs them of power—be dismissed as extremist? If so, extremism is a quality of which Scotland stands desperately in need. Mention has been made of only a few of the tendencies in modern Scottish life afflicted with indirection through related causes. Nothing has been said yet of the rapid transformation of the racial basis of the Scottish population—nothing of the alienation of the people from immense areas of the country, capable in the past of supporting a considerable population, and capable in the future of supporting a very large agricultural population, especially if modern intensive methods of cultivation are used (apart altogether from the question of exploiting the possibilities of the areas in question as mountain holiday centres)—nothing of the assimilation of Scots Law to English—nothing of the subordination of Scottish commercial and industrial interests to those of England—and, most important of all, nothing of the moral and spiritual loss involved in the denationalisation of Scotland and the destruction of Scottish national culture. In all these directions the same need manifests itself—the need for the development of a new national *will*; the need to overcome in some way or another our present inability to make our representations effective, to get wrongs righted, to devise a reconstructive national policy. [. . .]

It is of special significance that the saltatory development of the Labour movement in Scotland, the intensification of Scottish Home Rule propaganda, the awakening of the Churches to a new realisation of the moral and spiritual values of Scottish nationality and the need to conserve them, and the recreation of distinct tendencies in Scottish Literature when almost on the verge of complete submersion in English literature, should synchronise. That mere fact of simultaneity shows them as aspects of one and the same force in Scottish life. The danger is that they should not develop proportionately to each other. The Labour movement, owing to the exaggerated importance attached to mere politics, and also to the fact that it has a double appeal—spiritual and material—is conscious of its peril. The lessons of Russia (and by that I do not mean that the Soviet System has failed) are being learned. In Scotland less than in any other country in Europe is Labour contemptuous of culture or inclined to disregard the spiritual factors which alone can consummate its programme. In this connection it is particularly noteworthy that already Labour MPs who were formerly all out for economic change and 'Internationalists' of the old type, have become passionately nationalistic with benefit to their internationalist outlook. The Scottish Labour Movement is already modifying its Socialism as Mussolini modified his. It has got out of the rut of mere theory; and takes service as the touchstone of social values. As soon as it ceases to work for 'Socialism' and makes its goal 'Scottish Socialism', it will have purged itself of the elements which make for false progress and be within measurable distance of complete triumph.

Just as Fascism in Italy must incline to the Left, as has been pointed out, just because nationalism is opposed to capitalist materialism, so already in Scottish literature and religion tendencies are manifesting themselves to meet Labour half-way and make common cause in the interest of 'Scotland First'. [. . .]

The entire Fascist programme can be readapted to Scottish national purposes and is (whether it be called Fascist or pass under any other name) *the only thing that will preserve our distinctive national culture.* Mere Parliamentary devolution is useless. Every individual and every association interested in anything Scottish can only ensure the success of the particular

aim in view by joining with every other individual and every other association interested in anything Scottish.

(C.M. Grieve, 'Programme for a Scottish Fascism', *Scottish Nation* 7, 19 June
1923, p.10.)

9.2 Edwin Muir, from letter to Mr and Mrs Thorburn (December 1923)

> bei Frau Antner
> 7 Hahngasse
> Wien IX
> Austria
> 20 December 1923

Dear Lizzie and George, [. . .]

How are you all getting on? Write and let us know whenever you have
time. The Scottish election results, combined with the recent temper of the
Glasgow group in Parliament, gave us quite a thrill. Things have changed
enormously since I lived in Glasgow, only a little over five year ago (It
seems far longer). The Scottish members should make a move for Scottish
Home Rule, and then they would have the field to themselves. Do you
know if that idea has taken hold of the Socialist parties in Glasgow or not?
There's a man C.M. Grieve, a Socialist, running the idea in *The Scottish
Nation*—a very bad paper which I sometimes see. When I see things
stirring up so much I would like to be back to take a hand in the work. We
will certainly (D.V.) be back in Scotland to stay next summer. [. . .]

Good luck to you all. Perhaps in a few years Scotland will be a Socialist
republic. I shouldn't wonder: things are moving so fast. [. . .]

Yours affectionately,
Edwin

(Edwin Muir, letter from Vienna to Lizzie and George Thorburn, 20 December 1923;
reprinted from *Selected Letters of Edwin Muir*, pp.29–30.)

9.3 *Scots Observer*: inaugural editorial and statement of purpose (October 1926)

OUR PURPOSE

The *Scots Observer* is the fruition of an idea which is nearly forty years
old. Two generations of Church people in Scotland have discussed proposals for a weekly newspaper which should express the collective aims

and ideals of the Scottish Protestant Churches and reflect their main activities. The need for such a paper is indicated by what has been done elsewhere. The Church of England is represented by several important weeklies, the Methodists by two, the Baptists and the Ulster Presbyterians by one each, the Roman Catholic Church in Britain by more than forty, including local editions; while the Christian Scientists have a full-sized daily paper. Why the Scottish Churches should have lagged so long behind in this respect is a purely historical question which need not be discussed. Our concern is with the present and the future. It is sufficient for our purpose that the need has now been met.

That the need is widely felt is proved by the thousands of congratulatory letters which we have received. That it is greater to-day than ever before is shown by the purport of many of these letters. During the last twenty years, and particularly since the war, there has been a progressive intensification of industrial strife and class antagonism. Simultaneously there has been, at least in urban centres, a perceptible decline of public interest in religion as represented by the Churches.

That these two tendencies are co-related is beyond question. The most dangerous of social maladies has strengthened while, and because, the only possible antidote to it has weakened. If such a process were to go on unchecked, the logical result would be a social convulsion, followed by a regime which might be Fascist or Communist, but in any case would be autocratic and materialist. Political freedom is a product of Christianity. British Constitutionalism implies all that is connoted by the Church. It implies spiritual sanctions and the operation of the Golden Rule.

Experiential religion goes ahead of institutional, but it is only through the Church that it becomes socially effective. And the Church must go definitely ahead of the State and the average citizen. Its leadership is tacitly acknowledged by the secular Press, which, while at its best it is an indispensable and an active agent for good, does not claim to be much more than the mirror of the age and the exponent of conventional morality. The Church must lead or perish.

To strengthen and make socially manifest the spiritual leadership of the Scottish Protestant Churches is the main purpose of the *Scots Observer*. It is the purpose which will govern our presentation of Church and general news, our selection of articles, and our provision of wholesome entertainment for all sorts and conditions of Scots folk. But it is a purpose which involves acknowledgement of a higher leadership than that of any ecclesiastical institution.

The *Scots Observer* does not trench upon the functions of the recognised organs of the respective Churches. It is not the mouthpiece of the Churches, but their journalistic comrade-in-arms, owning no sway but that of their Founder. Bound to no syndicate or party, but owned by a multitude of members of all the Churches it represents, it is free to measure all things by the standard of the New Testament. Such a paper, under such a directorate as ours, is a unique and a priceless possession for any country, and we appeal to Scots people everywhere to become co-partners in this enterprise.

The heaviest obligations are those of absolute freedom. We shall use our liberty with careful discretion, but we will not hesitate to break windows if it is necessary to let in more air, and we shall be as frank as language will allow in expressing our sense of the bearing of Christianity upon the vital social problems of the day. And all we do shall be dedicated *ad majorem Dei gloriam*, and to the spiritual and temporal welfare of the Scottish Nation.

(Inaugural editorial [William Power], *Scots Observer: A Weekly Journal of Religious & National Interest* 2 October 1926, p.1.)

9.4 C.M. Grieve, from *Albyn or Scotland and the Future* (1927)

The forces that are moving towards a Scottish Renaissance are complex and at first sight incompatible. The movement began as a purely literary movement some seven or eight years ago, but of necessity speedily acquired political and then religious bearings. It is now manifesting itself in every sphere of national arts and affairs, and is at once radical and conservative, revolutionary and reactionary. Engaged in traversing the accepted conceptions of all things Scottish, it is in keeping that it should not have set the heather on fire. But it has made far greater headway than what has appeared about it in the English or Anglo-Scottish Press would indicate. For obvious reasons these are concerned to minimize or ignore its manifestations. The movement has had various more or less short-lived organs of its own; it will undoubtedly acquire others. But in the meantime it lacks any and its progress is correspondingly obscure but none the less real. Its inception synchronized with the end of the War, and in retrospect it will be seen to have had a genesis in kin with other post-war phenomena of recrudescent nationalism all over Europe, and to have shared to the full in the wave of Catholic revivalism which accompanied them. It took the full force of the War to jolt an adequate majority of the Scottish people out of their old mental, moral and material ruts; and the full force of post-war reaction is gradually bringing them to an effective realization of their changed conditions.

At first blush there may seem little enough connection between such phenomena as the Clyde Rebels, the Scottish Home Rule Movement, the 'Irish Invasion' of Scotland, and the campaign to resuscitate Braid Scots and Gaelic. But, adopting the Spenglerian philosophy, the Renaissance movement regards itself as an effort in every aspect of the national life to supplant the elements at present predominant by the other elements they have suppressed, and thus reverse the existing order. Or, in terms of psychology, the effort is to relieve the inhibitions imposed by English and Anglo-Scottish influences and to inhibit in turn those factors of Scottish psychology which have rendered it amenable to the post-Union state of affairs. In closer consideration, then, it will be seen that the four phenomena mentioned correspond to pre-Union conditions in Scotland. The first takes us back beyond the demoralizing concept of the Canny Scot, which has conduced so largely to Scottish denationalization, and re-establishes a psychology in keeping with the independent traditions of the country. The majority of the Scottish Labour members returned to the House of Commons went there as 'internationalists'. They were very lukewarm Home Rulers. A short experience of Westminster transformed them completely. They found the vote of the majority of the Scottish electorate systematically vetoed by an English majority, and saw how Scottish affairs were treated in the House of Commons. This saltatory emergence of a Socialist preponderance in the Scottish representation is a post-war product, and is interpreted from the Renaissance point of view as a significant reassertion of the old Scottish radicalism and republicanism. [. . .]

The Scottish Home Rule movement is re-orienting itself along realist lines, and has ceased to be mainly sentimental. For the first time it is looking before as well as after. It is concerning itself less with the past and more and more with the present and the future, and its membership is growing in direct ratio to its increased practicality.

(C.M. Grieve, *Albyn or Scotland and the Future* London: Kegan Paul, 1927, pp.5–8.)

9.5 Non-political 'Manifestos' (1927 and 1936)

a) International P.E.N. Scottish Centre (1927)

The P.E.N. Charter, to which all members of Scottish P.E.N. subscribe, is based on resolutions passed at its International Congresses and may be summarised as follows:

P.E.N. affirms that:

1. Literature, national though it be in origin, knows no frontiers, and should remain common currency between nations in spite of political or international upheavals.

2. In all circumstances, and particularly in time of war, works of art, the patrimony of humanity at large, should be left untouched by national or political passion.

3. Members of P.E.N. should at all times use what influence they have in favour of good understanding and mutual respect between nations; they pledge themselves to do their utmost to dispel race, class and national

hatreds, and to champion the ideal of one humanity living in peace in one world.

4. P.E.N. stands for the principle of unhampered transmission of thought within each nation and between all nations, and members pledge themselves to oppose any form of suppression of freedom of expression in the country and community to which they belong, as well as throughout the world wherever this is possible. P.E.N. declares for a free press and opposes arbitrary censorship in time of peace. It believes that the necessary advance of the world towards a more highly organised political and economic order renders a free criticism of governments, administrations and institutions imperative. And since freedom implies voluntary restraint, members pledge themselves to oppose such evils of a free press as mendacious publication, deliberate falsehood and distortion of facts for political and personal ends.

b) The Saltire Society (1936)

The Saltire Society has been formed with the object of restoring Scotland to its proper position as a cultural unit.

Scotland in the past has possessed a national culture. As late as the 18th century Edinburgh was a centre of intellectual life famed throughout Europe. The Saltire Society, however, looks back to the past only to move forward. Its main concern is with the future, and it envisages a new Scotland with a vigorous intellectual life, drawing on the past for inspiration to new advances in art, learning and the graces of life.

The nation that forgets its past is dead. The Saltire Society, therefore, seeks to revive the memory of famous men and to make Scots conscious of their heritage. It is to the break with tradition caused mainly by the Industrial Era which smote Scotland with especial violence, that one must ascribe the meagreness of her social amenities; the gloom of her cities; the decay of scholarship; the lack of imagination and invention that characterise Scotland today.

That section of the Constitution which speaks of preserving and developing the Scottish tradition in the arts is of paramount importance, and the encouragement of the best in all the arts will play a prominent part in the activities of the Society.

Since the sense of the past is mainly developed at school through the teaching of history, the Saltire Society is deeply interested in the history taught in schools. It will endeavour to promote the teaching of Scottish history as a serious study for young and old and not, as it often is at present a mere fairy tale for small children.

The Saltire Society is entirely non political. It might well take as its motto the words of the 'very wise man' quoted by Andrew Fletcher of

Saltoun. 'If a man were permitted to make the ballads, he need not care who should make the laws.'

(Charter of International P.E.N., formed 1921, adopted by the Scottish Centre of P.E.N. when formed in 1927, and included in official publications of the Centre. Statement of intent on formation of the Saltire Society in 1936, published in first Annual Report of the Society and reprinted in George Bruce, *The First Fifty Years of the Saltire Society* Edinburgh: Saltire Society, 1986, pp.16–17.)

9.6 Lewis Spence, from 'The National Party of Scotland' (*Edinburgh Review* July 1928)

The National Party of Scotland, which will function through parliamentary representatives at Westminster, as well as by means of propagandist effort on Scottish soil, has emerged from the deliberations of representative leaders belonging to the four existing Scottish nationalist bodies. Long experience making it apparent that none of the existing political parties can be relied upon to place a measure for Scottish self-government in the forefront of their programmes, far less upon the Statute Book, it has been resolved, after the most careful deliberation, to depart from the policy of depending for support on these, and to establish a separate Scottish nationalist party, distinct in aim and effort, which will endeavour to secure the suffrages of Scottish electors in support of a policy of autonomy for Scotland, based on her peculiar needs as a separate community and aiming at the reconstruction of Scottish national life. [. . .]

The main objects of the party, as expressed in its draft constitution, are 'self-government for Scotland with independent national status within the British group of nations, together with the reconstruction of Scottish national life'. This policy will be maintained by representation in the House of Commons and in the local authorities throughout Scotland, as well as by disseminating propaganda over the length and breadth of the country. A panel of approved parliamentary candidates is to be drawn up, who will be required to sign a declaration that if elected they will support the party on all questions, and will retire from the House of Commons if called upon to do so at any time by the governing body. It is believed that Nationalist members sitting at Westminster could safeguard the interests of Scotland there more satisfactorily than Scottish members belonging to the now existing parties, whose hands are too often tied by sectional and partisan interests.

The promoters of the party have been inspired to its establishment by a keen consciousness of the ruinous conditions which at present obtain in Scotland through her neglect under the existing régime and the existence of a policy of gradual and increasing encroachment upon her institutions. [. . .]

The Liberal and Labour parties have, indeed, disappointed Scottish nationalist expectations time and again. An extraordinary notion appears to prevail that the National party of Scotland is in some manner associated with the extreme left wing of Labour. As a matter of fact, if Labour has not proved absolutely hostile to the inception of the party, the Labour delegates to several of the unifying bodies have intimated their inability to join the National party, which, so far as having any Labourist or Liberal affiliations, stands completely alone and will permit no political association between its officials and other partisan institutions. Scottish Liberals have recently expressed themselves officially as fundamentally sharing 'the considered views of the English Liberals', and Scottish Labourists adhere too strongly to the English caucus to take up an independent attitude on Scottish affairs, though it is noteworthy that on the inception of the National party a somewhat panicky delegation of the Scottish members approached Mr Ramsay Macdonald with a request that the question of 'Home Rule' might receive greater consideration from the Labour party than heretofore—a request which met with no definite or satisfactory response.

So far, officials have not been appointed, as the first conference of the party will not take place until September, but already a number of prominent Scottish Nationalists have identified themselves with the party and are acting on its provisional council. These include Mr R.B. Cunninghame Graham, the well-known literateur and authority on Latin-America, Mr Compton Mackenzie, the novelist, who is taking a prominent part in the formation of the party, Mr R.E. Muirhead, Secretary of the Scottish Home Rule Association, who has been adopted as Nationalist candidate for West Renfrewshire, the Hon. R. Erskine of Marr, widely known as a Scottish publicist and Celtic enthusiast, Mr C.M. Grieve, J.P., the leader of the 'Scottish Literary Renaissance', and many others closely identified with and representative of Scottish public life and opinion.

(Lewis Spence, 'The National Party of Scotland', *Edinburgh Review* July 1928, pp.70–87 [70–73].)

9.7 John Barbour, from 'Scotland—The New Dominion' (*Edinburgh Review* April 1929)

The wave of nationalism which flowed over Europe at the close of the war has penetrated to the Presbyterian fastnesses of the Northern Kingdom. A Scottish literary renaissance is in the air, fighting hard to break through the long mists of national self-denial. Scotland to-day swarms with minor poets—heralds, let us hope, of some new 'surpassing spirit'. Mr

Cunninghame Graham, Mr Spence himself, Mr C.M. Grieve (the Nationalist candidate for Dundee), the Hon. Erskine of Marr—these are typical figures in the Scottish literary renaissance. Their chief weakness is their impatient versatility—best exemplified in the work of the ubiquitous Mr Grieve, who aspires to be the Pooh-Bah of Scottish nationalism, and is at once poet, philosopher, publisher, journalist, economist and politician. Diffused as it is, this cultural movement has a cumulative importance. It is purging Scotland's brain of the belief that all Scots' poets except Burns must be minor poets—unless they are English. Not from Burns, and still less Barrie, but from Dunbar and the old Scots Makars of the fifteenth and sixteenth centuries, this movement seeks its inspiration. As yet perhaps it savours more of Coué than of culture. But auto-suggestion is as powerful an influence in a revival of national as of individual confidence, and the renaissance group are preaching from the text that the only way to kill provincialism is to turn it into nationalism. They are groping their way to a new Scottish outlook on life which will be something richer than a hypocritical compromise between the claims of God and the bank-manager on the one hand, and something more individual than the second-hand gossip of the London correspondent on the other.

All these tendencies reveal a nation slowly waking to the fear of being about to lose its soul, and striving to convince itself, with the aggressiveness of self-distrust, that it still has a personality of its own. They have a definite influence on the growth of a national political sentiment. Nations, like individuals, cannot stand still. Can any nation regain—or even sustain a distinctive national culture, unless it possesses the fullest political attributes of nationhood? The answer of the Scottish renaissance movement is to be found in the fact that its chief exponents are also leaders of the National Party.

Their political leadership, however, perhaps for that very reason—is still more spirited than inspired. The deeper source of the revival of Scottish Nationalism, of which indeed the Scottish renaissance is as much a symptom as a cause, is the growing uneasiness among thinking men and women of all classes at the social condition of the country. For that condition the war was not, of course, responsible. But the war, by accentuating its worse features, for example in housing, has revealed it in all its horror. Mr Spence in his article in the *Edinburgh Review* draws a terrible picture of Scotland's condition. An even more desperate account is given by Mr George Malcolm Thomson in his *Caledonia—or The Future of the Scots*. Mr John Buchan, M.P., by no means a hot-headed Nationalist, confesses to a surprising amount of misgiving. [. . .] Is it surprising that men whose minds are blinded with discontent should gladly embrace self-government when it is held out to them—as it is by the National Party—as the last chance of the national regeneration which they have expected so long and so vainly from other sources? This tragic delusion is the mainstay of the National Party, and the one plank on which above all others they have elected to fight their case. The reasons for their choice are clear if hardly creditable. The vast majority of Scotsmen are not interested in their abstract right to a Parliament in Edinburgh. They are profoundly interested in the social and economic ills which face them day by day. The battle of Bannockburn will not win the party a single seat at the general election. The patriotism of Fletcher of Saltoun will fall flat on slum audiences paying high rents for verminous property out of scanty parish relief. By dispirited fathers and pinched wives the Nationalist candidates will be asked the one over-powering question: 'How will self-government help us?' To tell them that Scotland, being a nation, has an *a priori* national right to Dominion status would be like giving a stone to those who ask for bread. [. . .]

But the credulity of the party does not stop there. They seem to believe there is some divine necessary connection between national prosperity and national self-government. Is there? [. . .] Why should self-government, which has not apparently been effective in ending industrial depression in England, Northern Ireland, or the Irish Free State, suddenly acquire a sovereign efficacy because it holds aloft the cross of St Andrew?

(John Barbour, 'Scotland—the New Dominion', *Edinburgh Review* April 1929, pp.211–31 [216–18, 221].)

9.8 Neil M. Gunn, from 'Nationalism and Internationalism' (*Scots Magazine* June 1931)

The other day I happened to meet a Scottish painter and etcher who was kind enough to invite me to a private view of some of his recent work. It was distinguished work, full of vision, and aware of all the ways of the moderns, but by no means the least interesting part of my visit was the artist's own ideas and experiences elicited by, let me hope, natural questions. For example, a couple of his canvases were concerned with ploughed fields. The serpentine furrow was the motif in a bare Scottish landscape. Not possibly, what would popularly be called a 'picture'. Yet the artist had been intimately attracted by the subject, and, though believing that the attraction was peculiar and personal, had nonetheless had it included in a group of subjects from different parts of the world for a one-man show. Consider his surprise when the bare furrows caught the particular attention of the metropolitan dealers. It was almost enough to make him conclude that trips to North Africa may be fascinating, but not necessarily essential for the production of masterpieces! And if this theme provided a nearly endless one for speculation at least the one fact had emerged, namely, that by the artist's doing what he knew intimately, and what had appealed to

327

him deeply in his own country, he had attracted the closest attention of art lovers in other countries.

I mention this experience because it happens to be the most recent of many that have, from time to time, seemed to explain to me the relationship of nationalism to internationalism. Nationalism creates that which internationalism enjoys. The more varied and multiple your nationalism, the richer and profounder your internationalism. Conversely, where the nation would disappear and the world become a single body governed by the same machinery of laws and ideas, the common stock of culture would tend to become uniform and static. For cosmopolitanism does not readily breed the intense vision or rebellion of the native or individual spirit. On the contrary, its natural attitude is to deplore it as being unnecessary, often wasteful, and nearly always in bad form. Cosmopolitanism working through this man-of-the-world conception might out of an ultimate logic create its own idea, but it would be the deathly or neutral idea of the perfection of the beehive.

Now the question arises here: Why, then, is there in the world of affairs today the idea of antagonism between nationalism and internationalism? If internationalism is nationality's flower, why war? And it is precisely in this awful region of war that so many of us lose our bearings. For nationalism breeds patriotism; patriotism, it is asserted, breeds antagonism; and antagonism needs the mailed fist.

But patriotism, as a true emotion, is full of life; it has kinship with poetry and music and none with destruction and death. From the earliest times it has been the world's singing subject. In the history of each nation it has been a unifying and precious possession. Each nation has been prepared to fight for it, when it would not quite have been prepared to fight for its music and poetry, or, indeed, for any other of the mind's preoccupations except religion. Patriotism, indeed, fed such arts as poetry and music. Possibly no other single emotion is more responsible for the creation of the world's culture.

But that sort of patriotism has as little to do with jingoism as music has with a factory siren. [. . .]

Patriotism (even already the word is beginning to have a false note) is founded in tradition, and we can no more get away from tradition than ourselves. Indeed, immediately we get away from tradition we do get away from ourselves. A nation's traditions are the natural inspirations of its people. How much the child is the product of heredity and how much of environment may be a debatable point, but that he is the product of both is unquestionable. Out of his environment, acted upon by a traditional or national unity, he creates most profoundly. And to create is to cause or give delight. In the pure conception of patriotism there is pure pleasure just as there is in any true function of the arts. And it is only when a man is moved by the traditions and music and poetry of his own land that he is in a position to comprehend those of any other land, for already he has the eyes of sympathy and the ears of understanding.

How then has patriotism in idea got debauched by war? Simply because in time of war patriotism is so strongly roused to protect its frontiers that it has been confounded with the cause of war. Nations are the natural units in the war game, just as the family is the natural unit in the nation. But it would be as ridiculous to destroy our natural unities in the hope of destroying the war game as it would be to remove our teeth in the hope of getting rid of a pain caused by our stomachs. For, as has been said, patriotism is never a cause of war, but is merely used by war, just as other emotions are, only more profoundly. For even when nations group into compact empires or into scattered commonwealths, when they lose their nationhood and traditions, war can still use them. War can use them without patriotism. War can enjoy the spectacle of patriots of the same nation fighting each other. War is insatiable, and in the last resort cares nothing for nations. It cares only for destruction, and the earth laid waste would be its final triumph. [. . .]

Internationalism carried to its logical conclusion of a single centralisation of all power—arms, finance, law-making—could result in the greatest tyranny the mind of man is capable of conceiving. While the nation is still the unit (and history has shown the small unit to be singularly important—consider Greece and Palestine) the individual factor comes into play, and in a myriad personal contacts the finer elements of humanism are retained and tyranny suffered briefly, if at all. But when the governing machine becomes single in control, remote in place, and absolute in power, then hope of reform or progress—which generally means the breaking of an existing mould—would not have the heart to become articulate. Standardisation would be the keyword not only in the material things of life, but also in the spiritual. And whenever conditions got too desperate it would mean revolution, or world war on a basis of class hatred.

The small nation has always been humanity's last bulwark for the individual against that machine, for personal expression against impersonal tyranny, for the quick freedom of the spirit against the flattening steamroller of mass. It is concerned for the intangible things called its heritage, its beliefs and arts, its distinctive institutions, for everything, in fact, that expresses it. And expression finally implies spirit in an act of creation, which is to say, culture.

Culture thus emerges in the nation, is the nation's flower. Each nation cultivates its own natural flower. The more varieties, the more surprise and pleasure for all. For nationalism in the only sense that matters is not jealous, any more than music is jealous. On the contrary, if we are gardeners or musicians we are anxious to meet gardeners or musicians of other lands and rejoice when their blooms are exquisitely different from our own. In this way life becomes enriched, and contrast is set up as a delight and an inspiration. To have no longer these means for discrimination, to lose the charm that unending variety gives, to miss the spur in the shadow of difference, 'is, on this short day of frost and sun, to sleep before evening'.

(Neil M. Gunn, 'Nationalism and Internationalism', Scots Magazine 15:3 June 1931,
pp.185–88.)

9.9 From unsigned review 'Wyndham Lewis on German Nationalism' (*Modern Scot* Summer 1931)

Hitler is a disappointing book to have been written by the author of *Time and Western Man* and *Tarr* and *The Childermass*. True, Mr Lewis admits at the outset that he came to write it as the result of 'some weeks' spent on a business trip to Germany recently and that it does not pretend to be a full-dress criticism but a mere exposition of Hitlerism; but that is no excuse for him frittering away so many pages in sheer inanity.

There are many objections to the book, and one of the gravest is the note of empiricism so often struck (a strange phenomenon in one as opposed as Mr Lewis to the 'flux' of modern thought). In *Hitler* he becomes one of the treasonous *clercs* M. Benda trounces. Alarmed at the much-discussed threat to the civilization of the west, he forsakes his intellectual perch and throws in his lot with the most promising 'man of the people' Adolf Hitler, the anti-Semite, pro-Aryan, anti-communist, and individualist. 'Really', he says, 'we "Aryans", or whatever we are, are faced with extinction. We cannot afford just now to be philosophers, nor yet humanitarians. . . . We are compelled, I think, to lay more stress upon what is pragmatical and *useful*, and less upon what is perhaps eternally true. It is a case of *force majeure*. . . .We are in the greatest danger. Gentleness, beauty, sweet reason must veil their heads, they must give way to arguments of power. . . .', and so on. It is, however, at all times the business of a thinker of the calibre of Wyndham Lewis to philosophize, to court 'sweet reason', as best he can, and most especially at such a juncture as the present. His duty is to think as hard as ever he can: other people, otherwise gifted, will do the 'useful' things: he can best serve mankind by keeping to his own plane and relying on a process of percolation for his ideas to work their way through society. If he shuts himself up in an ivory tower, he will have no lack of 'popularizers', like Einstein. It is not a little regrettable to find Mr Lewis, turned pragmatist, writing such sentences as the following, marked at random: 'All revolutions are means to ends. Experience tells us that the ends are usually not found to justify the means. It is a matter of opinion.' Wyndham Lewis of all people knows that such things are *not* a matter of opinion.

Even if he deliberately chooses to write on that plane for once in a while, Mr Lewis owes it to himself to rise superior to the prose style of the *Daily Mail*. Let us, he says, try to understand Hitler's credit reform policy, 'then we shall know just where we are with these lads of Hitler's, what!' That wretched journalistic jargon is matched by the irrelevance of such portions of the book as the chapter headed 'The Berlin *Eldorado*'. 'I think that it argues a great deal of good sense on the part of the Nationalsocialists that they have ignored this feature of the glittering west-end of their city', he says—after which he devotes seven pages to a melodramatic description of what he calls this 'Perverts' Paradise, the Mecca of both Lesb and So'.

The book's shortcomings are legion, and we regret it all the more because we have a tremendous admiration for Mr Lewis and, being good Nationalists, are very interested in Hitlerism. Adolf Hitler is the most remarkable political figure in modern Germany, and Germany, in the words of Dr Benes (December 1930), 'holds the key of the new Europe. What happens there within the next few months will decide the course of European politics for years to come'.

('Wyndham Lewis on German Nationalism', unsigned review of *Hitler* by Wyndham Lewis, *Modern Scot* 2:2, summer 1931, pp.175–78 [175–76].)

9.10   D.S. Mirsky, from *Lenin* (1931)

If Lenin's relations with people were conditioned by their relation to his revolutionary work and unaffected by his personal sentiments, these latter were not necessarily affected by changes in behaviour. When political dissensions with former comrades made it impossible for him to continue his political collaboration with them, this unavoidably led to a cessation of personal relations, but it did not always kill his human feelings. [. . .] With workmen, peasants and soldiers, with the rank and file of the party, he was invariably patient and tolerant, confident that 'blood will out' and that the organic revolutionary instincts of the people may be relied upon. He was equally patient and tolerant with men whose main business was not politics. Thus his friendship with Gorky was not put an end to when the latter supported Lunacharsky in his 'religious' propaganda. Lenin was ready to make allowances for the subconscious and irrational ways of the imaginative writer. But he did not mince his words in telling Gorky exactly what he thought of the whole business. [. . .]

But what gave Lenin a unique and entirely personal popularity was the way in which he saw and spoke to thousands—workmen, peasants, administrative and party workers from every end of the country. At the numerous congresses he mixed with the peasant delegates, often unrecognized by them, listening to their talk, and taking stock of their grievances. He received hundreds of provincial administrative workers, listening to their reports, often knowing beforehand what they would say but waiting for a new confirmation of what he knew. While Trotsky moved from one end of the country to the other in his spectacular propaganda train, Lenin never left Moscow and yet remained in closer touch with all the moods and feelings of the country. From his central position he saw the country to its remotest corners and was, alone, better informed than the whole administrative apparatus put together. His attitude to that apparatus was characteristic. He insisted in general on strict discipline and allowed of no compromise in the application of essential and fundamental measures, but he knew at the same time that the work of government was—of necessity—being conducted in an inexperienced, inefficient way and that it would not do to erect into absolute rules measures that were nothing better than gropings after a not easily to be reached solution. He encouraged disobedience if it sprang from sincere and intelligent initiative. When Party workers in responsible posts in the Provinces found the measures prescribed from Moscow absurd, he would advise them simply to ignore them. When a decree was passed discontinuing City Soviets, he remarked to a provincial administrative worker who criticized it, that it was a good way of testing their fitness: a City Soviet that was really any good would never permit itself to be dissolved. Against bureaucratism, procrastination, and formalism he waged a relentless war. Unable to make an end of them, he intervened personally whenever he could and, by telephoning himself to half a dozen offices, would finish in a quarter of an hour an affair which in the normal course of officialdom would have taken days or weeks to settle. But this, of course, could only palliate the evil, which could be unrooted only by a lengthy re-education of all concerned. [. . .]

But problems of internal organization were only part of Lenin's work. The foreign policy of the Soviet Government was directed by him. He conducted it in the spirit in which he had signed the Peace of Brest and nationalized industrial enterprises against the protest of Germany. There was no compromise he would refuse to consider, subject to two conditions: that it was really necessary; and that it did not affect the fundamental political principles of the Soviet polity or jeopardize the survival of the Socialist Republic. [. . .]

Ever since November 1918 the international situation was materially modified by the birth of an International Revolutionary movement, which at once became a principal concern for Lenin. It is important to be quite clear about Lenin's respective attitudes to the Russian Revolution and to the Communist Revolution abroad. Attempts have been made to minimize his internationalism and to make of him a revolutionary patriot. This is entirely false. We have already seen his readiness to sacrifice the Russian Socialist Republic to the success of the more important cause of Socialism in Germany, if only the German Revolution became as much a reality as the Russian was. His attitude in this question was that of a soldier.

There were only two sides in the struggle—international Capitalism, and the international Proletariat. The proletariat of one nation was only a unit of the international army, and its leaders were as well entitled to sacrifice it, if this was necessary for the common victory, as a general is entitled to sacrifice his division to save the army. The question in each case was only whether such a sacrifice would really contribute to the victory of the common cause or be only an ineffective gesture. [. . .]

What has been given the name of Leninism is precisely the application of the relatively abstract formulas of Marx to the concrete context of a different age: it is 'the Marxism of the age of Imperialism and of Proletarian Revolution'. It follows that Leninism itself is a relatively abstract formula in so far as 'the age of Imperialism and of Proletarian Revolution' is a relatively long period of time, falling into a succession of more concrete historical situations. The practical application of Leninism in the thirteenth year of the Dictatorship of the Proletariat must obviously be different from its application in the fourth year; and, for instance, to advocate in 1930 a policy on the ground that it was supported by Lenin in 1921 would be only to display a complete misunderstanding of the very essence of his ideas.

Leninism is related to Marxism as species to genus. But Leninism is not identical with the sum of Lenin's outlook. The Marxist precedes in him the creator of Leninism, and the vindication and re-establishment of genuine Marxism was one of his principal tasks in life. I have spoken in another chapter of Lenin's defence of materialism and of his fight against the insinuation of Idealist and quasi-Idealist philosophies into Socialist theory. Next to the dialectical method, the philosophical problem that interested Lenin most, was the problem of the immanence of movement in matter. His interest in the classics of philosophy was conditioned by their relevance to these two problems. Apart from Hegel and the French materialists, he was particularly attracted to Heraclitus, whose philosophy is, as it were, the dialectical method at the mythological stage, and to Spinoza, whom he valued particularly highly for having destroyed the idea of a transcendent cause.

The insistence on dialectical, as opposed to mechanistic materialism, was part of Lenin's work of restoration of true revolutionary Marxism against the aberrations of the Second International. In the hands of the anti-revolutionary Socialists the determinism of Marx (a determinism inseparable from the scientific mind, which is by definition a mind operating in terms of cause and effect) had degenerated into a philistine fatalism, which found expression in the doctrine, for a long time implied rather than stated, of the ultimate inevitability of Socialism, apart from the efforts of Socialists. In practice this fatalism reflected the anti-revolutionary tendencies of the Socialists of the pre-war period and a complete abandonment of the idea of the dictatorship of the Proletariat. It is superfluous to insist on the fact that such fatalism is completely opposed to the real teaching of Marx.

But in his time Lenin was almost alone in insisting on the active nature of Marxism, whose greatest and most quintessential expression is the famous closing proposition of the *Thesen über Feuerbach:* 'Philosophers have done nothing more than explain the world, it is our business now to change it.' In all these points, as in the political conclusions drawn from them, Lenin did nothing but re-awaken the revolutionary soul of Marxism that had been lulled to sleep by the Second International, and his teaching is nothing more than Marxism as opposed to pseudo-Marxism.

(D.S. Mirsky, *Lenin* London: The Holme Press, 1932, pp.17–18; 157–58; 163–65; 192–94.)

9.11 From editorial article on Douglasite economics: 'Shall Scotland Lead the World to Economic Emancipation?' (*Free Man* March 1932)

The most important article which has appeared in the columns of the Scottish Press for many years was published in the *Glasgow Evening Times*, on Friday last. It is written by Major C.H. Douglas, whose name has been so closely associated with the Douglas proposals for Credit Reform, during the past twelve years. It is interesting to record that when Major Douglas approached the problem which is presented by the obvious failure of orthodox economic principles to bring our capacity to produce goods into a sane relationship with our desire to consume goods, he did so with the trained mind of a scientific engineer. He was also free from any misconceptions which might have been instilled by the teachings of the orthodox schools. [. . .] The purpose of this paper is to support and encourage any and every plan which we consider is designed to enlarge our industrial liberty and to place the control of Government where it ought to be, in the hands of the people. We believe that Major Douglas' plan is one which will achieve these ends. We believe too that Scotland is one of the few countries in the world which could *immediately* put the plan into operation. Shall Scotland do this thing? [. . .]

The following is Major Douglas's draft scheme of reconstruction for Scotland on the lines of social-credit policy:

1) Obtain from existing sources, such as company balance-sheets, land registration offices, and insurance companies, such information necessary to place a money valuation upon the whole of the capital assets of Scotland, such as land, roads, bridges, railways, canals, buildings, drainage, and water schemes, power schemes, minerals, semi-manufactured materials. No distinction between public and private property. Replacement values to be used where the property is in use.

Add to this the sum representing the present commercial capitalised value of the population. Such a figure exists and varies with the actuarial expectation of life and the plant capacity of the country, and is something like £10,000 for a citizen of the United States at the age of 25. From the grand total thus obtained a figure representing the price value of the Scottish capital account could be obtained. Financial credit to an equivalent amount can be created by any agency such as a Scottish Treasury empowered by the Scottish people.

2) As from the initiation of this scheme, the holding of any stock, share, or bond by a holding company or trustee will not be recognised. It is the intention that no shareholding in any industrial undertaking shall be other than in the form of equity shares of no par value, i.e. Preference or Common shares or stock. Bonded indebtedness will be recognised for purposes of compensation where held by individuals, upon a proper investigation, but where held by corporations will be subject to such terms of redemption as may seem desirable.

No real transfer of real estate directly between either persons or business undertakings will be recognised. Persons or business undertakings desiring to relinquish the control of real immovable estate will do so to the Government, which will take any necessary steps to re-allot it to suitable applicants. No Government Department shall administer, either directly or indirectly, any business, whether agricultural, productive, or distributive, other than the administration of the financial and credit schemes, or receive payment for any services rendered to the public, other than in bulk.

The Initial National Dividend

3) For the purpose of the initial stages an arbitrary figure, such as 1 per cent of the capital sum ascertained by the methods outlined in clause 1), shall be taken, and a notice published that every man, woman, and child of Scottish birth and approved length of residence, with the exception mentioned in the paragraph that follows, is to be entitled to share equally in the dividends thus obtained, which might be expected to exceed £300 per annum per family. It will be clearly understood that no interference with existing ownerships, so-called, is involved in such a proceeding. The dividend to be paid monthly by a draft on the Scottish Government credit, through the post office and not through the banks.

Any administrative change in the organisation of the post office should specifically exclude transfer of the money and postal order department and the saving bank. No payments of the national dividend will be made except to individuals, and such payments will not be made where the net income of the individual, for personal use, from other sources is more than four times that receivable in respect of the national dividend. The national dividend will be tax-free in perpetuity, and will not be taken into consideration in making any returns for taxation purposes should such be required.

'Assisted Price' for Registered Businesses

4) Simultaneously with the publication of the foregoing notice, publish a figure to be known as the discount rate to replace the existing bank discount rate, a suitable value of this for initial purposes being 25 per cent. It is important that the figure should not be less than 25 per cent, and it might very reasonably be higher.

5) Simultaneously, publish an announcement that any or all business undertakings would be accepted for registration under an assisted price scheme. The conditions of such registration would be that their account, as at present required under the Companies Acts, should contain an additional item showing the average profit on turnover, and that their prices should, as far as practicable, be maintained at a figure to include such average profit, where this is agreed as equitable for the type of business concerned, the suitable profit being, of course, largely dependent on the velocity of turnover. Undertakings unable to show a profit after five years' operation to be struck off the register.

How Free Credits Would Be Issued

6) In consideration of the foregoing, all registered businesses would be authorised to issue with sales to ultimate consumers an account on suitable paper for use as explained in the following clause.

7) Payment for goods would be made in the ordinary way, either by cheque or currency. The purchaser would, however, lodge his receipted account for goods bought with his bank in the same way that he now pays in cheques, and the discount percentage of the amount of such account would be re-credited to the consumer's banking account. Unregistered firms would not be supplied with the necessary bill forms for treatment in this matter, with the result that their prices would inevitably be 25 per cent, at least, higher than those of registered firms. It is obvious that the larger the discount rate can be made the greater will be the handicap of the non-registered firms.

The total of the sums credited by the banks to private depositors in respect of these discounts would be reimbursed to them by a Scottish Treasury credit. The capital account would be 'depreciated' by such sums, and 'appreciated' by all capital development. The existing banks would be empowered to charge an equitable sum for the services thus rendered.

Hours and Wages

8) The hours of Government offices to be reduced to four hours per day. To meet the temporary congestion of work, additional staff to be employed, such staff, however, doing identical work with the existing staff in the form of a second shift, and sharing with the existing staff the chances

of promotion irrespective of seniority. The object of this is to discourage the wellknown bureaucratic tendency to enhance the importance of existing staffs by employing additional numbers of persons ranking by virtue of seniority below the original officials, and, at the same time, to afford an opportunity of appointing a duplicate set of officials to check reaction without dislocation of existing routine.

9) Wage rates in all organised industries to be reduced by 25 per cent, where such reduction does not involve a loss to the wage-earner exceeding 20 per cent of the sums received in the form of national dividend. The wage rates ruling in 1928 to be taken as the basis against which the reduction would be made.

Any trade union violating a wage agreement to render its membership liable to suspension of national dividend, and any employers' organisation committing a similar offence, to be liable to suspension of price assistance.

Must Accept Employment, Or—

For a period of five years after the initiation of this scheme, failure on the part of any individual to accept employment in whatever trade, business, or vocation he was classified in the last census, under conditions recognised as suitable to that employment (unless exempted in a medical certificate), would render such individual liable to suspension of benefit in respect of the national dividend.

10) Taxation of specific articles, or specific forms of property, to be abolished. Any taxation found out to be necessary to take the form either of a flat non-graduated taxation of net income or a percentage ad valorem tax upon sales, or both forms of taxation together.

NOTES:—The price level of 1928 has been taken for the rough estimate of the items which, when added together, make up the Real Assets or Real Capital account of Scotland.

The Financial Credit, which is equivalent to this, appears in a National Account as a contra-item. Money and Real assets are on opposite sides of the account (and should balance) not, as in a commercial account, on the same side of the account.

(Editorial article on Douglasite Credit Reform, 'Shall Scotland Lead the World to Economic Emancipation? How It Can Be Done', *Free Man* 1:7, 19 March 1932, pp.3–4.)

9.12   Naomi Mitchison, from 'A Socialist Plan for Scotland' (*Modern Scot* Spring 1932)

The year 1932 was blown in by an apocalyptic wind. It seems at last really likely that there will be a great change in our lives and in the lives of all men and women in Western Europe before the year is out. It seems likely that we shall see, while we are still young enough to profit by it, the beginnings at least of a social revolution. We brace ourselves like swimmers to dive into the current, to be swept on with it and borne up by it, to glorify it and enjoy it for ever. Yet, while we are still standing on the safe brink, we have to consider the future, and—here in this paper, among friends—the relation between Socialism and Scottish Nationalism.

I am not a politician or an economist, or even a prophet, and I can only put the thing into the form in which I have seen it myself, especially during the last few months, and in the light of certain obvious social tendencies. When an ideal is still visionary it can remain vague and indefinite, shimmering with emotion, but when it is almost practical it has to become clear. Socialism will have to face a number of problems and make a number of decisions, not necessarily the same in all countries or under different conditions. Two alternatives from which it may have to choose seem likely to be: either producing more things and using them—having an increasingly high standard of life: or not producing more things but having more leisure. Closely connected with this, seem to be two other alternatives, and it is obviously wise to consider them before a mere current of accidents drifts Socialism definitely into one or the other.

One alternative is that the Socialist state should be organized on an urban basis, with the country considered and used merely as a food factory. This is the U.S.S.R. method, and was perhaps inevitable there, considering the previous history of Russia. It seems in a way to be the obvious modern economic organization. The alternative is less clear, but does, I think, exist. This would be a state based not on the town, but on the country, on a basis not of individual ownership but of a co-operative group which would in practice work out as something like the Scandinavian or early Scottish steading. In this civilization, the country, and the good life which it is possible to lead in the country under reasonably favourable economic conditions, would be the basis of civilization; the towns would be comparatively accidental, the necessary producers of certain commodities, including the more complicated agricultural machinery.

Now at present the urban civilization seems the only possible one, mostly because of the immense pressure of population, but we are beginning to see its dangers. Its chief dangers are, roughly, that it is desperately antiindividualistic, as a factory culture is bound to be, and that it encourages a most fierce form of militarism. This latter danger comes largely because the urban and industrial state needs to organize itself into as large areas as possible, which yet speak the same language and have the same basic economic needs. These large areas tend and will tend to be large national areas. It is no use denying that the U.S.S.R. is now as militarist a state as post-revolutionary France.

What is to be done with these militarist, nationalist instincts? Can they be denied or set to working the wheels of science? Only with the intelligent. The alternative seems to be to split them. Split up this dangerous nationalism into small cultural groups, where the nationalist spirit can easily manifest itself in other ways than by force of arms.

Small, intense cultural states, whether independent or federated, seem most unlikely to be dangerous. Small nationalities in the past have only been dangerous when they have been suppressed. They turn their energies inwards into producing some peculiar form of living, in setting their stamp upon things and art forms. The larger the nationality, the less it seems to produce. I need not, here, go into the evidence that small nationalities produce much.

Yet how, after any change, can Socialist states of this sort come into being? Or, better, where? And here I think the answer is: obviously, in Scotland.

Scotland is comparatively isolated, yet completely civilized (as civilization goes, that is to say!). Scotland is not hampered by any overpowering, anti-Socialist religious organization. Above all, there are a great number of intelligent people in Scotland who are still living in the country and on the whole want to go on living in the country.

Scotland is, of course, by no means all country or small country town. There is Glasgow and Edinburgh and the whole industrial belt stretching across the centre of Scotland and up the east coast. There is the rapidly growing industrial Ayrshire. Yet it seems to be that the main industrial belt, including Glasgow, could quite well be separated from the rest, becoming culturally united, perhaps, to some extent at least, with the industrial Midland belt of England. In these days of transport and very rapid communication it seems ridiculous to suppose that places which are apart on the map should not be in practice as united as they may think fit. It also seems possible that this industrial belt of Scotland is not so necessary or admirable as it is sometimes supposed to be. It is largely a product of private enterprise and private profit-making. It is a belt, not of magnificent factories and laboratories and workers' flats and great halls and parks where the working communities can meet, but of accidental slums, of cottages from which the green fields have been taken away, of poor shops and mean streets which house the immense surplus of unemployed which modern capitalist enterprise finds necessary for its fantastic economics. All that can go.

There is immense waste everywhere, waste brought about by competition. It should be possible to use the Scottish mines to make an electricity and gas grid across the Lowlands, supplying power to the country communities; for it is no part of the good agricultural life to waste the strength and beauty of men and women—especially women—on work which should be done by simple machinery. Apart from the mines there are infinite possibilities of using the water-power of the Highlands. Such schemes, when they get going, need comparatively few skilled men to look after them, who would easily assimilate themselves into the countryside, for its good and their own.

Edinburgh and Glasgow are both artificially large and crowded, full of unskilled labour, semi-unemployed at the best of times. Redistribution is wanted. But the Clydeside docks are part of something world-wide, something bigger even than Scotland.

This country civilization cannot, of course, be completely agricultural. There must be country factories, with good communications, which will employ hundreds or thousands of workers, who will live near it, but will, nevertheless, never get into real, crushing, urban conditions, never lose touch with the soil, the seasons, nor with the sense of being part of an intense culture, a small nationality. All kinds of industries can best be located in the country, not only these connected with food-stuffs and timber, including paper, but also some kinds of textiles, and some kinds of printing. All that seems as though it would fit in very well with Scotland as we know it. [. . .]

All this, of course, is in the future. Yet one must look at the future, if possible, in detail. We have to consider Scotland, not only as Scotland alone, but as Scotland in the Socialist world, and this is how I see that Scotland, as a force and a power and, above all, as a new experiment.

(Naomi Mitchison, 'A Socialist Plan for Scotland', *Modern Scot* 3:1, spring 1932, pp.25–30 [25–28].)

9.13 Willa Muir, from letter to Helen Cruickshank (May [1932])

Crowborough
26 May

My dearest Helen,

This is a private, unofficial account of many things which we do not care to put into an official report. Generally speaking, first: we were never so glad to leave any country as to leave Hungary. The official welcome, the official sprees, etc., were all very grandly and lavishly done, but the psychological tension behind it all oppressed us almost to misery. (1) Barely a fortnight before the Congress the Hungarian PEN was riven in two by Nationalist, or rather, by Chauvinist interests. A prize founded by Rothermere for the best Hungarian book was awarded by the then existing PEN committee (President, Kostolanyi) to a book which everybody admitted to be really a good book. The Government however intimated that this book was not to get the prize, since it was merely a study of peasant life and in no way furthered the Chauvinist aspirations of Hungary. The Government added that should the PEN persist in awarding the prize to this book it would not grant a single pengo for the International Congress. Result, uproar, and the resignation of all the members of the PEN who put good literature above propaganda. [. . .] (2) The *general* atmosphere was the same thing written larger: the same Government that received us so grandly in the Prime Minister's Palace and the Royal Palace has the great mass of the people cowed, unless they are content to be fed on daily hate of other nations around them, and enthusiastic for the secret military designs of the country. Shortly before we came, a tailor (I think a tailor), suspected of giving out Socialist pamphlets, was bound hand and foot, hung upside down in his house on a bar between two chairs, and bastinadoed on the soles till he was unconscious: when he came to he was beaten again and, finally, he jumped out of his window, bound as he was, and broke both his ankles. His wife, who was pregnant, was forced to witness his bastinadoing, and when she heard her husband land with a thud in the courtyard below she thought he was killed, and she died herself of shock. [. . .] In short, the general atmosphere is filled with hatred, revenge, and cruelty. Perhaps this should not have depressed us, but it did; and I spent Thursday afternoon of Congress week in roaring and greeting in my bedroom over the state of Central Europe! [. . .]

(3) Our personal difficulties as Scottish delegates must be added to this. From the very start we were treated as members of the English delegation, not as independent representatives. On the list of delegates we were described as 'angol', English, and we had to go to the Central Bureau and protest before we were allowed free quarters in our hotel. In fact, we had to assert ourselves continuously as being at least on the same independent footing as the delegates from Esthonia(!) The climax came in the Royal Palace, when the official reception by Horthy was arranged: the nations were arranged in a semi-circle, the head of their delegations in front and the others behind, and there was no separate provision made for Scotland: we were to be lumped together in one crowd with the English. Of course we protested: we had the satisfaction of making old Pekar hastily scribble us in in pencil on the typed list, and although we stood beside the English we did so with a little gap between us, and Edwin, as the Head of the Delegation (wha!!!! that was a story!) was separately presented to Horthy. All this made Edwin so nervous that he forgot to present me, I might say; and I had the dubious distinction of being the only person in the room who did not grab Horthy's hand. [. . .] Next year in Ragusa it will *not* happen, for we drummed it into Stefanović and Čurčin, both of them exceedingly pleasant men, and they know anyway about the Scottish Women's Hospital in Serbia, etc., and have some notion of how Scotland stands up to England [. . .]

From all this I would add that a Congress in Scotland will be the best and most immediate method of driving the fact home to the smaller nations of Europe. The Congress invitation was given in the name of *Scotland*, and a thoroughly Scottish Congress in 1934 would educate a vast mass of opinion throughout Europe. Of course, we cannot both eat our cake and have it: as an independent Scotland we must rank with the smaller nations, and cannot have the prestige of England or France or Germany. But it will be our own prestige, and we must establish it. . . .

Much love,
Willa.

(Willa Muir, letter to Helen Cruickshank, 26 May [1932], reprinted from *Selected Letters of Edwin Muir*, pp.72–76.)

9.14 W. Aitken, 'The Puzzle of Mr Grieve' (*Free Man* August 1932)

Sir,—As a keenly interested reader of Mr C.M. Grieve's stimulating weekly causerie, I have been rather puzzled of late with what seems to be his appalling inconsistency. The man, of course, who never changes his mind is a poor creature—his consistency is a pleasant name for what is usually pig-headed obstinacy. But how does Mr Grieve reconcile his Douglasism, Comunism [sic], and Hitlerism? What have they in common, apart from a general opposition to the present state of affairs? *Is* Hitler engaged in anti-Capital activities, or is the *Manchester Guardian* Berlin correspondent, who states the contrary, entirely mistaken? Does Mr Grieve expect us to accept this naive statement—'Though Hitler is armed, he is no military menace'? What does Mr Grieve mean when he says that 'little is heard over here of the Nazis' anti-semitic tendencies', when every paper in the country, without exception, harps on this one thing to the point of nausea?

Does Mr Grieve wish to see a Scottish Communist state, or a Scottish state incorporating Douglas principles? He can hardly have both. No doubt the application of Douglasism would make Scotland an infinitely better place, but it certainly would not incur equality of income or the destruction of our stupid class system.

Mr Grieve is a Communist. Hitler's principles are the direct antithesis of Communism. He loathes it. Since Mr Grieve can hardly admire Hitler for his principles can it be for his personal appearance?—because he is a more charming man than say, Maxton? Does Mr Grieve share Hitler's anti-semitic views, and if so, does he make exceptions of Stalin and Lenin?

Or do Mr Grieve's Communism, Douglasism, and Hitlerism consist, not in any devotion to the principles involved, but in a merely objective admiration for anything which claims to oppose the existing order? That, I confess, seems to be the most charitable explanation, and, if the true one, arouses a certain amount of sympathy. But sympathy is poor consolation for the disappointment we feel that the energies of so acute an intelligence should be diffused over so wide a range of policies—policies so strangely conflicting and incompatible.—I am, &c., W. AITKEN.

(W. Aitken, letter to the Editor, 'The Puzzle of Mr Grieve', *The Mercat Cross*, *Free Man* 1:28, 13 August 1932, p.7.)

9.15 From 'Whither Scotland? The *Free Man* Symposium' (*Free Man* October 1932)

a) From 'A Prefatory Note' by C.M. Grieve

Regarding the recent Conference of so-called 'Moderates', convened by the Duke of Montrose as an attempt to subvert the Scottish National Movement by a clique of Right Wingers who had not only contributed nothing to its development, but in some cases actually opposed it [. . .] it has been deemed essential to bring together in the form of this symposium the views of Scots, and particularly of younger Scots, of definite personal achievement, or representative of the more radical, and preponderating, elements in the Scottish electorate, or known for their concern with and competence in regard to those economic and financial issues which are of paramount importance to-day.

The expressions of opinion elicited are given below. I need not state my own views; it is sufficiently well known that I am out for an entirely independent Scottish Republic—that I am anti-English, anti-Imperialist, and pro-Irish—and that I have been an active protagonist of Social Credit for many years.

b) 'The Main Problem' by Edwin Muir

It seems to me the main problem is still to rouse Scotland to a genuine (not merely conventional or sentimental) consciousness of itself. Until that is done nothing of much value can come of any Nationalist movement, practical or otherwise, except indirectly; such movements are extremely useful, for instance, as symbols. But symbols are at best makeshifts for the real thing, and unless Scotland transcends them, all that independence will mean to her, if she does achieve it, will be a little Edinburgh House of Commons as like as two peas to the Westminster one, and that would not be worth lifting a finger for. It follows that an intellectual renascence is far more needed in Scotland than a political one—though that so far has been immensely useful. Ideally both should proceed side by side; but in

343

practice political activity almost invariably kills every other kind, and is particularly deadly to free intellectual enquiry. For that reason an energetic group of Scottish writers and intellectuals living in Scotland, with a popular organ in which to express their policy, is absolutely essential at present to the national revival; but so far as I can see it is also an impossible dream. Nevertheless, without something of the kind I can see no future for the national movement in Scotland except a purely bourgeois one, in which case it would deserve no more attention than Prohibition or Empire Free Trade.

c) 'Revolution Necessary' by Naomi Mitchison

Politics cannot be separated from economics, nor can we consider Nationalism apart from the social system where one class has money and power, and, knowingly or unknowingly, oppresses the other which is thus almost completely debarred from expression. Scottish national expression has got to come from the people, and is beginning to do so. In so far as we Anglo-Scots can help we should and will, but we must not lead from above or shove our culture down the throats of the real Scots. We must realise that national self-expression cannot come without a revolution of some kind. If Great Britain were socialist, probably Scotland would get all she wants, as the autonomous Russian republics have; yet perhaps Scotland may lead the way here. Her economic problems are rather different, especially that of agriculture, and Scotland probably needs a division of land. In the meantime nationalism must be expressed in a revolutionary way, and I hope in alliance with both Socialist and Communist parties.

d) 'The Danger of Caution' by J.H. Whyte

I think it is plain that by now the Scottish Movement is in its second phase. We no longer have to shout for a Scottish Revival when even Lord Beaverbrook has declared that the preservation of the Scottish spirit is important. The business of intelligent Nationalists is now to ensure that the revival takes the proper form.

The political aspects of the Scottish question interest me only in so far as political reform must precede or accompany cultural reforms in Scotland. Because of the relation of spiritual to material issues, I therefore join with the *Free Man* in deploring the attempts to effect a compromise between the Scottish Nationalists and the three large English-controlled political parties who have up to now complacently subordinated Scottish to English interests, and must by virtue of their constitution continue to do so; in insisting on Scotland's right to complete and unconditional autonomy; and in demanding this independence so that Scotland may break free from the trammels of outmoded English finance and inept parliamentarianism.

In literature, as in the other arts, our obvious need is still to make up the leeway between Scottish literature and the literature of Ireland, Poland, Czecho-Slovakia, and those other 'new' countries that have developed a national literature following the gaining of national independence and now move on a European plane. To aid in this, it is essential to eschew the log-rolling indulged in by those mediocrities who see in the Scottish Renaissance merely a new publicity medium for their mouldy wares; to judge our literature as good or bad, rather than as Scottish, as do so many—and to remember when extreme 'moderates' preach caution at us that caution, by which they mean inaction, has landed us where we are.

e) 'Wanted—A Workers' Scottish Republic' by Guy A. Aldred

From choice I am a domiciled Scot, but I have nothing in common with Scottish earls and landowners. I am a Socialist and want the end of all feudalisms, frontiers, sovereignties, nationalisms, exploitations. I believe in the poetry of social usefulness. The question of a Scottish Republic I would leave to the decision of the workers, assembled in Scotland at the point of production or of struggle towards the conquest of the right to produce. I have no faith in the irresponsible and ignorant parliamentarism of exploitation functioning in spendthrift London. I would have the workers seize Scotland instead of marching to London. I would industrialise the Highlands, for freedom comes through industry and machinery, not through rural backwardness. I would expel all parasites, destroy the vested-interest Press, and have the Press controlled by the workers living and working here. I would throw up Industrial Councils against present municipalities. I would emancipate the Church from all dogmas and make it a great free pulpit. I would ask to be voted into a pulpit myself, because today everything is sham—sham Nationalism, sham Freethought, sham Christianity, sham Brotherhood, and sham Division. I would have Robert Burns understood for the grandeur and happiness of his simplicity. I would not wait on England to solve our economic problems, but taking full advantage of the existence of a border, I would raise the Red Banner in Scotland and establish directly and immediately a Workers' Scottish Republic. I prefer a Workers' Scottish Republic to a Scottish Workers' Republic. I would expect a Workers' English Republic to follow AT ONCE.

Give me a pulpit in Glasgow or Edinburgh for six weeks, two addresses each Sunday, and I will tell you what I believe; tell it those who have never heard me confess. I would have a living people and living land: vitality resurgent everywhere.

f) 'Brief and to the Point' by Eric Linklater

Only an advertising expert can compress his opinions into 100 words; but if you permit me the right to qualify, shade, and condition the following statements you may declare them to be mine.

1 POLITICS: I believe that small nationalities would make the world safer, sounder, and more interesting.

2 ECONOMICS: a) Scotland might become practically self-supporting; Great Britain never could. b) Contrary to a recently established belief, I think that smaller economic units could find advantages denied to larger units.

3 CULTURE: It would, indeed, be as well if we got some.

g) 'Towards an Indigenous Communism' by William Soutar

There is little doubt that Scotland will be an autonomous country in the near future, and there is as little doubt that she will gain practically nothing if the foundations of self-government are set on a disrupting capitalistic system. The old truism holds good—a nation must have a faith which is visionary. What is to be the faith from which the reborn Scotland is to win strength to act? It must be such that it stirs all the types of men to action—so that the economist acts because he is primarily a man of faith and not because he is an economist; and so the artist, the theologian, the statesman. Scotland is not alone in this need, but the need is especially urgent here for she is about to take more power to herself, and power without vision becomes futile or destructive. If 'patriotism is not enough', neither is Douglasism though social credit may possibly help us over a hiatus between the death of capitalism and the birth of a new faith. An indigenous Communism comes nearer to our need, and the disintegration of the Church may be a pointer; a necessary preliminary to our faith in MAN.

h) 'Is This the Hour?' by Compton Mackenzie

To be frank, I find this a difficult moment to write about the road that free Scotland may follow. My whole attention is concentrated on doing and saying nothing which might make us miss a turning that could take Scotland nearer to that high road of the future. Is it of more practical value to push everything on one side in order to secure a Parliament as soon as possible, to the capture of which 'extremists' can devote themselves until that 'fanatical majority' feared by one of the debaters at the Liberal Conference is attained; or is it better to rely on our ability to convert the nation to our point of view before we accept a Parliament which in the present state of Scottish opinion will be nothing like what we want? In other words, will the appetite for freedom grow with tasting a faint flavour of it, or will that faint flavour satisfy the appetite for the time and perhaps ultimately destroy it altogether?

Some of your contributors seem to regard Nationalism as nothing more than a means to assist economic and political revolutions in the utility of which they believe. I have no doubt that a free Scotland will be a more fertile ground for ideas than a tied Scotland; but freedom is the aim, and those who want to free Scotland for a specific object of their own run the risk of being classed with Liberal politicians. I stand firmly for Social Credit, but if I believed that a free Scotland would be fatal to that great monetary revolution I should still be a Nationalist. In short, nothing matters at the moment except the achievement of independence, and if I were truly convinced that I could help that achievement by voting for a Liberal candidate I would do even that.

('Whither Scotland? The *Free Man* Symposium' 1:37, 38, 39; 15, 22, 29 October 1932, pp.3–4, 5–6, 3.)

9.16   From 'Editorial Notes: The Basis of Modern Nationalism' (*Modern Scot* Winter 1932)

We have argued—or maintained—in these pages that all art can be regarded as national art: the great universal artists are also national artists. But what of *Nationalist* art?

It is true, as André Gide has said, that 'it is by becoming national that a literature takes its place in humanity and acquires significance in its assembly. . . . What could be more Spanish than Cervantes, more English than Shakespeare, more Italian than Dante, more French than Voltaire or Montaigne, Descartes or Pascal, what could be more Russian than Dostoevsky, what is more universally human than these?' The writers M. Gide here names are imbued with a national spirit, are the products of a distinctive national culture; but they could not be called Nationalists. Just as there were not Nationalists, but patriots, in the England of Shakespeare's day, so Shakespeare was not self-consciously a national writer of the sort that is found today all over Europe where 'national particularism' is fostered. Shakespeare could not help being a national poet, but modern Italy, for instance, wants to *make* national poets: is this brand of Nationalism as harmful in the sphere of art as we have held it may be in the realm of politics?

No worth-while artist, of course, will allow himself to become a propagandist for Socialism, Conservatism, Nationalism, Catholicism or any other 'ism'. If he is a devout Catholic, for instance, his work may reflect the fact, but his concern in the act of creation will be for his art and not his Catholicism. [. . .] The artists who seek to 'put over' Nationalism in the way that H.G. Wells does Socialism or 'sex reform' are transparent failures, and the Nationalist writers who have caused concern to such critics as Julien Benda have not been so much the crude propagandists, the writers preaching a gospel of *l'égoisme sacré* and indulging in all sorts of racial glorification, but the writers who have sought to revive or create distinctive national modes of expression, the painters and musicians who have indulged in the exploitation of national idioms. What ought to be our attitude to them?

The Italian Minister of Education and Fine Arts said in a speech a few years ago, 'Italian artists must prepare for the new imperialist function which must be carried out by our art. Above all, we must categorically impose a principle of *Italianata*. Whoever copies a foreigner is guilty of *lèse-nation* (an insult to the nation) like a spy who admits an enemy by a secret doorway.' If such rulings had prevailed in the Middle Ages, the Catholic Church would have stood small chance of civilizing Europe, there would have been no Renaissance, none of the thousand and one interchanges between nation and nation that have had such fruitful results in art, philosophy and science.

To insist on erecting unsurmountable walls between nation and nation is as absurd as to refuse to acknowledge the existence of natural boundaries. To cultivate 'national particularism' like a hot-house plant in the name of tradition is a most untraditional thing to do: it is to fall into the errors of reaction that mark the entire neo-classical movement being fostered in so many quarters today. The classicism of Renaissance Europe was a dynamic thing; neo-classicism is static. To be Scottish was at one time to enjoy the freedom of a Dunbar or an Urquhart, whereas to be Scottish today, in the fashion of some Little-Scotlanders, is to paint in this way but—horrors!—not in that, to write music with a 'Scottish snap' and leave Stravinsky and his contemporaries out of mind, to imitate Burns but on no account Gerard Manley Hopkins. Such Nationalism is deplorable.

To some extent Nationalism must be reactionary, in a world tending towards a pernicious pseudo-Internationalism; but at its best it is not inhibitory. A true artist or philosopher would prefer to be a patriot rather than a Nationalist. When he becomes a Nationalist it is merely to combat the anti-national forces of the day. [. . .]

The Italian Minister of Education called on Italian artists to 'impose a principle of *Italianata*'. There is no doubt that the artists to whom he addressed his remarks *are* Italian artists, born into a great Italian tradition: artists in those countries where the national tradition has been destroyed or interrupted by a foreign ascendancy are in a very different position. In these latter countries a tradition has to be created, not merely exploited. Such a country is Ireland, where (at the time of writing) there wages a heated dispute as to whether the foremost Irish writers of the day *can* be considered Irish.

It is by no means an academic question. In the present atmosphere of Ireland it is deemed more important that a man be an Irish artist than that he be a good or even a great artist. When it was announced that W.B. Yeats and other Irish writers were constituting themselves into a body to be called the Irish Academy, storms of protest arose from every parish in the Free State, the objections to the proposed Academy being not that the members are not patriotic Irishmen and the best artists in Ireland, but that they were not Catholics and did not write in Erse, and consequently could not be considered Irish writers, commanding the respect of the people of the Irish Free State. This dispute over the Irish Academy raises some of the most important of the questions bearing on Nationalism and the artist. [. . .]

What is called the 'Irish consciousness' is largely the national memory, and in that memory W.B. Yeats and the rest of the members of the Irish Academy must in the future have a place; Ireland will never be able to wipe out the memory of its English-speaking past. That is not to say that the artists of the future Ireland ought not to be taught to regard Irish as their native language, but it is to insist that the circumstances governing an educational curriculum do not all apply to the appreciation of art and the honouring of artists.

Catholic, official Ireland, at the moment preoccupied with politics that will have cultural fruits in the distant future, withholds from the greatest Irishman of the day the honour that foreigners, versed in his writings, everywhere accord him. The thought should make doctrinaire Nationalists pause in some of their generalizations.

([J.H. Whyte], 'Editorial Notes: The Basis of Modern Nationalism', *Modern Scot* 3:4 winter 1932, pp.282–86 [282–85].)

9.17 'Encountering the Nazis: Some Personal Experiences' (*Free Man* July 1933)

A reader has sent us a communication, received from a friend, on his personal experiences of life in Germany at the beginning of the Hitlerite regime:

'Towards Easter, 1930 (he writes), a friend turned up, who asked me to go to Germany and teach in a Landschulheim that she was interested in. So in March I left Paris and went to this school, a co-educational and partly progressive one, five miles out of Ulm. This was quite a new experience for me, especially as I knew no German. There were 50–60 children, aged from about 6 to 17, and the place was run by a woman who had been for some 30 years in the States, where she had gathered a few ideas on new ways in education. I acquired an enthusiasm for the reform of schools and learned a good deal besides German. It was great fun, on the whole, and the children were frightfully nice and we got on famously together. The neighbourhood was delightful; the rolling pine and fir-covered hills of the Schwäbische Alb. The local inhabitants were friendly, good-natured people, very much like the yokels of Somerset, and speaking their pretty dialect. For the holidays it was ideal. Ulm lies just about the middle of Europe, almost equi-distant from Berlin, Paris, Vienna, and Prague, and you can easily slip down to the Bodensee and over to Switzerland. I went down the Danube to Vienna, visited various parts of Switzerland, including the Lago Maggiore, spent one holiday in Italy, as well as seeing parts of South Germany. It was really most agreeable. So I stayed on at this Land-schulheim till the end of last December, when I went to Dresden. I was being put up for a job in a German University, when Hitler arrived, and that finished that. My Ministerialrat was himself immediately out of office, and anyhow the new-born Germany had no further use for foreigners. It was an exciting time. The house where I was staying was raided three times, once illegally by Nazis in the middle of the night, and twice legally by a mixture of Nazis and police, who on one occasion were there from 11.30 a.m. till 6 p.m. Many people, of course, disappeared from view, and will never be seen again. Terrible things happened even in our neigh-bourhood, which was a peaceful suburb of Dresden. The change was so sudden and complete, though, and the control so strict that after the first few terrifying days it was almost impossible to find out what was going on, except through foreign papers. The German press became quite useless as a means of getting information, and people only told what they had seen or experienced to friends they felt quite sure of. You had to be extremely cautious in conversation, because denouncers were hanging about every-where—in public places, in trams, trains and 'buses, even listening outside houses to catch what was being said inside—and the legal punishment for telling a story of Nazi cruelty or making impolite reference to Hitler and his government was one year's imprisonment, while you stood a good chance of being beaten up in one of the Nazi Brown Houses. It has all become even stricter now, and you are to be regarded as 'in league with Marxist agitators' if you fail to report anyone who tells you such a story or makes discontented remarks about the Hitler regime. The fact of being a foreigner makes no difference; every consul in Germany knows of cases where foreigners have been maltreated. Some, including at least one Englishman, have been killed, and one of the assistant correspondents of *The Times* has actually been beaten by Nazis in the street, for overtaking a car of Nazi leaders. It is noteworthy that the other nations are definitely not bringing pressure to bear on Hitler's government, although they work themselves up over anything that the Russian government does.'

('Encountering the Nazis: Some Personal Experiences', anonymous report *Free Man* 2:26, 29 July 1933, p.5.)

9.18 N.K.W. [Nannie K. Wells], from 'The 20th Century Man's Ideals: Fascism and the Alternative' (*Free Man* August 1933)

Our ineffable contemporary, the *Morning Post*, is running a series of articles in which the great inventor and only true Apostle of Fascism defines his platform—Mussolini claims not only to have built up and consolidated a new form of national government: he claims to have ushered in a new era in Civilisation. The age of Constitutional Government is over, we are told. What Balfour called the 'organised quarrel' in Westminster no longer suffices to cope with the demand of modern legislation. [. . .]

Fascism might almost be considered as the logical outcome of the Trade Union Mind. Anyhow, Mankind, it seems has '*forsaken Liberty for Leadership*'. Upon this the new era of Mussolini will be built. 'Demo-Liberalism' is dead. A new ideal has taken possession of the twentieth century Man. '*Millions of men*', says our Dictator, '*have seen and understood*'. The phrase is significant: not, 'chosen' or 'willed', or 'decided', or 'believed'—simply 'seen and understood'—it implies somehow an inarticulate mass—one sees them a dead-weight or *live*-weight if you like—on board of transport—or as a class of intelligent children with a teacher standing by the blackboard, pictures into which one cannot fit by any stretch of imagination, the argumentative and fissiparous Scots: a picture, nevertheless, which appears to furnish a pattern sufficiently attractive to other nations to induce imitation, for to that formula in the end can be traced both the Nazi regime and the Roosevelt dictatorship. [. . .]

Let us not underestimate the power of this Challenge. Democracy is hardly even on its trial any more; it has been condemned and dismissed in too many countries. Even France, the Arch-Apostle of the sacred principles—doubts and speaks with too many and varying voices—[. . .]

Every fresh revelation of the origin of both Fascisti and Nazi organisations show that the money on which they were reared came from great capitalistic sources and that means also militarist sources. Both had their first origins in Socialism, borrowed the sheep clothing to attract the flock and when they had gathered the multitude together betrayed them. The American financing of Mussolini is now authenticated history: the militaristic sources of Nazi funds are only hinted at, as yet anonymously. But by their fruits ye shall know them and as these shew more plainly the parent tree is more plainly recognised. A time of heart-searching—of courageous decision, of endurance, of determined resistance to these false ideals awaits all Free Men.

Maybe it is for them that our Scotland has lain fallow these years—so that within us, Leadership and Liberty—may again be reconciled, as they have been more than once in our history as a Nation.

(N.K.W. [Nannie K. Wells], 'Fascism and the Alternative', *Free Man* 2:30, 26 August 1933, p.4.)

9.19 Compton Mackenzie, from 'Quo Vadis?' (*Free Man* September 1933)

Only one argument with any practical bearing on the future of Scotland as an independent nation has emerged from the controversy which has nearly wrecked the National Party within five years of its birth—that at whatever cost to individual aspirations and beliefs the prime need for the country is a Parliament sitting on Scottish soil, even if the full effectiveness of such a Parliament should be temporarily hampered by the limitations imposed upon itself in a spirit of compromise.

Would such a Parliament serve as a spring-board for the nation to leap forward and seize ultimately a true independence, or would it act as a feather-bed on which national hopes would be forever drowsed into a comfortable nonentity? The Nationalist who can feel sure of the answer to that question need have no hesitation according to the answer in supporting or opposing the coalition of the National Party with the Scottish Party, for it is clear that a coalition between those two parties will bring the attainment of some kind of Parliament in Scotland perceptibly nearer.

Unfortunately the discussion of this coalition has been embittered by so much personal recrimination that the outsider may be excused for supposing that the protracted dog-fight which has been going on for nearly a year now is an earnest of the dog-fight on a larger scale that will be started by the restoration of the Scottish Parliament. Before attempting to suggest an answer to what I regard as purely a question of political strategy I will put down my own beliefs.

(1) I believe more fervidly than ever that the only hope of Scotland's escaping the maelstrom in which the greater part of Europe must be involved within a comparatively short time is an independence as complete as the independence of Norway.

(2) I believe as a natural corollary of this that the Union of 1707 between Scotland and England should be dissolved as soon as possible.

(3) I believe further that the dissolution of the Union between the two countries cannot be really effective unless there shall be a simultaneous dissolution of the Union of the Crowns. I am not yet convinced that a republic would be an ideal form of government for Scotland, and therefore I would support with absolute loyalty any member of the reigning House who would bring back with him from Westminster the Stone of Destiny and be crowned at Scone as an independent monarch.

(4) I believe that, since there is no evidence for the present existence of the British Empire conceived by sentimental imperialists, it is otiose for England and Scotland to argue about the claims and responsibilities of maternity, and that the only practical way in which Scotland can justify her claim to be a motherland is to enter into direct relations with the Dominions. I believe that we may confidently expect from such a relationship a more solid

basis for mutual help than the present utterly unsatisfactory relationship between what is called Great Britain and the British Dominions overseas.

(5) I believe that all Crown Colonies should be offered an opportunity to declare themselves English or Scottish Crown Colonies.

(6) I believe that absolute neutrality during the next European War is vital to Scotland's existence, and for that reason that any surrender of Scottish harbours or air-bases into English control is unimaginable.

(7) I believe that the economic life of Scotland can only be saved by a financial revolution which will cut free from the antiquated financial system to which England is chained.

(8) Finally, I believe in the repudiation of all treaties, agreements, conventions and debts which are not acknowledged and ratified by a Scottish Parliament elected five years after the dissolution of the Union. [. . .]

We extremists have to face the fact that any Scottish Parliament is unlikely at first to be more than an extension of a County Council, and we have to decide whether the existence of such a glorified County Council would help or hinder the fruition of our aims. Of one thing I am perfectly certain, and that is the absurdity of there being two Parliamentary parties aiming at what seems in the most favourable light to be nothing more than a measure of 'Home Rule', and therefore every nationalist who believes in the policy of fighting Parliamentary elections should sacrifice his personal prejudices to promote a coalition between the National Party and the Scottish Party. Dogfights have a distressing effect on the public ear, and the allotment of the right proportion of blame to the dog that began it is apt to appear of less importance than the unpleasant row. Recent squabbles have undoubtedly had a most depressing effect on the popular attitude towards Nationalism. A rapprochement between the National Party and the Scottish Party would certainly have a favourable effect on public opinion. No Nationalist who believes in the policy of the Parliamentary approach should hesitate to work for unity between the National Party and the Scottish Party. Any other course will present itself to public opinion as illogical and petty. [. . .]

(Compton Mackenzie, 'Quo Vadis?', *Free Man* 2:35, 30 September 1933, pp.4–5.)

9.20 James Leslie Mitchell, letter to James Barke (January 1934)

Welwyn Garden 658

107 Handside Lane
Welwyn Garden City
24.1.34

My dear Barke,

(I wish you wouldn't sign yourself simply Barke—it makes me think you've got a peerage!) many thanks for the letter. I've been looking forward to reading *The Wild MacRaes*, but so far Collins have neglected to send a copy! They're pretty dud people, anyhow—especially if they're afraid to go full out on a second novel.

Sure I'll let you have a private as well as a public opinion—a quite unbiassed one!

Mungo Park (*Niger*) is coming on 1st Feb. Shameful to relate, it's a strong Book Soc recommand [sic]. On the same date my *Conquest of the Maya* (a Mitchell book) is coming from Jarrolds. I regard it as about twice as important as the Gibbon. It's going to raise such a howl here and in America among the historical Confusionists!—it's the first sane attempt at an explanation of the development of ancient Amerindian civilization.

Glad you're finding holes in the Diffusionists. Let's hear of them. After having disposed of Breasted, Flinders Petrie, Leonard Woolley and Imbelloni, we'll be only too pleased to whet our teeth on the historical materialists. . . . But remember—facts and dates—not pious affirmations of 'the similarity of the human mind' or imaginative datings of a site from mould-deposits or the like! (I take some pleasure in demolishing that kind of data in *The Conquest*.)

I haven't read the Soviet book, but I'll get my library to order it. Only too glad if the Russians have anything new to say: such of their anthropologists as I've read are (their own territory and Central Asia apart) the most absurd of all the Confusionists, mouthing infantile theses and unsupported affirmations with an energy which can only be described as fatuous. . . I'm hoping for something better.

So you've met the Douglasite-Nationalist-Communist-Anarchist Grieve? What a boy! I think his sections (and probably mine!) of *Scottish Scene* will move you to tears when it come out in May . . .

Holy God—I must get on with some work! We all flourish here. I hope Mrs Barke and the progeny and yourself are very well. I'm coming to Scotland in May and I hope to see you all.

Blessings,

Yours, Jas. Leslie Mitchell.

(James Leslie Mitchell, letter to James Barke 24 January 1934, James Barke Archive, Mitchell Library, Glasgow.)

9.21 Edwin Muir, from 'Bolshevism and Calvinism' (*European Quarterly* May 1934)

My purpose in this essay is to draw a comparison between Calvinism and Bolshevism (which seem to me to resemble each other in important respects), hoping that this may lead to a clearer understanding of both, and hence to a clearer awareness of what is happening in our own time. I shall try to remain as impartial as I can, for the fight for and against Communism is bound to go on; and to try to see clearly the logic that directs the combat and the fighters, though at first glance a purely passive act, is yet one which should be attempted for the sake of clarity, and one which, seeing the communists are still in an inconsiderable minority, may be of some use.

Calvinism has historically run its course; it has helped to change the face of society and as a factor in historical development has disappeared; it has thus for the student a double advantage over Bolshevism: we can see it completely in its rise, triumph, decline and fall, and we can estimate some of its consequences. I shall use Calvinism, therefore, as a light to examine the contemporary movement.

I shall begin with some of the resemblances between the two creeds. The following statements are true of Calvinism. First, it was a deterministic theory holding that certain changes were inevitable and that its own ultimate triumph was assured. Secondly, to concentrate its forces it possessed one central scripture reinforced by a mass of guiding exegesis, and encouraged the unremitting study of that scripture, attributing to all secular literature, of whatever nature, a secondary importance. Thirdly, on the model of its scripture it set up a complete new system of life and created a new machinery which was designed to be at once theoretically sound and practically efficient. Fourthly, in its secular policy it was eminently realistic, employing the pretext of liberty, as all young movements do before they attain power, but using the same weapons as its enemies: that is, repression and discipline within, and craft and force without. Fifthly, while in its triumph still hostile to literature and other forms of traditional culture, it showed an extraordinary enthusiasm for education and an almost fanatical belief in its efficacy. Sixthly, it essentially sought and secured the victory of a class which was at the time under a stigma, for 'the elect' were roughly the new commercial stratum which was already beginning to rise to the top. Seventhly, once it had triumphed it set up a dictatorship by committees and preferred the claims of the mass to those of the individual, exercising a strict control over people's private affairs. Eighthly, it revolted against the traditional conception of love and marriage, and while disgusted by the Romantic attitudes of chivalry, made divorce easier, at once rationalizing and loosening the marriage tie. And finally, it was in its policy international and revolutionary, from a convenient centre encouraging rebellion against the old order in other countries.

Let us see how this picture fits Bolshevism. Bolshevism, too, is founded on a deterministic theory, envisages an inevitable triumph, is inspired by one book to which it attributes infallibility, relegates secular literature to a secondary position, has elaborated a complete system and machinery of politics founded on its chief scripture, and is trying to perfect that

355

machinery so as to achieve the utmost efficiency. It is eminently realistic in its policy, essentially seeks the victory of a single class, once under a stigma, and rules now in its triumph in Russia by a dictatorship of committees. It is in revolt against whatever romanticizes the relations between the sexes, and to its adherents women are 'comrades' just as to the early Calvinists women were 'sisters'. And finally it has an antipathy to traditional culture and a sanguine faith in education, and is both international and revolutionary.

These correspondences seem to me to be more than merely curious. But before going further I wish to make it clear that I am not attempting anything so foolish as an identification of Calvinism and Bolshevism, but only suggesting a parallelism. The creeds of Calvin and Marx do not coincide at any point. The Calvinist was essentially concerned with his relation to God; the Marxian is not concerned with God at all. The Calvinist wished to create a society completely governed by a religious discipline; the Bolshevist's ideal is a society purely secular. The two theories are so far apart that they seem to apply to separate worlds; everything in these two worlds is different: the objects themselves, the terms in which the mind conceives them; yet when one has admitted all this the haunting sense of a parallelism remains: it is as if the one world were a copy of the other, a copy in which all the objects are altered even to their names, but are yet recapitulated in the same logical order. To put it briefly, in content these two creeds are quite dissimilar, but in logical structure they are astonishingly alike.

And both have this further resemblance: that they are essentially logical. The central scripture, the water-tight system, the determinism assuring ultimate victory, the practical and realistic temper, the unity of aim rejecting everything which lies beyond its scope—literature, for instance— the direction of that aim towards the advancement of a chosen class, the rigid internal discipline: all these things follow self-evidently from one another. [. . .]

The type of man who produces and is in turn reproduced by such theories is well known to us in history from such figures as William the Silent, Cromwell and Knox. His virtues, with the exception of his central virtue of faith, from which all the others spring, are almost exclusively practical. He is admirably fitted to accomplish political, economic or religious changes in the objective body of society; he is often masterly in dealing with affairs and institutions, with objects in general. He accepts institutions simply as institutions and asks: How can they be made better, more rational, more in accordance with sound theory? He does not generally foresee the suffering which is caused by his changes, and when it appears he refuses to admit its justification. So after revolution comes repression tempered by education, for the same virtues which enable him to direct the change now compel him to master its consequences. The

Calvinist type, in general, has thus an unrivalled capacity for action, and a less than normal capacity for living. [. . .]

But here an interesting question might arise. What if Calvinism had not lost finally in its main fight against the European tradition; what if, instead of contributing to modify that tradition in the long run, it had itself become the norm of European life, accepting only such scattered elements of the older order as it could use and digest? This speculation may seem idle, but it is very apposite to the present situation, for if Communism triumphs something like this is bound to happen. Communism is not only an exclusive creed, like Calvinism; it becomes, once it has triumphed, an all-inclusive one. For while the secular aim of Calvinism was to emancipate a single class, that of Communism is to free the last class of all; and to do that is not merely to stand out against society, to set up a smaller civilization within a greater one, but to transform civilization radically in all its parts and leave nothing as it was before. If Communism triumphs there will be no returning to the old European tradition [. . .] Communism sees only one choice for society, a choice relished by communists and disliked by their opponents, yet exercising almost as great an influence on the one as the other; for by persistently suggesting that there are only two possible attitudes, its own and the reverse, it circumscribes its opponents' way of thinking as strictly as its own. To believe that society can be both economically just and free, without being ruled by a dictatorship or subject to a political inquisition, requires a certain degree of freedom of mind, and freedom of mind on political questions is becoming more and more difficult to achieve. The whole Marxian argument is directed to proving that Communism is the necessary and inevitable next stage of historical evolution and it amounts in reality to an overpowering suggestion.

(Edwin Muir, 'Bolshevism and Calvinism', *European Quarterly* 1:1 May 1934, pp.3–11
[3–6, 8–9, 11].)

9.22   Lewis Grassic Gibbon, from *Scottish Scene* (1934)

a) From 'Glasgow'

In those days of Nationalism, of Douglasism, (that ingenious scheme for childbirth without pain and—even more intriguing—without a child), of Fascism, Glasgow, as no other place, moves me to a statement of faith. I have amused myself with many political creeds—the more egregious the creed the better. I like the thought of a Scots Republic with Scots Border Guards in saffron kilts—the thought of those kilts can awake me to joy in the middle of the night. I like the thought of Miss Wendy Wood leading a Scots Expeditionary Force down to Westminster to reclaim the Scone Stone: I would certainly march with that expedition myself in spite of the risk of dying of laughter by the way. I like the thought of a Scots Catholic king-dom with Mr Compton Mackenzie Prime Minister to some disinterred Jacobite royalty, and all the Scots intellectuals settled out on the land on thirty-acre crofts, or sent to recolonize St Kilda for the good of their souls and the nation (except the hundreds streaming over the Border in panic flight at sight of this Scotland of their dreams). I like the thought of the ancient Scots aristocracy revived and set in order by Mr George Blake, that ephor of the people: Mr Blake vetoing the Duke of Montrose is one of my dearest visions. I like the thought of the Scottish Fascists evicting all those of Irish blood from Scotland, and so leaving Albyn entirely deserted but for some half-dozen pro-Irish Picts like myself. I like the thought of a Scottish Socialist Republic under Mr Maxton—preferably at war with royalist England, and Mr Maxton summoning the Russian Red Army to his aid (the Red Army digging a secret tunnel from Archangel to Aberdeen). And I like the thought of Mr R.M. Black and his mysterious Free Scots, that modern Mafia, assassinating the Bankers (which is what bankers are for). . . .

But I cannot play with those fantasies when I think of the hundred and fifty thousand in Glasgow. They are a something that stills the parlour chatter. [. . .]

There is nothing in culture or art that is worth the life and elementary happiness of one of those thousands who rot in the Glasgow slums. There is nothing in science or religion. If it came (as it may come) to some fantastic choice between a free and independent Scotland, a centre of culture, a bright flame of artistic and scientific achievement, and providing elementary decencies of food and shelter to the submerged proletariat of Glasgow and Scotland, I at least would have no doubt as to which side of the battle I would range myself. For the cleansing of that horror, if cleanse it they could, I would welcome the English in suzerainty over Scotland till the end of time. I would welcome the end of Braid Scots and Gaelic, our culture, our history, our nationhood under the heels of a Chinese army of occupation if it could cleanse the Glasgow slums, give a surety of food and play—the elementary right of every human being—to those people of the abyss.

b) From 'The Land'

That is The Land out there, under the sleet, churned and pelted there in the dark, the long rigs upturning their clayey faces to the spear-onset of the sleet. That is The Land, a dim vision this night of laggard fences and long stretching rigs. And the voice of it—the true and unforgettable voice—you can hear even such a night as this as the dark comes down, the immemorial plaint of the peewit, flying lost. *That* is The Land—though not quite all.

Those folk in the byre whose lantern light is a glimmer through the sleet as they muck and bed and tend the kye, and milk the milk into tin pails, in curling froth—they are The Land in as great a measure. Those two, a dual power, are the protagonists in this little sketch. They are the essentials for the title. And besides, quite unfairly, they are all so intimately mine that I would give them that position though they had not a shadow of a claim to it.

I like to remember that I am of peasant rearing and peasant stock. Good manners prevail on me not to insist on the fact over-much, not to boast in the company of those who come from manses and slums and castles and villas, the folk of the proletariat, the bigger and lesser bourgeoisies. But I am again and again, as I hear them talk of their origins and beginnings and begetters, conscious of an overweening pride that mine was thus and so, that the land was so closely and intimately mine (my mother used to hap me in a plaid in harvest-time and leave me in the lee of a stook while she harvested) that I feel of a strange and antique age in the company and converse of my adult peers—like an adult himself listening to the bright sayings and laughters of callow boys, parvenus on the human scene, while I, a good Venriconian Pict, harken from the shade of my sun circle and look away, bored, in pride of possession at my terraced crops, at the on-ding of rain and snow across my leavened fields. . . .

How much this is merely reaction from the hatreds of my youth I do not know. For once I had a very bitter detestation for all this life of the land and the folk upon it. [. . .]

Not, I think, that I have gone the full circle and have returned among the romantics. As I listen to that sleet-drive I can see the wilting hay-ricks under the fall of the sleet and think of the wind ablow on ungarmented floors, ploughmen in sodden bothies on the farms outbye, old, bent and wrinkled people who have mislaid so much of fun and hope and high endeavour in grey servitude to those rigs curling away, only half-inanimate, into the night. I can still think and see these things with great clarity though I sit in this warm room and write this pleasant essay and find pleasure in the manipulation of words on a blank page. But when I read or hear our new leaders and their plans for making of Scotland a great peasant nation, a land of little farms and little farming communities, I am moved to a bored disgust with those pseudo-literary romantics playing with politics, those refugees from the warm parlours and lights and policemen and theatre-stalls of the Scots cities. They are promising the New Scotland a purgatory that would decimate it. They are promising it narrowness and bitterness and heart-breaking toil in one of the most unkindly agricultural lands in the world. They are promising to make of a young, ricketic man, with the phthisis of Glasgow in his throat, a bewildered labourer in pelting rains and the flares of head-aching suns, they are promising him years of a murderous monotony, poverty and struggle and loss of happy human relationships. They promise that of which they know nothing, except through sipping of the scum of Kailyard romance.

For this life is for no modern man or woman—even the finest of these. It belongs to a different, an alien generation. That winter that is sweeping up the Howe, bending the whins on Auchindriech hill, seeping with pelting blasts through the old walls of Edzell Castle, malagarousing the ploughed lands and swashing about and above the heavy cattle-courts where in darkness the great herds lie cud-chewing and breath-blowing in frosty steam, is a thing for most to be stared at, tourist-wise, endured for a day or a week. This night, the winter on the countryside, the crofter may doze contentedly in the arm-chair in the ingle-neuk and the mistress yawn with an equal content at the clock. For you or I or young Simon who is taking his girl to the pictures it is as alien and unendurable in permanence as the life of the Kamtchatkan.

c) From 'Religion'

Definition is the better part of dissertation. Before one sets to a sketch of Religion in Scotland it is as well to state what Religion is not. It is not altruism, it is not awe, it is not the exercise of a super-conscious sense. It is not ethics; it is not morality. It is neither the evolution of primitive Fear into civilized Worship nor the deified apprehension of an extra-mundane Terror.

Instead, a Religion is no more than a corpus of archaic science. The origin of Religion was purely utilitarian. Primitives—the food-gatherers, the ancient folk of all the ancient world—knew no religion. Their few and scattered survivors in this and that tiny crinkle of our planet are as happily irreligious as our own remote ancestors. They are without gods or devils, worship or cities, sacrifices or kings, theologies or social classes. Man is naturally irreligious. Religion is no more fundamental to the human character than cancer is fundamental to the human brain. [. . .]

Religion for the Scot was essentially a means of assuring himself life in the next world, health in this, prosperity, wealth, fruitful wombs and harvests. The Auld Kirk in Scotland is the greatest example of an armchair scientific Religion known to the world since the decay of the great State cults of Egypt and Mexico. In the case of all three countries the Gods were both unlovely and largely unloved; and in the case of all three definite discomforts of apparel and conduct were undergone in return for definite celestial favours manifested upon the terrestrial scene. [. . .] In Scotland the human mind and the human body were in thrall to what the orthodox would call a reign of religion, what the Diffusionist historian recognizes as the reign of a cultural aberration, what the political student might appre- hend as a reign of terror. The fears and hopes of long-defunct Levantines, as set forth in the Christian Bible, were accepted as a code of conduct, as a science of life, and foisted upon the Scottish scene without mercy and greatly without favour. This is an attempt at impartial statement, not an expression of anti-Christianity. Had they been the codes of the Korân or the Rig-veda the scene would doubtlessly have been even more farcical objectively, if in subjective essence the same. [. . .]

Debating those elementary facts with regard to Religion in Scotland the present writer before this time has met with the surprising complaint: 'And what is going to happen now? What are you going to put in the place of Religion?' The question shows some confusion of mind. The present writer had no hand in bringing about the decay of Religion; nor, alas, is he likely to have any hand in planning its succession. That succession lies with great economic and historical movements now in being—movements which may bring to birth the strangest of progeny on which we may look aghast. Of the future of Religion ultimately the historian can have little doubt: he sees its coming in ancient times, in the world of the Simple Men, as a cortical abortion, a misapprehension of the functions and activities of nature inter-larded and interwoven with attributes mistakenly applied to human rulers. He sees its passing from the human scene—even the Scots scene—in the processes of change, immutable and unstayable. But—

But there may be long delays in that passing. Another abortion of inactive brains—that of Fascism—looms over a tormented world, a creed of the *must* jungle brute, the cowardly degenerate who fears the fine steely glimmer of the open spaces of the heavens, the winds of change, the flow and cry of strange seas and stars in human conduct and human hope—who would drag men back into economic night, into slavery to the state, into slavery (all slaveries aid his purpose) to the archaic institutions of Religion. What has happened in Italy and Germany may happen in Scotland. The various Scots nationalist parties have large elements of Fascism within them. There is now a definite Fascist Party. If ever such philosophy should reach to power then again we may see deserted streets of a Sabbath, crowded kirks, persecutions and little parish tyrannies, a Free Kirk minister's millenial dream. If such should be the play of chance it is to be hoped that the historian (albeit himself on the way to the scaffold or the pillory) will look on the process with a cool dispassion, seeing it as no more than a temporary deviation, a thing that from its nature cannot endure. Man has survived this disease far too long either to perish in its last bout of fever or permanently retire into delirium tremens. [. . .]

Yet [. . .] men are not merely the victims, the hapless leaves storm-blown, of historic forces, but may guide if they cannot generate that storm [. . .].

(Lewis Grassic Gibbon, <i>Scottish Scene or The Intelligent Man's Guide to Albyn</i>,
pp.139–41; 293–94; 313–15, 325–26.)

9.23 'Controversy: Writers' International (British Section)' (*Left Review* February 1935)

A discussion was begun in the December LEFT REVIEW *on the statement of aim adopted at the conference which established this section of the Writers' International, and this discussion is continued. The text of the statement was published both in the October and the December issues of* LEFT REVIEW.

a) From Lewis Grassic Gibbon

A great part of the thesis seems to me to propound ideas which are false, and projects which are irrelevant.

It is nonsense to say that modern literature is narrowing in 'content'; there was never in the history of English letters such a variety of books on such a variety of subjects, never such continuous display of fit and excellent technique. One need do no more than glance through an issue of *The Times Literary Supplement* to be convinced of this.

To say that the period from 1913 to 1934 is a decadent period is just, if I may say so, bolshevik blah. Neither in fiction, sociological writing, biography (to take only three departments) was there work done half so well in any Victorian or Edwardian period of equal length.

So-called revolutionary statements on decadence (such as that contained in the resolution) seem to me to be inspired by (a) misapprehension; (b) ignorance; or (c) spite.

It is obvious that such revolutionists imagine that modern fiction means only Aldous Huxley, modern drama Noel Coward, modern biography the Lytton Stracheyites, and modern history the half-witted Spenglerites.

So much for misapprehension and ignorance. But the spite is also very real. Not only do hordes of those 'revolutionary' writers never read their contemporaries (they wallow instead, and exclusively, in clumsy translations from the Russian and German) but they hate and denigrate those contemporaries with a quite Biblical uncharitableness and malice. With a little bad Marxian patter and the single adjective 'bourgeois' in their vocabularies they proceed (in the literary pages of the *Daily Worker* and like organs) to such displays of spiteful exhibitionism as warrant the attentions of a psycho-analyst. From their own innate secondrate-ness they hate and despise good work just as they look upon any measure of success accruing to a book (not written by one of their own intimate circle) with a moronic envy.

Not all revolutionary writers (I am a revolutionary writer) are cretins. But the influence of such delayed adolescents, still in the grip of wishfulfilment dreams, seems to have predominated in the drawing up of this resolution. Capitalist literature, whether we like it or not, is not in decay; capitalist economics have reached the verge of collapse, which is quite a different matter. Towards the culmination of a civilization the arts, so far from decaying, always reach their greatest efflorescence (the veriest tyro student of the historic processes knows this).

That efflorescence is now in being. It is not a decayed and decrepit dinosaur who is the opponent of the real revolutionary writer, but a very healthy and vigorous dragon indeed—so healthy that he can still afford to laugh at the revolutionist. If revolutionary writers believe they can meet in fraternal pow-wows and talk the monster to death by calling it 'bourgeois' and 'decadent' they are living in a clown's paradise.

Having said all this in criticism, I'll proceed to a little construction:

First, I'm in favour of a union of revolutionary writers. But this union would

(a) Consist only of those who have done work of definite and recognized literary value (from the revolutionary viewpoint). It would consist of professional journalists, novelists, historians, and the like, who before admittance would have to *prove* their right to admittance.

(b) Exclude that horde of paragraphists, minor reviewers, ghastly poetasters and all the like amateurs who clog up the machinery of the left wing literary movement.

(c) Set its members, as a first task, to drawing up a detailed and unimpassioned analysis of contemporary literature and the various literary movements.

(d) Be a shock brigade of writers, not a P.S.A. sprawl.

I hate capitalism; all my books are explicit or implicit propaganda. But because I'm a revolutionist I see no reason for gainsaying my own critical judgment—hence this letter!

b) From Hugh MacDiarmid

Alec Brown is wrong in what he says about the 'proletarianization of our actual language'. Apart from the fact that to speak of 'getting right down to spoken English' in literary work is a misleading phrase, suggesting an essentially unrealizable objective and depending upon an altogether false equating (almost identifying) of life and literature, the whole attitude means just a kind of 'talking down to the people'. It threatens a short-circuiting of human consciousness and a stereotyping of the cultural disabilities that have been forced upon the working class by capitalism.

Far more allusive writing (or oral literature) than any contemporary work (except only its remnants in the music halls and in certain strains of working-class talk which are excessively allusive) was not over the heads of working-class people in Elizabethan days, in Gaelic Ireland in the Penal Age, and at many other times, and appeals to a deep-seated human desire, just as the obvious, the over-simplified, the pre-digested 'pap' is abhorrent.

The literature of the future cannot be 'thirled' to limitations that have had their roots in lack of educational opportunity and other methods of mass mutilation. Lenin was right when he insisted upon the full rigour of the word, upon the retention of the entire jargon—the technical terms—of Marxism, and refused to give Russian workers 'Marx-without-tears'. Similarly, in regard to the sciences, the technical terminology is indispensable to an understanding of the points at issue; simplification is falsification. There is no easy way—no short cut—to proletarian culture.

I would add that I am amused to note Alec Brown's insistence on English this and English that, and, similarly, Simon Blumenfeld's quite irrelevant remarks on 'English, the language of forty millions in Britain, millions overseas, and a hundred and twenty millions in America'. Proletarian culture—like every other culture—depends upon considerations of quality, not quantity, and there is no ground whatever for concluding that any better work is likely to be done in a language that hundreds of millions speak and read than in one that is only used by a fraction of a million.

('Controversy: Writers' International (British Section)': responses by Lewis Grassic Gibbon and Hugh MacDiarmid to the Conference statement of aim, *Left Review* 1, 1935, pp.179–80; 182.)

9.24 Edwin Muir, from *Scottish Journey* (1935)

Thus far I have been merely trying from an inadequate knowledge of Scottish history (and all Scottish history is inadequate and confusing; it has still to be written) to show why Scotland's existence as a nation was always unstable and incomplete, and why it finally dissolved. The reasons for this were partly geographical and partly racial, if the Celtic legend is to be given the credence that it is more and more acquiring. [. . .] These various obstacles then—geographical inaccessibility, local culture, separate language—have almost vanished, and there seems to be no palpable hindrance to the union of Scotland as a nation. If there was a really strong demand for such a union, England could not withhold it, nor probably attempt to do so. The real obstacle to the making of a nation out of Scotland lies now in the character of the people, which is a result of their history, as their history was in a large measure of the things of which I have been speaking, geographical and racial. And that obstacle, being the product of several centuries of life, is a serious one; it is, in fact, Scotland.

It is these things that make the National Party of Scotland so unconvincing. One can see that self-government for Scotland is a desirable ideal, but like all Utopian ideals it takes no account of history, past or present; indeed, it takes less account of present than of past history. That being the case, where is the force that will drive the people of Scotland to proclaim themselves a nation? In the heads of a few people, mainly middle-class, with an admixture of the intelligentsia, who see that Scotland a nation is a desirable aim. But meanwhile the people themselves, like the people of every industrial country of Europe, are being driven by the logic of necessity to a quite different end, the most convenient term for which is Socialism. Who in such circumstances can take Scottish Nationalism seriously, or even wish that it should enjoy a brief triumph, when processes so much more serious and profound are at work in the whole of society? [. . .] A hundred years of Socialism would do more to restore Scotland to health and weld it into a real nation than a thousand years—if that were conceivable—of Nationalist government such as that to which the National Party of Scotland looks forward; for even if the country were governed by Scotsmen, the economic conflicts within it could still generate the same intestine hatreds as they do now, and would still deserve to do so.

Looking, then, at Scotland as impartially as I could, in the little room of the hotel on that last evening of my run, I seemed to see that it was ripe for two things: to become a nation, and to become a Socialist community; but I could not see it becoming the one without becoming the other.

(Edwin Muir, *Scottish Journey*, pp.231–34.)

9.25 Catherine Carswell, 'Mackenzie *versus* Knox', review of *Catholicism in Scotland* by Compton Mackenzie (*Spectator* March 1936)

Accounts of persecution on either side in any great human dispute diminish with time in their effect upon us if narrated without particular reference to their causes. Allowing for this, Mr Mackenzie's book contains much that will win the sympathies of even non-Catholic readers, and the most rabid anti-Catholics will be able to learn much from it while doubtless strengthening their own convictions. There will remain a sceptical minority, perhaps a majority, who hold that Catholicism and Protestantism alike failed Scotland, or, what comes to the same thing, that Scotland failed them.

Mr Mackenzie's narrative is certainly full of horrors, and in a manner as lively, if not also as deadly as vitriol, he tells us what he thinks of the Scottish Reformation and John Knox. More than once he states his case by comparing the coming of Protestantism in Scotland with the forcing of Communism upon the unwilling majority of the Russian nation by a minority in the early days of the Soviets. And he extends the parallel by reminding us that both Fascism and Hitlerism owe their being to minorities. While admitting the aptness and the justice of the analogy, the reader may wish to ask why and in what circumstances minorities are so potent to become majorities. These questions Mr Mackenzie does not seriously try to answer. He ends, none the less, on a note of triumph and hope by informing us that the Catholic minority in Scotland is increasingly powerful and by proclaiming that 'the real Presence of God upon her altars will be more precious to Scotland than the real presence of a Parliament in Edinburgh'.

Thus we know where we are and that Mr Mackenzie has no objection to minorities as such. He is whole-souled and magnificently biased, so that he marshalls his material in full fighting trim, with that neglect of fairness which, as we all know, is fair in love and war and religion. To him the Tudor blood is 'black' and calamitous to England as to Scotland. Elizabeth 'lacked at once the essential bodily and spiritual characteristics of womanhood'. Knox is stigmatised as a coward—did he not slink out of Edinburgh when he knew that the Queen with 8,000 troops was advancing on the city and was he not avowedly nervous about his own election and salvation? But Ninian Winzet is commended for escaping to France when threatened with arrest. And Cardinal Beaton is ranked with Bruce and Wallace as a national hero. Wishart perceived that 'the right of private judgement carried with it as a corollary the validity of private action'. Beaton magnanimously had him strangled on the scaffold before committing his body to the flames. (And it is known that Catholics were often burned alive.) Of Charles Stuart's changes of religious front we find no mention in the long and eloquent account of Protestant wrong-doing and only one paragraph is allowed for the failure in Scotland of the main body of the Catholic clergy. Yet what could Protestantism have done but for that failure?

(Catherine Carswell, review of Compton Mackenzie's *Catholicism in Scotland*, *Spectator*
6 March 1936, p.410.)

9.26 Catherine Carswell, from letter to C.M. Grieve (May 1936)

International Association of Writers for the Defence of Culture
(British Section)
ROMNEY'S HOUSE, HOLLYBUSH HILL, LONDON, N.W.3.

17.5.36   17 Keats Grove
                                                       London. N.W.3.

My dear Christopher,

I never thanked you for your letter giving the required references (the sources *were* a disappointment, but never mind).

This, among other things is to suggest that you cough up 10/- (yes, I know, but we are all Jock Tamson's bairns there) and join the above Association if you haven't already done so. I felt I had to as there is nothing else of the sort except the P.E.N. which, being strictly non-political, is different. This means out & out anti-Fascism for members. All the most distinguished French writers of the Left are members & the Conference in Paris was a great success last summer I understand. I was asked to go & to speak, but couldn't rise to it financially or otherwise. Now, Chris, think about this, & if you decide to come in, write direct to Amabel Williams-Ellis. They will welcome suggestions from members. [. . .]

I wonder if you saw also my review of your *Eccentrics* in the *Spectator*? I hope the book is going as well as can be expected. The proofs of our Week End book—interminably held up—have not yet come home, & now the book won't be out till late autumn or even Christmas. Blast all publishers! [. . .]

I'm moving surely & rapidly toward the Left—& by that I mean Communism. It has taken me some time. Ever yours Cathie.

(Catherine Carswell, letter to C.M. Grieve, 17 May 1936. Edinburgh University Library Special Collections MS 2946.1, 22.)

9.27 James Barke, from 'The Scottish National Question' (*Left Review* November 1936)

Nationalism—political, economic or cultural—is not a deep or fundamental issue in Scotland. The overwhelming majority of the Scottish people do not feel that they are suffering from the oppression of a conquering nation. Unlike certain sections of the Irish people, they do not feel that they are a subject race forced to submit to an alien domination. Only a small section of the Scottish people are conscious of any wrong and injustice resulting from their incorporation in the 'United Kingdom'. The strength of this section is drawn almost entirely from the middle class, particularly the professional class, university students and the so-called Scottish 'intelligentsia'. It is from this section that the Scottish National Party sprang. Prominent in its membership are such figures as Compton Mackenzie (an Englishman), Eric Linklater (from the Orkneys), Neil M. Gunn, the Duke of Montrose, and the late R.B. Cunninghame Graham. The main object of the S.N.P, is 'national independence', which, being interpreted, means: 'There shall be established a Parliament which shall be the final authority on all Scottish affairs, including taxation and finance' (Scottish Prosperity pamphlet No.1).

It is true that the Scots are not without a sense of nationhood. Indeed, they are deeply imbued with a sense of national pride. Manifestations of this may be witnessed in relation to certain sporting events, particularly at

Wembley and Twickenham; and there is the taken-for-granted attitude of infinite mental, moral, physical and cultural superiority to the English.

Here, however, we are concerned mainly with the Scottish writers and the 'Intelligentsia' generally. How are we to account for the fact that 90 per cent of the Scottish writers including minor poets and a host of petty scribblers—are actively or loosely associated with the S.N.P.?

The biggest factor contributing to the growth of Scottish Nationalism had its source, significantly enough, in Fleet Street: not in the editorial departments, but (again significantly) in the advertising and circulation departments. When the race for circulation between the big dailies (Beaverbrook, Rothermere, Berry Bros., Odham's) was at a crucial stage, they discovered Scotland: the Scots actually bought newspapers. Now the Scottish Press had never evinced any interest in Scotland from a nationalist standpoint. The phrase 'Scotland a Nation' would have sounded rank separatist sedition to editors whose policy was predominantly Unionist. They would much sooner have published an article on Cornwall broccoli or Devonshire cream than an article on Tartan or Edinburgh Rock; much sooner 250 words of Sanskrit or Arabic than fifty words of native Scottish Gaelic.

But the English dailies altered all that. Out came a Scottish edition of Lord Beaverbrook's sheet and Mr H.V. Morton set out in search of Scotland. Auld Mither Scotland, neglected and despised, suddenly became news; she found herself prominently displayed in the headlines; soon it became impossible to buy a newspaper that did not claim to be Scotland's National newspaper. They proudly displayed such emblems as the Lion Rampant, the Auld Blue Blanket, and a miscellany of Pipers, Heather and Cocks o' the North.

One of the results of this was that editorial policy in Scotland changed overnight. Ex-policemen were engaged (at half rates) to write Gaelic articles consisting of translated English balderdash. When a volume of Scots (synthetic) doggerel was published, it got a full page to itself and the signal honour of a double-barrelled review by a couple of prominent publicists. And when a Scots novelist (whose previous novel had been barely mentioned) became a choice of the Book Society, the literary and national heather was not only thought to be on fire, but in full and riotous blaze. Now every aspirant to the Book Society Choice Stakes flaunted the national colours. And many Scots who had been forced across the Border to earn a decent living with their pens came scurrying back with a brief case of articles dealing with such topics as Scottish Licensing Hours, Edinburgh Castle, Deer Stalking, the Glorious Twelfth, etc., all ready to be set up.

Thus, in brief, did the English Press barons, in their drive for a redivision of the circulation market, re-discover and re-conquer Scotland.

There were other smaller agencies at work, of course. There was the influence of the B.B.C., for example. In order to justify the appellation 'Scottish Regional' they had to sweat blood to provide some tit-bit of something or other (music was the obvious standby) to differentiate themselves from the English regional stations. And their success in this is neatly summarised by a correspondent in a recent number of the nationalist monthly *Outlook*, as the work of 'jejune undergraduates and feckless hoydens'.

Not that there was ever a hint of all this. Instead, there was a great chatter about the Scottish Renaissance. Sad to relate, however, the average Scot remained cruelly indifferent to all this Nationalist ballyhooing. He selected the best free insurance (together with some volumes of Charles Dickens: what ailed them at Walter Scott?) and tuned in to the National programme. And even yet the finest and most truly national item on the Scottish wavelength—the strings of the station orchestra playing Scottish Dance Music—cannot hope to compete in popular favour with Mr Henry Hall.

But the important point for us which emerges from all this is that much strength that ought to accrue to the Left in Scotland is actually diverted into reactionary channels. Many important writers in Scotland are side-tracked by the political tenets of the S.N.P., and this has vitiated much of their work.

Nevertheless, an effort must be made to understand the problems and difficulties of Scottish writers. The best of them feel that Scotland has something unique and valuable to contribute to the world (as distinct from the Press barons) even when they sometimes make the mistake of thinking the world's boundaries lie between the Tweed and the Solway.

They are obsessed with the idea that 'the English' have destroyed and degraded Scottish national characteristics. They forget that English national characteristics have been equally degraded and debased. Capitalism in its ruthless days of ripening maturity destroyed everything that did not serve its purpose. And to-day the only use capitalism has for national traditions and characteristics is to debase them for imperialistic ends.

What our nationalist writers fail to understand is that there is no line of demarcation between English and Scottish capital. All the terrific power of gold, steel, coal, iron and political necessity has welded them together. [. . .]

The most that can be done, in conclusion, is to reassert that (1) there can be no true development of Nationalism under Capitalism, as there can be no true development of Nationalism without Internationalism (i.e. without some form of mutual co-operation and understanding by the nations of the world). (2) All that is truly national, all that is best and worthy of preservation in the various national cultures is the heritage of the workers and peasants concerned, of the class in whose hands the future lies. (3) All those writers and intellectuals (and their readers and followers) *must* ally themselves with the working class and the organisations of the working class, and so assist and be assisted in the realisation of their ideals and

369

aspirations if they are (a) genuine humanitarians, (b) real lovers of their country's best traditions, etc., (c) haters of war and Fascist bestiality and barbarism, (d) striving honestly to end the human misery and degradation which arises from the exploitation of man by man, and therefore necessarily striving for the betterment and advancement of humanity.

There is no other road out. Must there be in Scotland another 'burning of the books', concentration camps, and the degradation and denigration of culture (to mention only one aspect of Fascism); must the blood of Scotland's manhood be shed in yet another Capitalist war before the Scottish intellectuals and writers generally will open their eyes to the class nature of society and the realities of history?

Despite much disturbing evidence to support this view there is also evidence of dawning sanity and courage. Already the writers in Scotland are beginning to see their way towards unity with the workers, towards the path that will lead them towards real Peace, real Prosperity: in a word, *towards Socialism.*

(James Barke, 'The Scottish National Question', *Left Review* 2:14 November 1936, pp.739–44 [739–41, 743–44].)

9.28 From correspondence between James Barke and Neil M. Gunn (May 1938)

a) From James Barke to Neil M. Gunn (20 May 1938)

My dear Gunn, [. . .]

It was handsome of you to write P.E.N. on my behalf. I am really touched (I should be glad to know how Smith replies—in due course).

And my God, Gunn, why do you think there is always a sting in the tail of my remarks? When I speak of your art I mean your art—as I would speak of Theodore Dreisser's art, or Tolstoy's art or Gorki's art. The bourgeoisie have no special claim to our common language. Art is simply a word—neither is it bourgeois nor proletarian. I have never thought of you as bourgeois—even if you were that would be nothing to hold against you. I think that on several points you are dominated by certain philosophical and political ideas which are the ideas of the bourgeoisie as a class. But this is a sow with a very different snout. I may shout and bawl and denounce fortissimo—but I never sniff or sneer.

The German reference. I don't see anyone getting their books translated into German and published in Germany unless they support in one way or another the ideology of Hitler fascism. The censorship there is more strict than anywhere else. Nor are they above cooking translations and interpolating the desired Nazi ideology. Now I once wrote words to this effect and you took exception to them. 'The identity of Gunn's nationalist ideology with that of the Aryan theoreticians of Hitler fascism may not be so fortuitous as its superficial form and expression might indicate.' Do I make myself clear? Damnit, man, by getting published in Germany you now prove my case up to the hilt. I'd give a lot to have been proved wrong.

I don't understand what you mean by coming out for poverty, clarity—and temperance. What harm did Faith and Hope and Chastity [sic] do? Do you want to drive me nuts? When you get back we're going to have a talk and we're coming all out for Scotland and the Scottish people. I'm going to start a magazine (how I don't know—but even if it starts as a duplicated sheet it's got to start. We're going 'to raise the Scarlet Standard high' and plant the thistle in the middle of it. I'm not a Calvinist. But I've got Covenanting blood in me. Chamberlain isn't going to be the Political Patron Saint of Scotland. Now's the day and now's the hour—Oliver Brown's joined the Labour Party!!!)

On your way—and blessings on you! May you get a bigger Prize next year—big enough to take you to Russia. Drop me a card so that I'll know you're not in a concentration camp! And thanks for everything.

Bon voyage,

Ever,
[James Barke]

b) Neil M. Gunn to James Barke (21 May 1938)

My dear Barke,

Thanks for your letter and the fine spirit of it. I am still not quite clear about the PEN decision—the exact *why* of it. Did the Comm. really take dictation from an outside source? It will be interesting to find *that* out! [. . .]

About the rest of your matter, I am disappointed—principally because it shows you have not thought things out far enough. You see me dominated at several points by 'certain philosophical and political ideas which are the ideas of the bourgeois as a class'. From my books, how do you substantiate that? Even in my last—a travel book—the philosophical and political ideas are all of and for the people, the poor folk themselves, and very explicitly against the class that has exploited them. Landlordism, with all it connotes—the place is the West—is condemned not merely in the past but in the present. I had a lengthy fight with my publishers over extensive 'cuts' and had to give in (after taking legal opinion on my own) because it was proved to me that libel action against us (publishers, printers, too) would be successful. Truth, I found, can be a damning form of libel. And not merely in the economic, but in the spiritual or creative, I took the same line. I even show myself being moved in the sort of way 'communist poets' are moved. I took it from the economic to the spiritual (poetry, music). And so on. To say that this is the bourgeois attitude is unintelligible to me. In my last novel (called *Highland River*) I have the same fundamental attitude, going so far at one point to say that those who talk of 'glittering prizes' (the bourgeois to me) should be . . . 'bombed to smithereens'.

But it's no good going on, because if you haven't seen what I'm getting at you'll never see it. I suppose that what troubles you is my method of expression. You confound a certain shall we say apparent philosophic calm or joyousness or something of the sort as connoting satisfaction with things as they are. Can the manner be of more significance here than the matter? And now when you ask me, as quoting your 'The identity of Gunn's nationalist ideology with that of the Aryan theoretician . . .', if you make yourself clear, I not only reply no, but—as happened when I first read it— am left still in the dark. Not that I am here judging the Aryan theoretician. I am merely trying to get a slant on your insight or lack of it and challenging you to produce from my writings any expressed idea anywhere in support of your thesis. (Unless, of course, your new fine concern over what you are going to do for Scotland—and cheers for that!—is also of the order of Aryan theory!) To be precise—the book of mine published in Germany is *Butcher's Broom*. Go through it with some care—and then let me hear your verdict. If, in fact, you find in that book an ideology akin to that of early Christian communalism, possibly expressed today in Anarchism, I may at least see some intelligence at work! Whether I agree or not. Because I have never been a member of a church, good Xians call me an atheist. Am I to abhor Christ and what he said, because Rome ritualised him? Must one be a churchman or an atheist—with no more to be said? Do you expect me to argue seriously about that? Must my life always be restricted by the need to adhere wholly to a positive or wholly to a negative—when my intelligence can demonstrate that the whole truth is in neither? I can play the party game as well as anyone. Have done it for years. Committees an' all. But as writers, surely we have a bit of individual thinking and synthesising to do on our own. If I honestly feel that there is something of our common humanity in *Butcher's Broom*, should I not naturally want Germans and other peoples to read it as well as my own people? For the Germans as a people, a folk, I have always had a deep respect, and feel that I owe them something for the hours of intense delight I have got out of their music alone. How on earth are we to let the Germans or the Russians or other peoples know that we believe we are all of the common people unless we contrive to let them know?

From your ideological point of view, I simply have no idea why Germany published B.B. I assume that publishers publish in order to make money primarily. It may be that your remarks about me may have helped! They may be saying things about me that I know nothing about. And B.B. does not hit at any order of society except the order of society which prevailed at its period, which was landlordism (capitalism) rampant, and which is exposed, I hope, pretty ruthlessly and certainly without palliation. What more do you expect me to do as a writer trying to do a certain thing? If art is not a bourgeois possession entirely—as you so rightly say—then it has got to be applied to or used appropriately in given circs.

Perhaps you would like me to 'come out' and join something. Not at the moment, thank you. I have come out and joined too often. I am getting the impression that the masses of the people in all countries,—irrespective of proclaimed creeds—are being humbugged to a hell of an extent. Your idea of doing something for our own country—English Chamberlainism was bound to get you sometime!—seems more practical to me. I have plenty zeal for reform or revolution, but I am getting distrustful, or a bit tired, of those who think their advanced ideas (I have used more than once, with due acknowledgment, your brilliant remark that most of our young London communist poets have merely had their school ties dyed red) should be applied to Germans—with Scotland as it is and particularly this northern part of it I happen to know fairly well. And Christ! This appalling prospect of the abomination of war!

But enough. I am going to Germany and shall keep my own brand of politics to myself in the chance that I may see what another people thinks about it all. I shall try to be detached and when I come back I shall try to tell you what I think. In another year or so I hope to go to Russia. [. . .]
[P.S.] Your references to 'cooking translations' have not applied in my case. In an essay on Modern Scot. letters in a German lit. magazine I used your name flatteringly. No alteration.

In any case—what about Russia? A young fellow in Edinburgh who had done some mild criticism of Communism wasn't even allowed to land in Russia. What do you expect, in my case, given certain conditions? I am only asking you to think. I'm not criticising.

(James Barke, letter of 20 May 1938 to Neil M. Gunn [typed copy]; and reply from Neil M. Gunn to James Barke 21 May 1938 [original], both in James Barke Archive, Mitchell Library, Glasgow.)

9.29 [C.M. Grieve, editor], from 'Notes of the Quarter' (*Voice of Scotland* June–August 1938)

This is not a Communist periodical, although the editor is a member of the Communist Party. But it will be restricted to left-wing writers, and may be defined as Left in tendency yet free of organisational commitments, and partisan to Marxism yet not subject to Communist Party discipline. Tory, religious, and anti-Communist writers will not be accepted as contributors. It will, of course, be absolutely anti-Fascist, anti-Imperialist, opposed to

Imperialist War, and to the conception of the supremacy of brute instinct over intelligence, the perversion of science for the myth of racial superiority, and the deification of state. Equally it will be absolutely opposed to philistine 'common sense', to self-satisfied anti-intellectualism, and to the 'common touch'—e.g. William Gallacher's citation in his autobiography, *Revolt on the Clyde* of his mother's saying: 'Oor Wullie'll no' gang faur wrang,'—and to the whole pawky Harry Lauder–Will Fyfe–Sir Hugh Roberton type of chortling 'wut' which, as Lin Yutang says of the same sort of thing in China, has been largely responsible for the ruin of Scotland. The general editorial standpoint is that laid down in 'The Red Scotland Manifesto' in this issue, and our principal aim is advocacy of Independent Scottish Workers' Republicanism *à la* John Maclean. It will, in fact, be a Scottish counterpart of the new Irish left-wing monthly journal, *The Workers' Republic*. Since we hope to serve Scottish arts and affairs in exactly the same way, some notes on the contents of the first (May) issue of the latter will serve also to indicate the nature of our own intentions. *The Workers' Republic* subjects the De Valera–Chamberlain Agreement to a thorough analysis, and shows that in return for certain concessions De Valera has abandoned the struggle for an Irish Republic, agreed to partition, and signed a treaty of amity to tie Ireland's hands in the struggle for its complete independence. 'The Anglo-Irish Agreement', it says, 'will be used by the English reaction to stabilise the tottering Government in London and prolong the anxieties of European democracy and the agony of the people of Spain'. To prevent the growing Scottish Movement being used by reaction in the same way, to insist upon nothing short of Scotland's complete independence, and to make common cause with Irish and Welsh separatist Workers' Republicans—and with those in England who side with these movements and look forward to the emergence in turn of an English Workers' Republican movement, is the principal aim of this quarterly. Signed articles only express the views of their writers and must not be taken as expressions of the editorial opinion.

([C.M. Grieve, editor], 'Notes of the Quarter', *Voice of Scotland* 1:1 June–August 1938, pp.24–32 [24–26].)

9.30 Wendy Wood, from 'We Will Fight No More in England's Wars. Eirich Alba' (*Voice of Scotland* June–August 1938)

'We will fight no more in England's wars. Eirich Alba'—so ran the slogans which were lately stencilled all over the Capital. '1715, 1745, 1938, Third time's lucky' is to be found, since the new year, adorning many Scottish towns. 'Join Scottish Regiments' on a British recruiting poster, has been improved by the addition 'and fight for England'. The Culloden celebration this year found the roads marked 'Remember what these men died for'.

There is reason for the approaching challenge to united military action between England and Scotland, for seldom, except by ruse, have the two countries agreed on this subject of life and death. During the 231 years of our defence-association across the Border, we have never been called upon to defend either country from invasion. On the other hand, since the date of the Union, we have never been at peace; Scotland has been drained of her money and her blood for wars of imperialist aggression contrary to her national idealism. Never, while she had control of her own foreign policy, did Scotland make wars for loot or territory. Since then, the havoc we have wrought and the punishment we have taken is terrible. One graveyard of one of the wars and a millionth part of the money, would have won us our freedom, and exemption from the rest of the wars. Since the Union, we have fought in 21 countries of the world, never in our own name, and only once (by a stretch of the imagination) in the interests of democracy or justice; never for the necessity of defence and never to anything but our own detriment. In 1707, we sank in one day from a debt-free Scotland to be a part of Britain sharing a £20,000,000 debt with its resulting burden of taxation. The ever increasing debt, taxation, death and danger, without reward or the decencies of common justice, makes the companionship costly, and disagreement of policy leading to them, makes the conditions insupportable. To act as mercenaries is no noble calling, to do so against the individual and national conscience is utter degradation. In our own day, Scottish opinion has disagreed with the English policy of the Boer War, the Irish War, the Hore Laval pact, the Chamberlain muddle, the treachery to Spain. That same national opinion is questioning the necessity of the coming war. Even Scots who do not consider themselves nationalists are asking 'Why should we be involved in war simply because of our association with England? Have we not a right to neutrality?' They begin to realise dimly, with the bayonet at the neck, that we have a national moral right, and even a right under International Law (by the violation of the Treaty by England) to declare peace in our own name. No country at variance with England would be so idiotic as to violate our neutrality, lest it throw us on to England's side again, and Scotland alone is not worth conquering and would be too expensive to hold.

A manifesto in favour of declaring Scotland's neutrality as soon as possible, has lately been passed unanimously by the nationalist parties comprising the Scottish Self-Government Federation. [. . .]

He who in the coming war chooses to die for fascist England is a traitor to his own land and to world democracy. He who fights for the freedom of Scotland and its national expression, cries challenge to tyranny not only at home, but in every land where the imperialist union-Jack flies.

So eirich Alba! and be damned once again to John Bull!

(Wendy Wood, 'We Will Fight No More in England's Wars. Eirich Alba', *Voice of Scotland* 1:1 June–August 1938, pp.15–17.)

9.31 Catherine Carswell, from letter to C.M. Grieve (October 1938)

7.10.38.   35 Gloucester Crescent
                                                           London, N.W.1.

Dear Chris,

Sorry to have been so long in answering your welcome letter, but apart from the usual day to day struggle and some worrying extras, I am trying to pull off a scheme of a Scottish settlement—rather a special thing—of refugees from Austria, and such things take time as you know. I do hope this will come to something and that any Scottish contributions will be kept separate from the English conscience money funds, which will help Hitler to build roads etc. My lot of refugees are a complete community who have lived as neighbours in the country in Austria near the Hungarian Border for many generations. There are from 70 to 80 families, all young people, mostly with one child or two and all well-doing, vigorous, and used to a hard life, wishing only the chance to be self-supporting without hostility round them. They are mostly farmers, but there are wrights, builders, electrical engineers, a tailor, a doctor, etc. When Hitler came to their part, their 'pure Aryan' neighbours begged and prayed that they should be allowed to stay there unmolested. But driven out they were, and it was they who had to live for some time in the woods and on a barge on the Danube with nowhere to go on either side. Their leader is a most distinguished agricultural expert who has made a huge success of the vast farm lands of Count Harrach, after many other farming schemes there had failed. This man is Jewish, but the others have only some Jewish blood, having freely intermarried with the Austrians in their part of the countryside for generations. Between them they have at least £2,500 of capital safely somewhere (they have a clever lawyer among them fortunately) and each family has about £60 of ready cash. Hence they are not beggars, save for ordinary neighbourliness, and any money advanced would in time be repaid by their work. At present they live in daily terror of being sent to concentration camps, but most of them are at present in Vienna. They saw some of the Hebridean Islands advertised by a London agent and were set on buying one, but after many inquiries we have decided that this would not be practicable for them and we hope to get a stretch on the mainland where there are some farms that could be used at once. Sir Robert Greig and others are interested. Here's hoping!

Thanks for *The Voice of Scotland*, which has some good things in it. I think the Muirs might be let alone now though, don't you. It is too easy, and life too short. I agree with the sentiments expressed in your 'When the Gangs Came to London' and feel honoured by seeing my name on it. What a hell's broth it is. But it may as well boil up and show us all where we stand. [. . .] Today Don has gone to Scotland to take part on Tuesday in a broadcast discussion on Calvinism. This may just pay his expenses for the trip if he stays partly with friends, and he will try to see useful people and also to set up a committee that will be in direct touch with our Austrian friends. [. . .] My Boccaccio book has not gone well either here or in America, and I have not started another yet. I have one in mind, though, and hope to start soon. It's a sair fecht.

Love from us to you all. Ever yours, Cathie.

(Catherine Carswell, letter to C.M. Grieve 8 October 1938, Edinburgh University Library Special Collections MS 1946.1 35–36.)

9.32   Eric Linklater, Edwin Muir, Willa Muir, Open Letter concerning the Munich Agreement [1938]

Sir,

The sacrifice of Czechoslovakia has clearly revealed the danger in which democracy stands to-day, not only in Europe, but in Britain.

Mr Chamberlain is the head of a Government which, three years ago, was returned to power in response to a pledge given by its prospective members to defend the principles and observe the Covenant of the League of Nations. It was elected in order that it should pursue a certain policy, which was then the clearly expressed will of the majority of the people. But in the three years of its office it has failed consistently to observe that policy, and by repeatedly breaking its promised word has created anarchy in Europe. The crisis produced by Herr Hitler's threat to Czechoslovakia was made possible by the weakening of international law and the decay of justice, for which this government is largely responsible by reason of its failure to fulfil its original mandate. The crisis produced an emotion in Britain which was in many places frankly discreditable, but not incomprehensible. Fear is the obvious reason for the widespread gratification with which the Munich Pact was received. The people of this country found themselves in a position wherein the issues were, for many, not clearly defined; and being confronted with a danger whose origin was obscured by time, were momentarily grateful of anyone who could extricate them from it. But that danger was recognised in the Covenant of the League, and measures laid down for dealing with it. Had the danger arisen while our signature to the Covenant was still valid, the people of Britain would have acknowledged their responsibilities and faced them more calmly. It was because their responsibilities had already been denied by their Government, and their will ignored by its anti-democratic conduct, that they were bewildered, and permitted themselves to act in a fashion of which many are now ashamed.

We, the undersigned, representing a certain body of opinion in Scotland, deplore the Munich Pact and the recent conduct of the Government for their gross and manifest injustice to Czechoslovakia, and for the added dangers they have bequeathed to the principles of democracy and the people of Britain. We are realists, but not in the sense in which Mr Chamberlain uses the word: for we believe that among the true realities of the world are justice and honour. We believe in democracy, and recognise that if democracy is to survive it may have to fight for its existence. We urge, with all the strength of which we are capable, that the League of Nations be resuscitated, and our pledges under the covenant be re-affirmed. We abominate the thought of war, but cannot reconcile ourselves to peace with ignominy. If we were committed to war on behalf of the Covenant, we would know it to be morally defensible, inasmuch as war would be waged, not for self-aggrandisement or political advantage, nor in a despairing cause of self-preservation, but for the principles of justice, under which is the world's only hope for peace with honour.

We pray that the people of Scotland, in whom love of democracy is an ancient thing and once was valiant, will unite in strengthening its weakened forces, and will recognise that in the League of Nations is the greatest security for the welfare of mankind and future.

We are, Sir,

Yours faithfully,

[Signed]   Eric Linklater

Edwin Muir

Willa Muir

(Open typed letter signed in ink by Eric Linklater, Edwin Muir and Willa Muir, Acc.10282 National Library of Scotland, pp.1–3.)

COMMENTARY

Preliminary: What *is* Scottish Literature?

1.1 Stevenson begins this first letter to Kailyard novelist Crockett: 'Dear Minister of the Free Kirk at Penicuik,—for O, man, I cannae read your name!' The Yale editors draw attention to 'stabbed in the house of my friends' and its similarity with Zechariah 18:16: 'wounded in the house of my friends'.

1.2 W. MacNeile Dixon: Regius Professor of English Language and Literature at Glasgow University 1904–1935.

1.4 For Grieve, Gregory Smith's 'Caledonian Antisyzygy' offered a theory of Scottish literature which was distinct from English and fitted with his own wish to be 'whaur extremes meet'. Gregory Smith, trained at Edinburgh University, was Professor of English Literature at Queen's University, Belfast.

1.5 It is surprising that, as an American with a strong distinctive literature developing in his own country, Eliot does not accept that literature using the English language need not be *English Literature*.

Language, Identity and the Vernacular Debate

2.1 William Will and John Anderson became Joint Secretaries of the Vernacular Circle. John Anderson gave Catherine Carswell access to his extensive Burns collection when she was writing her *Life*.

2.2 Of those asked to become Honorary Members of the Vernacular Circle, only Professor J.H. Millar (author of *A Literary History of Scotland*) refused. See also 8.7.

2.3 W.A. Craigie was Professor of Anglo-Saxon at the University of Oxford. He began the project of the *Dictionary of the Older Scottish Tongue*.

2.4:2.5 J.M. Bulloch was editor of the *Graphic* and Chairman of the Vernacular Circle. 'Albyn Place English': perhaps 'upwardly mobile Scottish English'; not the English of England. Bulloch may be punning here on Alba (Scotland) and Albyn Place, an up-market Aberdeen residential area. The phrase does not appear in the *Scottish Tongue* publication of his lecture. The conflict with the Circle, even when Grieve, as MacDiarmid, became converted to Scots, was essentially rooted in the difference between ambitious literary use of language and language revived for everyday purposes. Excerpts 2.7, 8, 10 chart Grieve's movement towards 'synthetic Scots',

379

although at all stages he is insistent that it must be capable of expressing the 'newest tendencies of modern thought'.

2.6   Pittendrigh MacGillivray: sculptor and poet.

2.9   An early statement of Muir's equivocal views about language.

2.13   Lorna Moon, born Nora Wilson Low in Strichen, Aberdeenshire, emigrated to America, eventually becoming a script-writer in Hollywood.

2.15   Gunn's point about recapturing the *spirit* not the actual language of Dunbar is an important one. Yet such misunderstanding continues. As a civil servant until 1937, Gunn may have chosen to adopt a pseudonym when speaking on public matters.

2.16   Gibbon's irony makes it difficult to be certain about his position regarding language and identity which here appears similar to Eliot's in 1.5.

2.17   Muir recognises that MacDiarmid uses Scots for modern purposes and that the new writers write for a Scottish, as opposed to an external audience. His statement that the Scots talk in Scots but think in English appears to contradict contemporary concerns about the loss of the capacity to speak Scots.

2.19   Muir's argument in a) has much in common with MacDiarmid's Drunk Man's experience, where taking on 'the burden o' his people's doom' leaves him 'impaled' on the thistle (Riach & Grieve, Penguin *SP*, p.112); and with MacDiarmid's own departure for London in 1929. Nevertheless, Muir's views caused a breach with MacDiarmid which was never healed. Muir's attack on Calvinism was challenged by Dr Mary P. Ramsay in *Outlook*, July 1936, and in her later book *Calvin and Art*, while in 2.22, Catherine Carswell, with her 'English writers with Scottish souls', appears as confused as Muir. Muir wrote little Scottish criticism after the attacks on *Scott and Scotland*.

2.23   This must be one of the earliest articles by David Daiches (b.1912) who offers a young scholar's view of the dialect question.

A Scottish Literary Renaissance? Responses and Reviews

3.1   See 8.7 for the Introduction to *Lyra Celtica*, reprinted in 1924. Grieve recognises the importance of Patrick Geddes as against the Celtic revival of Sharp/Macleod. 'Book Reviews' (written here by Grieve) contains what is probably the first use of the term 'Scottish Renascence' in the 1920s; 'La Jeune Belgique': famous periodical of the Belgian literary revival in the late nineteenth century founded by Max Waller. Grieve also discusses the revival's parallels with Scotland in 'Scottish Books and Bookmen', *Dunfermline Press* 5 August 1922, p.6.

3.2   Denis Saurat taught French at Glasgow University before becoming Professor at the University of Bordeaux. In this excerpt, Saurat draws attention to a new literary movement in Scotland which he sees as one of the most interesting and promising developments in current Anglo-Saxon literature. He singles out Grieve as editor of the three important publishing organs *Scottish Nation, Scottish Chapbook* and *Northern Numbers*, describing him as 'this young, spirited, intellectual revolutionary and mystic poet [who] deserves a study all to himself'. Although his article limits itself to literary identity, he points to the idea of Scottish autonomy at the heart of the movement and to its belief that Scottish literature has something unique to offer European literature, something distinct from English. And he emphasises the universal dimension in their ambition, an ambition to judge world culture from a Scottish point of view and for the world to ask 'What do the Scots think?'

3.3   George Kitchin: literary scholar. His 'one of the chief voices in the Northern Numbers group' refers to Grieve (see 2.8).

3.4   William Power, on the editorial staff of the *Glasgow Herald*, was an early supporter of the new movement. His autobiography *Should Auld Acquaintance* (1937) provides useful information about Scottish culture in the interwar period. He became editor of the *Scots Observer* in 1926 and was President of Scottish P.E.N. 1935–38.

3.6   Grieve consistently had a high opinion of Muir as critic which must have made the 'betrayal' of *Scott and Scotland* all the more painful. Gunn was later displaced in his interest by Fionn MacColla.

3.7   Thomas Henderson, editor of the *Scottish Educational Journal*, commissioned Grieve's series of *Contemporary Scottish Studies* between 1925 and 1926.

3.8   Muir, in Europe and the south of England in the early 1920s, does not seem to realise here that Grieve and M'Diarmid are one person; the first of several important reviews of MacDiarmid's poetry by Muir.

3.10   Lewis Spence: poet and nationalist. He later became disenchanted with Grieve, omitting him from his *Scots Magazine* article 'Literary Scotland: 1910–1935' in May 1935 and writing to F. Marian McNeill in August 1929 that Grieve 'froze himself out of Scotland by his persistent caddishness to everyone, including those who would have liked to help him' (NLS MS 26194).

3.15   'no wonder she loves Grieve': Carswell wrote to Helen Cruickshank in February 1933: 'If I were rich I'd give Grieve £2 a week & ask for nothing in return. He has the sacred fire'. (Cruickshank correspondence, Stirling University MS1.)

3.17   Muir's novels were highly thought of at this time as was his criticism. Neither the *Modern Scot* nor Muir himself was an early enthusiast for Lewis Grassic Gibbon (see 3.20, 3.22, 3.23). Nor was Gibbon enthusiastic about the 'funny little quarterlies' (3.25).

3.21   James Barke: Marxist and proletarian novelist in the 1930s.

3.30   Robert Bain: poet, critic and dramatist whose *James the First of Scotland* was performed by the Scottish National Players in Glasgow in May 1925.

Transforming Traditions

4.1 A somewhat 'mythical' view of Burns by Muir, writing without reference books from Europe.

4.3 *G.O.C. Magazine*: *General Omnibus Company Magazine* which became *S.M.T. (Scottish Motor Traction) Magazine*.

4.6 Grieve has returned to an anti-Burns stance here after 4.2, while his reference to the English Romantics is a reminder of continuing Romantic period influence and of the prominence of English literature generally in the educational curriculum in Scotland. After their argument over Burns, he and Carswell became firm friends.

4.9 Excerpts from Carswell's *Life* were serialised in the *Daily Record* during September 1930 and provoked the kind of responses represented here. See also *The Bibliotheck* 22, 1997, pp.72–78.

4.11 F. Marian McNeill, friend and correspondent of Carswell, Willa Muir, Helen Cruickshank and other Scottish Renaissance writers, female and male; author of *The Scots Kitchen* and the four-volume *The Silver Bough* as well as the novel *The Road Home*. She was a founder member of Scottish P.E.N. and a Vice-President of the Scottish National Party in the 1930s.

4.17 See the Theatre Archive in Glasgow University Library for documents on Community Drama, the Scottish National Players and other aspects of the re-emergence of drama in this period. Neil Gunn strongly supported the Community Drama movement, writing several plays for it; as did former miner Joe Corrie. There were many tensions, especially in relation to the inclusion of Scottish material. The now promised but still awaited National Theatre was high on the interwar agenda.

4.18 The *Modern Scot* was incorporated into *Outlook* in 1936. J.H. Whyte's papers are in the National Library of Scotland.

4.21 Murray McClymont: critic and playwright whose plays were among those performed by the National Players.

Europe and the Impact of the Modern

5.1–5.11 present some of the ideas which influenced a modern consciousness in Scotland as elsewhere, especially in the creative writing of the time. Freud's and Jung's writings on the unconscious and on dreams and archetypes were especially influential on both poetry and prose fiction, as was symbolism also. Bergson's thinking on duration and the operation of memory was similarly influential, as was Proust's fictional exploration of this in *À la Recherche du Temps Perdu*. Bergson's Gifford lectures in Edinburgh University in spring 1914 were well covered in the Scottish Press. Several excerpts demonstrate the awareness of European literature being brought into Scotland through the influence of the *New Age* which became a model for the *Scottish Nation*, by Muir's residence in Europe in the early and mid-1920s and his essay writing and translation of European writers. In the early 1930s, the *Modern Scot*, edited by J.H. Whyte, took over this avant-garde role.

5.8 In later years, Muir denounced *We Moderns* as immature. However, the excerpts included here present a vital sense of the ideas of the emergent new age while simultaneously offering a critique of 'the modern' from a humanist perspective.

5.9:5.10 The key elements presented in these Eliot excerpts were influential in reshaping English criticism in the interwar period. In the Scottish context, the idea of impersonality in art was especially influential on Edwin Muir's poetry while the dissociation of sensibility theory in 5.10 may well have been transferred to Muir's diagnosis of the Scottish separation of heart and head in *Scott and Scotland*.

5.11 Grieve here takes a positive view of Spengler, whose *The Decline of the West* was more usually seen as contributing to a sense of a civilisation in crisis.

5.12 Muir travelled from Italy to attend the Salzburg Festival with the musician F.G. Scott during his first period of residence in Europe between 1921 and 1924.

5.13 Muir was introduced to the poetry of Hölderlin when staying at A.S. Neill's international school at Hellerau in 1922. It remained a life-long interest and influence.

5.14 For Scottish artists of the interwar period, see Tom Normand, *The Modern Scot: Modernism and Nationalism in Scottish Art 1928–1955* (Ashgate, 2000). See also cover image and 5.18.

5.15 The first of his two essays on Paul Valéry (see also Riach, ed., *Raucle Tongue* II pp.216–19 for the other). Significant in this excerpt is the quotation from Mallarmé which has affinities with MacDiarmid's 'It's soon no' sense that faddoms the herts o' men' from 'Gairmscoile' in *Penny Wheep*. Both quotations point to an interest in words and their sounds, although Mallarmé may have been less interested in their *associative* power than was MacDiarmid, who was also very much a poet of *ideas*.

5.16 Kafka was a lasting influence on Muir's poetry, although the 'lost way' theme appears in Muir's work long before he translated Kafka's fiction.

5.17 Mary Baird Aitken at this point was teaching in Edinburgh after living for some years in Denmark. See also 6.2 for Carswell's 'Proust's Women'. In the essay 'Scottish Renaissance' (*Scottish Field* August 1962) Neil Gunn remembers 'reading the Parisian magazine *Transition* in the Highlands when James Joyce's Work in Progress was appearing in its pages'.

5.20 Hermann Broch, author of *Die Schlafwandler* trilogy (*The Sleepwalkers*) which the Muirs were translating. He fled Germany when the Nazis came to power, staying for a time with the Muirs in St Andrews. In 'Willa Muir: Writer', Peter Butter quotes Broch writing to Willa: 'The translation is wonderful . . . I am quite delighted with it and utterly in your debt. . . . Oh Willa, my dear, you ought always to write in German, it is wonderful, and if ever you were to write a book in German, you would earn a great deal of money by it.' (*Edwin Muir: Centenary Assessments* 1990, p.62) Willa would appear to have been the principal translator so far as linguistic accuracy and devoting time were concerned.

5.22 Gibbon's awareness of the modern movement in literature as exemplified by Woolf and Joyce is shown here, as is his dislike of the avant-garde *Modern Scot*, perhaps because his own fiction was reviewed unfavourably there; see also 3.20 and 3.24.

5.23 Rilke's poetry was an early and continuing interest for MacDiarmid who welcomed the 'difficulty' of the German poet's work. His translation/adaptation of Rilke's *Requiem: Für eine Freundin* is a notable inclusion in *To Circumjack Cencrastus*.

Women on Women: Gendering the Renaissance

6.1 Prague provided the Muirs' first experience of a European city when they travelled abroad between 1921 and 1924.

6.2 Carswell's interest in the operation of memory can be seen in her fiction and unfinished autobiography, the epigraph of the latter being: 'To be bound for ever to the arbitrary accidents of one's memories: what an idea of immortality.'

6.3 Readers who come to 'Women: An Inquiry' fresh from *Imagined Corners* may be baffled by this essentialist essay which seems to belong more with Ruskin's *Sesame and Lilies* view of woman as the creator of 'the place of peace' than with the exploration of female self-determination in the later novel. Freud's and Jung's writings on the unconscious are significant here and in her novel, as is Bergson on time and memory; also Willa's own study of educational psychology. The explanation for her obsession is given in 6.4.

6.5 Carswell also seems to take an essentialist view of woman here. There are resonances of D.H. Lawrence in her comments to McNeill together with good creative writing advice.

6.6 Lorna Moon is relatively unknown in Scottish writing and what comment there has been tends to place her alongside Kailyard writing— even if to make the point that she departs from it. As she insists here, she should be read in the context of 1929, which is where her thinking about female identity belongs.

6.7 'Had Gibbon read Shepherd's *The Quarry Wood* with its anticipation of the "two Chrisses" predicament?' is a tantalising question. He does, however, give a dismissive account of Shepherd's *A Pass in the Grampians* in 3.25. Elizabeth Kyle was a popular novelist from the 1930s onwards, her last book being published in 1981. She died in 1982.

6.8 The ending of *Imagined Corners*, with its two principal female characters leaving Scotland together for the south of France, has aroused much gender and nation speculation. Here Muir answers her interwar and present-day readers.

6.9 Mitchison's entire Russian Diary has never been published.

6.10 Marion Lochhead went on to be a significant writer of social histories, especially concerned with family history. At this point, she was herself writing poetry and novels and contributing articles on women's issues to newspapers such as the *Bulletin*.

6.11 Nannie K. Wells was Secretary Depute of the National Party of Scotland, and then of the Scottish National Party, and was also secretary of the Edinburgh Women Citizen's Association. She was a friend and correspondent of many writers of the period and looked after Donald and the young John Carswell when Catherine was in Russia in November 1934. In 9.18 she speaks out strongly against fascism.

6.12 Muir wrote two essays about women in Scotland in the 1930s, the other being 'Mrs Grundy in Scotland', written for the *Voice of Scotland* series. Here Muir still appears trapped by the idea of a woman's child-bearing role in her analysis of women in society, while in 'Mrs Grundy' she explores ironically the negative effects of being responsible for the 'creation of human beings'.

6.13 Mitchison's account from Carradale of waiting with her family, friends and house servants for the official announcement of the outbreak of war with Germany: Dick is her husband; Avrion, Denny and Valentine three of her children.

The Condition of Scotland

7.1 See 9.3 for the *Scots Observer* as a platform for the Protestant Churches which were becoming increasingly concerned about social conditions.

7.2 *Caledonia* and Thomson's *Scotland: That Distressed Area* provided wide-ranging and influential analyses of decline in Scotland. As with Andrew Dewar Gibb in *The Eclipse of Scotland* (7.4), Thomson's reputation has suffered from his attacks on Irish immigration and the Catholic Church. 'Inge': Dean Inge of St Paul's cathedral.

7.3 A belief in the economic theories of Major Douglas (see 9.11) was omnipresent among writers of the revival and supported by the *Modern Scot*.

7.4 Ironically, as section 8 shows, such attacks on Irish immigration were contradicted by the attempt among nationalist creative writers to create a Celtic identity for the new Scotland by drawing on the common Gaelic heritage of Scotland and Ireland. Writers such as MacDiarmid and Muir saw Catholicism as having a leavening influence on Scottish Calvinism. Dewar Gibb was Professor of Scots Law at Glasgow University.

7.6 The *Free Man* was edited by Robin Black. Although independent of any specific political affiliations, it was sympathetic to nationalists seeking new social, economic and cultural ways forward for Scotland.

7.9 For this period in Grieve's life, see Alan Bold's *MacDiarmid: Christopher Murray Grieve* (1988), chs 10–12. 'Couéism': a system of optimistic auto-suggestion as psychotherapy, developed by the French psychologist Émile Coué who died in 1926.

7.11 David Cleghorn Thomson: Regional Director of the BBC in Scotland. His book, although its contributors can be critical, is less fierce than *Caledonia* and *Scotland in Eclipse*.

7.12 Muir's diagnosis is sharp, but his conclusion equivocal. 7.13 provides a sympathetic account of the Carfin Grotto, while 7.15 provides a powerful review of the state of Scotland provided by the statistics in Thomson's book with Muir temporarily converted to 'Home Rule'.

7.17 George Blake: novelist and joint editor (with George Malcolm Thomson) of the Porpoise Press from 1930.

Celtic Connections and the Situation of the Highlands

8.1–8.3 The regeneration of Gaelic was an early part of the Renaissance agenda. Corkery's book was influential in affirming shared Scottish/Irish traditions. MacDiarmid drew on the *aisling* tradition and the poetry of Aodhagàn Ó Rathaille in *To Circumjack Cencrastus* (1930). *Aisling ghear*: A vivid vision I beheld last night as I was in bed spiritless and weak. Sharp's *Lyra Celtica*, reprinted in 1924, presented an 'Anglo-Celtic' view (3.1).

8.5 *Dia'na thoiseach*: God willing.

8.6 Lecky: William Edward Hartpole Lecky, author of *A History of Ireland in the Eighteenth Century* (1913). Gunn draws on *The Hidden Ireland* here, which itself draws on Lecky's *History*.

8.7:8.8 Two important essays for MacDiarmid's position concerning the significance of the Gaelic tradition in relation to the balance of power in Britain and in Europe, something he admits may be primarily 'a dynamic myth', a creative inspiration for change. Less inspired is his apparent unquestioning transference of Hitler's 'Blutsgefühl' theories to the Gaelic situation in part V of the 'Caledonian Antisyzygy' essay (printed in full in Glen). In *Free Man* 3 September 1932 he denied any endorsement of such ideas. See also 9.8 and 9.14.

8.10 This shows the continuing nationalist fascination with Mussolini's fascism in 1931. In contrast see 9.18 and other references post-1933.

8.13 Fionn MacColla: pen-name of Tom Macdonald of Montrose, novelist and Gaelic learner who became a fierce defender of the language; *a' ae 'oo*: all of a kind (*oo/ou* = wool, so literally all one wool, all from the same flock).

8.16 *Earra-Ghaidheal*: An Argyll man; *An Comunn Gaidhealach*: the Highland Association, founded in 1891.

8.17 *Iain Ruadh*: Iain Roy.

8.19 *Sunny Memories* by Harriet Beecher Stowe, author of *Uncle Tom's Cabin*, praised the Sutherland Estate's 'benevolent' improvements and provoked *Gloomy Memories* by Donald MacLeod, the Strathnaver stone-mason active in the fight against the evictions. See Alexander Mackenzie's *History of the Highland Clearances* (1883, repr. 1979), referred to also by Corkery in 8.2; also Neil Gunn's *Butcher's Broom* (1934).

Competing Ideologies

9.1 A representative example of the loose linking of Mussolini's fascism with effective nationalism found in the 1920s.

9.2 An uncharacteristic perspective from Muir whose stay in Prague seemed to influence him in favour of small nations. See also his *The Story and the Fable* (1940), p.228.

9.4 *Albyn* was advertised as a response to *Caledonia* in Kegan Paul's *To-Day and To-Morrow* series. The opening offers a realistic assessment of the Scottish Renaissance position.

9.5 The Scottish Centre of P.E.N. was founded by Grieve/MacDiarmid and supported by many writers of the period. Helen Cruickshank became Secretary in 1929. See also 9.13. The Saltire Society was founded by a group including Andrew Dewar Gibb, Mrs Bonfield, the first Secretary of the Society, Eric Linklater and William Power and had wide support among cultural activists.

9.7 *Coué*: As in 7.9.

9.10 Prince D.S. Mirsky belonged to the group associated with the *New Age* under Orage and influenced Grieve/MacDiarmid's understanding of Russian literature. In the excerpts given here one can recognise the heroic and Christ-like Lenin presented in the Hymns to Lenin of the 1930s, while Lenin's belief in a dynamic Marxism relates to the poet's belief in creative change. The metaphor of Lenin's willingness to 'sacrifice his division to save the army' has some resemblance to MacDiarmid's 'What maitters 't wha we kill/To lessen that foulest murder that deprives/Maist men o' real lives?' in 'First Hymn to Lenin' which is dedicated to Prince Mirsky. In a forthcoming article in the *Bibliotheck*, John Manson discusses specific points of reference between MacDiarmid's ideas in the Hymns and Mirsky's *Lenin*.

9.11 This is one of the most helpful expositions of Douglasite economics. Major Douglas's book *Credit Power and Democracy* was published in 1920 and reprinted in 1921 and 1931.

9.13 The Scottish conference referred to here was held in Edinburgh in 1934 and is discussed in her *Octobiography* by Helen Cruickshank.

9.14 For Grieve's response see *Free Man* 3 September 1932.

9.16 J.H. Whyte, editor of the *Modern Scot*, distinguishes between national and *nationalist* art here. See also Neil Gunn in 9.8.

9.17 This account of the coming to power of the Nazis in 1933 has similarities with Edwin Muir's poem 'The Good Town' which relates to the communist take-over in post-ww2 Prague.

9.18 Nannie K. Wells shows the change in nationalist attitudes to fascism by 1933.

9.19 What seems contradictory about the nationalist position as stated here is Mackenzie's acceptance that Scotland, when freed from London control, will itself exert power over colonies who 'choose' to be Scottish.

9.21 Muir's position here is similar to that in his poem 'The Incarnate One' from *One Foot in Eden*. He started the *European Quarterly* in association with Janko Lavrin in 1934.

9.22 The 150,000 mentioned in section a) refers to the opening of the 'Glasgow' essay and the description of 'a hundred and fifty thousand human beings living in such conditions as the most bitterly pressed primitive in Tierra del Fuego never visioned'.

9.23 'P.S.A. sprawl': I am grateful to John Manson, whose Chambers Dictionary glosses 'P.S.A.' as 'Pleasant Sunday Afternoon', which seems to fit with Gibbon's ironic sense of humour! In 1937, MacDiarmid was also one of a group of prominent writers who took a stand for 'the legal government and people of Republican Spain' in a Writers International pamphlet published by the *Left Review*. In 1939 he wrote the long poem *The Battle Continues*, his attack on Roy Campbell's support of Franco, although it was not published until 1957.

9.28 The correspondence suggests that Barke had been rejected as a Scottish P.E.N. conference delegate because of his politics. The excerpts here and in 9.29 are interesting for Gunn's defence of being published in Germany and his forthcoming visit to Germany. His response suggests more that of a P.E.N. member (see 9.5) than a Nazi sympathiser.

9.29:9.30 *Voice of Scotland* was edited from Whalsay and managed by the young W.R. Aitken in Edinburgh. Wendy Wood's refusal to fight for 'fascist England' contradicts MacDiarmid's own anti-Chamberlain poem 'When the Gangs Came to London', dedicated to Catherine Carswell and Karl Čapek and sent to Carswell after the Munich Agreement: a poem he unsuccessfully tried to persuade Aitken to find space for during the next nine months. See W.R. Aitken papers, NLS Acc.10488 and *Scottish Studies Review* 1.1 Autumn 2000, pp.94–98. *Eirich Alba*: Scotland arise!

9.32 In the absence of accompanying papers, it is not clear whether this Open Letter from the Muirs and Eric Linklater was sent to any newspaper or official organisation, or whether it was one of a number of signed copies sent to associates at this time. It is typed and signed in ink by all three.

THE ASSOCIATION FOR SCOTTISH LITERARY STUDIES

ANNUAL VOLUMES

Volumes marked * are, at the time of publication, still available from booksellers or from the address given opposite the title page of this book.

COPYRIGHT ACKNOWLEDGEMENTS

The editor and publisher are grateful for permission to reproduce copyright material in this collection of source documents. We are especially grateful for the support and encouragement of the estate-holders for the principal Scottish authors represented here by the several excerpts listed. We regret that, despite every effort having been made, it has not yet been possible to trace estate-holders for all authors. If such information is brought to our attention, the necessary arrangements will be made at the first opportunity. Full information about provenance and publication details for each item included is given in the text after presentation of the item.

Grateful acknowledgement is made to the following:

David Higham Associates for permission to reproduce excerpts by George Blake; Alistair Barke for those by James Barke; Continuum International Publishing Group for excerpts taken from *Henri Bergson: Key Writings* (2002); A.P. Watt Ltd for material by John Buchan; Harriet Wilson and Deborah Kaplinsky for the several listed excerpts reprinted in this collection by Catherine Carswell and Donald Carswell; the extracts from *The Hidden Ireland* by Daniel Corkery are reproduced with permission of its publishers Gill & Macmillan, Dublin; David Daiches gives permission for his essay from *Outlook*; Faber & Faber and the estate of T.S. Eliot for extracts from 'The Metaphysical Poets' and 'Tradition and the Individual Talent' and for 'Was there a Scottish literature?'; The Master and Fellows of Trinity College, Cambridge, for excerpts from *The Golden Bough* by Sir James Frazer; Penguin Books for excerpts from Sigmund Freud's *The Interpretation of Dreams* reprinted from the Penguin Freud Library edition; Nigel Dewar Gibb for extracts from *Scotland in Eclipse* by Andrew Dewar Gibb; Rhea Martin for the several listed excerpts by Lewis Grassic Gibbon; Deirdre Grieve and Carcanet Press for the several listed excerpts by C.M. Grieve (Hugh MacDiarmid); Dairmid Gunn for the several listed excerpts by Neil M. Gunn; Malcolm Hunter for the letter by Violet Jacob; excerpts from *Jung: Selected Writing* (1983), introduced and selected by Anthony Storr are reprinted by permission of HarperCollins Publishers Ltd; A.M. Heath for 'Modern Women Authors' by Elizabeth Kyle; excerpts by Eric Linklater are reproduced by permission of PFD on behalf of the Estate of Eric Linklater; the London Burns Club for excerpts from their Minutes and for Vernacular Society material; Margaret McCance for 'Idea in Art' by William McCance, together with cover image acknowledged separately;

COPYRIGHT ACKNOWLEDGEMENTS

Francesca Hardcastle for excerpts by Fionn MacColla; the Society of
Authors as Literary Representative of the Estate of Compton Mackenzie
for excerpts by Compton Mackenzie; David Fletcher Associates on behalf
of the F. Marian McNeill Estate for 'The New Burns'; Lois Godfrey for
excerpts by Naomi Mitchison; Richard de Mille and Black & White
Publishing for excerpts from letters by Lorna Moon; Kenneth Ross of the
Muir Estate for the several listed excerpts by Edwin and Willa Muir; Faber
& Faber and the Estate of Ezra Pound for excerpt from 'A Retrospect';
Lilias Scott Forbes for the F.G. Scott material in 'Edwin Muir and F.G.
Scott: A Conversation'; the National Library of Scotland for excerpts by
William Soutar; Anne B.M. Ettlinger for excerpts from *Caledonia* by
George Malcolm Thomson; PFD for the *Modern Scot* review by Rebecca
West; Cora Cuthbert for the *Voice of Scotland* essay by Wendy Wood; the
Society of Authors as Literary Representative of the Estate of Virginia
Woolf for excerpt from 'More Dostoevsky'; A.P. Watt for excerpt from
'The Symbolism of Poetry' by W.B. Yeats. Acknowledgement is also made
to the Saltire Society and to Scottish PEN for the reprinting of their non-
political 'manifestos' and to Special Collections and Manuscript
departments in the National Library of Scotland, Edinburgh University
Library, St Andrews University Library and the Mitchell Library, Glasgow,
for the reproduction of excerpts from unpublished manuscript material
deposited with them for which estate-holders have given permission.
Acknowledgement is made to the *Times Literary Supplement* for kind
permission to reproduce anonymous reviews from the interwar period; and
to other still-continuing periodicals and newspapers of the time in whose
pages some of these excerpts first appeared, including *Burns Chronicle,
Daily Record, Dunfermline Press, Glasgow Herald, Radio Times, Scots
Magazine, Scotsman, Scottish Educational Journal, Spectator.*

SELECTED INDEX OF PRINCIPAL NAMES AND TOPICS